BEYOND ENTITLEMENT

BEYOND ENTITLEMENT

The Social Obligations of Citizenship

LAWRENCE M. MEAD

THE FREE PRESS
A Division of Macmillan, Inc.
NEW YORK

Collier Macmillan Publishers
LONDON

The Free Press
A Division of Macmillan, Inc.
866 Third Avenue, New York, N. Y. 10022

Collier Macmillan Canada, Inc.

Printed in the United States of America

printing number

3 4 5 6 7 8 9 10

Library of Congress Cataloging-in-Publication Data

Mead, Lawrence M.
Beyond entitlement.

Bibliography: p.
Includes index.
1. United States—Social policy—1960–
2. Responsibility. 3. Economic assistance, Domestic—United States. 4. Public welfare—United States.
5. Political participation—United States. I. Title.
JK1764.M4 1986 323'.042'0973 85-16227
ISBN 0-02-920890-4

For
my parents

Contents

Preface

WHY does poverty still exist in America twenty years after the War on Poverty? Most critics direct our attention to the scale of public effort. Advocates of big government like Michael Harrington would increase spending on the needy and unemployed, while conservatives like Charles Murray would cut it back.

I think the main problem with the welfare state is its *permissiveness*, not its size. Today poverty often arises from the functioning problems of the poor themselves, especially difficulties in getting through school, working, and keeping their families together. But the social programs that support the needy rarely set standards for them. Recipients seldom have to work or otherwise function *in return* for support. If they did, the evidence suggests they would function better, bringing closer an integrated society.

Most studies of the welfare state view it economically, in terms of the resources it gives to the needy. As a political scientist I approach it as an institution that helps to govern, or misgovern, society. My training, which centered on how government institutions evolve, included several years' study in Britain, a more orderly nation than our own. I came away with a conviction that civility is essential to a humane society, but it is not a natural condition, as Americans tend to assume. It is something societies must achieve, in part through public authority.

When I joined the Department of Health, Education, and Welfare in 1973, however, I discovered that authority played virtually no role in federal social policy. All the programs were conceived as distributing benefits to people and expanding their claims on society. The behavioral problems among the poor were already evident, yet everyone assumed that the responsibility for change lay entirely with government. One reason programs fail is simply poor implementation, a subject I studied for several years at The Urban Institute. I concluded, however, that the central problem in social policy was something more fundamental—Washington's inability to obligate the recipients of its programs, even for their own benefit.

This book is the first to approach social policy in terms of those authority problems. It traces the poor record of Great Society programs, in part, to their failure to set standards for their clients. Special attention is given to work requirements in welfare and other programs, since it seems that work must be enforced for many workers today, especially the low-skilled. The work tests, which are still very limited, demonstrate both Washington's reluctance to obligate and the potential that requirements might have to improve functioning. The permissive nature of programs is deeply rooted in federal politics, yet some politicians already call for a more demanding policy, and the public would support one.

New York University's excellent support facilities have eased my labors. I am grateful to Peter Allison and his staff at the library's social science research center and to Bert Holland, George Sharrard, and Ed Friedman at the computer center. A number of dedicated research assistants have helped me: Julie Mostov, Seth Benjamin, Dave Gerould, Beatrice Lewis, Paul Garrido, Craig Chin, and Ben Moore.

The book melds technical with theoretical reasoning, and conservative with big-government politics, combinations that made it difficult to fund. Thus I especially appreciate the grants I received from the Institute for Educational Affairs and the Earhart Foundation. My department contributed a light teaching load. I acknowledge, as well, encouragement and support from R. Randolph Richardson.

My critics have saved me from many errors and omissions. Parts of the manuscript was read by my colleagues Mark Roelofs, Ron Replogle, and Robert Pecorella at NYU, and by Thomas Main and

Malcolm Goggin. Another colleague, Alan Altshuler, as well as James Q. Wilson, Leslie Lenkowsky, and Nat Semple, read the entire first draft and made detailed comments, a Herculean labor. The Lehrman Institute graciously sponsored two seminars on the book at which groups of experts gave excellent feedback. For the final argument, however, the responsibility is very much my own.

I am grateful to a number of public officials for expediting my research on welfare work programs and for answering my questions about them, especially Ron Putz and Rita Treiber of the Department of Labor, Jo Anne Ross and Ken Lee of the Department of Health and Human Services, and many members of the departments of labor and welfare in New York City and New York State.

I have been fortunate in my editors at The Free Press. Erwin Glikes and Joyce Seltzer sometimes grasped what I wanted to say better than I did. With her comments and substantive expertise, Joyce has made this a better, and a shorter, book than I could have written alone.

A number of other persons for whom I have the greatest respect have given me encouragement: Samuel Beer and Samuel Huntington, my former teachers, Irving Kristol, Nathan Glazer, Ken Auletta, Richard Nathan, Hugh Heclo, William Julius Wilson, Blanche Bernstein, Robert Curvin, Peter Salins, Philip Marcus, Richard Pious, Hadley Arkes, Gerald Benjamin, and Suzanne Woolsey. They do not all agree with me, but they helped me to believe that I had something to say.

One cannot write a book as wide-ranging as this without a long and fortunate education. My parents made possible the early stages of mine. Through their sacrifice, they ensured that the limits to my opportunities would only be my own. They also taught, by example, a willingness to give oneself to large challenges without fear. Without these gifts, I could not have written this book. In love and gratitude, it is dedicated to them.

New York, N.Y.
April 1985

LAWRENCE M. MEAD

BEYOND ENTITLEMENT

1

The Problem of Obligation in Social Policy

THIS is a book about social policy, but also about American politics. My question is why federal programs since 1960 have coped so poorly with the various social problems that have come to afflict American society. These twenty-five years have seen a succession of new programs for the needy, disadvantaged, and unemployed pour forth from Washington. But during the same period welfare dependency and unemployment have grown, standards have fallen in the schools, and rising crime has made some areas of American cities almost uninhabitable. In all these respects there has been a sharp decline in the habits of competence and restraint that are essential to a humane society. The public never wished for this state of affairs, but government has seemed powerless to affect it.

Part of the explanation, I propose, is that the federal programs that support the disadvantaged and unemployed have been permissive in character, not authoritative. That is, they have given benefits to their recipients but have set few requirements for how they ought to function in return. In particular, the programs have as yet no serious requirements that employable recipients work in return for support. There is good reason to think that recipients subject to such requirements would function better.

Policy is permissive, in turn, for reasons rooted in the libertarian nature of American politics, especially at the federal level. Because of the way social policy is approached in Washington, as well as for electoral and constitutional reasons, federal politicians tend to use social programs simply to give deserving people good things, seldom to set standards for how they ought to behave. Thus dependent groups are shielded from the pressures to function well that impinge on other Americans. A more authoritative social policy has begun to emerge, but it faces stiff resistance from the benefit-oriented habits of federal politics.[1]

The term "social policy" is less abstract than it sounds. Federal social policy is summed up in the specific programs Washington has developed over the years for meeting the needs of vulnerable Americans. They include programs like Social Security and Medicare that serve the general public without regard to need, but in this book the focus is mainly on programs for the needy and disadvantaged, particularly welfare and employment programs. In essence federal social policy amounts to the specific things these programs do for, and expect from, their recipients.

The "welfare state" is more than a metaphor. By what they do and do not expect, social programs directly govern their recipients. The fatal weakness of federal programs is that they award their benefits essentially as entitlements, expecting next to nothing from the beneficiaries in return. The world the recipients live in is economically depressed yet privileged in one sense, that it emphasizes their claims and needs almost to the exclusion of obligations.

The approach to social policy taken here emphasizes the balance of rights and duties that programs imply for recipients. Such an approach has not been usual. The programs have been planned and studied mainly by economists, who seldom address their legal and administrative aspects. Lawyers, who do, have usually been interested in defining the claims of the recipients against government even more clearly, not in strengthening government's claims on them. Political scientists tend to see programs as occasions for political dispute between the parties, politicians, Executive and Congress. Very little attention has been paid to the potential the programs have to set norms for the public functioning of citizens.

This history reflects the fact that American politics has largely been about the *extent* and not the *nature* of government. The main questions have been where to divide public authority from individual rights, and government regulation from the unfettered free market. Those are the issues that chiefly divide Republicans and Democrats, and have done so since the New Deal. Firmly in that tradition, most prescriptions for American social policy say that Washington is doing either *too much* or *too little* for the poor.

There is substantial agreement about the nature of the social problem. A class of Americans, heavily poor and nonwhite, exists apart from the social mainstream. That is, it has very little contact with other Americans in the public aspects of American life, especially in schools, the workplace, and politics. This *social* separation is more worrisome to most Americans than the material deprivations that go along with disadvantage. Secondarily, problems of nonwork and low productivity have recently surfaced even among better-integrated members of the workforce, helping to account for the country's declining economic competitiveness. While performance difficulties are greatest among the underclass, they are not at all confined to it. There is also substantial agreement that the solution for the disadvantaged must mean integration, that is, an end to the separation so that the disadvantaged can publicly interact with others and be accepted by them as equals. I shall use "social problem" to mean this separation and "integration" to mean overcoming it.

The disagreement is over the role of government in that solution, and specifically over the *scale* of government. Conservatives, for example George Gilder or Charles Murray, say that an overblown welfare state has undermined the vitality of the private economy and deterred the needy from getting ahead on their own.[2] Liberals say that the "war on poverty" achieved much, and would have achieved more if spending had not been cut by the Republican Administrations since 1969.[3] Those further left, for example Michael Harrington, deny that the "war" ever amounted to much at all.[4]

These criticisms have weight, but mainly in ways their makers do not intend. Washington does give too much to the poor—in the sense of benefits given as entitlements. It also gives too little—in the sense of meaningful obligations to go along with the benefits. What undermines the economy is not so much the burden on the private sector as the message government programs have given that hard work in available jobs is no longer required of Americans. The main problem with the welfare state is not its size but its permissiveness, a characteristic that *both* liberals and conservatives seem to take for granted. The challenge to welfare statesmanship is not so much to change the extent of benefits as to couple them with serious work and other obligations that would encourage functioning and thus promote the integration of recipients. The goal must be to create for recipients *inside* the welfare state the same balance of support and expectation that other Americans face *outside* it, as they work to support themselves and meet the other demands of society.

The liberal and conservative critiques both assume that greater freedom is what recipients need to progress in American society. Some impediment, it is said, must be holding them back. Liberals say it is the oppressive, unfair, sometimes racist demands of the private economy. Employers refuse to hire the poor or to pay them enough to escape poverty. Only government action can overcome these "barriers." Conservatives say the obstacle is government itself, whose programs keep recipients dependent and unable to get ahead on their own. The answer is to cut back the programs. For one persuasion freedom for the disadvantaged means to extend government's reach into society; for the other, to pull it back.

Neither prescription, however, would fundamentally change the welfare state we have. Experience shows that big-government programs in the liberal or Harrington mode, which increase benefits without expecting any return, would not make the poor any less dependent. However, simply to cut back welfare as Gilder and Murray advise, while it would force independence on the recipients, lacks the political support to be carried very far, as the Reagan Administration has discovered. Most Americans, and their leaders, want to continue a humanitarian social policy. Also, many dependent people could not immediately cope on their own. They need support and guidance, even if the goal is overcoming dependency.

Once we face these realities, the welfare problem emerges as one of authority rather than freedom. The best hope for solving it is, not mainly to shift the boundary between society and government, but to require recipients to function where they already are, as dependents. Even more than income and opportunity, they need to face the requirements, such as work, that true acceptance in American society requires. To create those obligations, they must be made *less* free in certain senses rather than more.

Even to speak of obligation as a goal of social policy, however, is novel in the American context. The idea that government might act to enforce social order may sound like a truism, but it has not been prominent in American politics. For most commentators and academics, American politics has been about freedom rather than order. Its essence is to be found in our freewheeling elections and in the jockeying for power among the various institutions and interests in Washington. It is a game played out among lobbies, parties, and politicians to decide, in Harold Lasswell's phrase, "who gets what, when, how."[5] The game is played by rules designed, by James Madison and the other Founders, to disperse and divide power rather than concentrate it. The political system offers access to all interests. Each meets limitation from the force of competing interests rather than government itself. There is no state separate from society, but only a political process through which social forces compete for power. Government does not make demands on the people; they make demands on it.

The Madisonian view of government, however, centers too much on the high politics of Washington. The average American actually has little interest in politics in this participatory sense. Public opinion studies show that his knowledge of government is usually quite limited, and his desire to participate in it even more so.[6] His concerns are usually closer at hand, rooted in his daily life of job, home, and family. He gets interested in government to the extent public policies make leading that life more or less difficult. His immediate attention is on law enforcement, the quality of the neighborhood schools and other public services, and employment prospects for himself, his family, and friends. In assuring these conditions the face of government as public authority, not as political arena, is most salient. As Hobbes said, government's essential, if not only, purpose is to maintain public order.

"Order" here means more than just "law and order" in the narrow, police sense. It encompasses all of the social and economic conditions people depend on for satisfying lives, but which are government's responsibility rather than their own. It includes, in other words, all of the *public* conditions for the *private* assurance of what Jefferson called "life, liberty, and the pursuit of happiness." Which conditions are a public responsibility is, of course, for politics to decide. In modern conditions the public agenda is broad. Even conservatives believe that government must manage overall economic conditions and assure equal opportunity to all, alongside basic public services.

Even the most liberal government, however, could never assure the conditions for order by itself. Policymakers in Washington sometimes forget that order is not a service that they can provide just by spending money. It depends on the concurrence of people with government, and with each other. The frontispiece of Hobbes's *Leviathan* shows that the sovereign is literally made up of "his" citizens. Government is really a mechanism by which people force themselves to serve and obey *each other* in necessary ways.

"Compliance," further, is too passive a term for what order requires, particularly in complex modern societies. People must not only refrain from offenses against others but fulfill the expectations others have of them in public roles, as workers on the job, as neighbors, or simply as passers-by in the streets of our cities. Order requires not only self-discipline but *activity* and *competence*. It is achieved when a population displays those habits of mutual forebearance and reliability which we call civility.

American political culture gives pride of place to the value of freedom. But a "free" society is possible only when the conditions for order have substantially been realized. People are not interested in "freedom" from government if they are victimized by crime, cannot support themselves, or are in any fundamental way insecure. They will want more government rather than less. Nor are they likely to vote or otherwise participate politically unless they are employed and have their personal lives in order. A "free" political culture is the characteristic, not of a society still close to the state of nature, as some American philosophers have imagined, but of one already far removed from it by dense, reliable networks of mutual expectations.

The conditions for order also extend across the border between the public and private sectors in the usual meanings of those words. Obligation usually connotes governmental duties such as paying taxes, obeying the law, or serving in the military (if there is a draft). But order also requires that people function well in areas of life that are not directly regulated. They must be educated in minimal ways, able to maintain themselves, able also to cooperate with others for common ends, whether political or economic—what Samuel Huntington has called the "art of associating together."[7] The capacities to learn, work, support one's family, and respect the rights of others amount to a set of *social* obligations alongside the political ones. A civic society might almost be defined as one in which people are competent in all these senses, as citizens and as workers. For people to fulfill these expectations or not is what I shall mean by their functioning or not functioning well.

Social policy should be seen as one of government's means of achieving order. Social programs define much of what society expects of people in the social realm, just as other laws and the Constitution do in the political realm. By the benefits they give to and withhold from different groups, the programs declare which needs government will help people manage, and which they must manage for themselves. The structure of benefits and requirements in the programs, then, constitutes an *operational definition of citizenship*. One of the things a government must do to improve social order is to use these programs to require better functioning of recipients who have difficulty coping. The tragedy of federal social programs is that they have only begun to do this. Federal political culture has such difficulty setting requirements for recipients that the programs have undermined social order rather than upheld it.

Functioning in American society has declined since 1960. Each column of Table 1 shows a fall in one kind of competence that American society has traditionally expected of its members. The

TABLE 1
Trends in Social Functioning, 1960–83

Year	*Recipients of AFDC (1,000's)*[a]	*Unemployment rate (percent)*[b]	*Serious crimes (1,000's)*[c]	*SAT scores*[d]
1960	3,005	5.4	3,384	969
1965	4,329	4.4	4,739	967
1970	8,466	4.8	8,098	941
1975	11,346	8.3	11,257	899
1980	10,774	7.0	13,295	893
1981	11,079	7.5	13,290	892
1982	10,358	9.5	12,857	890
1983	10,761	9.5	12,070	894

[a] Average monthly number of recipients of Aid to Families with Dependent Children, the main federal welfare program. Source: U.S. Department of Health and Human Services, Social Security Administration, *Social Security Bulletin, Annual Statistical Supplement, 1983* (Washington, D.C.: U.S. Government Printing Office, 1984), p. 248. Figure for 1983 from Office of Family Assistance, U.S. Department of Health and Human Services.

[b] Percentage of the civilian labor force unemployed. Source: U.S. Department of Labor, Bureau of Labor Statistics, *Employment and Earnings*, 31, no. 12 (December 1984):6.

[c] Serious crimes include murder, forcible rape, robbery, aggravated assault, burglary, larceny, theft, and motor vehicle theft. Source: U.S. Department of Commerce, Bureau of the Census, *Statistical Abstract of the United States, 1976* (Washington, D.C.: U.S. Government Printing Office, July 1976), p. 153, and *Statistical Abstract of the United States, 1984* (Washington, D.C.: U.S. Government Printing Office, December 1983), p. 176; U.S. Department of Justice, Federal Bureau of Investigation, *Crime in the United States, 1983* (Washington, D.C.: U.S. Government Printing Office, September 1984), p. 41.

[d] Sum of average math and average verbal scores of all students taking the Scholastic Aptitude Test in the school years beginning in the indicated years. Figures differ somewhat from published averages for college-bound seniors. Source: College Entrance Examination Board.

rise in Aid to Families with Dependent Children (AFDC), the main federal welfare program, reflects the inability of increasing numbers of low-income families to stay together and support themselves, since eligibility is usually limited to one-parent families in need. Most recipient families are headed by mothers separated from their spouses. The rise in unemployment means that increasing proportions of the labor force are unable to find jobs—or to accept the jobs available to them. The rise in crime reflects mainly the explosion of violence against persons and property in the large cities. The steady decline in SAT scores indicates a fall in the academic skills of students seeking to go to college.

Each trend appears a little less worrisome on examination. Welfare has risen mainly because more broken families in need have decided to seek assistance, not because there are more such families, though both trends are involved. While joblessness is greater, especially among the unskilled, the proportion of the adult population working or seeking work has actually risen. Higher crime is partly due to the huge "baby boom" generation passing through its youth, since greater numbers of young people always produce more crime. Declining SAT scores partly reflect the fact that relatively more test-takers in recent years have been disadvantaged or nonwhite, groups that on average were less well prepared for college than the middle-class whites who dominated earlier cohorts.[8] Some of the rise in crime and dependency is due simply to population growth. The trends in crime and SAT scores had reversed by 1983, but dependency rebounded.

The magnitude of the changes, nevertheless, is so great that nothing can fully explain them away. Many Americans evidently are less able to take care of themselves and respect the rights of others than in earlier decades. The numbers give credibility to the concern over the decay of "traditional values" that has colored American politics since the late 1960s. The mystery is why the decline occurred in spite of sharp public disquiet.

Not all the causes are regrettable or governmental. A disproportionate number of criminals and welfare recipients are nonwhite, although all races are well represented. A rising willingness of black Americans to make demands on white society, though it inflated the welfare rolls, was also essential to the civil rights movement and to civil rights reforms needed to advance integration. Rising unemployment results, in part, from the fact that many people have become impatient with the demands of low-paid jobs because of rising affluence, in itself a good thing. The decline of social order, which most Americans regret, was also related in diffuse ways to political disillusionments, particularly over Vietnam and Watergate, which many would say were warranted.[9]

Is government also to blame? Liberal and conservative criticisms about the scale of government have already been mentioned. Some other critics disillusioned with American politics, whom I call radicals, believe that society unfairly burdens the poor, to the point where they are forced into dysfunction. Michael Harrington is one exemplar. That belief contributes an important idea—that one purpose of social policy can be to discipline the poor. But where radicals say that welfare programs regiment the dependent and should not, my conclusion is that they usually do not but might, in ways that would serve the poor themselves.

Federal benefit programs set the rules under which a good part of the population lives. People learn social mores initially from their families, but public institutions have a lot to do with whether they are taken seriously. There is little disagreement in American society that people should observe social obligations—work, support one's family, and obey the law, among other things. There is a good deal of disagreement, however, about how closely those norms must actually govern personal behavior. Whether the values are treated as obligatory ultimately depends for many—perhaps most—citizens on the presence of enforcement. Like duties to obey the law or pay taxes, obligations to function at school, at work, and in other social roles would wither to formalities unless noncompliance ultimately drew some kind of sanction.

But federal programs have special difficulties in setting standards for their recipients. They tend to shield their clients from the threats and rewards that stem from private society—particularly the market place—while providing few sanctions of their own. The recipients seldom have to work or otherwise function to earn whatever income, service, or benefit a program gives; meager though it may be, they receive it essentially as an entitlement. Their place in American society is defined by their need and weakness, not their competence. This lack of accountability is among the reasons why nonwork, crime, family breakup, and other problems are much commoner among recipients than Americans generally.

The authority of programs is decisive for a different reason too: It is in principle subject to public control. Americans cannot be said to have chosen the social and economic changes that have swept over them in recent decades, contributing to disorder. Politically, however, they have accepted a permissive welfare state, and they could demand a more exacting one. The search for social solutions, James Q. Wilson has said, must emphasize factors that are subject to public control, not those that are not.[10] Federal policymakers must start to ask how programs can affirm the norms for functioning on which social order depends. There are serious problems in doing so, but they are political problems subject, in principle, to public debate and resolution.

At first such an approach may seem nothing more than an elaborate way of "blaming the victim." Social policy is supposed to help the weak and vulnerable. How could one justify burdening them with the responsibility for succeeding in school or at work when the conditions they face are difficult? The answer is simply that social programs have failed partly because they expect too little of their recipients, not too much, and there is evidence that clearer standards would improve functioning. A judgment against the poor could be accomplished simply by throwing them off programs to fend for themselves, the traditional conservative prescription. The idea of an authoritative policy, rather, is to *combine* requirements with support in a balance that approximates what the nondependent face outside government. This treats the dependent like other citizens in the ways essential to equality. Far from helping the poor, exaggerated fears of victim-blaming have themselves become a leading cause of dependency.

That fear expresses too crude a view of the role of authority in social order. As every political theorist—and policeman—knows, government can rarely control people if it merely blames or coerces them. Rather, citizens must *accept* its demands as legitimate, transmuting mere power into authority. Only then can compliance be widespread. Far from blaming people if they deviate, government must persuade them to *blame themselves*. This sense of responsibility, though it is individual, is not something individuals can produce alone. It rests ultimately on public norms and enforcement that are collective in character. It cannot last unless individuals finally get something out of compliance, unless they derive success and social acceptance from being "good citizens." That again only society can assure.

The idea of programs inculcating values may nevertheless seem foreign to American political mores. It conjures up a brutal, Hobbesian image of government deciding what is good for people and then imposing it on them by force. For policy to involve itself in the personal competences of individuals is inherently sensitive, and whatever is required can seem invidious. It is important to emphasize that what standards to require is not for any one person to decide, and there is no one right answer to it. It is a political question, indeed the supreme question in social policy. Some social requirements, such as work, may reasonably be treated as enforceable, because there is good evidence that the public views them this way. However, the main point here is not to advocate a specific set of mores but rather to show that programs embody a decision about norms, not only for recipients, but for citizens in general. For that reason social policy should be made in a political way by politicians, not, as it often is in Washington, in an expert and technical way, clothed in the language of economics, that admits only liberal goals or suppresses value questions entirely.

Americans are easily tempted to seek technical, nonpolitical solutions to the social problem that avoid behavioral issues. Confronted by the problem of nonwork by the poor, many people respond that either the economy must be denying work to the poor, or they are disabled or otherwise unemployable and hence exempted from the normal work expectation. The question of employability is obviously crucial and prior to any talk of obligations, but it is also substantially a political question. Within very broad limits it cannot be settled on medical or economic grounds alone. There are a great many nonworking poor who may be termed employable or not depending on how demanding society wishes to be of its members. It is precisely the groups who do not work regularly yet are not clearly disabled—unskilled men and welfare mothers with children—who have been the crux of the social problem and will be the main focus here. Are they too burdened to work, or are they employable and hence "undeserving"? It is a political question, and welfare and employment policy increasingly revolves around the answer.

Even a very authoritative social policy would not involve imposing values on recipients that are foreign to American life. American politics is a good deal less demanding than American society. Benefit recipients live under a regime of political values that allows individuals to make demands on government rather than vice versa. But in private society pressures to perform are strong, and most people have to function reasonably well just to maintain their economic and social postion, let alone improve it. The task in social policy is, not to invent values supportive of order, but to *elevate* those that already exist from the social realm into the political. The problem is to overcome the political and ideological reflexes that drive social policymakers to emphasize only benefits for recipients, denying the more orderly values in which both they and the dependent also believe.

To speak of obligating the poor may sound like abandonment of the goal of equality in the sense of mainstream income and status for the poor, the traditional aim of social policy. In reality, the lack of standards in programs has probably increased inequality in this sense by undercutting the competences the disadvantaged need to achieve status. But more important, equality to Americans tends not to mean middle-class income or status at all, but rather the enjoyment of equal citizenship, meaning the same rights *and* obligations as others. While we usually think of citizenship as something political, specifying rights like free speech and duties such as obedience to the law, it has a social dimension too. Benefit programs define a set of social rights for vulnerable groups, while Americans tend to regard minimal social competences like work or getting through school as obligatory even if they are not legally enforced. These *social* obligations may not be governmental, but they are public in that they fall within the collective expectation that structures an orderly society. Both political and social duties are included in what I shall call the common obligations of citizenship.

The great merit of equal citizenship as a social goal is that it is much more widely achievable than status. It is not competitive. It does not require that the disadvantaged "succeed," something not everyone can do. It requires only that everyone discharge the common obligations, including social ones like work. At the same time no one is exempted on grounds of disadvantage. All competent adults are supposed to work or display English literacy, just as everyone is supposed to pay taxes or obey the law, without regard to income or social postion.

Current programs infringe equality in this sense as much as they serve it. They raise the income of the needy, but they also exempt them from work and other requirements that are just as necessary for belonging. The novelty of an authoritative social policy would be to enforce social obligations, at least for the dependent, just as political obligations are enforced for the population in general. To obligate the dependent as others are obligated is essential to equality, not opposed to it. An effective welfare must include recipients in the common obligations of citizens rather than exclude them.

The next two chapters concern the emergence of functioning and obligation as issues in federal policymaking during the Great Society, the era of rapid innovation in social policymaking between 1960 and the late 1970s. Before that period social policy followed what may be called a progressive agenda. Government's job was to liberate the most vulnerable groups and classes from the external limitations imposed by destitution, mass unemployment, and racial discrimination. After 1960 the progressive search for social barriers persisted even though opportunity was much more widespread. The main impediments to a more equal society were now the functioning difficulties of the remaining poor themselves, especially problems of family instability and nonwork. Those problems government cannot solve without setting some behavioral standards for its dependents. Yet the many programs and policies of the Great Society never did that; they merely transferred increasing income and other benefits to recipients. The programs were justified, also, by an understanding of the social problem that assigned all of the responsibility for social change to government, none to the poor themselves.

Chapters 4 through 7 concern work, the strongest and clearest social obligation and also the one with the longest policy history in Washington. There are good grounds to think that work, at least in "dirty," low-wage jobs, can no longer be left solely to the initiative of those who labor. The unskilled have too many other sources of income, including government benefits, for them to work reliably unless programs require them to. At least for these workers, employment must become a duty, enforced by public authority, rather than an expression of self-interest. That is so regardless of how we interpret the mysterious phenomenon of nonwork, or irregular work, among many low-income people.

A growing perception of the need for enforcement explains why work requirements came to dominate the debate, during much of the Great Society period, over proposals to "reform," or expand, welfare. Most treatments of that struggle interpret it as a typical New Deal battle over whether to enlarge government. In reality few Congressmen of either party had much problem with liberalization as such. The critical issue was work, not welfare. Congressmen divided mainly over whether employable recipients should have to work *in return* for support. Reform lost primarily because moderates and conservatives demanded stronger work provisions than liberals would grant. The struggle dramatized the power of the functioning problem, once it was grasped, to shift the debate from the *scale* to the *nature* of goverment.

Welfare reform was only the most dramatic episode in a long struggle by congressional conservatives to strengthen work requirements in all the main federal income programs. Support for welfare and unemployment benefits is too strong to enforce work simply by refusing assistance to the employable; increasingly, rather, they are subjected to pressure to work from within the programs. None of these requirements as yet has had much effect, however, because of the very difficult administrative and political problems of work enforcement. My own studies of the Work Incentive (WIN) program, the main federal welfare work program, demonstrate both the importance of work tests and the ways in which they are, or are not, enforced. The studies show that whether recipients work depends heavily on the degree of work obligation they face from WIN. The economic "barriers" usually stressed in Washington, such as the low skills of the recipients and the limited jobs available, are not decisive.

The last four chapters deal with the politics of social obligation. The questions raised are why federal programs have such difficulty setting standards, and how clearer requirements might be justified. The impediments include the limitations of federal constitutional authority, the tradition that federal programs should merely subsidize social groups, the ways policy analysts in Washington approach social policy, and implementation difficulties. Even more important, perhaps, are the political beliefs, on the part of both conservatives and liberals, that oppose the use of federal authority for social ends.

On the other hand, the welfare reform struggle caused some Congressmen to articulate a new approach to social policy—which I call the civic conception—that justified work requirements much along the lines already suggested. Welfare had to require work as well as offer support, these members said, if the recipients were to be integrated and not just subsidized. That philosophy is alien to the permissive culture of Washington but is supported by public opinion. The idea of coupling benefits with enforcement of the common obligations might at last provide a political and ideological basis for a more effective social policy, but major changes toward a more authoritative and perhaps paternalist kind of program would be involved.

The sources for the chapters on the development of policy are mainly histories of the Great Society and evaluations of its programs. The chapters on work requirements draw heavily on the employment policy literature as well as my own research on welfare work and the legislative history of work tests. The chapters on the politics of obligation are based on analyses of federal policymaking as well as surveys of public opinion as it bears on social policy issues. The treatments of welfare reform and of the attitudes for and against requirements also rely heavily on citations from the many congressional hearings, reports, and debates on welfare work and reform between 1967 and 1979.[11]

The mix of historical and technical, qualitiative and quantitative sources is unusual for a study in public policy. There is a tendency, especially in social policy, for analyses to run to extremes. There are qualitative, historical treatments of programs and issues like welfare reform that are accessible to laymen and deal well with the political and administrative aspects of programs, but do not evaluate them with much authority or suggest alternatives. Conversely, there are evaluative studies that say much more about the worth of programs and alternatives, but are inaccessible to the nontechnical and say little about politics and administration. That division largely reflects a division of authorship between political scientists, public administrators, and journalists on the one hand and economists and evaluators on the other. Some recent studies of program implementation, including most of those reported in Chapter 7, merge institutional and economic perspectives, but in general the two seldom meet.

That is unfortunate for both social science and policymaking, since it takes both viewpoints either to understand programs or to improve them. The effects programs have reflect the politics behind them as well as the benefits they provide, yet political scientists tend to study only the first and economists only the second. Analysts who do not know statistics have largely been driven out of social policymaking by economists and other technicians. Yet welfare reform failed, in part, because the economists behind it were politically naive. They would not, or could not, face up to the functioning problems in welfare to the extent Congress wished. The present analysis combines political and economic reasoning in an attempt to understand social policy more fully than either approach can do alone.[12]

This treatment of the social policy problem does not supplant all others. The traditional, conservative and liberal approaches that want to change the scope of support for the poor remain important. Part of the answer to dependency still is to eliminate benefits that tempt people to dysfunction, or to provide new ones that might help them in decisive ways. Another imperative, which would exist under any approach, is simply to administer programs more effectively. Many of their problems, not only in levying obligations, come down to poor implementation.

To establish the need for standards is only the beginning of new thinking in social policy. Then other, equally difficult questions come into view. *How much* impact on the social problem would standards have? *How exacting* must the standards be to improve functioning to the levels necessary for integration? Clearly, a lack of standards is not the only reason for dysfunction; European social programs are generally as permissive as American ones, yet those countries do not experience social problems on the same scale. The potential and proper scope of standards probably cannot be known until there is more experience with, and research about, work and other requirements in programs. At this point it can be said only that clearer obligations are a necessary, if not sufficient, condition for a successful social policy.

There is uncertainty as well simply because the nature of dysfunction remains mysterious. No one really knows why some individuals master their environment while others are overwhelmed by it. The quest for answers is at least as old as the Industrial Revolution, when poverty and dependency were first seen as problems for government to solve.[13] Time and modern research methods have not unraveled the mystery. There are competing explanations even for nonwork among the poor, a more researchable problem than most.

The most fundamental question is political: How could behavioral requirements for the needy be reconciled with the mores of a humane polity? The idea of a publicly sponsored ethos for citizens sounds contrary to the nature of an open society. Some political footing for such standards can be found in Congress, in public opinion, and in American values. But there is also strong resistance from the anti-authoritarian, benefit-oriented habits of federal politics. A more directive policy could be realized only after a long struggle to justify it politically, implement it in detail, and build up its authority. That struggle has only just begun. For years to come it will remain easier for liberals simply to vote more benefits, or for conservatives to cut them back, than to link requirements to them.

It is already clear, however, that the thinking behind policy in Washington has been too narrowly economic. The programs claim to serve equality, but essentially all they do is transfer benefits to recipients. As long as equality in America requires competence as well as income, programs must set standards as well as support people. The most vulnerable Americans need obligations, as much as rights, if they are to move as equals on the stage of American life.

2

Functioning: The New Shape of the Social Problem

PERHAPS the greatest obstacle to an effective social policy today is the memory of earlier periods of successful social reform. Up through the mid-1960s, it was possible for reform to proceed in the ways most congenial to American politics, by the elimination of barriers to the advancement of competent citizens. Turn-of-the-century regulation of big business, New Deal measures for working people, and civil rights reforms to eliminate official race discrimination all presumed, with good reason, that the main impediments to a more just society lay in unfair social structures and, secondarily, in the political forces defending them. Those who suffered organized themselves to demand redress. They believed, also with good reason, that if government would only remove the barriers, ordinary Americans would have no trouble making use of the new opportunites open to them.

Since about 1965, however, this progressive tradition has been a poor guide to integrating poor and disadvantaged Americans at the bottom of society. For these individuals the main barrier to acceptance is no longer unfair social structures but their own difficulties in coping, particularly with work and family life. The Great Society period saw a string of new approaches to helping the disadvantaged, but their success has been very slight. Today the social problem appears, not mainly in the destitution of functioning citizens and their families, but in widespread dependency, with millions of Americans, including many working-age adults, subsisting on federal benefit programs. The progressive approach to social reform has begun to contradict itself. Further attempts to emancipate the poor, if functioning problems are ignored, will produce a society that is *less* free and equal rather than more.

Progressive Reform

There have been three main periods of social reform in the progressive style. The Progressive era proper, in the decades around 1900, saw the first substantial federal regulation of the economy, the bare beginnings of national social legislation, reforms to clean up politics such as the secret ballot and primary elections, and measures to strengthen government itself such as civil service and the graduated income tax. The New Deal, in the 1930s, instituted further business regulation, the first large-scale federal social programs, and a number of new protections for workers and farmers. The Great Society of the 1960s and 1970s had several themes, the most purely progressive being the civil rights measures of the mid-1960s, outlawing official forms of racial discrimination.

Such reforms reflected the progressive view of the nature of social change. They addressed economic social impediments that were believed to make society inefficient, uncompetitive, or unfair to working people and, later, to minorities. The barriers included the overweening power of the "trusts," corrupt political machines, railroad exploitation of farmers, business resistance to trade unionism, and Jim Crow laws, especially in the South. Worst of all, an economy controlled by big business rather than government was prone to periodic panics or depressions, leading to mass unemployment and hardship for ordinary Americans.

Progressive reforms involved large-scale political conflict. They were pressed by coalitions of middle-class reformers, labor, and civil rights groups and resisted by business and the better-off. In general the Democratic party was in favor of change, the Republicans opposed or skeptical. While the civil rights acts were not as divisive at their passage as earlier progressive measures, the busing and affirmative action policies stemming from them and from Supreme Court decisions have been intensely controversial.

However, progressive reformism had, in some ways, very

limited goals. There was no desire to remake American society, even to the extent of the kind of democratic socialism seen in Western Europe. The point was to even up somewhat the advantages of different classes and interests. Political and economic power was redistributed much more than wealth or status.[1] Even business, though it generally opposed the new government controls, benefited from regulations that controlled prices and limited competition in some industries.[2]

Progressivism was also much more radical in economic than in social terms. The crucial issue was the extent of government intervention *in the economy*. Reformers wanted to increase regulation and taxation and bring key aspects of business operations—prices, wages, working conditions, finance—under public control. Corporate forces resisted. This "New Deal" question is still the main issue dividing the parties. But progressivism did not change the nature of American *society*. Reform concentrated narrowly on the *economic* bars to opportunity. It was assumed that workers were competent to run their own lives and get ahead once their prospects were widened. That was why the New Deal did little to educate, train, or otherwise socialize people. It also took only small steps to assist those who could not support themselves. A number of relief and welfare programs were enacted, but they were either temporary or confined to the unemployable. Unemployment Insurance was conservatively administered, while Social Security was limited to the retired. At least implicitly, the New Deal rejected dependency by the working-aged.[3]

The competence that the progressive approach assumed in ordinary people came out in several ways. One was simply the political tactics needed to achieve reform. In view of the resistance, reform leaders did not expect government to bestow the desired changes unasked. Pressure had to be exerted on it from outside, and that made demands on both leaders and followers. Pressure from unemployed workers and unionists helped push through the principal New Deal enactments,[4] while nonviolent marches, demonstrations, and lawsuits were critical to the civil rights victories of the 1960s. Unemployment Insurance and Social Security also assumed that the working class would support itself, since both were based on social insurance, whereby those who were working paid payroll taxes to support those who were jobless or retired. Neither program, at least initially, involved much redistribution from rich to poor.

Most important, the beneficiaries of progressive reform did indeed make good use of new opportunities with little further help from government. During and after World War II, a generation of workers and their families advanced toward middle-class income and status simply through participating in a growing economy and to some extent through trade union activity. It was enough that the social rules now gave a better break to working people. The most important postwar programs for workers were probably the housing and highway subsidies that helped many of them move to the suburbs. The massive expansion in university education in the 1950s and 1960s was also progressive in spirit, since it widened access to white-collar careers, but the initiative came mainly from the state level. Most workers effectively entered the middle class, and they did it with only indirect help from government. The civil rights reforms, similarly, set the stage for the rapid emergence of a black middle class in the 1960s and 1970s. Many of today's black professionals participated in the civil rights movement in their youth, then benefited from the enlarged opportunities that came to them as a result of it.

The success of progressivism seemed to prove, as reformers said, that there were reformable abuses in society. The experience has entered deeply into the American political consiousness. The moral we still tend to draw is that all social problems are due to denials of freedom. We forget reformism's unspoken premise that those at the bottom of society could take care of themselves. A great many of those who were poor in resources were rich in abilities to work, learn, and raise families. Public action and private competence worked together for effective social change.

The Social Problem Today

The dilemma for social policy is that, following civil rights, no further formidable social barriers were discovered that could explain the persistence of poverty among some Americans. From the late 1960s onward it was no longer plausible that poverty was due primarily to economic injustices or systematic discrimination against minorities. While government took a number of expensive new steps to aid the needy, none has led to integration, to a healing of social wounds, in the manner of the New Deal or civil rights. The main reason for this is that lower-income people today often lack the coping abilities that reform earlier assumed. Thus it is no longer possible to help them simply by extending new opportunities or benefits.

Since 1960 the main preoccupation of federal social policy has not been demands by large strata for opportunity but the risk of social exclusion for a number of groups at the bottom of society. Of these the most important has come to be called the underclass or lower class. Experts are in close agreement about its nature. It comprises those Americans who *combine* relatively low income with functioning problems such as difficulties in getting through school, obeying the law, working, and keeping their families together. These characteristics, in turn, are traceable to an unstable family life, marked by absent fathers, erratic parenting, and low self-esteem and aspiration. I shall use "underclass" or "lower class," not pejoratively, but simply to designate this group.

The underclass is most visible in urban slum settings and is about 70 percent nonwhite, but it includes many rural and white people as well, especially in Appalachia and the South. Much of the urban underclass is made up of street hustlers, welfare families, drug addicts, and former mental patients. There are, of course, needy people who function well—the so-called "deserving" or "working poor"—and better-off people who function poorly, but in general low income and serious behavioral difficulties go together. The underclass is not large as a share of population, perhaps 9 million people, but it accounts for the lion's share of the most serious disorders in American life, especially in the cities.[5]

While the underclass functions less well than earlier out-groups, it is if anything more conformist. Studies have shown that the group is alienated and populist but not radical. Its members want expanded social programs but not any great change in the economy or society. Few of them vote, but if they did, contrary to the conventional wisdom, election outcomes would change little, and Republican candidates would probably benefit as often as Democrats.[6] Nor are the social mores of the underclass unusual. Lower-class people profess attachment, just like other Americans, to the family, work, and obeying the law. They are distinctive not in their beliefs but in their inability to conform to them as closely as other people. One reason many lower-class people are demoralized is that they *know* they should work, stay in school, support their families, and so on, even if they do not.[7] The orthodoxy of lower-class belief is itself a good reason to blame much of the disorder of the group on the permissive character of social programs. For if needy recipients themselves accept mainstream mores but live otherwise, the programs they rely on must get much of the blame.

Most often federal social planners define their concern, not as the underclass, but as "the disadvantaged." The connotation is of a somewhat larger group, perhaps 20 million, that suffers low income and cultural deprivation but may or may not have lower-class functioning problems. Since 1960 federal education and job training programs have usually been targeted on the disadvantaged, defined as those with low income who also have, or might have, serious language, learning, or employment problems. The disadvantaged are seen as people who already function marginally and may become lower-class unless their "deficits" in income and skills are dealt with.

A related group that has drawn federal attention since the early 1960s is the "poor," meaning individuals and families without sufficient income by official measures. The poverty line was defined as $9,862 for a nonfarm family of four in 1982, and 15 percent of the population, or 34.8 million people, were below it. The figures drop to perhaps 8 percent or 18.6 million at present if noncash government benefits such as food stamps are counted as income.[8] Much of federal domestic policy since 1960, not only social programs, has aimed to reduce poverty. Yet much of the real concern, as with disadvantage, stems from the belief that poverty causes problems such as crime or family breakup that are much more damaging to integration.

As even more important group to federal policymakers has been nonwhites, especially blacks, who have been the "special objects and beneficiaries" of federal policy since the civil rights movement.[9] Eligibility for federal education, training, and welfare programs has always been framed in race-blind terms, chiefly poverty, low income, or disadvantage, yet a plurality and even a majority of recipients in many of these programs have been black. While, because of slavery and discrimination, blacks in general have special claims on federal attention, policymaking attention has focused mainly on that share of black America with the income and behavioral problems associated with the underclass.

While there were 26.5 million black Americans in 1980, most of them not lower-class, almost a third or 8.6 million were poor. The comparable figures for Hispanics were 14.6 million and 3.5 million.[10] While blacks are only 12 percent of the population, they make up 43 percent of AFDC recipients and 23 percent of the unemployed. Of those who are poor or welfare recipients over long periods, the majority are black, and two-thirds of blacks depend on some kind of welfare benefits at least temporarily.[11] Blacks comprise half or more of those arrested for most violent crimes and over 40 percent of jail inmates.[12] And while blacks are rapidly closing their educational gap with whites, they are still overrepresented among illiterates and high school dropouts.[13] While there is no necessary connection between race and lower-class status, blacks do face special difficulties because so many members of their group have functioning problems.

Finally, Washington's preoccupation with the underclass overlaps its concern, inherited from the progressive period, for the unemployed. The two groups are much the same size, the latter running 8 million to 10 million in recent years.[14] The presumption, stemming from the New Deal, that unemployment is due to economic collapse and is government's responsibility was codified in the Employment Act of 1946 and again in the Humphrey–Hawkins Act of 1978.

Today, however, a lot of unemployment has more to do with functioning problems of the jobless themselves than with economic conditions. The administrators of federal training programs find that their clients have more difficulty keeping jobs than finding them. Since the early 1960s, except in the most depressed areas, most of the long-term unemployed have been unmarried men, youths, or women, not older men or heads of household. What they have needed most was training in the basic skills and attitudes needed to hold any job, such as literacy and punctuality, not advanced skills. That is still true, since today's supposedly "high-tech" economy produces many low-skilled jobs. To find a constituency, federal training has had to become an antipoverty effort and serve the disadvantaged.[15]

In the 1970s unemployment became more widespread and was apparently less attributable to disadvantage. Some of the increase was "cyclical" joblessness, due to recessions, and some was "structural," due to the decay of the automotive, steel, and other "smokestack" industries. But again, a decline in functioning was also involved. Many observers say that the American workforce may be less skilled and motivated than it once was. One cause may be the decline in school standards, another the higher proportion of women and youths (who tend to be less skilled) now seeking work, still another the effects of unionism and protected industries. The fall in capability, along with low investment, were the main reasons why productivity growth declined in the 1970s compared to previous decades, and even reversed in some recent years.[16] That in turn led to the collapse of the industrial Midwest. Compared to their competitors in Japan and elsewhere, American workers often produced less relative to what they were paid. Problems of commitment and capacity at work, previously confined to the disadvantaged, now seemed to stretch much more widely.

During the 1970s federal service programs served the disadvantaged and better-off workers with less distinction than formerly. Training programs provided public jobs to both groups. Federal education programs, which were supposed to serve the disadvantaged, in fact benefited a wide range of students, especially in their early years. One reason was that the criteria for eligibility were loosely drawn and administered,[17] another that local educators did not think learning problems were confined to a narrow group. Recent efforts to raise educational standards have focused on the schools in general.

All this suggests that competence problems are not narrowly confined to the specific groups mentioned earlier. The aggregate trends in unemployment and SAT scores seen in Table 1 could not have been produced by lower-class, disadvantaged, poor, or nonwhite Americans alone—they are too few in number. While the working and middle classes still usually avoid the crime and overt welfarism that are so destructive for the underclass, functioning is an issue for American society as a whole.

The Great Society

By the time of the Great Society, the challenge to social policy had clearly changed from freedom to functioning. After the civil rights acts there was little more that government could do to help the poor by emancipating them from obvious limitations of opportunity. The programs of the 1960s and 1970s, therefore, made much less demanding assumptions about the competence of their recipients.

Where New Deal policies had forced change on the economy in favor of the worst-off, most Great Society programming was directed at the disadvantaged themselves. It aimed either to increase their skills, so they would be more competitive in the job market, or simply to support them. Where the New Deal gave greatest emphasis to changing the economic rules so that workers could make their own way, policy after 1960 seldom assumed that government clients could support themselves, either individually or collectively. Instead, antipoverty and other Great Society programs[18] emphasized giving recipients services, income, and other benefits directly. Of the new programs, only Medicare was paid for by the claimants themselves, through payroll taxes and other contributions. All the others were funded out of general revenue. They were also mostly means-tested or focused in other ways on the disadvantaged. Thus, they constituted "welfare" in a broad sense, as against the more respectable social insurance emphasized by the New Deal.

The Great Society was at least creative. Five phases or themes can be discerned in the policies of the period. Each was driven, in part, by the perceived shortcomings of the preceding phase. The inability of the government to deal well with the social problem drove it to continual new policymaking.

The earliest phase, already mentioned, was civil rights. The reasoning was that equal rights were not only just but an effective antipoverty policy, since so many poor people were black. The most important civil rights measures were the Supreme Court decisions outlawing school segregation and the Civil Rights Acts of 1964 and 1965. Those edicts ended at least overt, legalized forms of discrimination in education, employment, and voting. Because of affirmative action, equal rights have been pressed furthest in government hiring and among state and local governments, universities, and contractors dependent on federal funds. The public sector in this enlarged sense has become a vanguard for black advancement and has gradually drawn the rest of society in its wake.

A second approach, almost contemporaneous, emphasized job creation through macroeconomic policy. Keynesian economists reasoned that the manipulation of taxing and spending to maintain full unemployment would be of special benefit to the poor. People with low income were usually low-skilled; they stood at the back of the "hiring queue." They would be hired only if unemployment were so low that employers had no alternative. This argument, by the economists who crafted the "Kennedy tax cut" of 1964, illustrates the tendency in the 1960s for "What does it do for the poor?" to become a criterion for federal policies of all sorts.[19] The 1964 tax cut, along with Vietnam War spending, launched the late-1960s boom. Between 1969 and 1978 Congress cut taxes several more times in an effort to sustain the boom and overcome the recessions of the 1970s.

A third approach of the early and mid-1960s was special education and training programs. Some planners recognized that many low-income people might not benefit economically from more equal rights or employment. Their skills were too limited for them to compete in the job market, even if the economy were booming. This was the closest the Great Society came to recognizing the coping problems of the disadvantaged. The new programming was supposed to "compensate" for those "deficits." The education programs included Head Start, a preschool program for disadvantaged children; Title I, which funded remedial programs in the schools; other programs for the handicapped and non-English-speaking; and a number of grants and loans to help the low-income go to college. The main employment programs were the training and jobs services provided successively under the Manpower Demonstration and Training Act (MDTA, 1962–73), the Comprehensive Employment and Training Act (CETA, 1973–82), and the Job Training Partnership Act (JTPA, since 1982). The antipoverty effort also funded a number of training programs, of which the most notable was the Job Corps, an intensive residential program for disadvantaged youth.

Funding for the compensatory programs was substantial. Federal spending for education grew from $4 billion to $16.5 billion between 1965 and 1975. In employment, spending jumped from only $450 million in 1964 to $4.7 billion in 1974 and $11.2 billion in 1978, when 3.9 million clients were served. Between 1962 and 1980, there were 32.6 *million* enrollments in the training programs.[20]

Nevertheless, the record of the compensatory effort was disappointing. Evaluations suggested that the programs often provided worthwhile services, but they had very limited impact on the skills of their recipients. Head Start and Title I did not much improve the learning abilities of poor children, though some recent evaluations have been more favorable. The "Coleman report" on education, published in 1966, suggested that schools might never be able to overcome the learning advantage that better-off children derived from the superior background of their parents.[21] The training programs, similarly, generally raised the earning power of their recipients very little. The gains usually exceeded the cost of the programs, and for some trainees, notably younger welfare mothers, they could be substantial. The Job Corps had some clear impact on its trainees, but it was costly. The recipients, however, seldom improved enough to escape need or dependency on a permanent basis.[22]

By the late 1960s disillusionment caused thinking in Washington to shift again, toward the possibility of abolishing poverty more directly, simply by transferring income to the poor. The number of poor had declined to the point where an "income strategy" seemed feasible. The idea originated with liberals, but it appealed to some conservatives as well, since it would require less bureaucracy than service-oriented antipoverty strategies.[23] Proposals to guarantee all Americans an income were defeated in Congress, but income programs were expanded in other ways that, collectively, had much the same effect. AFDC, which normally covered single-parent families, was extended in 1961 at state option to cover two-parent families, if the father was unemployed. Supplemental Security Income (SSI, 1972) federalized and liberalized welfare for the aged, blind, and disabled. Important new welfare programs were added: food stamps (1964), which assured sustenance to all the needy, and Medicaid (1965), which covered health care for the welfare poor.

Most important of all, benefits were expanded in existing income programs, often without explicit decisions in Washington. Disability (which covers disabled workers) and Unemployment Insurance were administered more leniently, allowing many people out of work to become dependent. States raised benefit levels in AFDC, increasing the pool of eligibles for the program by 35 percent between 1967 and 1971. By 1970, 30 percent of the recipients were above poverty.[24] Benefits have since declined in real terms by about a quarter, because of inflation. Congress regularly increased benefits in Social Security, finally indexing them to inflation in 1972, steps that led to massive new transfers to the elderly.

More than any other strategy, income maintenance led to staggering increases in social spending. Table 2 shows the trends. The nation's overall social expenditures rose more than eleven times between 1960 and 1982. The increase was four times even allowing for inflation, and more than three times adding in population growth. Even sharper increases were seen in social insurance and welfare programs, and in all categories federal spending rose most quickly. The result was a virtual doubling of the share of national wealth going to social welfare. Since the social insurance programs cover the middle class, only 40–45 percent of this spending went to

TABLE 2
Social Welfare Spending, 1960–82

	1960	*1970*	*1982*	*Ratio of 1982 to 1960*
Total Social Welfare[a]				
Current dollars				
Total spending (billions)	52.3	145.9	592.6	11.3
Federal spending (billions)	25.0	77.3	366.6	14.7
Per capita (dollars)	285	699	2,519	8.8
Constant (1982) dollars				
Total spending (billions)[b]	148.9	322.6	591.2	4.0
Per capita (dollars)	815	1,550	2,519	3.1
Social Insurance[c]				
Current dollars				
Total spending (billions)	19.3	54.7	300.7	15.6
Federal spending (billions)	14.3	45.2	249.3	17.4
Per capita (dollars)	105	262	1,277	12.2
Constant (1982) dollars				
Per capita (dollars)	301	580	1,277	4.2
Public Assistance[d]				
Current dollars				
Total spending (billions)	4.1	16.5	80.8	19.7
Federal spending (billions)	2.1	9.6	52.4	25.0
Per capita (dollars)	22	79	344	15.6
Constant (1982) dollars				
Per capita (dollars)	64	176	344	5.4
Total Social Welfare				
As % of Gross National Product	10.3	14.7	19.3	1.9
As % of all government spending	38.4	48.2	55.5	1.4
Federal share as % of all federal spending	28.1	40.1	52.4	1.9

[a] Includes spending by all governments on social insurance, public assistance, health, veterans, education, housing, vocational rehabilitation, children, and community action programs.

[b] These spending figures omit expenditures abroad for several programs, so the 1982 figure is slightly less than the current dollar equivalent.

[c] Includes Social Security, Disability, Unemployment Insurance and workmen's compensation, Medicare and other health insurance, and special programs covering railroad workers and public employees.

[d] Includes Aid to Families with Dependent Children, Supplemental Security Income, food stamps, Medicaid, social services, and local general assistance.

SOURCE: Ann Kallman Bixby, "Social Welfare Expenditures, 1981 and 1982," *Social Security Bulletin*, 47, no. 12 (December 1984):14–22.

the poor. However, federal spending specifically for the needy also grew explosively, by more than 10 percent a year between 1965 and 1974 even allowing for inflation.[25] The cumulative impact of such increases transformed the economic position of most poor people in the United States. Though it was unplanned, the combination of social programs constituted by the mid 1970s, according to one liberal assessment, a "relatively generous, complete, and comprehensive social welfare system" covering "most basic needs."[26]

Of themselves, however, welfare programs led only to dependency, and lack of work provisions had doomed proposals for guaranteed income in Washington. Thus, there was pressure to deliver more help to the disadvantaged through work instead of welfare. That could no longer be done simply through macroeconomic policies to generate jobs, since to lower unemployment to the point where unskilled workers were hired seemed, by the early 1970s, to carry too high a cost in inflation. Therefore, policy shifted again, toward labor market policies, the last of the Great Society strategies. Government would promote hiring of the poor by changing the job market rather than the jobless.

This effort was rationalized by a new academic theory that contended that the labor market was "dual" or "segmented." The earlier strategies had optimistically assumed that even if the unskilled could initially obtain only low-skilled, low-paid jobs, they or their descendents would be able to move up into better-paying positions. The new theory said that such advancement was unlikely. Low-skilled workers could usually obtain work only in the "secondary" economy of fast-food restaurants and the service trades, where pay and conditions were poor, seldom in the "primary" sector of government and large or unionized industries, where pay, benefits, and job security were much more attractive. Primary employers used applicants' race or educational credentials as "cues" to "screen" out the disadvantaged, with little attention to actual skills. That meant these workers could seldom get "good" jobs no matter how much training they received. Therefore government had to take more regulatory steps, reminiscent of the New Deal, to force the hiring of the disadvantaged.[27]

The main device to this end was government employment. Clients who did not get worthwhile jobs in the private sector would be employed in government itself. Earlier antipoverty programs had already generated a fair amount of employment for their staffs, who themselves often had disadvantaged backgrounds. What was new in the 1970s was massive funding for "public service employment" (PSE), or short-term government jobs created for the jobless in local government or nonprofit agencies. PSE, most of which was funded under CETA, offered little training; it assumed that recipients would be socialized into better work habits simply by holding a "good" job in government for a short period. In 1975–79 there was also a national experiment in a more intensive form of PSE called "supported work," where jobholders also received training, counseling, and peer group support to help them overcome fears of failure. Secondary aspects of the labor market strategy included tax credits given to employers for hiring welfare recipients or other disadvantaged, and affirmative action, which caused government agencies, contractors, and grant recipients to hire more minorities and women.

These programs, too, had little favorable impact. The main disappointment with PSE was that few recipients "transitioned" to regular employment in the private sector. Trainees tended to keep their positons as long as allowed, then go on Unemployment or leave the labor force. They seldom moved on to unsubsidized private jobs, which usually offered less attractive pay or conditions than PSE. In 1977 only 22 percent of disadvantaged holders of CETA PSE slots left the program. Only 9.5 percent left for regular, unsubsidized employment, and most of that was in government itself rather than the private sector. This record—along with widespread diversion of PSE to support regular municipal workers—was why the program faced increasing opposition in Congress and was cancelled in 1981. The supported work experiment recorded clear benefits for welfare mothers but little or none for other recipients. The hiring incentives demonstrated little effect, and while affirmative acton expanded government hiring of nonwhites, it raised questions about how real this integration was since it depended so heavily on preferences.[28]

As the nature of the social problem changed, compared to the progressive era, so did the nature of political conflict over social policy. Compared to the earlier period, Great Society policymaking was much more problem-solving and experimental, much less partisan. The last issue that aroused a generalized battle between reforming and conservative forces was the enactment in 1965 of Medicaid and Medicare, which cover the major health expenses of the poor and elderly. During much of the 1960s and 1970s the two political parties groped for answers to the social problem side by side. Republicans played an important role in building the arsenal of new programs. Opposition came, not so much from the GOP as a whole, as from conservatives of both parties (notably conservative committee chairmen) who doubted that Washington could or should deal with poverty. Even business got into the act by helping the government develop several of its new employment programs.[29] Only at the end of the 1970s did the Republicans adopt a more hard-line attitude opposed to most new programs.

The Reagan Administration, with its strenuous efforts to cut social spending, has to some extent restored ideological conflict over social policy, but the change is more apparent than real. The effort to control spending actually began under the Carter Administration, and many of the Reagan cuts have had bipartisan support. The cuts in social spending through 1983 totaled $35 billion to $40 billion a year, only 7 to 10 percent of the federal social budget, and they were aimed at recipients above the poverty line. The reductions hit vital income programs like welfare much less than service programs like CETA. While working families near the poverty line were hurt, most of those under it remain protected. There are holes in the social "safety net," but they mostly predate Reagan. Rhetoric aside, the Reagan program is mostly an effort to eliminate waste, not to terminate the federal role in social policy.[30]

One reason for diminished conflict was simply that the new programs did not threaten conservative economic interests in the way that New Deal policymaking had done. They did not, on the whole, regiment business with new regulations. The chief expenses were due to the social insurance programs (Social Security, Unemployment Insurance, Medicare, Disability) that covered rich and poor alike and thus had a secure constituency; programs specifically for the poor were politically more vulnerable but also less costly. The main advantage of solving the social problem would be further integration and a decline in all the forms of disorder seen in Table 1, something in which all classes had an interest. Besides, most of the new programs operated by means of grants to state and local governments, something popular with the constituents of both parties, rather than through more heavy-handed economic controls.

Another important difference from the New Deal was that the new policies generally came from *inside* government rather than outside. The style of progressive politics was for groups to come to government with their own ideas for reforms, many of which government enacted. That made for conflict, but it also reflected one facet of the competence that progressivism presumed in the beneficiaries of reform—the political skill to lobby for redress of grievances. After the climax of the civil rights crusade in the mid-1960s, there were no further mass movements bringing demands to Washington. Even the hard times of the 1970s failed to inspire such a movement on behalf of either workers or minorities. Policymaking became much more elitist and paternalist. Most of the education and employment programs of the War on Poverty and Great Society were designed by experts within government or working closely with it. Reform ceased to be political in the old sense and became professionalized.[31]

The Great Society was not economically radical, as the New Deal had been. The labor market policies were the only ones that sought to reshape the economy, and in very minor ways. One reason for economic conservatism was that the most prominent Great Society planners were social scientists, especially economists, rather than lawyers as most of Roosevelt's "brain trust" had been. The urge of economists was not to remake the market but to liberate it for social ends. In fact, at economists' urging much regulation of prices and competition dating from the New Deal, especially in energy, airlines, and banking, was undone during the 1970s. The argument was that these industries were competitive and did not need regulation. Increasingly, American domestic policy is market-based. The main impetus of Great Society policy, therefore, was to give the disadvantaged the income and skills they needed to function in the free market, not to change the economic rules in their favor.[32]

The new programs were radical, however, in social terms. They tended to shield their recipients from the usual demands of American society, as the New Deal had not. Because most were welfare programs without serious work or other requirements, they did not assume or enforce social functioning as the New Deal insurance programs had. So far as basic income and services were concerned, the recipients were exempted from the pressures to perform that normally emanate from schools, neighborhoods, and workplaces. They were assured a secure, if depressed, place in American society almost without reference to behavior.

As a result the social, not economic, aspects of recent domestic policy have been the most controversial. In the 1930s resistance to government was led by businessmen afraid that Washington meant to undermine the free economy. Since 1960 it has been led mainly by neighborhood, religious, and other conservative forces afraid that school desegregation, residential integration, lenient law enforcement, and permissive welfare policies were undermining social standards. In the 1930s unemployment was the preeminent symptom of social disarray. Much of the time since 1960 crime, welfarism, and declining school standards have been at least as prominent.

The Record

The record of the Great Society gives good grounds for concern. The period recorded substantial progress against the remaining barriers to opportunity in American life, but apparently at great cost to the ability of government's clients to cope on their own. The question must be asked whether federal programs are making the social problem better or worse.

The main achievements of the period were to improve opportunities for nonwhites, expand employment, and reduce poverty. The first meant the sharpest break from the past. The civil rights acts abruptly increased voting among blacks, so that by 1972 no discernible discriminaton against them remained.[33] Along with the Supreme Court decisions, the acts also broke up dual school systems in the South, although *de facto* segregation due to housing patterns remains strong in the North. Partly owing to federal programs, black attendance in school and at universities rose sharply, and the educational gap between the races started to close. In 1960, 26 percent of whites, but only 13 percent of blacks, had finished high school; by 1982 the figures were 39 and 33 percent. The black proportion of college students rose from 5 to 9 percent between 1960 and 1972, and by the latter year 18 percent of blacks aged 18–24 were in college.[34]

Economic advance was also rapid, partly because of government antibias policies. In 1959 the median black male worker made 58 percent as much as his white counterpart; by 1978, the figure was 76 percent. During 1958–74, the proportion of blacks in managerial, professional, and skilled jobs doubled, while the share in service or laboring jobs dropped by a third, changes outpacing those for whites. The gains have been realized mainly by younger black men. Around 60 percent of blacks now appear to have entered the working or middle classes, escaping disadvantage.[35]

Besides these concrete advances, racism declined. The public became more accepting of equal rights for blacks, both in the abstract and in the specific forms of blacks entering schools, workplaces, public office, and neighborhoods alongside whites. Change was greatest among the young, educated, and non-Southern, but it reached all groups to some extent. While many whites still dislike or distrust blacks, most appear to feel that the case for fairness in public matters is overriding.[36]

Job creation was prodigious during the Great Society, due in part to the expansive economic policies of the period. The increase in positions was 13 million, or 20 percent, in the 1960s, then 21 million more, or 26 percent, in the 1970s. As planners hoped, unemployment dropped from 5.4 percent of the labor force in 1960 to only 3.4 percent in 1969.[37] The jobless rate grew in the 1970s, not because job creation faltered, but because of the massive rise in the labor force as the "baby boom" generation matured. To be sure, many of the new jobs were in the "secondary," service and support sector and hence relatively low-paid. They did not confer immediate middle-class status like many white-collar or unionized factory jobs. But they were also relatively low-skilled, hence better for absorbing the disadvantaged and uneducated than more demanding jobs would have been. Even the "high-tech" world of computers and data processing generates as many low-skilled as high-skilled jobs. Entry-level jobs in the new environment demand somewhat different skills from those the manufacturing economy did—literacy more than manual dexterity—but still limited skills.[38]

As many as 10 million illegal aliens have entered the country in recent years—between 500,000 and 1.5 million in the New York area alone. They are not eligible for welfare but have had little trouble finding employment,[39] another sign that at least low-wage jobs are widely available.

Finally, the combination of economic growth and rising income transfers reduced poverty. The Census Bureau estimates the proportion of the population living in poverty at 22 percent in 1960, declining to 11–12 percent over the 1970s, then rising to 15 percent by 1982. The Census poverty measure, however, omits the income many poor people receive from in-kind benefit programs like food stamps, Medicaid, and public housing. If the measure is adjusted for this and other shortcomings, the figure drops to perhaps 8 percent at present. It would drop further if all the needy claimed all the benefits that are available to them.[40]

What has compromised all these achievements is evidence that work and family problems among the disadvantaged are getting worse, not better. Most notably, a bifurcation has occurred in black America. While better-prepared blacks have made good use of fairer opportunity to get ahead, large numbers have also descended into the underclass.[41] The share of black families headed by women rose from 21 to 41 percent between 1960 and 1982; the figures for white families, while rising, were only 8 and 12 percent. Between 1960 and 1980, too, the share of nonwhites born out of wedlock grew from 22 percent to 48 percent (55 percent for blacks); the white figures were 2 and 11 percent. In 1984, 47 percent of black households received welfare benefits of some kind, compared to 41 percent for Hispanics and 16 percent for whites.[42]

The effect of family breakup was to reverse black economic gains, since female-headed families are usually thrown onto welfare, which usually pays below poverty, and few welfare mothers work. According to an Urban League study, the number of poor black families headed by men dropped 34 percent between 1969 and 1978, reflecting the gains in earnings and opportunities for black workers. But the overall number of black families in poverty still grew by 19 percent in that period because of a 64 percent rise in female-headed black families, most of them on welfare. Though the gap between white and black *earnings* is closing, the gap in *family income* between the races is now growing, largely because of black female-headedness. The ratio of black to white median family income rose from .55 in 1960 to .61 in 1970, then fell back to .55 by 1982.[43]

These family problems, along with economic recession, are the main reasons poverty has risen in recent years, more important than the Reagan cuts. But for family breakup and other social changes, measured poverty would be two or three points lower than it is and the black–white family income ratio would have risen to nearly two-thirds rather than declined.[44]

The other important dysfunction has been nonwork by the poor and nonwhite. Despite greater opportunities for these groups, much of the underclass actually withdrew from the labor force during the Great Society period. Many unskilled adults, especially black men, stopped even looking for work, at least in the legal economy. The shift was sharp enough to affect the overall figures for the races, even though most black men are working. In 1960, 83 percent of both white and black men were working or looking for work. By 1982 the white figure was 77 percent, but the black figure was 70 percent, more than twice the drop. While black women in the same period sought work more often than whites,[45] their effort could not compensate. Nonwork by men, not women, is the main force undermining the black family.

Some of the men took advantage of easier access to Disability and other benefits to retire early. The effect was especially sharp for blacks because their earnings are usually low relative to what Disability pays.[46] Others, especially younger men, entered the underground or illegal economy, where activities like smuggling of untaxed goods and drug trafficking paid them more than they could earn in legal employment. The result was a large hole in the legitimate labor market. In New York City fully 7 percent of working-age adults, or 318,000 people, had gone on welfare by 1970.[47] The hole was filled chiefly by illegal immigrants, many of whom earn good wages doing jobs that Americans decline to take. In New York and other cities today, owners of many factories, restaurants, and laundries say that they simply could not operate without illegal workers.[48]

Nonwork has caused a fundamental change in the character of poverty. Before 1960, and especially before 1940, poverty cut across the low-income population generally. Many working people could not earn enough to escape need, and those unable to work were even worse off. But after 1960 most of the aged and disabled were lifted out of poverty by expanded benefit programs, while a growing economy assured above-poverty incomes for the great majority of workers. The remaining poor were mostly people who were not disabled enough to claim an income but nevertheless did not hold a job regularly. That generally meant female-headed families and lower-class men, groups that usually worked irregularly at best or subsisted on AFDC or meager local assistance programs.

In recent years, whether families have working members, and how long they work, have been the main determinants of whether they are poor, next only to whether the families are intact or single-headed. Already by 1972, a major reason poor black families were needy was simply that they lacked earnings; of these families, only a third had heads working full-time. By 1980, the poverty rate for male-headed black families was 14 percent, close to the overall rate for the nation, while for female-headed black families it was 47 percent.[49] What made the difference was that most of the male heads were working while most of the female heads were not.

The effect of more generous social benefits plus the family and work problems was to generate massive new dependency on government. Especially from the late 1960s on, millions of female-headed families and other low-income people signed up for AFDC, food stamps, and other programs rather than continue struggling to support themselves without assistance. Table 3 lists the caseloads for the principal federally funded programs intended to support the needy and unemployed and provide health care, compensatory education, or housing to the low-income and disadvantaged.[50] The figures demonstrate again that the welfare state is more than a metaphor. The caseloads have become greater than the population of many states. In 1981 there were more people on Disability than lived in the state of Washington (4.2 million), and more people on

TABLE 3
Caseloads in Federal Social Programs, Fiscal 1981

Program	*Caseload (millions)*
1. *Aid to Families with Dependent Children (AFDC).* Cash assistance to needy one-parent families (enacted 1935)	11.1
2. *Food Stamps.* Coupons for all needy to buy food (1964)	22.4
3. *Supplemental Security Income (SSI).* Cash assistance for the needy aged, blind, and disabled (1972)	4.1
4. *Disability Insurance (DI).* Income for the disabled under Social Security (1956)	4.5
5. *Unemployment Insurance (UI).* Income for the unemployed (1935)	8.9
6. *Comprehensive Employment and Training Act (CETA).* Training and jobs for the unemployed and disadvantaged (1973)	2.9
7. *Work Incentive Program (WIN).* Required work and training for employable welfare recipients (1967)	2.4
8. *Medicaid.* Medical care for the needy (1965)	22.0
9. *Compensatory education* (Title I of the Elementary and Secondary Education Act). Special schooling for disadvantaged children (1965)	5.3
10. *Housing assistance* (section 8 of the Housing Act). Subsidized rents and housing construction for lower-income individuals and families (1974)	3.4
11. *Public housing.* Publicly built and managed housing for lower-income individuals and families (1937)	3.2

TABLE 3
Continued

NOTE: Caseloads for the first four programs are for a given month or a monthly average over the year. For the other programs, they are the total number served or on the rolls at any time during the year. For the housing programs, the caseloads are estimates made by multiplying *Budget* figures for housing units or families served by the average size of family in these programs computed from the *Statistical Yearbook* (see notes 10 and 11).

SOURCES:

1. U.S. Department of Health and Human Services, Social Security Administration, *Social Security Bulletin, Annual Statistical Supplement, 1983* (Washington, D.C.: U.S. Government Printing Office, 1984), p. 248.
2. U.S. Department of Commerce, Bureau of the Census, *Statistical Abstract of the United States, 1984* (Washington, D.C.: U.S. Government Printing Office, December 1983), p. 131.
3. *Annual Statistical Supplement, 1983*, p. 233.
4. *Social Security Bulletin*, 47, no. 12 (December 1984): 30.
5. U.S. Department of Labor, *Employment and Training Report of the President, 1982* (Washington, D.C.: U.S. Government Printing Office, 1982), p. 53.
6. *Employment and Training Report, 1982*, p. 30.
7. U.S. Department of Labor, Employment Security Automated Reporting System (ESARS), National Report, September 30, 1981, table 30.
8. *Health Care Financing Review*, 6, no. 2 (Winter 1984): 104.
9. U.S. Department of Education, *Annual Report, Fiscal Year 1981* (Washington, D.C.: U.S. Department of Education, July 1982), p. 34.
10. Office of Management and Budget, *Budget of the United States Government, Fiscal Year 1982* (Washington, D.C.: U.S. Government Printing Office, 1981), pp. 260–61, and U.S. Department of Housing and Urban Development, *1980 Statistical Yearbook* (Washington, D.C.: U.S. Government Printing Office, 1981), p. 275. See note above.
11. *Budget, 1982*, p. 261, and *1980 Statistical Yearbook*, p. 262. See note above.

AFDC than in Ohio (10.8 million). Food stamps' caseload approached the size of California (24.2 million), the nation's largest state.[51]

The overall dependent population is difficult to judge, since the caseloads overlap, but it probably approaches 30 million, or 13 percent of the general population. If Social Security, the principal retirement program, is added, the figures rise to 61 million and 27 percent.[52] A recent survey discovered that 19 percent of American households receive some kind of means-tested benefit, while 37 percent draw benefits from non-welfare programs, usually Social Security.[53]

Questions about social functioning can be raised about most of these 30 million. While the programs cover many children and elderly, they also support many adults of working age. To qualify for them, one must be more than temporarily needy, a condition that in the last generation has usually indicated some inability to cope, not simply impersonal economic barriers.[54] The education and training programs tend to require not only low income but "disadvantage," meaning a history of, or reason to expect, difficulties in learning or working. AFDC, the most important welfare program, requires that one parent of the family (usually the father) be absent or unemployed. Only Disability and UI, as social insurance programs, require a prior work history, but their eligibility and benefit rules were eased in the 1960s and 1970s so that they came to support many workers who were simply unable to adjust to available low-wage jobs.

Dependency throws serious doubt on the nation's progress against poverty and disadvantage. Poverty did not really disappear; it was overwhelmed by cash. Although measured poverty declined to below 12 percent in the 1970s, after the late 1960s some 18 to 25 percent of the population would have been poor in the absence of government transfers, a group that Charles Murray has aptly called the "latent poor."[55] Policymakers have not really solved poverty, only exchanged it for the problem of large-scale dependency seen in Table 3.

Like family and work difficulties, dependency is especially acute for black Americans. Starting in the late 1960s, black single mothers and their children went on AFDC in large numbers, making welfare the economic mainstay of ghetto communities around the nation. Black reliance on government thus increased dramatically. In 1969 black families living in poverty still drew 63 percent of their income from their own earnings and 37 percent from other sources, mainly government income programs. By 1976 the proportions had more than reversed, with 65 percent of poor blacks' income now coming from outside sources and only 35 percent from earnings. The proportion of their income coming from welfare doubled from 22 to 44 percent. Black use of other income programs also increased. By 1973 nearly three-fifths of *all* black families received unearned income from some source, usually from government, and a quarter of them were on welfare.[56]

Many civil rights activists and other blacks also relied on government for employment. They were absorbed into the proliferating structure of federal programs for the poor, becoming directors or staff of antipoverty agencies or employment programs. The hiring of blacks in older education and social welfare agencies also increased. In 1960 only 15 percent of blacks employed outside agriculture worked for government. By 1976 the figure had almost doubled, to 27 percent. The comparable figures for whites were 13 and 16 percent. Fifty-five percent of all black employment gains over the period came in the public sector, compared to 26 percent for whites.[57] While working for government did not mean dependency in the same sense as welfare, neither did it expose blacks to the competitive pressures or give them the independence from government that greater reliance on the private sector would have. The massive dependence of the black leadership, as well as rank and file, on government may have put a premature end to civil rights as a reforming force.[58]

The swelling of dependency may be an expression of what some have called "postindustrial" politics in the United States. Wealth makes a society readier to fund a generous welfare state than it was in a less affluent age. People also feel less need to fulfill work and family obligations once government is willing, in effect, to do it for them. Perhaps capitalism, by its very success, undercuts the social discipline it depends on.[59] Already in 1840 Alexis de Tocqueville warned that affluence in America might lead to "a kind of virtuous materialism . . . which would not corrupt, but enervate, the soul and noiselessly unbend its springs of action."[60]

The Exhaustion of Reform

The trends suggest an exhaustion of the progressive style of social reform. That approach assumed that all great divergences from equal income or status were due to social or economic structures extraneous to people's own capacities. Equality could always be advanced by finding and removing further impediments. But it is difficult any longer to find "barriers" against the poor that government can easily remove. The distribution of income in America is unequal, but it is not rigid. Between 1971 and 1978, 60 percent of families experienced substantial gains or losses in income relative to other families. There is enough fluidity so that the main problem the poor face is limited skills in coping with everyday challenges. We may blame low skills ultimately on society, but this no longer helps solve the problem, since government has found personal incapacity even harder to overcome than more impersonal social impediments.[61]

Of course, there is no way strictly to prove that all the barriers are gone. Most would say that the worst disadvantages the poor have faced in the past, such as formalized racial discrimination or systemic joblessness, clearly did constitute barriers. Is the same true of the lesser impediments that typically remain for the poor today, such as relatively low income and substandard schools, or are the poor themselves now responsible for their fortunes? Especially, do we attribute today's behavioral, work, and family problems to the individuals involved, or do we still trace them back to putative social causes? Those questions are matters of opinion and, ultimately, political philosophy.

Among those who still perceive removable barriers, some are liberals, who believe that society is still unfair to the poor but that government can bring redress. Some are radicals, who believe that the failure of capitalism to provide adequately for out-groups is so deep-seated that reforms short of socialism are unlikely to improve matters. Such fundamental changes, however, are unlikely in view of the disproportionate influence of moneyed and corporate elites in American politics. Under capitalism social programs appear to be generous but are actually used to force conformity on the poor. The criticisms of social policy along those lines by Michael Harrington, William Ryan, and the team of Frances Fox Piven and Richard Cloward[62] have done much to cement a fear of "blaming the victim" in the minds of the analysts and experts who directly deal with social policymaking in Washington.

The radical view has enough plausibility to deserve serious assessment by students of American politics.[63] It hinges on pessimistic interpretations of the nature of political and economic power that cannot, strictly speaking, be disproved. Yet the more the worst limitations on opportunity for average Americans have been eased, the more tortuous the logic required to trace the remaining problems of the poor back to conditions that they do not control. The danger is that, through continued neglect of the functioning problem, social policy will begin to contradict itself. It will no longer serve democratic ends but may actually make the poor *less* free and equal rather than more.

Those who cannot manage their affairs well enough to remain independent are necessarily unfree. They will inevitably be governed, however permissively, by the programs on which they rely. As Edmund Burke wrote:

> Society cannot exist unless a controlling power upon will and appetite be placed somewhere, and the less of it there is within, the more there must be without. It is ordained in the eternal constitution of things that men of intemperate minds cannot be free. Their passions forge their fetters.[64]

Those who are free of responsibility for themselves cannot be free to make their own way in society.

Dependency also undercuts the claims to equality made by disadvantaged groups. For how can the dependent be equal, except in the most metaphysical sense, with those who support them? Orlando Patterson points to the contradiction in much of black claim-making: "The victim's cry for help and mercy concedes the nobility of the oppressor . . . ."

> There can be no moral equality where there is a dependency relationship among men; there will always be a dependency relationship where the victim strives for equality by vainly seeking the assistance of his victimizer. No oppressor can ever respect such a victim, whatever he may do for him, including the provision of complete economic equality. In situations like these we can expect sympathy, even magnanimity from men, but never—and it is unfair to expect otherwise—the genuine respect which one equal feels for another.[65]

Those who *only* make claims can never be equal, in the nature of things, with those on whom the claims are made. The claimants are liberated, but not elevated, by the right to make demands; those who receive the demands are burdened, but not humbled.

Freedom and equality require some capacities *internal* to the individual, and these the mere removal of *external* barriers can never assure. The paradox is that measures to obligate the dependent that seem contrary to those values are actually necessary to achieve them. There is actually a strong streak of respect for order and competence in the traditions of both liberals and radicals. As John Stuart Mill wrote, even a "free" society must regulate behavior in the interests of "self-protection." The behavior of individuals may be subject to "moral reprobation" any time it involves "a breach of duty to others."[66] Government, in other words, can refrain from binding the lives of people only if they bind *themselves* in the ways essential to civility.

Radicals easily admit the role of social standards because of their conviction that social forces mold the poor. If constraints collapse, they admit, serious social problems follow. In their analyses of American welfare, Piven and Cloward demonstrate that welfare programs have often been used to enforce the work ethic on the poor. Until the 1960s the programs often tried to confine assistance narrowly to the unemployable, mainly the aged and disabled, in order to force healthy adults, however poor, to accept low-wage jobs. This policy had "deep roots in the two main tenets of market ideology: the economic system is open, and economic success is a matter of individual merit (and sometimes luck)." The average worker must internalize such beliefs if capitalism is to function efficiently.[67]

The rapid upsurge in dependency in the late 1960s and early 1970s, the authors admit, led to serious difficulties for the poor themselves, notably an "erosion of the work role":

> When large numbers of people come to subsist on the dole, many of them spurning what little low-wage work may exist, those of the poor and near-poor that continue to work are inevitable affected. From their perspective, the ready availability of relief payments (often at levels only slightly below prevailing wages) undermines their chief claim to social status: namely, that although poor they nevertheless earn their livelihood. If most of them react with anger, others react by asking, "Why work?" The danger thus arises that swelling numbers of the working poor will choose to go on relief.
>
> Moreover, when attachments to the work role deteriorate, so do attachments to the family, especially the attachement of men to their families. For all practical purposes, the relief check becomes a surrogate for the male breadwinner. The resulting family breakdown and loss of control over the young is usually signified by the spread of certain forms of disorder—for example, school failure, crime, and addiction. In other words, the mere giving of relief . . . does little to stem the fragmentation of lower-class life. . . .

Social elites, the authors reasoned, would quickly act to curb welfare eligibility and benefits, impose work tests, and otherwise restore the "work-maintaining function of the relief system."[68]

That, however, is not what they have done. Efforts to enforce work or other civilities on the welfare class are as yet rudimentary. The permissive reflexes native to federal politics have proven stronger than the apparent self-interest of the affluent. The progressive tradition of extending new benefits and opportunities to the worst-off has made it next to impossible to address the behavioral difficulties at the bottom of society in their own terms. For to do that, authority, or the making of demands on people, would have to be seen as the tool, and not the butt, of policy.

3

Functioning Ignored: Permissive Programs

WHY was the achievement of the Great Society so limited? Why, particularly, did the programs accomplish little but to increase dependency? Right and left offer political explanations that focus on the scale of effort. Too much, or too little, was done *for* the poor by government, they say. No doubt some of the things government offered to the dependent did encourage dysfunction, while there were perhaps other services the poor needed and never received.

It is more persuasive, however, to look at the *character* of policy and the thinking behind it. Disappointment may have stemmed from the fundamental *political* assumption of the policies, which was that the responsibility for the poor and their problems lay entirely outside themselves, in the hands of society and government. Government persisted in a progressive style of reform, seeking barriers outside the poor, even though behavioral problems such as nonwork, crime, and illegitimacy had become at least as great a difficulty for the disadvantaged. Behavior stems in the first instance from the individual, and there is no way to change it unless at least some responsibility is imputed to the individual. The assumption of social responsibility blocked policymakers from recognizing those problems, let alone solving them.

The politics of programs caused them to be permissive. They

did not set standards for their recipients with any authority. They did not obligate them to function in integrating ways, such as work, in return for support. It stands to reason that one of the things a society must do to maintain order is simply to *tell* its members clearly what is expected of them.[1] This Great Society programs virtually never did. In the face of problems of personal *conduct*, they offered essentially only *benefits*.

The Usual Explanations

Why did work and family difficulties actually get *worse* among the poor just when the nation mobilized to help them?[2] It is the central mystery in American social policy. True to the American political tradition, the commonest explanations focus on the extent rather than the nature of programs.

Conservatives say that the Great Society did for the poor too much for their own good. Allegedly the new social programs overburdened the economy and led to the chronic inflation and recession of the 1970s. Because growth faltered, the poor along with other Americans suffered income losses far outweighing any benefits they received from government. Ronald Reagan declared, "With the coming of the Great Society, Government began eating away at the underpinnings of the private enterprise system." But for this, "black families and all Americans would be appreciably better off today."[3] Conservatives such as Charles Murray also charge that generous benefits created "disincentives" for the poor to work and get ahead on their own. Since government help flowed to the incompetent, not the "deserving," many of the poor decided that to be dependent offered an easier life than to assume the burdens of self-reliance.[4]

Critics from the left, such as Michael Harrington, say instead that government did too little for the poor. All the Great Society initiatives were in important ways limited. Busing and affirmative action were never pressed vigorously enough to root out the less official forms of discrimination against blacks. By the late 1960s economic policymakers began worrying more about controlling inflation than maintaining full employment. The antipoverty training and education programs were never fully funded because of the cost of the Vietnam War. The income maintenance system was never completed by the enactment of a comprehensive welfare reform, nor were national health insurance or guaranteed jobs programs approved. To some liberals poverty is the result finally of inequality, not of inadequate resources, and it can be overcome only by a dramatic reduction in social and economic differences.[5]

As Ken Auletta has pointed out, both of those diagnoses are too narrowly economic. It is difficult to believe that an excess *or* a deficiency of resources given to the poor explains their current problems. Most poor people today are needy in the first instance because of illegitimacy, family breakup, and inability to get and hold available jobs, none of which result automatically from economic conditions. While government programs may in some sense reward dependency, it is "rational" in only the most short-run sense for the poor to succumb to family and work problems or engage in crime. Nor would it obviously assuage those difficulties simply to give the poor more benefits.[6]

The political analyses by the two sides are also implausible. Conservatives suggest that a "new class" of government planners and academic experts fastened the Great Society on the nation unawares. This elite allegedly had an interest in big government, because it depended on government jobs and funding. If the main strategy for the social problem was dependency, more power would inevitably flow to the planning elite. Among other goals, the new class seeks social equality through government, a value not shared by the general public.[7]

Liberals, on the other hand, say the reforms fell short because of controversy and the inherent conservatism of the political system. Support for the antipoverty crusade was undermined by the urban riots and the demands pressed by radicals through Community Action, a network of local service and advocacy agencies funded by the antipoverty program. Those upsets led to Republican gains in the 1966 elections, ending the liberal Congress of 1964–66 that enacted most of the important Great Society measures. Fundamental change must always be difficult in a political system of dispersed power.[8] It has become still tougher with the decline of the liberal activist presidency. Johnson was the last president to press strongly for progressive legislation. His successors have mostly been Republicans, and all of them have been preoccupied with balancing the budget rather than with social change.

In essence, both those interpretations blame the failures on political conflict. Both right and left believe they had the answers to poverty—they were merely defeated by contrary political forces.

However, Great Society policymaking was by and large consensual. Planners did play a leading role, but their schemes were enthusiastically endorsed by Congress. The parties and factions mostly agreed on the need to help the poor. A variety of approaches were tried. Second-guessing by left and right came mostly after the programs had fallen short, not before. The real mystery of the Great Society is how the new efforts could have disappointed *even though* there was broad agreement behind them. Something about federal policymaking caused *all* the leaders and factions somehow to misread the social problem.

Lack of Obligations

A better explanation is that the programs failed to overcome poverty because they largely ignored behavioral problems among the poor. In particular, they did not tell their clients with any authority that they ought to behave differently. New benefits and services were given to the disadvantaged, but virtually no standards were set for how they should function in return.

Each phase of Great Society policymaking placed the responsibility for change on society, without *sharing* it in any important way with the client. The civil rights reforms attributed racial inferiority entirely to discrimination against minorities, a view that had much more substance in 1960 than in 1970 or 1980. The macroeconomic strategy placed the responsibility for employment entirely on policymakers at the center, not on workers seeking jobs. The compensatory programs, though they recognized the performance problems to some extent, were thought of as another kind of benefit to be given to clients, without conditions. The income maintenance and labor market strategies understood income or employment as benefits that could be given *to* clients *by* government, not as things involving *activity* by the recipients themselves.

Now that social problems closely reflected the behavior of people, the search for external barriers was no longer a sufficient basis for policy. Daniel Moynihan's report on *The Negro Family* attained notoriety in 1965 for its unvarnished portrayal of family problems among blacks, but its real point was the inadequacy of civil rights as a social strategy. Government could ensure blacks fairer chances to get ahead, but it could not *give* them in any simple way the capacities to make use of these opportunities. To some extent skills must be a black responsibility, but civil rights laid responsibility only on whites.[9]

The training programs presumed that government could give practical assistance to the jobless that would free them to work. That was often true for welfare mothers, and that is why this group generally showed the sharpest gains from training. The programs could help the mothers find a job and manage the logistics of transportation and child care, and then they could work steadily and make substantial income gains. However, disadvantaged men and youths, the other main group of hard-core jobless, often had too much resistance to low-wage work for benefit-oriented programs to succeed.

The dilemma the programs faced was how to get the contribution they needed from their clients if they were to help them. Since training seldom improved skills much, the motivation of the recipients was all the more important. The programs registered earnings gains, when they did, mainly by causing clients to work *more hours*, that is, avoid unemployment and withdrawal from the labor force, rather than by qualifying them for higher-paying jobs. But inability to commit steadily to any task, be it school, family life, or a job, was also central to the coping problems of the disadvantaged. Programs that set no clear standards and possessed no sanctions over their clients could do little to enhance commitment. The training efforts all suffered high dropout rates. Clients were free to use the benefits they received wisely or foolishly. Two sympathetic observers have well characterized the record of these problems: "A few participants benefited greatly, many somewhat, but large numbers also dropped out or simply marked time while accepting allowances. The government opened doors, but many potential clients did not seek entry."[10]

The Great Society systematically weakened the tie between income support and work obligation which the New Deal, at least implicitly, had upheld. Unemployment Insurance (UI) and Social Security had both been based on social insurance, and their proponents had always, for that reason, viewed them as more "respectable" than welfare.[11] Not only were most of the new programs "welfare" in some sense, because they were means-tested and noncontributory, but the contributory basis of the insurance programs was adulterated. In UI, Social Security, and Disability, benefits were increased in the 1960s and 1970s so that beneficiaries commonly received more than the payroll taxes paid for them would have justified on a strict actuarial basis. That was one reason for the financial crisis that hit all these programs toward the end of the 1970s.[12] In the case of UI, some of the new benefits were financed directly out of federal general revenues, giving up even the pretense of insurance. The trends broke down much of the real difference between the middle-class programs and welfare.

The traditional view had been that income was the result of work and other competence by the individual. The income strategy reversed that presumption. Some analysts believed that to guarantee income would actually produce equivalent coping abilities. "[P]rovide the poor with middle-class incomes," the argument went, "and middle-class behavior will follow—even though slowly—because poor people share the conventional values of the middle class and, basically, desire to conform." Asserted Harold Watts, a leading poverty economist, "the rehabilitative effect of cash by itself is not small. . . . Sheer money will serve some of the same purposes as our detailed service programs."[13] The experiment failed. The welfare boom occurred, yet the "human problems associated with poverty," admitted one liberal expert, were just as bad afterward as before.[14]

The labor market strategy attributed nonwork to the unpleasant jobs allocated to the disadvantaged by unfair hiring. Thus if government broke down those barriers by guaranteeing "better" jobs, the same workers would perform better. But the job market is far from arbitrary. Most low-paid workers really are less productive than the more successful *in the current economy.* Blacks, for instance, have no doubt suffered from the decline of the manufacturing economy, which paid good wages for manual skills, in favor of service and office jobs that more often demand literacy. But the immediate problem they face today is still predominantly one of skills, not arbitrary exclusion from jobs they could do.[15]

Research has failed to corroborate that disadvantaged workers are confined to unrewarding jobs in an invidious way. The income of workers seems more closely related to their *personal* characteristics than to the features of their jobs. Most low-paid workers are young, female, and nonwhite; whether they work in the "primary" or "secondary" sector is less important. Even more telling, the income of individual workers relative to others varies a great deal over time, and this is true for blacks and other low-paid groups as well as the better-off. Rigid barriers in the labor market are not apparent.[16]

What would it have meant to share responsibility for change more evenly between government and the disadvantaged?[17] Essentially, to support the needy but require in return that they function in minimal ways essential to integration, especially work. That would have meant setting standards for recipients by conditioning the benefits they received in some way on their behavior. This Washington essentially never did, not even in the training and education programs whose explicit purpose was to improve the skills of clients. Of course, to set and enforce behavioral standards is very difficult, as later discussion will show. The point here is that there was next to no discussion of requirements even at a policymaking level. Even the need for standards was barely perceived.

The clearest instance of such standard-setting occurs in the military, where enlistees accept definite obligations to obey their superiors and conform to military law in return for pay, training, and eventual veterans benefits. The sanction for noncompliance is more than severance and loss of benefits; it can include a dishonorable discharge and other penalties. However, the government has special powers to obligate for defense purposes. While the current military is volunteer, Congress can draft soldiers if it wishes without any recompense at all. In social policy the government cannot simply force its recipients to work, but it can condition benefits on work or other functioning requirements. The social insurance programs involve an implied contract of work in return for support. People contribute while working to Social Security, Unemployment Insurance, and others programs so that they may draw benefits when not working. Welfare programs do not require prior work, but they can levy work or other stipulations upon or after receipt of benefits.

However, none of the regular compensatory education and training programs set norms for the performance of recipients from the national level. The programs regulated the local agencies that provided services quite heavily, but not the beneficiaries themselves. No program required work in available jobs as a condition of receiving benefits. A perception of the need for standards, and an effort to enforce them, has occurred only in the older income programs, especially AFDC. But those requirements were, until the Reagan Administration, imposed by Congress against the will of Executive planners. They have also been halfhearted for political and administrative reasons to be explored below.

Standards have sometimes been set in service programs at the local level, but not with explicit warrant from Washington. The Jobs Corps and the supported work demonstration were noted for being demanding of their clients, which was one reason they showed results, but the norms were set and enforced at the project level.[18] This reflects the tradition in federal welfare policy of financing benefits from Washington but leaving behavioral requirements to decision at the local level. Benefits are thus more salient politically than obligations. Federal politicians can take credit for giving deserving groups good things, while leaving to obscure local officials the unpleasant task of enforcing social standards.[19]

The only instance of statutory functioning requirements in compensatory policy came in youth employment. The Neighborhood Youth Corps, enacted in 1964, provided government jobs to poor youth over the summer and after school in an effort, largely unsuccessful, to reduce school dropout rates. The Youth Incentive Entitlement Pilot Projects (YIEPP), a Carter Administration experiment of 1978–81, formalized the connection by *requiring* that youth remain in or return to school as a condition for receiving such jobs. While YIEPP raised the incomes of youth who were still in school, who took the jobs avidly, it did not cut dropout rates or lure dropouts back to school. Apparently, the dropouts did not feel they needed the jobs, which were low-paid, enough to make them accept the school obligation.[20]

Although regular service programs set no standards for recipients from the center, they might nevertheless have been more demanding if local administrators had been required by Washington to show results. Federal regulation of local programs has been pervasive, but its main concern has been to ensure that federal funds were spent for the activities specified and on disadvantaged clients, not on other things or the better-off, strictures that localities have often evaded. Much less frequently programs have been subject to performance standards designed to enhance achievement of program objectives. The most notable instances have been based on a computerized reporting system run by the Labor Department that tells the agency, among other things, how many clients its programs have placed in jobs. In the past some welfare work and job placement programs have been subject to performance funding requirements based on this reporting. State agencies were funded, in part, on the basis of how well they had done relative to other states in placing clients in jobs and keeping them there in the previous fiscal cycle.

However, CETA, the main training program, was never subject to such a system. Congress authorized one in 1978, but it was never used to allocate actual funding. Low-performing agencies claimed attenuating circumstances and refused to accept the verdict of the new system. They feared that centralized performance pressure would force them to give more attention to placing clients in private sector jobs. They invoked the tradition of local autonomy in CETA, which began in 1973 as a "revenue sharing" program. Under the Job Training Partnership Act (JTPA), which replaced CETA in 1982, centralized evaluation was effectively abandoned. The Reagan Administration insisted that the job of evaluation be delegated to the states, with at best an advisory role for Washington. The Carter Administration also proposed a performance system for youth programs, largely run by CETA, where there was a sense that benefits were being "ripped off." Youth would often take the government jobs or spending money offered without making much effort to adjust to regular employment, and staff has little incentive to make them do so. Again, internal resistance defeated the plan.

In education the tradition of federal control was even weaker, and attempts to set performance standards were still more modest. Initially, Title I, the principal remedial program for disadvantaged students, was very loosely administered by the Office of Education. School districts were allowed to spend Title I funds and assess the results pretty much as they chose. Pressure for more accountability developed only after early evaluations suggested the program had little impact, mainly because a lot of the money was spent on better-off students and local evaluations were poorly done. Administration was tightened up, and over the 1970s targeting and results improved.[21] But no meaningful performance standards were set. In 1974 Congress mandated that states use more rigorous and uniform evaluation methods. Some progress in that direction was made, but such was the resistance to federal "paperwork" that the requirement was rescinded in 1981. Linking funding to performance was never seriously considered.

The Sociological Approach

Thus, federal programs were not conceived or structured to require recipients to help government solve their problems. Much of the reason for that, in turn, lay in a way of understanding the social problem which may be called the sociological approach. Starting in the early 1960s the poor and disadvantaged were understood to be so conditioned by their environment that to expect better functioning from them, such as work, became almost inconceivable. The responsibility for their difficulties, even behavioral ones, was transferred entirely to government or society.

By "sociological approach" I do not mean sociology as an academic discipline but a political ideology held by policymakers and academics alike of which academic sociology was only one origin. It is true that academic developments in the 1950s and early 1960s prepared social science to play a leading role in Great Society policymaking. In that era the writings of Talcott Parsons, Robert K. Merton, C. Wright Mills, and others extended sociological theory and applied it to contemporary states and societies. Simultaneously, the emphasis on rigor and quantification began that was to transform all the social sciences in the 1960s and 1970s. The rapid development of government data on society, survey research, statistical methods of data analysis, and computerized data processing seemed to promise that social science might become as quantified and predictive as the natural sciences. Economists following the precepts of Keynes believed they could manage the economy so as to avoid recession and inflation, a claim that the success of the Kennedy tax cut in the mid-1960s seemed to validate. All this emboldened the more political social scientists to believe that they could solve social problems like poverty as well.[22]

Politically, the significant fact about the new social science was its determinism. Any science must assume that the phenomena under study are "caused" in some sense by identifiable outside forces. Quantified social science applied that assumption to human problems more literally than before. Problems of social competence were seen as the direct product of adverse social forces. Poor children's learning problems in school, for example, were "caused" by their parents' own limited background, plus the deficiencies of public programs. Implicitly this cast the government's clients as the passive products of their environment, including public policy.

This approach was attractive to federal politicians because it helped solve the serious dilemma posed by the poor. After 1960 it became more and more difficult to find reformable conditions on which the disarray at the bottom of society could be blamed. Poverty and disadvantage seemed rooted mostly in the limited skills of the poor themselves, yet government could do little to raise skills simply with benefits. Politically, that left unpalatable alternatives. Either equality must be achieved by a leveling of income or status without regard to the capacities of the poor, the prescription of the far left, or the poor themselves must be seen as malingerers or congenitally incompetent.[23] Sociological analysis offered a way out. It defined a set of less obvious social barriers permitting further reformism. By providing further benefits and services, it was argued, government could push back the barriers of "disadvantage" without either embracing revolutionary change or blaming the poor for their condition.

Some observers have attributed the policy role of sociological ideas to the personal influence of intellectuals. It is true that academics had uncommon influence in Washington in the early years of the antipoverty effort. Poverty was first publicized as an issue by John Kenneth Galbraith in *The Affluent Society* (1958) and then, much more pointedly, by Michael Harrington in *The Other America* (1962). Government economists like Robert Lampman argued that economic growth alone would not suffice to reduce poverty.[24] Most notably, Harrington, Lloyd Ohlin, and Richard Cloward were advisers to the task force that drafted the antipoverty program in 1964. Ohlin and Cloward had already analyzed juvenile delinquency as a product of social pressures on youth, and Cloward, with Frances Fox Piven, was later to interpret welfare as a form of social control of the poor. Critics of the War on Poverty like Daniel Moynihan see in such influence a case of the "direct transmission of social science theory into governmental policy."[25]

However, the intellectuals' approach was strongly seconded by politicians. Presidents Kennedy and Johnson both seized on the antipoverty program as a welcome new agenda for progressive government. So did most of the larger political class. An early reviewer of Harrington's book, for example, found in it the simple moral that "every citizen has a right to become or remain part of our society." Escape from poverty was one more right that a generous government should guarantee its citizens.[26] Thus, the new social analysis of poverty and the political interests served by it came together spontaneously, a process that Max Weber called routinization or "elective affinity."[27] Liberal political goals posed a problem that the new social analysis promised to solve. The two naturally merged to form a new ideology.

The keystone of the sociological approach was to attribute even the behavioral problems of the poor to hostile social conditions. To some degree this extended the solicitude the New Deal had shown toward the dependent. Part of the ideology of social work, which received steady federal funding in the New Deal for the first time, was that recipients should not lose any of their rights as citizens simply because they were dependent. However, in their initial decades federal welfare programs were so conservatively administered that they never dealt with behavioral problems on the scale that became common after 1960. By confining assistance fairly narrowly to the unemployable, the New Deal programs still gave the message, at least implicitly, that government took responsibility only for narrowly economic problems like unemployment. The individual was still responsible for the personal behavior and skills needed to take advantage of opportunity.

Great Society social analysis, however, treated even personal problems like nonwork or family breakup as if they were outside forces acting on the poor, just like economic need or discrimination. There was, Daniel Moynihan says, "a near-obsessive concern to locate the 'blame' for poverty, especially Negro poverty, . . . outside the community concerned."[28] In that respect government analysis closely resembled the radical understanding of poverty developed by Michael Harrington, William Ryan, and others. Ryan wrote:

> The crucial criterion by which to judge analyses of social problems is the extent to which they apply themselves to the *interaction* between the victim population and the surrounding environment and society, and, conversely, the extent to which they eschew exclusive attention to the victims themselves—no matter how feeling and sympathetic that attention might appear to be. [A]nalysis will fasten on income distribution as the basic cause of poverty, on discrimination and segregation as the basic cause of racial inequality, on social stress as the major cause of the majority of emotional disturbances. It will focus, not on problem families, but on family problems; not on motivation, but on opportunity; not on symptoms, but on causes; not on deficiencies, but on resources; not on adjustment, but on change.

The point of sociological reasoning was exactly to exempt those at the bottom of society from responsibility for their condition.[29]

In much the same way, the Council of Economic Advisers in 1964 traced the attitudinal problems of the poor to social forces outside themselves:

> Lack of motivation, hope, and incentive is a more subtle but no less powerful barrier than lack of financial means. . . .

> Escape from poverty is not easy for American children raised in families accustomed to living on relief. . . . It is difficult for children to find and follow avenues leading out of poverty in environments where education is deprecated and hope is smothered. This is particularly true when discrimination appears as an insurmountable barrier.

The poor person was prey, not only to low income, but to "ignorance, disease, delinquency, crime, irresponsibility, immorality, indifference." Virtue could not be expected from people living in ghetto environments "where honesty can become a luxury and ambition a myth."[30]

A good example of the shift in attitudes is the federal response to illegitimacy, a critical problem for the disadvantaged, particularly blacks. The traditional attitude, embodied in state child support laws, was that parents were responsible for their own procreation. Fathers, even if they abandoned their spouses, should be tracked down and made to contribute to the support of children. In testifying on an antipregnancy program in 1978, however, Secretary of Health, Education, and Welfare Joseph Califano characterized illegitimacy as a curse "likely to befall the teenage mother." It was caused by "large social forces" such as "changing moral standards" and the "declining authority" of church and school. It gave rise in turn to "other, pervasive social problems" such as "poverty, unemployment, poor education, family breakdown." In so impersonal an analysis, the individual played no role, in either the problem or the solution. While "personal self-discipline" was desirable, Califano said, it could no longer be the basis for public policy. Government must provide services to forestall pregnancy and, if it failed, provide for the mothers and children. It could not simply expect the mothers to behave otherwise than they did.[31]

The sociological approach was often echoed at the local level, among the providers who delivered social services for government. Soon after the Califano proposal, a conference of family planning counselors expressed the consensus that even women who had repeated abortions "could not be held culpable." For each, said one expert, "had what was to her a valid reason," either "a problem with the relationship" or "nonuse or failure of a contraceptive." Another averred that the women were not "poorly motivated to use contraception"; rather, the available methods were "inappropriate to their particular life situations."[32] Such comments illustrate the major reflex of the sociological outlook—the tendency to view social problems always from the viewpoint of the client, not of society.

Since most people understand their behavior in self-justifying ways, the effect is to deny government any authority to ask them to behave differently.

A second theme of sociological thinking was to shift responsibility for the poor, including behavioral problems, to government. Michael Harrington wrote that individuals usually could not escape the "vicious cycle" of poverty by themselves. "Neither can the group, for it lacks the social energy and political strength to turn its misery into a cause. Only the larger society, with its help and resources, can really make it possible for these people to help themselves."[33]

Official thinking took much the same line. In an important speech at Howard University in 1965, President Johnson extended the federal responsibility for black Americans from freedom to functioning. The government must assure to blacks not only equal rights in a formal sense but the "human ability" needed for them to succeed on a level with other groups. This was the only way rights guaranteed by the government could extend "beyond opportunity to achievement."[34] That promise could be kept, wrote the Council of Economic Advisers, if government could find a way to give poor children the "skills and motivation" they needed to escape poverty.[35]

New Deal policy had confined government's responsibility to providing certain new economic protections and opportunities; it was the responsibility of ordinary people to make good use of them. In the Great Society conception the public responsibility was potentially unlimited. Government could never say it had done enough for the poor, because the burden of change was not shared with them. That feeling helps to explain the restless innovation of Great Society policy. Planners had to keep coming up with new programs until they found something that "worked," that is, some benefit to which poverty responded without obligating the poor themselves.

A final theme of sociological thinking was to shift responsibility, not only to government, but to the social elite in a broader sense. The "privileged" were supposed to take the lead in social change, rather than be pushed into it by political pressure from below—the reverse of the New Deal assumption. John Kennedy struck this note of *noblesse oblige* often, especially in a speech at Amherst College just before his death:

> There is inherited wealth in this country and also inherited poverty. And unless the graduates of this college and other colleges like it who are given a running start in life—unless they are willing to put back

> into our society those talents, the broad sympathy, the understanding, the compassion—unless they are willing to put those qualities back into the service of the Great Republic, then obviously the presuppositions upon which our democracy [is] based are bound to be fallible.

Government could not discharge its tasks, at home or abroad, without "the service, in the great sense, of every educated man or woman."[36]

The novelty was the idea that the elite should discharge its responsibilities *through government.* The better-off had always felt some duty toward the poor, but they had expressed it largely through philanthropic and other private endeavors. The Great Society suggested that actual *public service* was necessary. Kennedy spoke just as the "baby boom generation" was entering the universities, and it responded to his challenge. A higher proportion of that generation became bureaucrats, social scientists, public-interest lawyers, and other policy professionals than ever before.

One of the paradoxes of the Great Society was that government never became so elitist as when its main domestic purpose was to help the underprivileged. The vogue of policy analysis in Washington after 1960 made policymaking increasingly technical. To get a staff job, advanced skills in statistics became necessary. Economists came to rival lawyers as the dominant professional group in the capital. Yet the new elitism actually opened government to the claims of the disadvantaged. The new analysts were mainly technicians, interested in using their skills to develop new programs. They therefore welcomed new demands on government. The challenges posed by poverty were especially intriguing to them. The analytic class joined the politicians in conceiving of government's responsibility toward the poor in expansive terms.[37]

The sociological approach crystallized as an orthodoxy during the controversy over the "Moynihan report" on the black family in 1965. At the time Moynihan himself leaned toward sociological thinking. He wrote the report as an Assistant Secretary of Labor to stimulate fresh thinking about poverty within the government. He blamed family problems on "American society" rather than on blacks. The report provided the intellectual basis for President Johnson's Howard University speech, mentioned above. Yet the study spoke so graphically of the "tangle of pathology" in the ghetto that many liberals and black leaders smelled "blaming the victim" in it. Their outrage made clear that the private problems of poor Americans could no longer be discussed publicly without sociological caveats even stronger than Moynihan's.[38]

Prominent later analyses of poverty observed that convention. Kenneth Clark, in *Dark Ghetto*, also published in 1965, did not deny the destructive nature of ghetto culture any more than Moynihan, but he characterized it as a social "epidemic" for which blacks were not individually responsible. He also called more clearly for "a concerted and massive attack on the social, political, economic, and cultural roots of the pathology."[39] In 1968 the Kerner commission explained the urban riots in similar terms. Social problems of the ghetto such as crime or drug addiction, it said, were not to be blamed on blacks but seen as an "environmental 'jungle'" of which they themselves were victims. The life-style of "hustle," nonwork, and family instability was due, not to blacks, but to a "system" for which "white racism is essentially responsible." Again, "only a greatly enlarged commitment to national action—compassionate, massive and sustained" could change that situation.[40]

The taboo against discussing the behavioral side of disadvantage openly, except in the vaguest sociological terms, lasted for a decade. Only in the middle 1970s were conservatives in Congress able to institute child support enforcement and other controls in welfare that presumed that the needy could, after all, be responsible for their actions. The black family problem has continued to worsen, to the point where black leaders themselves have begun to talk openly about it. They still do so, however, in abstract terms that transfer responsibility to society.[41] Sociological logic still blocks government from expecting or obligating the poor to behave differently than they do.

The Effects of Permissiveness

The emphasis of Great Society programs on social, as against individual, responsibility helps explain why they sometimes seemed to undermine the ability of recipients to cope rather than improve it. In this respect, the antipoverty and training programs had the most influence, even though they were much smaller, in cost and caseloads, than the income programs.

Social changes alone could not explain the "welfare explosion" of the late 1960s. While the number of needy female-headed families eligible for AFDC was growing, a much sharper change was the sudden determination of more of those families to claim their benefits. The share of eligible female-headed families actually on

AFDC jumped from 63 to 91 percent between 1967 and 1970.[42] Something dramatic happened to break down the stigma surrounding welfare.

That "something," Piven and Cloward have shown, was very often the Community Action program. Community Action originated as a way to involve the poor themselves in overcoming poverty, but much of what it did in practice was to pressure regular government agencies to increase services to poor areas. Neighborhood service centers and legal services lawyers were both originally funded under Community Action. The former persuaded more mothers to apply for welfare; the latter brought class-action suits against many of the legal restrictions on access to welfare. Out of these activities grew the notion that welfare was a right that the poor should claim without shame or preconditions. The National Welfare Rights Organization (NWRO), which pressed these claims most aggressively, arose in 1966–67 very much as an outgrowth of Community Action.

Piven and Cloward err mainly in suggesting that the mothers and NWRO extorted increased welfare from the establishment against its will. Rather, they demanded assistance, and then the same rights-oriented thinking, working among welfare administrators and politicians, caused the claims to be granted. Benefits were raised and procedures eased in many Northern cities. Applications for relief rose, and so did the proportion accepted, from 55 percent in 1960 to 70 percent in 1968.[43] At the local level, as in Washington, a permissive approach came to dominate welfare.

What women got from welfare men got on a smaller scale from federal employment programs, especially those operating under the Comprehensive Employment and Training Act (CETA). Next to AFDC, CETA was the most ambitious welfare structure ever developed by Washington. At its height in 1978 the program spent $9.6 billion to provide more than 750,000 PSE jobs in public and nonprofit agencies, a wide range of training services, and special programs for youth and other groups.[44] Congress repeatedly pressed new funding and services on CETA to deal with the recessions of the 1970s. The program would have grown still further if Carter Administration reform proposals had passed.

Few men qualified directly for AFDC, which generally covers only female-headed families. But they could receive what amounted to welfare through the allowances and other benefits that CETA provided to clients in its training programs. They could also enter PSE jobs, which were typically less demanding than private sector work paying the same wage. The style of many CETA agencies was not to press clients into jobs already available, which tended to be menial and low-paid, but to hold out the promise that, through training or PSE, they could qualify for "better" jobs. This meant that in practice the programs often shielded their recipients from the job market rather than insisting they come to terms with it. They did not require that recipients work in order to receive benefits.

Often CETA agencies tried to substitute government jobs for private sector employment. CETA funded PSE positions, not only in regular government agencies but in local "community-based organizations" (CBOs), many of which worked for CETA itself as providers of training services. In these organizations PSE slots were often used to hire staff from among former recipients, at much more than they could command in the private sector. The distinction between staff and recipients often broke down. In many localities CETA seemed dedicated, not to preparing clients for work in regular jobs, either public or private, but to elaborating the PSE/CBO structure as an alternative to both. Legitimate doubts about whether that structure was anything more than disguised welfare contributed to the abolition of PSE. The better to concentrate on training, the Job Training Partnership Act (JTPA), which replaced CETA in 1982, disallows both PSE and training allowances for trainees.

Because they effectively relaxed the work obligation for many men, the employment programs probably increased joblessness rather than reducing it. Between 1964 and 1979, the period of greatest federal employment spending, the hard-core unemployed grew from 380,000 to 2.4 million. The problem of work discipline was the greatest among disadvantaged youth. Measured joblessness among black youth is between 30 and 50 percent, a figure that generates great pressure on the government to do something. But by 1979 a succession of federal youth programs had already served some 30 to 40 percent of *all* jobless black youth, to little effect. Much of the problem turns out to be that many youth will accept only temporary or part-time work, in part because of school. Many also decline easily available jobs as low-skilled and are erratic about sticking with the positions they accept. Employers say that they often do not know what is expected of them on the job.[45]

Research has shown something of how government income or

training, if it is permissive, can demoralize recipients. There has long been a suspicion that AFDC sets up "disincentives" against work and family unity. Recipients may feel little interest in working if the welfare agency reduces their grants in proportion to any earnings they make. Fathers may leave their families, since usually only female-headed families can qualify for welfare. Studies of AFDC suggest that both effects exist, although neither is as strong as is often asserted. The mechanisms are complex. Families seem to break up most often, not because anyone calculates that it is rational to do so, but because the mothers lose patience with the unemployment or low earnings of the father. The role of AFDC in breakup is mainly to provide an independent income to the mother, freeing her to leave or oust the father. Earnings from a job, if the mother has one, have much the same effect.

The government ran four experiments in income maintenance between 1968 and 1978 in order to gauge the behavioral effects of welfare more closely. The studies selected needy families, both intact and single-parent, guaranteed them incomes ranging from 50 to 135 percent of the poverty level, then compared them to equivalent families eligible only for existing government programs. The members of a family did not have to work, but if they did, their grant was reduced, not dollar for dollar, but by percentages ranging from 30 to 70 percent of earnings. Hence, the recipients still gained something from working. Planners hoped that this "work incentive" would minimize, if not eliminate, the reduction in work resulting from the income guarantee.

The results were disillusioning. Recipients in the four experiments reduced their work effort quite a bit more than expected, especially those who did not head families. In the last and most definitive of the studies, in Seattle and Denver, husbands reduced their hours worked by about 5 percent, wives (in two-parent families) by 15 percent, female heads of family by 12 percent. According to one estimate, those three groups would probably reduce their work effort by 4, 27, and 16 percent under an income guarantee like that proposed in the principal welfare reform plans, which would have been less generous but more permanent than the experiments.[46]

Less attention was paid to marital stability, but most planners assumed that guaranteed income would probably enhance it, since the experiments freed families from the need to split up to get assistance. That effect, however, was apparently overridden by the fact that the projects guaranteed both parents an income whether or not they split. In the Seattle/Denver study, rates of family breakup rose by more than 40 percent for both whites and blacks, though negligibly for Hispanics, findings whose meaning is still in dispute.[47]

The experiments also dramatized the dangers to work effort of providing the low-income training if it shields them from the need to accept available jobs. In the Seattle/Denver study some participants received job training and counseling of a "nondirective" kind. They were encouraged to channel their employment efforts toward jobs they would *like* to have, and they were paid allowances that freed them from the need to work. The findings were that such training actually *depressed* the hours clients worked after the program. Many trainees apparently embarked on training for positions that were, practically speaking, beyond their reach, and this made them more reluctant to do the more menial jobs actually available to them.[48]

Overall the results sharply undercut support for expanded welfare. They suggested that a benefit-oriented social policy might after a point produce *more* poverty rather than less, because of the behavioral changes it would induce. Nonwork and family breakup would reduce family income even as transfers from government tried to raise it.[49] The damage seems to be done, not by the benefits themselves, but by the fact that they are *entitlements*, given regardless of the behavior of clients. They raise the income of recipients but, more important, free them to behave without accountability to society. If the recipients in the experiments had not been supported unconditionally but required to work or avoid family breakup, the results might have been quite different.[50]

Guaranteed income and other benefits from government have helped to produce what Ken Auletta calls a "welfare mentality" among the poor. Clients in the supported work demonstration, which Auletta observed, tended to view themselves as barred from work by lack of training, child care, transportation, and so on. They thought of overcoming these obstacles as government's obligation rather than their own. They could hardly imagine going to work without a government guarantee or protection of some sort. Supported work was more hard-headed than most programs in pressing its clients to accept personal responsibility for their predicament. Such suasions, however, were overborne for most clients by the availability of welfare and other training benefits without conditions. The dependent could drift from program to program, "hustling" the benefits of each, and never share responsibility for themselves with government.[51] The very succession of programs made it all too evident that government was willing to assume that burden alone.

The permissive nature of programs placed local staffs in some ways in a thankless position. Many of them initially supported the benefit-oriented approach of CETA and other training programs. The whole point of the Great Society was to be more "responsive" and less demanding of disadvantaged workers than society had been. That meant dropouts from training should be given repeated second chances. No one, if possible, should be allowed to "fail." As time went on, however, the mood shifted. Many staff suffered "burnout" from bearing the burdens of difficult clients. Others came to feel that tougher standards, rather than benefits, were what many of the poor really needed.

As a result some divergence has opened between the public and private messages that programs give their clients. Local trainers and job counselors often say they have begun to make more demands on clients. They usually have the leeway to do so because of the discretion they enjoy about whom to serve and how. But federal policies still do not set clear standards for the clients, and this sets sharp limits to how demanding individual staff can be on their own. How, many ask, can they persuade clients to accept responsibility for their problems when government has promised that it will do so? They feel defeated by the rhetoric of their own programs.[52]

Other developments that have curbed the permissive approach at the local level include the Reagan cuts in social programs and the return of welfare to conservative administrative doctrines. The end of CETA and cuts in other programs have circumscribed the world of training and services where the tendency to exempt recipients from responsibility was always strongest. Local welfare agencies have largely abandoned the lax, client-oriented eligibility procedures they flirted with during the welfare boom. Even the New York City welfare department, the national symbol of permissive welfare, is now conservatively administered. Some social workers, disillusioned with the entitlement approach to poverty, left welfare and joined work programs in the belief that the poor now needed employment at least as much as income.

Federal programs transferred benefits *to* the poor, but they also took responsibility for their lives *from* them. It was a devil's bargain. The moral lessons most people learn, that they must work and take care of their families if they are to prosper, were blocked for much of the underclass by federal policy. Society normally exacts work or other contributions from its members in return for support.[53] Government demanded no such reciprocity from its dependents, and that helps explain why so many subsist on the fringes of American society.

The outcome has been most tragic for the poor black families first spotlighted by Moynihan's report. The irony is that black society was more coherent before civil rights than after. The Haley family dramatized in the *Roots* television sagas was one of numberless black families that kept their pride and unity despite the pressures of overt racism. Comer and Poussaint have well summed up the spirit blacks often showed in those years:

> A Negro spiritual says, "Keep your hands on the plow, hold on."
>
> Black parents advised their children, although living in a sea of racism, to "prepare yourself—your time will come."
>
> Black porters and domestics saved their nickels and dimes and sent five or six children to college.
>
> Without weapons or war, blacks overcame overt segregation laws and practices that powerful racists said would never fall. And this happened because the black church-based culture preached pride and determination.[54]

Racism *per se* was certainly harmful to blacks. The aim of Jim Crow, North and South, was to exclude and subordinate blacks. One reason black society often held together under that regime was simply that the most gifted individuals, denied advancement, devoted their leadership entirely to their own communities.

But at least racism did not exempt blacks from normal social demands as recent federal policy has done. Permissive programs have replaced the racist regime with one that is, in its own way, equally destructive. At least for the dependent, the unfair expectations blacks faced in the past have been replaced, not with constructive ones, that would reward competence with acceptance, but rather with none at all. The tragic misuse of authority in the past bars government from using it now, even in ways that would help blacks. Consequently, the promise of freedom held out by civil rights has yet to be fully realized.

The Search for Oppression

Permissiveness, unfortunately, is not just the error of this or that party or policymaker. It cannot be rectified by changing this or that officeholder or program, or even by eliminating all the programs. It is deeply rooted in the progressive approach to social policy and in the nature of federal politics.

During the Great Society, the urge to find new social barriers acquired a life of its own. Policymakers increasingly responded, not to the needs of their problem, but to the imperatives of political culture. In American politics, if oppression cannot be found, the tendency is to search for it all the more intensely.[55] Thus federal policy has never come to terms with the increasing importance that dysfunction plays in the social problem. The drive to liberate the poor has only driven government further toward assuming total responsibility for them.

Today's social problem is difficult for American politics precisely because it is *not*, on the whole, due to oppression. Since the poor are no longer usually excluded from society by external forces, to give them freedom in either its liberal or conservative meaning cannot be the answer. Benefits without obligations merely entrench dependency, while cutting back benefits will not much reduce dysfunction, at least cuts of the small magnitude that are politically feasible. Instead, government must couple benefits with functioning requirements. Standards are a good thing, not a bad thing, as good as the benefits programs give. Caring for the needy now requires governing them in some ways, not just defraying their needs.

It is a form of caring, unfortunately, that lies outside the American tradition. On the whole, federal domestic policy has been about freedom and not order. The regime much of the disadvantaged live under today is permissive precisely *because* it is governmental. Somehow, government lacks the standing that private authorities, like family or friends, might have to tell the dependent how to behave. The problem is not so much hostility to the needy as suspicious attitudes toward authority, especially at the federal level, that all classes share. The disappointments of social policy reach back to the limitations of the American regime.

4

Why Work Must Be Enforced

IT is reasonable, in general, to think that social policy must set at least some standards for the dependent if they are to function, and that failure to do so explains much of the travail of the Great Society. In the case of work, however, that need is especially clear. There is a good reason to think that disadvantaged workers are unlikely to labor regularly unless they are required to as a condition of support by society.

The assumptions made in the progressive era were that individuals would seek out and accept employment without prompting. Under current conditions, however, society's interest in work can be greater than the individual's, especially in the case of "dirty," low-paid jobs. For both rich and poor alike, work has become increasingly elective, and unemployment voluntary, because workers commonly have other sources of income, among them government programs. Jobseekers are seldom kept out of work for long by a literal lack of jobs. More often, they decline the available jobs as unsatisfactory, because of unrewarding pay and conditions.

Nonwork is most serious among the disadvantaged, There are a number of competing explanations, but whichever we choose, public authority seems indispensable to solutions. For the nondependent nonwork may not pose a public issue. For the dependent, however, government probably must enforce work as a condition of support if it wants to advance integration. For recipients, work must be viewed, not as an expression of self-interest, but as an obligation owed to society. At the same time, to fulfill this obligation would permit the poor a kind of freedom that government benefits alone never can.

Voluntary Nonwork

Much of the remaining poverty in the United States is due to high unemployment and nonwork among the poor.[1] If low-income men and welfare mothers worked regularly, the underclass would be well on its way to dissolution. In Washington the presumption that nonwork is due to external barriers like lack of jobs has been orthodox since the New Deal, when an economic collapse threw a quarter of the labor force out of work for reasons beyond its control. Unemployment was a comfortable issue for liberal politics, since it seemed to reflect so little on the jobless themselves. The same attitude carried over to the Great Society. "The memory of the Depression and a penumbra of Marxism lingered on," wrote Daniel Moynihan, with the moral that "individuals were not to be held accountable for their fate."[2]

The progressive interpretation of nonwork rested on two specific assumptions. One was that people would work if they could, because to do so served their own interests. What could be more self-interested than to offer one's labor in return for income? Each worker simply made his or her own best bargain with the labor market. While jobseekers wanted the pleasantest, best-paying jobs they could get, they would accept lesser positions if they had to. Some income was always better than none. That is, they were economizers—they accepted the constraints of their environment and adjusted to them as best they could. The other assumption was that the individual search for work served the social interest as well. It produced income for the jobseeker but also contributed to economic growth, which in turn meant opportunity for others and the wealth needed to finance public benefits for those who could not work. Full employment has always been a high priority in Washington simply because it expands the "pie" for everyone.

The trend in unemployment is unmistakably up, as Table 1 shows. Furthermore, much higher rates than the average have become usual for displaced factory workers and a number of groups of special interest to social policymakers—women, nonwhites, and black youth. However, where joblessness in the 1930s was due mainly to economic contraction, today it is due mainly to a growing labor force and greater job turnover. In the last twenty-five years, despite recessions, job creation has been very strong, but a much higher proportion of the adult population is working or looking for work today than in earlier decades; the figure rose from 59 to 64 percent between 1960 and 1982.[3]

The boom in workers, and in unemployment, partly reflected the maturing of the "baby boom" generation. The economy did well to absorb that massive cohort with no greater rise in joblessness than occurred. Since later cohorts are much smaller, fewer new workers will be entering the labor force in future. Over the next decade the prospect is for a much tighter labor market than the country has recently seen, a favorable omen for reducing poverty. Already, in the current recovery, there have been difficulties filling low-wage jobs in low-unemployment areas of the country. Employers will probably be forced to pay more for these jobs, offering the low-skilled more of a living wage.[4] Attractive, high-paying jobs are likely to remain competitive. But in terms of elemental job availability the nation is very distant today from the Depression, when there were insufficient jobs of any kind for those who sought them.

The other reason the labor force is growing is that more women and teenagers have been seeking jobs. While some members of these groups are responsible for their own households, many more of them, compared to adult men, are "secondary" workers, from families where the husband, parents, or other members are already working. Secondary workers tend to raise unemployment because they usually have limited skills and work experience and have less need to accept available jobs than primary workers; often they will take only part-time or temporary positions. In 1960, 35 percent of the unemployed were women, and 19 percent were aged 16 to 19. By 1980 the figures had grown to 44 and 22 percent. In 1976, according to one survey, secondary workers comprised 26 percent of employed workers—and 35 percent of the unemployed. While these workers clearly could use work, their joblessness cannot be viewed with the same seriousness as that of family heads, because they have other means of support.[5]

The signs are that unemployement has become more voluntary, in the sense that jobseekers often choose to remain jobless rather than take the jobs most accessible to them. The problem is not that jobs are *unavailable* but that they are frequently *unacceptable*, in pay or conditions, given that some income is usually available from families or benefit programs. Many unemployed, it appears, are no longer job*seeking* in the traditional sense of accepting the best job they can get, however bad it is. Rather, they are job*shopping*—seeking work but not accepting it unless it meets their conditions. As in other shopping they have the option not to "buy" at all, that is, to remain unemployed or withdraw from the labor force.

We tend to think of the unemployed as having "lost" their jobs or been "thrown out" of work, but on average that was true for only 47 percent of the jobless between 1970 and 1982. Thirteen percent quit their jobs voluntarily. Forty percent were people just entering or reentering the labor force, that is, who had not sought work in the period just prior. Even in 1982, a year of sharp recession, only 59 percent of the jobless had lost their jobs while 8 percent had left them and a third were new entrants. Intermittent employment is one reason why, although over 95 percent of nonfarm workers are covered by Unemployment Insurance, only about a third now have a steady enough work history to collect benefits when they are jobless—down from around half in the early 1960s.[6]

A special government survey done in 1976 revealed the demands that the unemployed now feel they can make on the job market. The average worker who had lost or left a job was prepared to enter a new one only if it paid 7 percent *more* than his or her last position. While 35 percent of these jobless were willing to return to work for less than they formerly earned, 38 percent demanded more money. Even after fifty weeks out of work the average respondent persisted in expecting nearly as high a wage as in his or her old job. If jobless demanding a wage increase were defined as voluntarily unemployed and excluded from the statistics, unemployment as officially measured would drop by more than a point, more than three points for nonwhites.

Furthermore, only 30 percent of the jobless were willing to commute more than 20 miles to a new job, and only a third were willing to move to one. Especially for married women, maintaining ties to one's existing home, property, and friends often took priority over working. The jobless often had the resources to hold out for an attractive job. The commonest means of coping with the loss of earnings were simply to reduce expenses and delay major purchases, followed by reliance on savings, Unemployment benefits, and the earnings of other family members. More demeaning steps such as seeking help from friends or relatives, borrowing, or going on welfare were mentioned much less frequently.[7]

These findings, which apply to the unemployed generally, demonstrate that a disinclination to accept many available jobs, if they are unattractive, extends to the population as a whole. Among the low-income and low-skilled, however, unemployment is compounded by nonwork in other forms. Many disadvantaged workers have simply withdrawn from the legal low-wage labor market. Their place has been taken largely by illegal immigrants.

When the low-skilled do work, the pattern is rapid turnover in jobs rather than steady jobholding. Among workers generally, the duration of unemployment is shorter than one would expect if joblessness were involuntary. In 1980, 43 percent of the unemployed were out of work four weeks or less, 67 percent ten weeks or less, and only 11 percent more than twenty-six weeks, the usual duration of Unemployment benefits. Among women, teenagers, and nonwhites especially, cycling in and out of work is frequent. These groups seem to be able to find jobs about as easily as those with lower unemployment, such as adult men, but they also leave them quickly, or leave the labor force entirely. Turnover rather than lack of jobs largely explains why they are so often unemployed.[8] Of course, as in musical chairs, if the turnover stopped there might not be enough jobs for everyone. Then government job-creation efforts would become more necessary than they seem now. But at present, for most jobseekers in most areas, jobs of at least a rudimentary kind are generally available.

This kind of joblessness is difficult to blame on the environment. It is not influenced much by the ups and downs of overall business conditions. Though the low-wage labor market has a lot of temporary jobs, the usual pattern is for the same job to be filled by a succession of low-skilled workers. No doubt discrimination plays a role, but the evidence suggests that the workers usually leave for their own reasons. It is most likely that they are impatient with menial pay and working conditions and keep quitting in hopes of finding better. This "pathological instability in holding jobs," rather than lack of jobs, is the main reason for the work difficulties of the disadvantaged.[9]

Voluntary nonwork seems to be common among welfare recipients. Until the 1960s the presumption was that needy mothers with children and without husbands were unemployable; that was why they were covered by AFDC. But the "welfare explosion" of the late 1960s brought onto the rolls a great many younger mothers with more education and fewer children. Table 4 shows the shift. The sharp drop in mothers with more than two children, from over half in 1967 to under 30 percent in 1979, is especially notable. The trends reflect, in part, rising educational levels in the population, especially among blacks, and increasing use of birth control and abortion to limit family size.

Of course, younger mothers more often have children too young for school, a condition also thought to preclude employment. In fact, such mothers are no less likely to earn their way off welfare than those with older children. The logistics of work for these mothers are no doubt difficult, but lack of *government* child care seems seldom to be a barrier; most prefer to arrange care with friends or relatives informally.[10] As a result of those trends, by the 1970s many welfare mothers could be regarded as employable. According to estimates for New York City, from a fifth to a half of adult welfare recipients might be employable depending on how much child care and support services were available.[11]

The other important change was that more women went to work in the population generally, calling into question the presumption that mothers with children belonged in the home. The proportion of married women with husbands who were working or looking for work rose from 31 percent in 1960 to 41 percent in 1970 and 51 percent in 1980. For separated or divorced women like those on AFDC the rates ran still higher, at least 45 percent after 1970 even for women with preschool children.[12] Meanwhile, as Table 4 shows, the proportion of AFDC mothers in the labor force rose only from 19 to 24 percent between 1967 and 1979, and the proportion actually working hovered around 15 percent. That raised an unavoidable question. To quote Senator Russell Long, "What makes [welfare mothers] so different from their sisters who choose to work?" In many cases, joblessness could reasonably be viewed, not as something forced on mothers, but as a choice they made in preference to the difficulties of work in low-wage jobs.[13]

The welfare work problem was once thought to be untroublesome, because recipients seemed to enter and leave the rolls rapidly. Because of "tremendous turnover," HEW Secretary Wilbur Cohen asserted in 1967, it was a "great mistake" to imagine the existence of a permanent welfare class on AFDC.[14] A lot of the turnover, however, turned out to reflect closing and reopening of cases for administrative reasons rather than families really leaving dependency.

TABLE 4
Work Readiness and Effort of AFDC Mothers, 1967–79

Percentage of AFDC Mothers	*1967*	*1969*	*1971*	*1973*	*1975*	*1977*	*1979*
With more than 2 children	52.5	50.2	47.9	40.7	36.1	32.4	29.4
Age 35 or over	42.7	38.9	34.8	32.8	29.0	25.9	26.2
High school graduates	17.7	18.6	22.2	26.2	28.3	23.9[a]	21.9[a]
On welfare 3 years or more[b]	39.0	36.4	31.4	34.7	44.4	39.3	42.4
In labor force[c]	19.2	18.9	19.2	27.6	25.1	24.4	24.2
Working full or part time	13.3	13.5	13.9	16.1	16.1	13.8	14.2
Looking for work	5.9	5.4	5.3	11.5	9.0	10.6	10.0

[a] These figures are biased, probably downward, by very high proportions of respondents for whom education was unknown in these two years—39 percent in 1977 and 48 percent in 1979. There is no reason to suppose that actual education levels dropped.

[b] The time on welfare is measured since the last opening of the case. Some mothers may also have been on welfare prior to that time, with a break before their most recent case.

[c] Labor force participation figures are for the month when the survey was done. Figures for mothers working or looking for work anytime during the year, if known, would be higher.

SOURCE: U.S. Department of Health, Education, and Welfare/Health and Human Services, *AFDC Studies* for the indicated years. The studies are based on a sample survey of recipients.

The average length of an AFDC case also dropped around 1970 simply because the "welfare explosion" brought so many new cases onto the rolls. The proportion of long-term cases fell, then rose again, as Table 4 shows. Despite appearances, most cases in urban areas are on the rolls for substantial periods. In New York State (mostly New York City) in 1975, for example, almost half of AFDC cases had been on the program more than four years, and 38 percent had been on longer than nine. A recent study of AFDC nationally found that, while half of all cases entering welfare leave in under two years, 38 percent remain on for five years or more. The population on the rolls at any time is heavily slanted toward these longer-term cases; more than three-quarters will eventually remain on welfare for five years or more, and nearly half will remain on longer than eight years.[15]

A similar picture emerges if we look at the larger population in poverty, which includes most welfare recipients. Again, turnover seems very high. Nearly a quarter of the population occassionally falls into poverty, while less than 3 percent stays there long-term. But movement across the poverty line, a fixed point on the income scale, exaggerates how far the poor usually escape need. Many families leave poverty only to return. Perhaps 40 to 45 percent of the poor in a given year remain poor most of the time.[16]

Work is unquestionably one of the keys to overcoming poverty and dependency. But given the trends toward selective employment, among the better-off as well as the poor, steadier work at the bottom of society is unlikely unless government does something to motivate it.

THEORIES OF NONWORK

Exactly why do so many welfare mothers and other needy people fail to work consistently, even though many seem employable? It is, says Robert Hall, the "central unanswered question" in employment policy.[17] There are a number of theories, a fact that indicates how mysterious dysfunction is.

The commonest explanation has been economic. Economists regard the decision to work, like other decisions, as reflecting a choice among options. If employable people decline work, the reason must be that they have alternatives preferable to accepting the available jobs. In the service economy of the 1980s many jobs are less skilled and less well-paid than was formerly the norm in the American economy. And on the other hand government has increasingly provided support even to the employable through expansions of welfare, Unemployment Insurance (UI), and other benefit programs. The income facilitates seasonal and intermittent work. It allows the jobless to pursue more extensive job searches than previously, to hold out for "better" jobs, and to avoid being stigmatized by lesser ones. Specifically, UI has shielded many of the factory unemployed from having to shift to worse-paying jobs in the service economy.

AFDC benefits vary widely across the states, and the more generous they are, the lower work effort is among welfare mothers. Similarly, receiving UI benefits tends to make a worker stay jobless longer and expect a higher wage before returning to work. In the 1976 job search survey, workers on UI were out of work beyond 26 weeks twice as commonly as comparable workers without UI (38 percent versus 20 percent). They also spent 20 percent less time job-hunting and stayed unemployed 25 percent longer, other things being equal. If there were no UI, measured unemployment would probably be a half to one point lower than it is.[18]

How much of a worker's prior earnings UI replaces also has an influence. The average replacement rate has been variously estimated at from half to two-thirds of after-tax income. It varies with the state and is greatest for low-wage workers. High replacement rates tend to produce more voluntary unemployment, that is, workers who demand a wage increase to return to work. A cut in replacement rates, say, from 70 percent to a half would reduce wage expectations and cut the time out of work for the average recipient by more than a third.[19] The human and political benefits of UI are not doubt great, but the program, again, means that we can no longer view most joblessness as strictly involuntry.

The other important alternative to low-wage work is the mushrooming underground economy, which has grown to account for perhaps 10 percent of national income. Underground jobs can compete with mainstream ones largely because they are *sub rosa*. Employers can avoid taxes, which in the legal economy can amount to half of wages, and split the savings with their employees. Enterprises like drug running also earn large returns because their illegality limits competition. Thus unskilled workers can earn much more than in mainstream jobs, where they would often be confined to the minimum wage. Many workers who say they are unemployed are really working "off the books," enabling them to take home, not only wages, but Unemployment and other benefits.[20]

Some features of nonwork, however, are difficult to explain with economic logic. The jobless often decline work even when it would seem to suit their immediate interests. Why do many unemployed stay that way for long periods when they could accept lesser jobs and then try for better ones while working? Why do most welfare mothers avoid jobs when working would usually raise their income? Such behavior is not self-serving in an economic sense, let alone conducive to the social interest.

The mistake may be to assume, as economists and most politicians do, that the jobless are economizers seeking only to adjust to the conditions around them. They may in fact be engaging in political behavior, that is, attempting to get *others* to adjust to *them*. There is an element of protest in their refusal to accept "dirty" jobs they feel are beneath them. While they do want to work, they insist that jobs meet social standards for the "good" or "decent" job. For an individual that protest usually means nothing more demonstrative than claiming government benefits when menial work is in fact available.[21]

The protest has taken a more assertive form in the case of urban blacks. Joblessness in the ghetto, especially among young men, certainly reflects more than economics. Frustration by unskilled black youth at low-wage jobs, the Kerner commission found, was one of the causes of the urban riots.[22] Erratic work behavior looks deviant at the level of the individual but is understandable as a kind of political behavior. Ghetto youth are trying to shift the terms of their burdens and opportunities within American society. Many apparently see underpaid "dirty" jobs as among the ways white society controls them. Through nonwork as well as protest, they demand better.[23]

From an economic perspective the minimum wage looks like a barrier to employment for the unskilled. Employers may resist hiring youths whose labor, at least initially, is not worth $3.35 an hour. If ghetto youth were economizers, they would want the minimum wage repealed so they could underbid more productive workers for their jobs.[24] But it is mainly economists, who believe in economizing, who suggest this. The youth themselves commonly demand work at well above the minimum wage. In reality, only better-prepared youth, both black and white, can usually obtain well-paying jobs. To lower the minimum wage would only increase the gap between what disadvantaged youth expect and what the legal labor market offers them.[25] To satisfy those expectations they frequently turn toward underground or illegal employment.[26]

Distrust born of militancy seems to be one of the reasons why ghetto youth often quickly leave the jobs they are able to get. A close observer explains:

> It appears that the militancy of the 1960s has given way to a new sense of racial pride and self-assertiveness that has been slowly diffusing through urban black communities. With raised consciousness, the young, unskilled black worker often perceives himself useful only to the most exploitative employer, in the most menial of jobs, and then receives little or no job security, advancement, benefits, and at times no pay. With the increased emphasis on self, young blacks are tending to be more selective about the jobs they will perform, and often will not accept employment and work conditions they consider to be demeaning. This attitude appears in striking contrast to that of an earlier generation of blacks, many of whom accepted almost any available work. The youth tend to feel they are entitled to and deserve "much better jobs" than they are presently able to obtain.

The problem for the black youth is to "reconcile his high concept of self with the menial work he usually must perform." That struggle causes friction with the boss, which often results in dismissal or in the worker just leaving.[27]

The same kind of tension makes it difficult for disadvantaged clients to profit from government training programs. They look to the programs to provide alternatives to "dirty" jobs, but they often resist accepting the authority of program staff. They do not want these authorities, any more than employers, telling them they must accept work beneath them.[28] In response, federal training and public employment programs have often provided them a haven from the demands of the private sector. But since the programs expect little, neither can they reward their clients with the self-respect that goes with "cutting it" in real jobs.

A third interpretation of nonwork is cultural. It says that the reason groups with high unemployment do not work reliably is the values they hold. They do not calculate economically that nonwork pays; they do not protest politically. They simply march to a different drummer.

At first glance, this theory seems implausible. The poor and disadvantaged profess the same commitment to work as the better-off. The principal study of work orientations among the needy, by Leonard Goodwin, found "no differences between the poor and nonpoor when it comes to . . . wanting to work." The poor "identify their self-esteem with work as strongly as do the nonpoor." In fact, "the poor and the nonpoor, blacks and whites, the young and the old, feel the same way about work." All are very much in favor.

But equally, Goodwin found that how strongly his respondents endorsed the work ethic was "unrelated" to whether they in fact worked. What governed work behavior, rather, was whether they were disposed to accept welfare, and that in turn reflected whether or not they had achieved "decent" jobs in the past. The poor may want to work in principle, but a great many in practice accept welfare as an alternative to low-wage jobs.[29]

On examination the work desires of many poor people turn out to be highly conditional. Welfare recipients and other low-income people want to work, but they feel work is impossible unless government first provides them with training, transportation, child care, and, above all, acceptable positions. Goodwin found that his welfare mothers, "while expressing a desire to work," did not "care for menial jobs." One mother herself stated in congressional hearings on welfare reform that

> . . . welfare recipients want to work. They want real jobs that provide benefit to society and pay decent wages. They do not want to work off their inadequate grants at depressed wages in jobs that provide them with no training and no chance for advancement.[30]

The advocates of welfare reform often struck a similar note:

> [T]he majority of those who are able to work among the poor either are working or would prefer to work if they had proper training or job opportunities, or if other barriers to finding work could be surmounted. In other words, the poor are not willingly so, and the majority among them would strive to better their economic position and improve their lot in life given some form of encouragement and assistance.[31]

We recognize here the familiar contours of the culture of poverty, so much more dutiful in intention than in execution. The poor would like to work, but only if barriers over which they have no control are first overcome by others. Since much of the burden of work consists precisely in acquiring skills, finding a job, arranging child care, and so forth, the effect is to drain the work obligation of much of its meaning.

What is missing is the idea of obligation. Work is normative for the poor, but it is not something they feel they *must* do, whatever the personal cost. Lee Rainwater writes:

> The great discovery that lower-class people make, which middle-and working-class people find so hard to understand, is that it is possible to live a life that departs very significantly from the way you think life ought to be lived without ceasing to exist, without feeling totally degraded, without giving up all self-esteem.

But from the viewpoint of integration it is a tragic discovery, for it means that mainstream norms cannot be held with the commitment necessary to achieve them.[32] To use Lon Fuller's distinction, the work ethic for the disadvantaged appears to represent a "morality of aspiration" but not of "duty."[33]

A more extreme interpretation is that the poor may not actually share the work ethic as much as appears. The desire they claim for work may reflect only "response set"—the tendency of respondents to tell researchers what they want to hear. According to one study by a sociologist, nonworking welfare mothers are usually "traditionalists" who, though they do not oppose work, much prefer to stay home and raise a family. Rather than accept a work obligation, they feel society should support them in their role as mothers.[34] Other studies suggest that the poor do display less achievement motivation on average than the better off, [35] even if the reason is ultimately social barriers.

The work ethic may also be declining for the population generally, in practice if not in belief. The notion that work carries moral meanings for the individual arose in an age before labor was collectivized. In the craft economy of the eighteenth century, artisans could see the results of their labors and were rewarded accordingly. As much as anything, Daniel Rodgers has written, it was "intense regional faith in the worth of labor" that spurred the creation of an industrial economy in New England, a region poor in many of the material prerequisites of wealth. The appearance of the factory and other forms of large-scale organization, however, increasingly separated the worker from his product. While belief in the work ethic remained strong, people worked increasingly for money, not for meaning. Unionism and other economic protests were driven in part by a feeling that big business had violated the proper moral order of the workplace.[36]

Today, according to sketchy polls, the tension between what

Americans would like to get out of work and what they do is sharp. About three-quarters of Americans still express satisfaction with their work, but the proportion has declined somewhat from the 1960s, and dissatisfaction has risen. A government study found that while workers want jobs to pay well, they are distressed by lack of meaning on the job—inadequate autonomy and challenge. According to one survey, people still believe in work, but they also see little connection between their personal effort and their own rewards. As a result less than a quarter say they are performing at the level they could.[37] Such feelings undermine the sense that hard, dedicated work is obligatory in any definite sense. If work commitment is declining among Americans generally, rising nonwork among the poor and dependent cannot be surprising.

The Need for Authority

All the interpretations of nonwork say, in one way or another, that the comfortable, progressive approach to work is no longer valid. Work, at least in low-wage jobs, no longer serves the individual's interest as clearly as it does society's. Whichever approach we take, the solution must lie with public authority in some form. If society seriously wants more of the disadvantaged to work regularly, to achieve goals like integration, then it must require them to. Merely to offer the jobless freedom and the opportunity to work will not suffice, at least under current conditions. Work must be treated as a public obligation, akin to paying taxes or obeying the law.

The commonest solution to the work problem in Washington, like the understanding of it, has been economic. Economists contend that welfare recipients and other nonworkers can be induced to work by making it worth their while. The preferred means is work incentives, or provisions that a recipient who works should have only part of his or her earnings subtracted from the family's welfare grant, leaving the rest to motivate work. Experience and research, unfortunately, have not been kind to the incentives theory. The leading test was a feature added to AFDC in 1967 that allowed working recipients to deduct (that is, keep) $30 plus one-third of their earnings per month. The incentive was actually stronger than that, perhaps 50 percent or more, because the 1967 deductions were added to allowances for work expenses already granted in 1962.[38] Yet studies found the impact of the incentives to be modest. Table 4, certainly, shows no upsurge in the proportion of welfare mothers going to work. Work incentives also made it less common for working families to leave welfare, since fewer earnings were subtracted from the grant and families stayed eligible for assistance longer as their income rose. Welfare directors complained that the incentives just cost extra grant money and made it harder to "close cases."[39]

Conversely, when the Reagan Administration reduced work incentives in 1981, very little fall in work effort resulted. The cuts limited the $30 and one-third deduction to the first four months a recipient was on the job; after that, all earnings beyond work expenses were once again deducted from the grant. Experts predicted that many working recipients would no longer find work worthwhile and would quit in droves, preferring simple dependency. But the propensities of recipients to work, or quit work, changed hardly at all.[40]

Further disappointments came from the income maintenance experiments. In those studies a number of different levels of grant and work incentive were tried. The results generally showed, as expected, that the decline in participants' work effort varied directly with their grant level and inversely with the strength of work incentives. But the effects were disappointingly small, and even strong incentives did not forestall unacceptable levels of nonwork.[41]

The incentives theory was perhaps too subtle for the realities of welfare. Recipients seldom work their way off the rolls gradually in response to incentives. They usually leave, as they enter, through large, discontinuous changes in family status or income. The mother loses or gains a husband, or she loses or gains a job. Going to work may immediately raise her income above the welfare level, so she is never subject to the incentives at all.[42] Today the main "disincentive" to work while on welfare is not the "tax" earnings place on the grant but fear of losing eligibility for Medicaid, the main health program for the poor, which is linked to welfare.[43]

Another serious problem with incentives surfaced during the debates over welfare reform. The idea behind incentives was to motivate work by letting recipients keep more of their earnings. But to do that conflicted with other economic goals. If fewer earnings were taken from the recipient to reimburse the grant, the cost of welfare rose. More serious, the tendency of incentives to keep working recipients on the rolls meant that much more of the population might qualify for welfare. Incentives extended welfare eligibility well up into the middle class by some reckonings. That consequence could be prevented only if the benefits given without work were very low, too low for the unemployable to live on, or if the work incentive was weakened, so that the benefits were "taxed" away more quickly as earnings rose.[44]

In Congress conservatives refused to consider welfare plans that would massively expand the rolls, while liberals insisted on generous benefits. The only way to combine these priorities was to abandon strong work incentives, and events tended that way. The incentive in the Nixon welfare reform plan was cut from a half to a third during consideration in Congress. The Reagan Administration largely eliminated even the AFDC work incentive in order to concentrate benefits even further on the "truly needy." The price of such shifts, however, was a greater and greater reliance on administrative work requirements as a means of promoting work.[45] That is, work was to be motivated, not by the prospect of adding to one's grant, but by the fear that the authorities would take it away if one did not work.

The real difficulty with incentives was that they appealed simply to *individual* self-interest. If a gap had opened between the individual and social interest in work, how could methods that served only the individual ever close it? For the employable not to work violated the social interest in one way. To pay them excessively to work was sure to do so in another. The same was true of other liberal approaches to the work problem. To raise the minimum wage, for example, would make low-paid jobs more attractive, but it would also make employers less willing to hire the unskilled, and it would risk greater export of jobs to countries with cheaper labor. Similarly, to provide public service employment (PSE) would cause more jobless to work, since such positions tend to be better paid and less demanding than the jobs the same workers could get in the private sector. But PSE is also costly and, like generous work incentives, raises questions of fairness: Why should unwilling workers be bribed to work when many other Americans, not on welfare, do "dirty" jobs every day?

Rather, the solution must lie in public authority. Low-wage work apparently must be mandated, just as a draft has sometimes been necessary to staff the military. Authority achieves compliance more efficiently than benefits, at least from society's viewpoint. Government need not make the desired behavior worthwhile to people. It simply threatens punishment (in this case loss of benefits) if they do not comply.[46] To some extent authority seeks to change individuals preferences as well as subordinate them to society's. Moral appeals are made to get people to accept compliance as legitimate, not simply prudent. Only then is compliance assured.[47]

The need for authority is even clearer if nonwork is construed as a political act. In an open political system rebellious actions, even if not overtly political, tend to provoke countervailing forces. The welfare politics of the Great Society period, both in and out of government, can be seen as a political dispute of which nonwork was a part. The radical forces that questioned welfare and other institutions in those years claimed to reject the "system," yet they were drawn ineluctably into political argument with those institutions. They were accountable at least to the communities for which they claimed to speak [48] and, in a looser sense, to the nation. The National Welfare Rights Organization, for example, originally concentrated on mobilizing welfare mothers to demand higher benefits, eschewing politics in any larger sense.[49] But when welfare reform was proposed, NWRO was forced to take a position and testify. Its view—in favor of very high benefits without any work tests—did not prevail, but it helped keep guaranteed income on the national agenda for a decade.

The repeated national debate over welfare since the mid-1960s can be seen as a struggle to define a new social contract. The questions were what sustenance the nation would guarantee its members, and what effort it would demand from them in return.[50] Only the extreme positions have clearly been rejected. Congress has not guaranteed the employable an income, but neither has it done away with all welfare benefits for them.

That debate goes on even when discussions of social policy appear unpolitical. Among economists in Washington, for example, there is argument over how much government should do to promote work. Liberals favor well-paid public employment as the only way to create enough "decent" jobs of the kind low-skilled workers aspire to. Conservatives resist, saying sufficient, if less pleasant, jobs are already available in the private sector. In the middle are those favoring stronger work incentives, more aggressive job placement to find attractive private jobs, or required work in low-paid public positions.[51]

The dispute appears technical, but is really about social standards. The contestants differ less than appears about the economic situation facing the unemployed. All will admit, if pressed, that low-wage jobs are available for most of the jobless, if they would accept them. The real issue is whether they should have to. That is, who must economize? Must government adjust the job market to the needs of the jobless, or must the jobless themselves adjust to it as it is? The issue is political, with no definite answer.

The debate, in and out of Congress, may foreshadow a bargain in which the jobless accept something closer to a work obligation in return for efforts to enrich the jobs available to them. While the low-skilled probably cannot be saved from work that is relatively "dirty," they might be subsidized in some way or given better benefits linked to work, such as health coverage, than they usually have now. Costs to employers must be minimized to prevent export of jobs, but that danger is greater in manufacturing than in the service economy that dominates the current low-wage labor market. Generally, service jobs must be done in America by Americans, so the costs of enriching them could be imposed on employers or taxpayers without the jobs disappearing. It would also be necessary to stop foreign workers from coming here to get the jobs through restraints on immigration, both legal and illegal. In return for improved jobs, however, society would enforce work more strictly, and any idea that work is voluntary for the employable would be given up.[52]

If nonwork has cultural roots, again freedom-oriented policies will not suffice. Experience shows that benefits and opportunities alone will not overcome a reluctance to work embedded in the attitudes of the welfare class. And while the conservative policy of just cutting back support would surely put more pressure on the jobless to work, whether they would respond with the kind of disciplined effort required by the American economy is very questionable.

Conservatives often suppose that welfare demoralizes the lower class, while to abolish welfare would automatically produce the kind of self-reliant behavior typical of the rest of the population. Actually, there is no reason to suppose that a more small-government, market-oriented society would achieve any particular level of social functioning. Conservatives tend, like economists, to view human beings as abstractions whose productivity is invariant. In reality, people differ enormously in their economic capacities for cultural reasons. Most differences in wealth within and among countries result from those differences, not from variations in more impersonal economic or political conditions.[53]

With less government there would surely be a market society of some sort, but the level of economic and other functioning found in it might be below, not above, the relatively high level still usual in the United States. In some societies with weaker governments than in America, the level of social cooperation is not far above the warfare of a state of nature; Lebanon and southern Italy are examples. In American cities the atrophy of public authority has produced not harmony and efficiency but crime and economic decline.[54]

Even a market society depends for its vitality on a habit of social trust, a proclivity to meet the expectations of others, that does not derive from the market alone. A market place involves a severely limited form of individualism. People compete to serve their own interests, but to avoid open conflict they must also behave morally. Buyers and sellers find that to succeed they have to serve others' interests with a dedication stretching beyond immediate reward. The faith to do so when the return is unsure is what distinguishes successful economies from others.[55] Government plays a role in producing such virtue, by supporting civic behavior when it does *not* serve self-interest. The role of public authority is precisely to make *obligatory* the norms that people commonly affirm but do not reliably obey, a gap that is especially wide for the underclass. For the unskilled and unmotivated to work regularly requires *more* government in this sense rather than less.

The more extreme, counter-culture interpretation of nonwork suggests an even stronger government role. Many young people today, especially at the bottom of society, simply are not as well socialized by adults as they used to be. They cannot be integrated unless they become something closer to the disciplined workers the economy demands. In some form government must take over the socializing role. It has been suggested that only "mass, socialized therapeutic measures," such as intensive casework with families, could begin to dissolve the culture of poverty.[56] The implications seem Orwellian. In reality, a number of institutions—schools, the police, the military—already exist to inculcate the functioning necessary to a civic society.[57] All reinforce the socializing efforts of private institutions—the family, churches, and voluntary organizations. To speak of work or other welfare requirements is only to add social programs to the other structures already engaged in the formation of citizens.

The need to enforce work is clearest in the case of young black men, the group perhaps most central to the work problem. A special survey of inner-city black youth done in 1979–80 showed all the forces for nonwork at play. The youths faced strong disincentives to work in regular jobs, because they could earn more through illegal work or crime. They were strongly alienated from mainstream social institutions, including school, where most had failed to progress. And cultural influences on work were palpable. If the youths went to church, they were more likely to work; if their families were on welfare, they were less likely to.[58]

But however we explain their joblessness, the overriding fact is that their behavior is not controlled by the normal expectations supporting work. They are, in Hobbes' phrase, "masterless men," living in many ways outside social norms. Only public authority in some form can restore order. The requirements for order, Hobbes reminds us, must be met even in a "free" society:

> For the prosperity of a people . . . cometh not from aristocracy, nor from democracy, but from the obedience, and concord of the subjects: nor do the people flourish in a monarchy, because one man has the right to rule them, but because they obey him. Take away in any kind of state, the obedience, and consequently the concord of the people, and they shall not only not flourish, but in short time be dissolved.[59]

Community has indeed dissolved in the low-wage labor market. For it to be restored, work must apparently become a duty for the least skilled, not just a matter of self-interest.

To show that work requirements are necessary, of course, does not settle what they would consist of in practice. How much impact would they have on nonwork or other dysfunctions among the poor? How strong must they be to have a significant impact on those problems? How would they be implemented? The little that is known about these issues is discussed further below.

Forms of Freedom

The most fundamental question is political: How could such demands be justified to a liberal polity whose leading value is freedom? To enforce work would unquestionably make the dependent less free than they are, at least in some senses.

If we think socially, in terms of what individuals require to make their way in life, justification is easy. A sense of personal obligation is in fact necessary to freedom. Parents teach their children to be "responsible," that is, to obey reasonable requirements levied by others and to be accountable for their behavior. Individuals must be *un*free in these senses in order to live independent lives.

The Coleman study of education found that social background largely determines how children do in school, but it also found that the strongest single determinant of success was the child's own sense of responsibility for his or her performance. Children who traced their fortunes to their own efforts, rather than luck or favor, tended to do well regardless of race or background. It was the children without a sense of responsibility whose performance was most predictable from their backgrounds. They were less burdened but also less autonomous.[60] Other research shows that even the victims of misfortunes like muggings recover more quickly if they accept at least some responsibility for the mishaps, for those who do implicitly assert their ability to control events in furture.[61] The moral seems to be that society will set its stamp on people in chosen or unchosen ways. Those who accept its just demands have the greatest, not the least, freedom to set their own directions.

It is much tougher to square obligations like work with the nation's public notions of freedom. Even if Americans are dutiful in their private lives, many blanch at the thought of government setting rules for personal behavior, even it it would benefit recipients. Fortunately, most Americans learn their public rights and responsibilities from families, friends, churches, and other private interactions; the role of public institutions like schools is important but secondary.[62] The trouble is that because the dependent already live under public auspices, there is no practical alternative to a public role in socialization. If government does not set standards for its recipients, no one else can.

Economic regulation is sensitive enough in American politics and business is a fairly impersonal activity. How much more sensitive must it be to regulate the intimate details of individual lives, as work or other performance standards would do? Such standards require government to decide, not only who is needy, but who is able to function and who is not. Unavoidably, the setting of social standards extends government's role from the regulation of conditions to the governance of individual need.[63]

From one point of view the enterprise is hopeless. As Edward Banfield has argued, politics forbids the most direct solution to urban disorders: simply to enforce the laws and institutionalize those who are unable to obey them.[64] But from another viewpoint movement toward a government role in functioning standards is inevitable. American *society* is a lot less permissive than American *government*, especially in Washington. Over time, those who want a more orderly society, and they are the majority, are bound to demand that federal programs set clearer standards than they do now.

The pressure for action from below should be reassuring to those fearful of authority. If government sets standards for work or other competences, they will not be arbitrary, but will reflect beliefs about social obligation that are already commonplace, among the poor as much as others. The political problem in social policy is large but limited. It is not to create new standards but to *elevate* into social policy those that already prevail outside the public sector. The important division over welfare requirements is not between the poor and other Americans but between government and society.

5

The Work Issue Defeats Welfare Reform

A REALIZATION in Washington that the character of work was changing came to overshadow the question of welfare reform. A number of proposals to expand welfare and guarantee an income to all Americans surfaced during the Great Society period. The welfare reformers operated within the progressive tradition. They saw low income as one more barrier that had to be eliminated if the poor were to join mainstream American life.

By the late 1960s, however, it was difficult to explain poverty any longer as simply a lack of income. Nonwork or irregular work by the poor themselves played too obvious a role. That was especially true among welfare recipients, who seldom worked. Thus it was less and less apparent that self-interest alone would lead recipients to work. Politicians, like researchers, began to ask about the nature of nonwork and what government could do about it.

Welfare reform failed, at bottom, because proponents never provided convincing answers to those questions. Reform planners either denied that nonwork existed or explained it away with sociological reasoning. The various reports that advocated guaranteed income in the late 1960s all boldly claimed that most needy, even able-bodied adults, were unemployable and hence entitled to support without working. The progressive reflex to provide new benefits overwhelmed attention to the growing functioning problem among the poor themselves.

The attempt to exempt the needy from a need to function, not the idea of welfare for them, was the most controversial aspect of reform. During hearings and debates on a number of reform plans between 1969 and 1979, the central issue was work, not welfare. There were conservatives who wanted to deny all welfare to the employable and liberals who would have guaranteed them an income without strings, but both those extreme positions were rejected in Congress. Most members wanted to give at least some benefits to the employable but require that they work, or at least look for work, in return. This stance was an expression of what I have called the civic approach to social policy.

In the short run the result was a stalemate. The disputes over work and, secondarily, benefits and costs were enough to defeat welfare reform. But over the decade there was movement toward the civic position. Congress more and more tried to *combine* welfare with functioning requirements like work and child support. Thus welfare began as a typical "New Deal" dispute over the proper *extent* of government; it ended as a question of the *nature* of government.

The Welfare Issue

As originally enacted in 1935, federal welfare programs had been deliberately confined to groups everyone agreed were unemployable so as to avoid a work issue. Eligibility was limited to those who, in addition to being needy, were aged, blind, or members of families with only parent, commonly a widow. Coverage for the disabled was added in 1950. Other people were supposed to support themselves by working or through social insurance (Unemployment Insurance or Social Security), for which they had to qualify by working.

By the 1960s, however, liberals had come to view the rules for Aid to Families with Dependent Children (AFDC), the family welfare program, as restrictive. AFDC benefits often paid well below the poverty level, since states, which shared the cost with Washington, controlled benefit levels. For the same reason, benefits varied widely from state to state. In 1965 the average benefit was $137 a month, but it was $197 in New York and only $33 in

Mississippi.[1] Coverage was usually denied to intact families, that is, those with two parents, often called the "working" or "deserving" poor, and to single adults, even though they might be as needy as single-parent families. The uncovered needy could obtain help only from scanty local "general assistance" programs not funded by Washington. Even families that were eligible for AFDC often had to accept demeaning treatment by local welfare agencies as the price of assistance. Social workers sometimes tried to regulate the personal lives of welfare mothers, on pain of cutting them off the rolls. In addition, there were suspicions, mentioned earlier, that welfare set up "disincentives" against family unity and work.

To an impartial eye those criticisms were overdrawn. The problem of low benefits was acute only in the South. In Northern cities, where most recipients lived, payments were often competitive with what low-skilled workers could earn. The exclusion of intact families and single people from coverage was based on the reasonable assumption that these groups could work. Instances of invidious welfare administration were uncommon outside the South and after 1960. Recent studies find that most recipients are satisfied with the way welfare agencies treat them, although they would like higher benefits.[2] Nevertheless, liberals said, it was "known beyond any doubt . . . that public assistance as it is now administered is arbitrary, degrading to the recipients, and spotty geographically, and that it reduces people's incentives to . . . work." Secretary of Health, Education, and Welfare Joseph Califano later repeated the litany: Welfare was "antifamily, antiwork, and prone to error and fraud."[3] Whatever the realities, a liberal government had strong motivations to make welfare a problem, for this provided what politically it most needed—a new way to locate the difficulties of the poor outside themselves, in programs and policies that government could change.

Changes occurred. New welfare programs, particularly food stamps and Medicaid, were inaugurated during the 1960s. Food stamps covered all needy without distinction of family type, exactly as the critics wanted. In most states AFDC benefits became markedly more generous. To improve incentives to work, recipients were allowed in 1962 and 1967 to protect as much as half their income from deductions to repay welfare. Starting around 1960 federal administrators exerted increasing pressure on states to administer welfare in a less discretionary and more client-oriented manner. That pressure was forcefully seconded by the courts. Responding to class-action suits brought by poverty lawyers, the Supreme Court in the late 1960s outlawed a number of devices some states had used to restrict access to AFDC—"man-in-the-house" rules (which denied aid to families where the mother was still seeing the father or another man), residency requirements (which disallowed aid to eligibles until they had been in the state for periods up to a year), and arbitrary terminations of benefits (forbidden by requirements that states observe due process and provide recipients legal counsel in disputes over benefits).[4]

These steps transformed welfare from a last recourse of the poor into an entitlement on which much of the disadvantaged population could live. At least for eligibles, in most localities by the late 1960s AFDC provided a minimum income distributed virtually without regard to the behavior of recipients. The new liberality and generosity of the system, at least relative to the past, was one reason for the massive growth of the rolls in those years. A great many low-skilled adults now chose dependency on government over struggling to support themselves in low-paying jobs. According to one study of New York City:

> In a numerically stable population of approximately 8 million, the number of dependents rose from 328,000 in 1960 to 1.2 million in 1970, or from 4 percent of the city's inhabitants to 15 percent. In terms of household heads, the comparable numbers are 137,000 and 454,000 of a total adult population (aged 18 and over) that grew only minimally from 5.6 million to 5.7 million over the same period of time.[5]

AFDC had become, in the literal sense, a welfare state.

Conservatives, for their part, attributed much of the growth to the liberalizing changes just mentioned. Lax administration, they asserted, allowed onto the rolls many people who were ineligible or could support themselves. They counterattacked with new regulations from the federal level. In 1973 Congress enacted a tough new "quality control" program that required states to reduce ineligibility and overpayment in AFDC or risk cuts in their federal funding. In 1974–75 tougher child support requirements were added. While states had always tried to track down absent fathers to make them contribute to supporting their families, the mothers now had to help the authorities do this as a condition of eligibility. In 1967 and 1971 work requirements were added to AFDC. Some welfare mothers might now be required to work, look for work, or enter training as a condition of eligibility. The conservative reform program reached its culmination in 1981, when the Reagan Administration enacted a number of cuts in AFDC eligibility, toughened the work requirements still further, and proposed—so far unsuccessfully—to devolve responsibility for welfare to the states.

These measures achieved important savings, but they did not shake the character of AFDC as an assured income for much of low-income America. Thanks to quality control the proportion of AFDC funds spent in error dropped from 16.5 to 8.6 percent between 1973 and 1977. State child support programs recover enough money to pay for themselves, but on average they collect from only 11 percent of absent fathers and reimburse only 5 percent of the cost of AFDC. The Reagan cuts saved all of $546 million annually out of a total federal AFDC budget of $6 billion in 1982.[6] Toward the late 1970s the AFDC rolls did begin to decline, as did the proportion of eligibles claiming their benefits. While the new rules and restrictions were one reason, another was simply that AFDC benefits declined in real value after 1970 because of inflation, so fewer eligibles found it worthwhile to claim them.[7] Yet AFDC and related benefits still constitute an entitlement that female-headed families, the core of the poverty population, can subsist on with few if any requirements in return.

Guaranteed Income

The welfare issue took a new turn at the end of the 1960s, when income maintenance became the preferred approach to the poverty problem. Federal planners reasoned that disadvantaged children, youths, and welfare mothers had not profited much from special government training programs, but perhaps they could be integrated simply by giving them enough income to buy a mainstream standard of living.

The idea was developed in several influential studies of welfare and poverty that appeared in the later 1960s. The sponsoring bodies included an HEW Advisory Council on Public Welfare, an Arden House conference on welfare convened by Nelson Rockefeller, the Kerner commission on the urban riots, the Heineman commission on income maintenance programs, and the Committee for Economic Development. The groups represented businessmen and labor leaders as well as public officials and academics.[8] Apart from details, they reached a remarkable consensus: The way to end poverty was to eliminate most of the traditional restrictions on welfare other than need. Specifically:

- Base assistance only on income level and the size of the family, eliminating AFDC's preference for female-headed families.
- Pay benefits sufficient to raise family income to the poverty level, either immediately or within a few years.
- Rely on strong work incentives, that is, on the right to keep part of earned income, rather than work requirements in order to increase work by the poor.
- Eliminate complex and degrading administration in favor of simplified, rights-oriented procedures, especially in determining eligibility.
- Federalize welfare financing and administration wholly or substantially, so benefits and practices would be more uniform nationwide.

The point was to treat welfare recipients more as middle-class claimants were treated in "respectable" programs like Social Security or Unemployment Insurance. They would no longer be "suppliants," said one academic study, but "rights-bearing citizens claiming benefits to which they are entitled."[9]

The difficulty for all the reports was to justify guaranteed income in the face of the traditional expectation that individuals should support themselves unless they were children, aged, or disabled. To do so the studies resorted to sociological arguments that the poor were not really responsible for their problems, even behavioral ones. Welfare recipients were "not dependent through choice," it was claimed, but were "victims of economic, social, or health circumstances beyond their control." They simply lacked the background or the opportunity to be self-sufficient. Most were already "doing what they can." It was "wrong that so much attention is focused on the few laggards," since the nation's "economic and social structure virtually guarantees poverty for millions of Americans."[10]

In particular, the poor could not usually be expected to work. Many were children or elderly, and most of the adults were occupied with young children or disabled for psychic if not physical reasons. High proportions of the needy, it was estimated, suffered "personal barriers" to work, including, not only school and family responsibilities, but "poor health," "low motivation," and "inhibiting cultural attitudes or values." Hence "only a small proportion of the adults can be helped to be self-supporting." Even if they worked, the needy could not always earn enough to escape poverty. The standard American assumption that "anyone who wishes to live well can achieve that objective by seeking and accepting work" had to be reevaluated.[11]

The responsibility for the poor, rather, must be transferred to government. The welfare system must "make up to individuals for all deficiencies of economic and social functioning"—not on their part but society's—that had helped make them poor. The problem lay not in the behavior of the poor themselves but in "widespread lack of public understanding and acceptance of our society's responsibility" for the needy. Two facts sufficed to establish that responsibility: "*The poor lack money, and most of them cannot increase their incomes themselves.*"[12]

Welfare reform, therefore, could only mean additional benefits for the needy. No behavioral requirements like work tests could be imposed, for that would place the responsibility for poverty on the recipient rather than society. Of the welfare studies, only the one by the business-oriented Committee for Economic Development endorsed a work requirement, and then only a mild stipulation that employable recipients register for possible work or training. All the others dismissed work tests as ineffective or demeaning. They relied for motivating work entirely on work incentives, the usual recommendation being that recipients have only half of any earnings deducted from their grants. Self-interest, not coercion, would then lead them to work. Wrote the Heineman commission, "We do not think it desirable to put the power of determining whether an individual should work in the hands of a Government agency when it can be left to individual choice and market incentives."[13]

The policymaking behind the proposals showed the consensual patterns characteristic of the Great Society. Guaranteed income drew surprising support from business as well as social workers and welfare advocacy groups. The welfare study groups all had business representatives, two were dominated by business, and yet all recommended assured income in much the same terms. Later, when proposals went before Congress, business groups divided, testifying as much for as against reform.[14]

One explanation, already mentioned, is that Great Society programs, including welfare, were less threatening to business interests than more regulatory social intiatives. Another is that the elite, big-company businessmen named to the study groups were usually more liberal than the average. Perhaps most important, the mere fact of serving on such commissions caused businessmen to think in progressive terms. The very question put to them—What should Washington do about poverty or welfare?—assumed that their job was to seek new barriers that government could eliminate.

Economists did most of the planning for reform, and their role showed that problem-solving had triumphed over partisanship as the impetus to policymaking. In Washington an "economist" means, not so much an expert on the economy, as someone equipped to use economic concepts and mathematical tools to analyze proposals in any policy area. "Policy analyst" and "systems analyst" are close synonyms. The vogue of economics in Washington began in the early 1960s, when Robert McNamara, as Secretary of Defense, employed systems analysts to take control of military planning from the armed services. In the later 1960s, when earlier service-oriented strategies had failed to overcome disadvantage, economists took over social planning in the bureaucracy.[15] They dominated the staffs of the welfare study groups as well as the planning offices of the Departments of Labor and Health, Education, and Welfare, the nerve centers of executive social policymaking where the major welfare reform proposals were drafted.

The economic approach to poverty was indifferent to the moralistic concerns that had animated earlier approaches to welfare. Economists defined poverty simply as a lack of income. They proposed to overcome it simply by transferring money to the poor. Their preferred means was some kind of negative income tax, or NIT. Where individuals above poverty were taxed positively, giving some of their wealth to government, those below poverty would be taxed "negatively," receiving additional income from government. Some economists wanted to administer the transfer through the federal income tax system, some through the welfare system, but the idea was the same.

To an economic eye many of the traditional restrictions on family welfare were nonsensical. Assistance was limited largely to female-headed families, when economic need should be the only criterion. States were allowed to limit benefits arbitrarily, when payments, like the poverty level, should be uniform nationwide.

Some welfare programs like food stamps and public housing gave recipients benefits "in kind" rather than in cash, thus constraining their freedom to spend their income as they wished. The restrictions all reflected moral judgments that the poor were in some ways less deserving or competent than other people. The abstract psychology of economics eschewed such judgments. To an economist, all individuals are self-seeking, the poor no more than the better-off, and each is the best judge of what serves his or her own interest.

Economists assumed that, if the dependent did not work, the reason must be that it was not worth their while. The solution was work incentives or some other device such as a wage subsidy that would strengthen recipients' economic interest in jobs. Work requirements, which mandated that recipients work or look for work on pain of cuts in their grants, were bound to be unenforceable, because they tried to make people work against their interest. Such tests were bound to cost more to administer than they would save in welfare.

The economic approach was indifferent to the size of government, the traditional nub of partisan controversy. While guaranteed income would have greatly enlarged government social spending, economists did not seek a larger government in administrative terms. By instituting national benefits and standards and paying grants through the tax system or equivalent procedures, planners hoped actually to reduce the size of the welfare bureaucracy, especially at the state and local level. They also thought that some service programs, like education or housing, could be replaced with either an equivalent amount of cash or with vouchers, meaning coupons (food stamps are an example) with which the recipients could buy the services from any vendor, public or private. That would force the providers to compete and would simplify social administration.[16] In welfare, these hopes were probably vain. The intricacies of case management and of interfacing any new income system with the old would probably have meant more bureaucracy, not less.[17]

Among economists guaranteed income has not been a partiasn matter. The inventer of the negative income tax was Milton Friedman, the best-known of conservative economists. For him the main virtue of the NIT was that it would simplify government; for liberals, it was that transfers could eliminate poverty. On several occasions economists of differing persuasions petitioned the government to reform welfare along NIT lines.[18] Their disciplinary conviction that *economic* tools of transfers and work incentives were the right basis for antipoverty policy overrode any political differences among them.

Concrete guaranteed income proposals began to appear in the mid-1960s. Economists at the Office of Economic Opportunity and the Department of Health, Education, and Welfare advanced a number of plans to reform welfare as an NIT. The two most important proposals were developed with White House support: the Nixon Family Assistance Plan (FAP) and the Carter Program for Better Jobs and Income (PBJI). FAP would have expanded welfare eligibility to cover the "working poor," that is two-parent needy families, as well as AFDC female-headed families. FAP's income guarantee, that is, the income a family was assured without working, was $1,600 for a family of four (the amount varied with family size), somewhat below the poverty level. To motivate work, there was a 50 percent work incentive; recipients could keep half of any earnings, the rest being deducted from their grants. FAP was before Congress from 1969 to 1972. From 1971 on it appeared in a modified form, called H.R. 1 (from the bill number). Where the original FAP had left food stamps standing as a separate program, H.R. 1 "cashed out" (replaced) those benefits with equivalent welfare, raising the guarantee to $2,400.

PBJI, proposed in 1977, was much more complicated. It covered single people and childless couples as well as families with children, and it had an elaborate employment facet. The guarantee for a four-person family was $4,200, cashing out food stamps, the increase over FAP due mostly to inflation. To motivate work, the benefit was only $2,300 if the family had employable members, but it rose to the full $4,200 if the employable members were still without work after eight weeks. Alongside the cash benefits PBJI provided up to 1.4 million new training and government job slots. They paid the minimum wage or slightly above it, and the only eligibility requirement was that the applicant be the main wage earner in a family with children. It was estimated that only workers with low skills and income would want these jobs; less than half would probably be current AFDC recipients, the rest adults from "working poor" families. Further, tax subsidies for low-income workers were liberalized to give more income to poor people already working in the private sector.

The only other important reform proposal to reach Congress was a plan called Allowances for Basic Living Expenses, or ABLE, the fruit of an extensive study of welfare done under the auspices of the Joint Economic Committee by Representative Martha Griffiths between 1968 and 1974. ABLE was an NIT with a $3,000 guarantee (again cashing out food stamps) and a 50 percent work incentive, but the benefits would have come from a combination of welfare grants and employment tax credits, the latter another economic device to tie benefits to work.[19]

The main feature that made all these plans "guaranteed income" was that none seriously required recipients, even the employable, to work or otherwise function as a condition of support. While each incorporated a work incentive to *motivate* work, none actually *required* employables to work on pain that aid would otherwise be denied. Martha Griffiths and the Executive political appointees involved in developing the proposals realized the appeal of work tests in Congress, but the economist planners who did their staff work successfully resisted including clearcut work requirements.[20] All the plans, therefore, fell within the permissive traditions of federal social policy.

In FAP a stipulation that employable recipients register for possible work or training was added only to placate Nixon Administration conservatives like Arthur Burns, who predicted trouble in Congress. It was already clear from experience in AFDC, to which a similar requirement had been added in 1967, that merely to mandate registration accomplished little unless the clients were actually required to enter work or training. FAP would have strengthened the AFDC rule by specifying more closely who was employable and mandating their referral to the work agency. But it would also have exempted mothers with children under six, as the AFDC rule did not. As Kenneth Bowler states, such provisions "did not in concept or effect make FAP any less of a low level, federal guaranteed minimum income for families." President Nixon himself admitted as much to Daniel Moynihan, at the time his domestic policy adviser. "I don't care a damn about the work requirement," he said. "This is the price of getting the $1,600."[21]

PBJI relied mainly on financial incentives, which were carefully tiered so that it would always "pay" a recipient more to work than not, and more to take a private job than a government one. Parents with children under seven, as against six in FAP, were exempted from any work requirement. Other adults had to register for work, but those with children under fourteen could be required to work only half-time. Even the half-time provision was added only after pressure from conservatives in Congress. PBJI could easily have enforced work by requiring welfare recipients to take the government jobs provided under the scheme, but planners never contemplated formalizing such a requirement. The Carter Administration's chief economist estimated that the plan, far from enforcing regular employment, would cause most eligible primary workers to quit low-paid private jobs in favor of public ones. Hearings revealed, furthermore, that the Administration planned to abolish the Work Incentive program, hitherto the main welfare work agency, and vest enforcement in the less work-oriented CETA program.[22]

Work was peripheral to the guaranteed income plans because functioning had been ignored in the thinking behind reform. Like other Great Society planners, the welfare reformers dismissed concern over dysfunction by the poor, especially nonwork, as a prejudice that could not be a legitimate basis for social policy. At best, wrote Richard Nathan, one of the Nixon planners, work was "a preachment and a symbol" to be tacked onto guaranteed income as window dressing, but not something that should seriously qualify income by right.[23]

The Defeat of Reform

In outline the defeat of guaranteed income is quickly told. Most of the proposals advanced by planners never got out of the bureaucracy. Some were rejected by political executives in Health, Education, and Welfare, others by the Office of Management and Budget or the White House. The reasons were either a desire to base antipoverty policy on existing programs or a conviction that the proposals would die in Congress.

The proposals that reached Congress did die there. FAP succeeded in passing the House with minor revisions in both 1970 and 1971 but was defeated in the Senate, where Russell Long and other conservatives on the Finance Committee never let it come to a vote. In both houses some liberals also opposed the plan as insufficiently generous to the poor. PBJI reached hearings in both houses in 1977–78. A special House subcommittee, drawn from all the regular committees with jurisdiction over the plan, approved, and even liberalized, the proposal. But it was then set aside by the leadership of both houses. The Griffith ABLE proposal was never considered seriously by either house.

Existing commentaries suggest that welfare reform, like the Great Society in general, faltered for ordinary political reasons. It is said that President Nixon was not really committed to FAP, President Carter was ineffective in selling PBJI, and Russell Long and other congressional conservatives were diehard, even racist, opponents of reform. Welfare reform was also, in the phrase of Joseph Califano, Carter's Secretary of HEW, "the Middle East of domestic politics," a reform that could never get enough support from the affected groups, even those that would benefit from it.[24] Most of the benefits of FAP would have gone to the South, because existing AFDC payments were lowest there, yet most Southern congressmen opposed the plan because most Southern recipients were black. FAP would have expanded welfare, yet the National Welfare Rights Organization (NWRO) opposed it because its own members, mainly from the high-paying Northern cities, would have gained little or nothing. Some Northern liberal congressmen feared an increase in racial turmoil if reform passed, while civil service unions feared that existing welfare personnel would lose their jobs if welfare administration were federalized. Most notably, the intact-family "working poor," who had the most to gain from expanded eligibility, never brought pressure to bear on Congress in favor of the plan.

Perhaps most common has been the interpretation, by Daniel Moynihan among others, that reform died because of conventional, New Deal disagreement over the scale of government. Both left and right overreached themselves and came up with nothing. Reformers insisted on proposing expansions of welfare that were anathema to conservatives, who in turn took out against reform their resentments over abuses in AFDC. Secondarily, some have seen welfare reform as a radical idea favored only by "new class" planners and not by regular politicians or the public.[25]

All these explanations have some truth to them, but they fail to explain the central mystery of reform—the fact that the issue of guaranteed income caused some conservatives to propose bigger government and many liberals to oppose it, the reverse of the New Deal pattern. Richard Nixon may have been an unpleasant personality, hated by liberals, but he did propose, in FAP, a revolutionary expansion of welfare. Despite their hostile rhetoric few congressional conservatives opposed the expansion as such. Wilbur Mills, who as chairman of the Ways and Means Committee twice guided FAP to passage in the House, said he was "perfectly willing to spend almost any amount of money within reason" on an effective reform. Russell Long, chairman of the Senate Finance Committee, opposed both FAP and PBJI mainly because they lacked serious work requirements, not because of cost. He asserted repeatedly that he was "willing . . . to help the working poor—provided that they are working, as well as poor."[26]

In opposition to the reformers, Long proposed, not no reform, but a statist version of it that would have coupled support for the employable with workfare, that is, a requirement that they actually work as a condition of eligibility. The plan had distinctly Big Brother aspects, including vast new agencies to provide child care and jobs. Abraham Ribicoff, one of Long's opponents, twitted him for being more big-government than the liberals. The Long plan helped turn some liberals against reform, fearing that it would serve only to repress and control the poor. The conflicting currents meant that neither party was anywhere near unanimous about the question. Al Ullman, who later replaced Mills as chairman of Ways and Means, remarked that the issue was "nonpartisan," and both parties were "split pretty well right down the middle" about it.[27]

A fresh reading of the hearings and debates surrounding reform suggests that in fact the critical issue was work, not welfare.[28] Congressmen divided, in the main, not over the preferred cost or extent of welfare, but over whether employable recipients should face serious pressures to work *in return* for support. Only a small minority on the right opposed welfare, or even its extension, as such. The real battle was over what kind of work requirements should be attached to the new benefits that most members wanted. Reform died, in essence, because conservatives and moderates demanded more onerous requirements than liberals would accept.

Defeat, however, was the womb from which a new kind of welfare policy emerged. Congress consistently rejected the extremes of either doing away with welfare for the employable or guaranteeing them an income. Instead most members wanted to preserve a generous welfare system but also to require some kind of work performance by employable recipients. The effort to combine welfare and work, or benefits with obligations, raised questions different from traditional New Deal struggles over the scope of benefits. Much of the confusion of the welfare debates arose because the issues were novel and the usual partisan reflexes did not apply well to them. The question of how demanding to be of recipients cut across positions on the size of government.

The leading role in the debates was played by the small group of Congressmen, whom I call the civic conservatives, who pursued the idea of combining work and welfare more deliberately than others. Most of them—Russell Long, Wilbur Mills, Martha Griffiths—were leaders of the Finance or Ways and Means committees, which had immediate responsibility for welfare on Capitol Hill. They developed their position both against and alongside the one represented by the chief reform proposals.

The politics of welfare reform was not a traditional battle between right and left but a competition for the mind of a moderate plurality or majority by three groups—liberal reformers seeking guaranteed income, traditional conservatives opposed to welfare, and the civic conservatives, who wanted expanded welfare only with serious work requirements. The immediate outcome defeated all three groups, in that welfare was neither cut nor expanded radically, while work tests remained weak. But over time Congress edged closer to the civic position, which therefore has great importance for the future of social policy.

The debate over welfare work began somewhat before the reform plans reached Congress. By the mid 1960s serious behavioral problems in welfare were already evident. The AFDC rolls were growing rapidly, yet fewer than a fifth of welfare mothers worked. The reasons for nonwork prompted intense debate. Liberals emphasized the supposed disincentives to work in AFDC, while conservatives said the mothers were not trying. Amendments enacted in 1967 reflected both theories. The "$30 and a third" welfare work incentive was instituted, but at the same time some employable recipients were required to register for work or training, the first "work test" in AFDC.

Those work measures were very mild, yet when Wilbur Mills, on behalf of Ways and Means, first proposed them to the House, there was a storm of protest. Liberals and welfare groups denounced the work test as virtual slavery for recipients. The reaction was out of all proportion to WIN's actual power to force recipients to work, as its limited impact proved. Mills protested, "What in the world is wrong with requiring these people to submit themselves, if they are to draw public funds, to a test of their ability to learn a job?"[29] To liberals, work violated the orthodoxy that only society could be held responsible for the problems of the poor. The work test passed, but partly because Mills was careful to package it in a larger bill including popular increases in Social Security benefits.

The affair served notice that work struck a nerve, that it cut to the heart of the issues in social policy.

Work also dominated congressional consideration of FAP, far more than the plan's benefits or costs. Nixon Administration officials tried to argue that the plan was closer to workfare than welfare for the poor. It did not provide a "guaranteed annual income," contended HEW Secretary Robert Finch, because it did "not guarantee benefits to persons regardless of their attitude; its support is reserved to those who are willing to support themselves."[30] But throughout the hearings and floor debates in both houses, the plan faced hostile questioning from conservatives, who dismissed the proposed test, in Al Ullman's term, as a "token."[31] In the Senate, Finance Committee conservatives questioned, in addition, whether the work incentives in the bill were really strong enough to motivate recipients to work without a firm work requirement. They argued that even if working recipients kept half their wages from welfare, they would still lose so many benefits from other programs, such as Medicaid and public housing, as their incomes rose that they could still be worse off working than not.

Liberal congressmen also concentrated their fire on the work provisions, but from the opposite direction. To them, to force mothers in need to work, or even register for work, was "degrading," "punitive," "humiliating," an attempt to "punish the poor for being poor."[32] Secondarily, they attacked the benefit levels in the plan as inadequate and demanded that they be raised at least to the poverty level. A minimal income even for the employable was a matter of right, they contended, and should not be contingent on work.

These divisions, especially over work, were what doomed FAP. The ease with which the plan passed the House in 1970 and 1971 was deceptive. As in 1967 Wilbur Mills handcuffed his opponents by bringing the plan to the floor submerged in a bill containing popular increases in Social Security and other programs, thus forcing even opponents to vote for it. In the Sentate a three-cornered battle developed between FAP, a more liberal version of the plan drafted by Abraham Ribicoff, and Russell Long's workfare proposal. The plans differed mainly in the severity of their work requirements, secondarily in the generosity of their benefits. After extended battles in 1971 and 1972 the Senate was able to agree only to test the three versions, a scheme rejected by the House. FAP and its competitors were all scrapped at the end of 1972. The only piece of welfare reform enacted was Supplementary Security Income (SSI), which federalized welfare for the aged, blind, and disabled.

The sensitivity of the work question was dramatized when simultaneously, in 1970–71, a large scale expansion of food stamps passed Congress with very little controversy. One explanation was that the bill included a much tougher work test than FAP's, at least on paper. Under the welfare plan, as in AFDC, an employable recipient who refused work would merely have his or her own welfare cut off; benefits for the rest of the family continued, which indirectly supported the sanctioned recipient as well. But under food stamps the entire grant could be cut off if the head of a family refused to work.[33]

The FAP debacle put Carter Administration planners on notice that they had to pay even more deference to work in their arguments for PBJI. In his own advocacy Carter, like Nixon, put the work, not the income, aspects of his plan up front. It would, he said, "combine effective work requirements and strong work incentives with improved private sector placement services, and create up to 1.4 million public service jobs."[34] The Carter planners contended that the jobs benefit would counteract the tendency of cash alone to reduce work effort. But, as with FAP, such assurances were not widely believed, and the hearings concentrated disproportionately on them. Opponents denied that recipients would really have to work. Liberals, on the other hand, objected that families with employable members would at first receive a lower benefit than those without. They demanded that all families immediately receive the higher benefit as a right. PBJI died as much as anything because of high costs—at least $17 billion more than existing programs.[35] The work disputes, however, would probably have killed even a cheaper plan.

The issue was not the value of work. Virtually all Congressmen hoped that welfare recipients would take jobs. Few endorsed the original presumption of AFDC, that welfare mothers should stay home and raise their children full time. The disagreement was entirely over whether the mothers should *have* to work. In the hearings and debates liberals, economists, and welfare advocates tended to treat work as desirable *for the recipient*, a kind of extra benefit alongside the welfare grant. While they hoped mothers would work and get off welfare, they opposed forcing them to work. As one AFL-CIO spokesman put it, "every mother should have the opportunity to work. It is the compulsion I am objecting to."[36]

Moderates and conservatives, on the other hand, viewed work as *obligatory*, as something the recipients *owed* to society in recompense for support, whether or not it served their own interests. Why, Representative Martha Griffiths asked Harold Watts, a welfare economist, should some women scrub floors and pay taxes to support welfare women in idleness? Watts replied that work incentives would make it in the *mother's* interest to work, missing the moral point. His reasoning reflected the economic approach to nonwork, which appealed only to the self-interest of the recipient. Senator Daniel Moynihan, however, admonished HEW planners that work was "not just therapy" for the recipient; it was also a matter of "social responsibility."[37]

The dispute came down in practice to which should come first, welfare or work. Was welfare an entitlement for the poor, after which they could also work if they chose, or did they have to show a work commitment as a condition for welfare? Liberals usually took the first position, conservatives the second. Russell Long said he was willing to support the needy in return for work, but he would not pay them *not* to work, as FAP and PBJI appeared to do. That "one little thing" kept him from supporting reform. In the FAP hearings he had a revealing exchange with Joseph Pechman, a leading economist. Long complained about the refusal of many recipients to take low-wage jobs, while Pechman asserted that stronger work incentives would solve the problem. Since they both wanted to combine work and welfare, Senator Ribicoff remarked on how close to agreement they seemed. But in truth a gulf divided them. Long wanted to make work a precondition of aid for the employable, as Pechman did not. Said the economist, his "only problem" with Long's position was that "you wish to limit assistance to people who are working."[38] That little "problem" was the lion in the path of reform.

Related to that difference were divergent views of the employment available to the poor. For liberals the goal of social policy was to raise the income and status of recipients. Since most jobs available to the poor were too "dirty" and low-paid to do this, the decision whether to take them should be left up to the recipient. To force aspiring poor people into jobs beneath their hopes was cruel and futile. Rather, the onus was on employers and government to improve the pay, prospects, and conditions of available jobs so that more needy would take them spontaneously. Reasoned Senator Charles Goodell, a liberal Republican:

> A work requirement is demeaning. If job openings are perceived as being worthwhile in terms of income and the personal satisfaction they provide, they will be filled voluntarily. If not, then we should be changing the nature of the openings available. Dead-end jobs inevitably result in high turnover, and no legal compulsion can change that fact.

Conservatives, however, were less concerned with status than with paying a debt to society. If work was an obligation, any job would discharge it. All legal jobs, therefore, even "dirty" ones, should be obligatory, at least for the employable. In any event, Russell Long said, the poor should be less choosy, since few of them could hope to be "president of the corporation or chairman of the board."[39]

The two perspectives collided when, in 1971, President Nixon defended the FAP work test along these lines:

> I advocate a system which will encourage people to take work. And that means whatever work is available. . . . Scrubbing floors or emptying bedpans is not enjoyable work, but a lot of people do it—and there is as much dignity in that as there is in any other work to be done in this country—including my own. . . .

He drew a tart reply from welfare rights organizer George Wiley: "You don't promote family life by forcing women out of their homes to empty bedpans. When Richard Nixon is ready to give up his $200,000 salary to scrub floors and empty bedpans in the interest of his family, then we will take him seriously." The work test, said Wiley, meant nothing more than "forcing mothers into a kind of servitude, cleaning Senator Long's shirts and President Nixon's john."[40]

These divisions made the detailed rules governing work obligation exceedingly sensitive. Exactly what kind of jobs should welfare recipients have to accept? One of the many ways the original FAP proposal was permissive was that it required employable recipients to accept only "suitable" work. That usage, borrowed from Unemployment Insurance, meant that clients could refuse jobs that were much inferior to their previous employment without suffering any cut in benefits. Liberals wanted this protection lest the work test force recipients into "underpaid and demeaning jobs" such as domestic or custodial work. Some wanted the restrictions spelled out in more detail.[41]

Conservatives and moderates, however, viewed such curbs with suspicion. They were more restrictive than the existing rules in AFDC. They might allow the employable to decline most low-paid jobs, usually the only kind they could get, and thus render any work test nugatory. How, asked John Byrnes, the Republican leader on Ways and Means, would the system deal with clients with too "high [an] opinion of what kind of job is a suitable job for them"? There was skepticism on the right that HEW, viewed as client-oriented, would ever force recipients to "accept a job in a restaurant, a hotel, a motel, a laundry," although other Americans took those jobs.[42] Rather than restrict acceptable jobs, the rules should require the employable to take any legal job that they were physically able to do.

These rather arcane work rules occasioned more conflict than the cost or benefits of FAP. In Congress the Administration and liberals pressed for language that would allow recipients to decline menial jobs if, in the judgment of the work agency, they could shortly get or train for better positions. Conservatives pressed to make any job obligatory, exempting only workers with demonstrated skills. Over time the FAP language became less and less permissive. Furthermore, the wage that jobs had to pay to be obligatory was cut from the full minimum wage to three-quarters of it. Suitable work became a key issue dividing the competing welfare plans in the Senate; Long's proposal contained fewer job restrictions, Ribicoff's more, than did FAP.[43] The original job rules in PBJI, as in FAP, were quite permissive, and had the plan survived longer they would surely have become an issue.

The most revealing passage of arms in this struggle occurred in 1970, when the House cleared FAP for the first time. Mills brought the bill to the floor containing language that gave local staff wide discretion to define suitable work. The rules for the debate forbade opponents to amend the bill on the floor; they could only move to recommit it to committee for changes. Had New Deal politics still governed, they would surely have used their motion to oppose the reform in principle or at least cut its benefits or costs. Instead they demanded that Ways and Means replace "suitable" with less permissive language. In the teeth of committee opposition, the motion carried, 248–149, and the amended bill then passed by an almost identical margin, 243–155.

The coalitions on these votes show how the civic approach to welfare came to define the consensus in Congress. Of the 393 members who voted on both recommittal and passage, a plurality of 146, or 37 percent, took the civic position of voting for *both* stiffer work rules and reform. Conservatives who voted for the motion but against the bill numbered only 101, while liberals who supported the bill but not the motion were only 95; each group was about a quarter of the House. Yet even these two groups shared the consensus to some extent. Conservatives, though they opposed expanded welfare, were willing to use it to set clearer work standards, while liberals accepted a bill that, as amended, paid strong obeisance to work requirements. Total opposition was limited to the fifty-one members, only 13 percent, who rejected both work rules and reform. This group was divided between a majority of doctrinaire conservatives who repudiated wider welfare in any form and a few militant liberals who refused to stomach either the work test or the low benefit levels in FAP.[44]

The outcome dramatized how guaranteed income had shifted the center of social controversy from freedom to functioning, and from the size of government to its nature. What most Congressmen wanted for the poor was neither income without work nor self-reliance without assistance, the positions of the far left and right, but rather welfare *and* work. The movement was toward the civic position of trying to combine support with obligations.

Shaping the Debate

The work issue shaped the reform struggle in other ways as well. One was that reformers found themselves under relentless pressure to treat employable recipients less favorably than the unemployable. It had been a principle of the thinking behind reform to reject any such distinction and base eligibility only on need. But the more Congress pressed for work provisions, the more difficult that was.

The main political difficulty for FAP and PBJI was that they provided essentially the same income benefits to all families whether or not they had employable members. The only difference was that employable recipients had to register for work, and in PBJI their families received a lower benefit for the first eight weeks. The elaborate employment aspects of PBJI did not change this, because the employable did not have to accept jobs as a condition of welfare eligibility. Unified benefits made it difficult to convince Congressmen that the employable were subject to any serious work requirement.

It was more expedient politically to place the employable and unemployable in separate programs. In the H.R. 1 version of FAP, Wilbur Mills removed employable families from AFDC. They were placed under a separate Opportunities for Families program, popularly known as OFF, where they could get aid only by satisfying tougher work registration and suitable work rules than in AFDC. Russell Long's workfare proposals carried the separation a step further. Now employable recipients actually had to work to receive support, since all support for them and their families was linked to work, via wage supplements, tax credits, or government jobs. Even the Carter welfare plan, though it did not mandate work, treated recipients who worked more favorably than others. Thus the distinction between "deserving" and "undeserving" recipients, which had been traditional in welfare, crept back into welfare reform.

Separation was also necessary to make work incentives look effective. Recipients viewed as unemployable, such as mothers with very young children, needed a high income guarantee, so they could live without working, but not a strong work incentive (a right to keep half or more of earned income) since work was not expected. But those expected to work, such as husbands and single men, needed just the opposite—a low guarantee so they would need earnings to live, but a strong work incentive, so work was economically rewarded. In any compromise benefit structure, as in FAP and PBJI, the guarantee would look too generous for those who could work, the work incentive too strong for the unemployable (also costly, because fewer earnings were deducted from the grant). Only separate programs could honor the different needs.[45]

Another result of the work issue was pressure on the reformers to deal more openly with the functioning issue in welfare. In their planning they had avoided it because of their conviction that nonwork and family instability were traceable to social conditions only government could change. By the time of FAP, however, the problems posed obvious barriers to helping the poor, even if their ultimate causes were environmental. Even some liberals admitted this. This was Senator Fred Harris's diagnosis:

> [I]t is going to be terribly difficult for [the poor] to break out of the cycle. We will find many cannot learn because of their long disassocia-

> tion from education. Many of them cannot eat properly because there is no one to tell them how. . . . It will be hard for many to get work, because they are not trained and educated to perform useful work in our technical society.

As Daniel Moynihan had long maintained, American welfare had a pathological, "custodial" character, and reform efforts had to address it.[46]

Administration spokesmen for FAP and PBJI, however, turned aside congressional questions about nonwork in welfare with abstract arguments that the enhanced work incentives in the plans would cure the problem. Therefore, asserted HEW planning chief Henry Aaron in 1978, the "burden of proof" was on the opponents of reform. Unfortunately powerful conservatives, especially in the Senate, were unconvinced. The Finance Committee said FAP proponents had "simply glossed over" and "avoided discussing" the behavioral issue in welfare.[47]

Daniel Moynihan was the leading voice for candor. He had been vilified in 1965 for pointing out the family problems of blacks, which had only grown worse in the interim. Now, as the Senator in charge of the Senate hearings on PBJI, he was in a position to press the issue. He pleaded with Labor Secretary Ray Marshall to "let it all hang out" and "make your people tell you the truth" about nonwork and the failure of efforts to overcome it. Few answers were forthcoming, and that was fatal to trust. The burden of proof, Moynihan assured Aaron, would not sit very heavily on the Finance Committee.[48]

When the reformers did discuss work, they preferred to speak not of welfare recipients but of the poor in general, a much larger group about which more reassuring statements could be made. Their rationale was that most of the poor, not just existing recipients, would be covered by the proposed reform. In his testimony for PBJI in 1977, HEW Secretary Joseph Califano pilloried "myths" that the poor were averse to work, permanently needy, mostly nonwhite, and so on. "Do the poor work? They work damn hard," he exclaimed. "Eighty-five percent of poor male family heads work during the year," 29 percent of them full time. But as Moynihan was quick to point out, the myths were much more true of the welfare population.[49]

If forced to speak specifically about welfare, reformers resorted to much the same sociological reasoning as the welfare studies. They asserted that only a small proportion of the adults on welfare were employable; 2 percent was the estimate of New York City welfare commissioners. The Labor Department found that few recipients could earn enough to get their families off welfare,[50] though that did not prove they should not work at all. The trouble was that reformers also claimed, to buttress their case, that a high proportion of the poor would work even if "unemployable," given support services such as child care. It was certainly true that many recipients had worked in the past and that alternation between work and welfare was common.[51] But if so, then a sizable portion of welfare adults were employable after all. The reformers could not have it both ways.

A further claim was that jobs were unavailable. This was why, planners said, employment had to be created for the poor, as in the massive public jobs component of PBJI. That view conflicted with the observation of conservatives that many low-paying jobs were going begging. When pressed in the hearings, Administration witnesses admitted that a lot of "dirty" jobs were in fact available. The problem was that many welfare recipients did not want to take them, and perhaps should not. The point of job creation was to create "better" jobs they would want to take.[52] That, again, shifted the issue from benefits to social standards. The question was, not so much whether jobs existed, as whether they should be obligatory.

The more dysfunction appeared at the heart of the welfare problem, the more pressure came from Congress to learn more about it. Exactly why were family breakup and nonwork so common among the poor? Senator Moynihan accused HEW of "obfuscation, sometimes lying, always avoidance of this issue." The Department had been "obscurantist" and refused to commission "5 cents worth of honest inquiry" about family problems in welfare.[53] Reform proponents had to rely initially on the available research, mostly by liberals, on the reasons for nonwork. One oft-quoted study, by Lawrence Podell, found that 60 percent of New York City welfare mothers with preschool children would prefer to work if "appropriate day care facilities" were available. Another study by Leonard Goodwin, previously mentioned, asserted that a lack of "good" jobs at which they could succeed, not refusal to work, was the main reason the poor did not work more consistently.[54]

Eventually HEW did commission research of its own, the four experiments in income maintenance. Planners confidently expected that recipients' own desire to work coupled with work incentives would limit nonwork to acceptable levels even under an income guarantee. The first experiment, in New Jersey, seemed to confirm those expectations by showing very little work reduction. Administration officials rushed the preliminary results to Congress to bolster their case for FAP. The data showed, they claimed, "very strong Protestant ethic work attitudes" on the part of the poor.[55] But the later experiments showed more work reduction plus, in the Seattle/Denver study, the disturbing finding that guaranteed income might sharply cut family stability. While some analysts continued to believe that correctly designed benefits and incentives could stem nonwork and breakup, that view was now much less widely persuasive. Far from publicizing the Seattle/Denver results, HEW downplayed them when Moynihan made inquiries.[56]

The Seattle/Denver results, as much as anything, killed the Carter welfare plan in early 1978. They also marked an important milestone in Daniel Moynihan's progress from proponent to critic of guaranteed income. Ten years earlier he had advocated a welfare system based only on "*need*" and "*right*," and he had been an architect of FAP. But in light of the experimental findings, he confessed, "We must now be prepared to entertain the possibility that we were wrong."[57]

Timing and Meaning

Questions of functioning and obligation had been consistently ignored during other phases of Great Society policymaking. Why did they suddenly erupt over welfare reform?

Most probably because welfare raised the issues more starkly than other programs. AFDC was in a sense the central antipoverty program, since it was so large and dealt directly with economic need. It also dramatized the functioning problem like no other program. The education and training programs at least claimed to prepare their clients for self-reliance; AFDC simply financed dependency. The aged and disabled poor raised little functioning issue, because they were seen as unemployable for physical reasons; AFDC supported women and children whose problems, including nonwork, were much more attributable to behavior. Welfare reform was also the issue where the sociological viewpoint, exempting the poor from responsibility for themselves, was asserted most aggressively; a political counterreaction was understandable.

For other reasons, too, the functioning issue could not be

avoided in welfare, even though federal politicians were uncomfortable with it. AFDC was growing rapidly during the period of FAP. But because it was an entitlement, guaranteeing benefits to everyone meeting the eligibility rules, it could not be curbed just by cutting back its budget. Costs could be cut only by reducing benefits or eligibility in law, something Congress has been loath to do. That meant measures aimed directly at the functioning problems were indispensable to controlling the program. Needy mothers could not be denied benefits, but they could be made to work, or at least look for work, and the fathers who had deserted them could be made to pay child support. Welfare statecraft after 1972 concentrated on such requirements, rejecting proposals to increase or to decrease benefits more than marginally. Welfare did not become much more or less generous, but it did become more demanding. Inexorably, the focus shifted from the scale to the nature of government.

Furthermore, the requirements had to be imposed from the federal level. The tradition in welfare had been for Washington to delegate the enforcement of behavioral norms in welfare to the local level. This was why liberal reformers believed invidious local welfare administration was one of the main barriers to helping the poor. But because of liberalizing regulations and court decisions, local agencies could no longer play the enforcing role on their own authority. They had to have a clear statutory mandate. That forced the questions of standards back on Congress. If federal politicians wanted work or other requirements in welfare, they would have to take the responsibility themselves.

After the early 1970s the work issue faded, also for a number of reasons. One was simply that the welfare rolls leveled off, another that the repeated recessions of the 1970s made nonwork by recipients seem more defensible. The economic issues raised by welfare reform now became more salient. Much of the opposition to the Carter plan was over costs, and much of the support for it came from mayors and governors seeking fiscal relief from the expense of AFDC, since PBJI would have largely federalized welfare costs. Even after the plan died, more modest proposals were advanced by several Senators, including Moynihan, in an attempt to provide at least some relief for states and localities.[58]

There was also a partial accommodation between the forces demanding and resisting work in welfare. Conservatives contented themselves with requirements that employable recipients register for possible work or training, something well short of making them work in return for support. Liberals learned that they could accept such stipulations without condoning forced work, and they saw that it was politic to do so.[59] On the surface PBJI, with its elaborate work provisions, paid even more deference to work than FAP. Welfare clients groups also become more accepting of work. The trend was for nondependent women to go to work, even when they had young children, so the prospect of welfare mothers working was less alarming to liberals. Work was also endorsed by the feminist movement, one of whose objectives was to help welfare mothers escape dependency. Accordingly, where the welfare groups had been threatened by FAP's work provisions, they tended to view PBJI's as an opportunity. In hearings they pressed for even more training, work incentives, and public jobs than the plan provided.[60]

The work issue subsided, furthermore, because reformers shifted to a more incremental legislative strategy. It was clear after PBJI that Congress would reject explicit proposals for a guaranteed income to the employable. But Congress might approve new programs and benefits that added up to a guaranteed provision less openly. In the same period when it defeated reform of AFDC, Congress enacted food stamps, Medicaid, SSI, and large public jobs programs. The accretion of benefits also made a large-scale welfare reform less pressing. The most serious needs of most poor people were already covered. As Richard Nathan told Ways and Means in 1977, "It is hard to be poor in this country now."[61] Welfare reform came down to filling gaps in existing benefits, mainly for non-aged single people and families headed by men.

There was even a tradition of piecemeal improvements in AFDC, the program that most resisted reform. Congress would not extend coverage to the "working poor," but in 1961 it did allow states to cover two-parent families where the father was unemployed. It also expanded social services linked to welfare in 1962 and employment benefits and services in 1967. The Johnson Administration, which rejected entreaties from its planners for welfare reform, did propose further liberalizations of AFDC in 1967, though Congress declined them.[62]

Following the demise of PBJI, Carter Administration planners came up with an incremental reform proposal for AFDC that would have done in miniature what the larger plan had contemplated. The proposal made mandatory the state option to cover families with unemployed fathers under AFDC, liberalized eligibility for that component, and required states to pay benefits in AFDC that, together with food stamps, brought recipient incomes up to 65 percent of the poverty level. These steps would have covered at least some of the "working poor" and linked benefits to the poverty line for the first time. Some fiscal relief for states and 600,000 new job and training slots were also included.

The fate of the measure, however, shows how tenuous the new welfare consensus was. Patience with work requirements that required only registration was running out. "We have seen how easy it is," Russell Long complained in 1972, "for people to get past the work requirement without taking a job,"[63] and more and more people agreed with him as the decade progressed. From this perspective the employment side of the Carter plan was bogus. It provided extensive work *benefits* to the needy, but there was no true work *obligation*. By the late 1970s conservatives were so disillusioned that more than before began to question whether there should be a federal role in welfare at all.

In the House the income aspects of the Carter incremental plan barely weathered conservative counterproposals that would provisionally have revenue-shared AFDC to the states and allowed them to decide their own work requirements. The effect of those steps, liberals feared, would be to "remove most of the Federal protections that we have written into the AFDC law." The plan died when the welfare changes were never taken up in the Senate and the jobs side of the scheme never got out of committee in either house.[64] The ground was laid for the Reagan efforts to cut welfare and return control of it to the states.

The outcome suggests that the work issue is only dormant, ready to break out again whenever the functioning issue surfaces in federal policymaking. While New Deal, size-of-government disputes are far from dead, welfare reform shifted the central dispute toward the character of government. Democrats have become the party of permissive as well as large government, Republicans the party of authoritative as well as small government. The same Reagan Administration that has cut welfare has pushed for the toughest work tests yet. The shift can already be seen in the 1972 platforms of the two parties, written in the heat of the controversy over FAP and George McGovern's proposals for "demogrants," a form of guaranteed income. Democrats wanted to make "economic security a matter of right," through either jobs or welfare, and opposed "the coercion of forced work requirements." Republicans accepted the principle of welfare but opposed "the idea that all citizens have the right to be supported by the government regardless of their ability or desire to support themselves and their families."[65]

As the reform debate proved, both liberals and conservatives find these new issues uncomfortable, yet unavoidable. Liberals wanted to continue progressive reform, but they could not do so without confronting the functioning problem, something their permissive social analysis did not prepare them to do. Conservatives could frustrate the drive for guaranteed income by pointing to dysfunction, but they were reluctant, beyond limited work tests, to press for a more authoritative approach to welfare themselves. They would rather cut programs than *use* them for conservative ends. For both, a reluctance to set standards stood in the way of a more credible social policy.

6

Federal Work Tests: Weakness and Potential

THE battle over welfare reform was only the most dramatic skirmish in a long struggle to deal with the work problem in welfare and other income programs. A work problem, and policies to promote work, have appeared, not only in welfare programs like AFDC and food stamps, but in the more "respectable" Unemployment Insurance and Disability, social insurance programs that supposedly cover the "deserving." This demonstrates again that a preference for nonwork, if jobs are unattractive, is not confined to the underclass. It also shows that Congress is moving away from attempts to motivate work simply through the addition of new benefits or the denial of established ones, the usual dictums of left and right. Increasingly the effort is to combine support with obligations *within* the welfare state.

Nevertheless, the various work policies have had, as yet, only slight effects. They have reduced nonwork or dependency only marginally. The explanation is partly that the existing work tests are halfhearted even in legislation, partly that work enforcement faces a number of very difficult administrative and compliance problems. To make people work is inherently difficult, especially when they are already receiving benefits from government. Institutions that enforce work, and a political climate supportive of them, must be developed over time. The answer to the work problem lies mostly in administrative statecraft, not in benefits or cuts in benefits.

AFDC

Work tests in AFDC arose as part of the conservative approach to welform reform. Their history is one of repeated implementation failures, each one followed by yet greater efforts by Congress to impose a real work requirement. The failures say much about the difficulty of levying obligations in social programs from Washington.

Typically, federal officials try first to get what they want from local authorities by persuasion or fiscal inducement, only later by clearcut mandates. Welfare work follows this pattern. The initial federal effort came in 1962, when Congress subsidized "Community Work and Training" (CWT) programs that states might set up to place welfare mothers in jobs. A similar program was inaugurated under Title V of the Economic Opportunity Act in 1964. But very little happened. Only ten states participated in CWT. Their incentive was weak, because the federal subsidy was small and the program was not required as a condition of federal AFDC funding.[1]

The enactment of the first AFDC work test in 1967 was supposed to change that. The test was administered by the Work Incentive (WIN) program. WIN was required of states in AFDC, and employable recipients had to participate in WIN as a condition of eligibility for AFDC. Previously welfare agencies could deny benefits to recipients who refused work, but they could not require them to do anything to seek work. Now the employable had at least to register and cooperate with WIN or face a cut in their welfare grants. WIN was to be run jointly by local welfare agencies, which would provide participants with child care and other support services, and staff from the Employment Service (ES), which would give them employment services such as training and placement in jobs. The ES, also known as the Job Service, is a federally funded employment agency for the jobless.[2]

Proponents of WIN made large claims that it would reduce the welfare rolls, and opponents seem to have believed them. That is why the "work test" became so controversial. In reality the test was mostly symbolic. Welfare agencies were given the power to decide which recipients were employable and hence "appropriate" for referral to WIN. This allowed the big-city departments with the largest caseloads to shield their welfare mothers from the work test, contrary to congressional intentions. The Department of Health, Education, and Welfare (HEW) also wrote the intitial WIN regulations so that WIN had to serve fathers, teenagers, and mothers who volunteered for the program before it could force mothers to participate against their will.[3] Furthermore, an early evaluation found, the very idea of "compulsory participation" in WIN "provoked such consternation among welfare rights representatives, union leaders, and others" that local agencies seldom could enforce the new requirement to the full extent of the law.[4]

As a result, WIN's impact fell far short of projections. Only a fifth of adult AFDC recipients were found "appropriate" for WIN (far fewer in the large cities), and fewer still were actually referred to WIN and enrolled. Most of those who did enroll were placed in school or training that spared them immediate pressures to work. While the training had measurable benefits for many recipients, it did not satisfy the work concerns in Washington. In the end only about 2 percent of adult recipients entered jobs.[5]

WIN faltered precisely at the time, in the late 1960s, when the AFDC rolls were exploding. The Senate Finance Committee noted with consternation that in WIN's first twenty-one months of operation the rolls rose by 641,000 cases, while only 13,000 cases were closed because of WIN—a ratio of 49 to 1. Out of 8,100 recipients who refused without good cause to participate in WIN and who could have been sanctioned, only 200 had their grants terminated as a result. WIN actually failed to spend even a third of its funding in fiscal 1969—unheard of for a government program—because it served so few clients.[6] The experience helps explain why congressional conservatives viewed the "work requirements" in the Nixon welfare reform plan so skeptically.

In 1971 Finance Committee conservatives, led by Herman Talmadge, succeeded in toughening WIN. The Talmadge amendments (PL 92-223, sec. 3) legislated what would have been the work provisions of FAP, had it passed, along with other features designed to strengthen work enforcement. Control over referrals to WIN was taken away from the welfare agencies. Now all those defined in the law as employable had to register with WIN. That included all recipients who were not under sixteen, still in school, aged, disabled, too far from a WIN office to participate, or—most important—mothers who had children under six or other relatives to care for in the home. These rules still define employability for most AFDC recipients today.

Financial incentives were applied to increase participation and services in WIN. States were required, not only to register the employable in WIN, but to work actively to train or place at least 15 percent of them, on pain of cuts in their federal AFDC funding. At the same time the federal subsidy for WIN services was raised to 90 percent of state expenditures—a strong incentive for more activity in the program. Limits were set on how much training recipients could receive, and the training was supposed to be more work-related, less academic. WIN programs were required to spend at least a third of their employment services money to put clients in on-the-job training (OJT) and public service employment (PSE). Evaluations confirmed that training keyed to actual jobs was usually more effective than classroom training in schoolbook skills, the kind WIN had favored.[7]

Institutional changes were made to implement the new approach. Regular welfare departments had dominated the first version of WIN. Talmadge shifted registration and the provision of support services to a special welfare unit (called the Separate Administrative Unit, or SAU), which was supposed to be totally dedicated to WIN. In 1975 registration was shifted again, into the hands of the labor, or Employment Service, side of WIN, and today the ES dominates most programs. Congress was determined that WIN at least not shield recipients from the job market.

As WIN shifted from training, which catered to the career hopes of recipients for "better" jobs, toward immediate placement in available jobs, it became less voluntary, more coercive. Infusing it was an ethos that all jobs, however different in social status, equally fulfilled the work obligation linked to welfare. As President Nixon said in signing the Talmadge bill, "No task, no labor, no work is without dignity or meaning that enables an individual to feed and clothe and shelter himself and provide for his family."[8]

The amendments had an immediate impact, demonstrating how critical authority is to work for the welfare poor. WIN now subjected more recipients to a work demand, and more work resulted. In fiscal 1973, the first year of the new rules, nearly 137,000 WIN registrants obtained jobs, more than double any previous year. The numbers went on rising, to nearly 278,000 jobs in fiscal 1977. In the same period the number of families that left welfare because of WIN rose from 34,000 to 136,000; about equal numbers had their grants reduced, if not ended, by WIN jobs. By 1977 WIN was saving as much in welfare grants as it cost.[9] Only increased obligation could explain such gains, since the welfare rolls grew little and the economy was in recession during much of this period. WIN now began to place around 20 percent of its registrants in jobs, much like other employment programs such as CETA.[10]

But even gains on this scale hardly dented the rolls. WIN has about 1.5 million clients on its rolls in a given year, about 1 million of them new entrants that year,[11] and *all* are officially defined as employable. While WIN has internal problems,[12] its main difficulty is that its authority over its clients is still severly limited. Even under the mandatory registration rules, only 38 percent of adult recipients have to sign up for WIN. The others are mostly disabled or have children under six. More important still, WIN works actively with only a part of those it registers. Only a third to a half of the registrant pool are ever called to participate regularly in training, job placement, or other activities.[13] The others are in practice exempted from the work test.

In addition the Labor Department, like HEW, has rarely run the program with a determination to enforce work. The bureaucracy remembers that Congress foisted WIN upon it. Until the Reagan Administration, it administered WIN in the same client-oriented spirit that informed the Executive welfare reform plans, with their half-serious "work requirements." Regulations and policy still tell WIN to serve mainly father, volunteers, and the job-ready, not the more reluctant mothers and youths who make up the bulk of the adult caseload.[14]

Conservatives in Congress have recently tried both to exclude more employables from AFDC—the Reagan cuts of 1981—and to toughen work tests further. In 1980 Congress said AFDC recipients could be made to search for work up to eight weeks a year (PL 96-265, sec. 401). Before that they were usually required only to interview for specific positions located for them by WIN staff. The next logical step was workfare, a requirement that employable recipients actually work, not just register or look for work, as a condition of eligibility for assistance. In workfare labor is enforced by guaranteeing recipients work in public or nonprofit agencies, unless they accept private jobs. Sometimes they receive something extra for working, but usually they simply put in the hours necessary to "work off" the welfare they are receiving.

Traditionally workfare had been found only in the state-funded general assistance programs that localities run for needy people (mainly two-parent families and single men) who do not qualify for federal welfare. Nineteen states had workfare in general assistance in 1978. Workfare was normally not allowed in AFDC, much the most important welfare program, because the more lenient WIN rules took precedence. But in the 1970s a number of states frustrated by the work problem—Utah, California, New York, Massachusetts—obtained waivers to let them run workfare demonstrations even in AFDC.[15] In 1977 Congress authorized a number of workfare demonstrations in both AFDC and food stamps. In 1981, at the behest of the Reagan Administration, it allowed states to replace WIN with workfare, called the Community Work Experience Program (CWEP), among other options. In CWEP, if jobs and child care are assured, mothers with children as young as three—not six as in WIN—can be required to work. However, Congress has so far rebuffed Administration proposals to mandate CWEP, so that most AFDC adults still fall under the more permissive WIN rules.

Workfare looks like the ultimate solution to the welfare work problem. Recipients must actually work, and because jobs are guaranteed, they cannot escape by claiming work is unavailable. But workfare so far has had little more impact than earlier programs. Just as in WIN, the main problem is that few recipients, even if employable, actually have to participate actively in the program. In general assistance workfare the proportion of recipients judged employable has ranged from 26 to 87 percent, but only 15 to 40 percent are ever placed in government jobs. In AFDC workfare, on average, adults in around 39 percent of cases have been found employable, but in only 21 percent of those cases (under 7 percent of all cases) have the adults participated actively—hardly enough to break the norm of nonwork in welfare.[16]

The trouble is that enforcing work is resisted by those immediately involved. Some recipients manage to avoid the requirement by entering other programs. Employment staff prefer to work with willing clients and place them in "better" jobs; they dislike forcing menial work on the unwilling. Public agencies often resist employing workfare clients, even if paid to do so, since they are often unreliable, turn over rapidly, and require close supervision. Municipal unions also resist lest low-paid welfare workers threaten the jobs, pay, and benefits of their own members. Agency reluctance means that programs rarely have enough positions to mandate work for eligibles. Even welfare authorities may raise questions, since workfare costs more per client than just paying assistance, because of supervision and other expenses.[17] Yet further, poverty lawyers have litigated and delayed many workfare programs, though the courts have upheld them in essentials. All these pressures shift workfare in the direction of earlier welfare work efforts: It provides work to some receptive clients but does not enforce work on the employable as a class.[18]

Workfare will not transform AFDC any time soon. As of 1983 only twenty-two states had opted for CWEP in place of WIN, and only six had instituted it statewide. Few of the states require that the employable work off their entire grant, and some allow training in place of work.[19] Many of these states also had earlier run fairly demanding WIN programs, so there is less change from the past than appears. Over most of the country WIN remains the norm for welfare work in AFDC.

Food Stamps

Food stamps is the largest national welfare program after AFDC. It provides coupons to needy families with which they can buy the food needed for a minimal diet. Food stamps does for food what welfare reform proposed for cash welfare: It covers all needy families without regard to family structure. Provided they are poor, two-parent families, childless couples, and single people are eligible right along with female-headed families of the AFDC type.

Because of wider eligibility few thought work would pose as much of an issue in food stamps as it had in AFDC. More of the food stamp poor would be "deserving," intact families in which at least the husband would work even while on assistance. Yet a work issue emerged. One reason was simply the growing cost of the program. Food stamps was established as a national program in 1964, then liberalized in 1971 and 1977. Its growth was precipitous, since richer benefits and rising food prices in the 1970s raised eligibility levels while recessions increased need. Between 1969 and 1976 the number of recipients rose from 3 million to 18 million, while costs rose from $272 million to $5.9 billion a year.

There were fewer working recipients than expected, because by the 1970s most "working poor" people were no longer poor enough for food stamps, simply because they were working. That left the nonworking. By 1975, 13 percent of the family heads on food stamps were unemployed, and 59 percent were not even looking for work. The comparable figures for the population were 5 and 27 percent. Two-thirds of the recipients were drawing other welfare benefits, 42 percent were on AFDC, 64 percent were in female-headed families, and 78 percent were poor.[20] The food stamp caseload, in other words, presented a work issue not much different from the one in AFDC.

The political response was much as in AFDC—a combination of cuts and work requirements. College students, whose abuse of food stamps had angered Congress, were excluded from the program in 1977. In 1981 the Reagan Administration, as in AFDC, cut eligibility somewhat so as to focus benefits more closely on the "truly needy." Pressure was put on employable recipients to work. In 1971 (PL 91-671) all recipients aged eighteen to sixty-five were required to register for work with the Employment Service. The sanction for noncooperation by a family head was in some ways tougher than in AFDC—a cutoff of benefits for the entire family. On the other hand mothers caring for children of any age were exempted. In 1977 (PL 95-113) adults over sixty were exempted from registration, but mothers with children over twelve were subjected to it. The employable had to register not once but every six months, and suitable work rules were toughened.

The 1971 and 1977 requirements were contained in the same legislation that expanded the program. The 1971 law raised benefits to ensure an adequate diet to all recipients, while the 1977 measure eliminated the stipulation that clients pay something to get their food stamps (the "purchase requirement"), which had caused many eligibles never to claim their benefits. The logic of social legislation was shifting from the approach either liberals or conservatives had favored in the past. Benefits were no longer extended without work requirements. Nor was work enforced just by confining support to the hard-core unemployable. Rather, many able-bodied adults were covered on grounds of need, then subjected to work demands from inside the program.

Later moves to stiffen the work requirements have paralleled those in AFDC. A stipulation that registrants look for work up to eight weeks a year was added through a change in regulations in 1981.[21] Fourteen demonstration projects in food stamp workfare were authorized in 1977, and in 1981 (PL 97-98) the states were allowed to institute workfare in food stamps much as in AFDC. But as in AFDC, Congress declined to mandate workfare.

The requirements did have some impact. During 1971–76, even the weak 1971 work registration rule caused 244,000 households to be dropped from the program for failure to comply; 224,000 others had their benefits terminated or reduced by obtaining jobs.[22] But the effect was slight alongside a high and rising caseload containing millions of potential employables. Like WIN, food stamps somehow lacks the power to obligate most of its recipients. In the workfare demonstrations only 12 percent of households were even mandatory participants at first, because of the many exemptions granted in the law. Whether the projects have saved more than they cost is unclear.[23]

A further problem for work in food stamps is that the program lacks an enforcement structure comparable to WIN in AFDC. Work registration for stamps is carried out in regular Employment Service offices. While ES is paid by food stamps to do this, it does not give the attention to placing welfare clients that can be counted on in WIN. As a result even fewer recipients face serious pressures to work in food stamps than in AFDC.

Unemployment Insurance

A work issue was still more unexpected in Unemployment Insurance. UI supports what might be called the mainstream unemployed. The program pays compensation to workers out of a job. How large a benefit a worker receives, and for how long, depends on his or her prior earnings, length of employment, and the policy of the state program. Benefits are financed by a tax levied on payrolls. States set benefits and taxes and administer the program under loose federal supervision.

Workers must have an employment history, to demonstrate their "labor force attachment," to qualify for benefits. Eligibility demands further that they be able to work and available to work while drawing benefits. They must also not be disqualified for "cause," meaning they must not have quit their previous job voluntarily or lost it through misconduct. Like other social insurance UI levies a work requirement *before* benefits are claimed, not after as in welfare.

Yet from its origins in the Social Security Act of 1935, there has been anxiety that UI would tempt workers not to work. During the Depression mass unemployment forced the government to give "relief" to large numbers of workers for the first time, the task UI would later asume. In his State of the Union address for 1935, the year UI was enacted, Franklin Roosevelt commented on the moral implications in stark terms:

> A large proportion of these unemployed and their dependents have been forced on the relief rolls. . . . The lessons of history confirmed by the evidence immediately before me show conclusively that continued dependence upon relief induces a spiritual and moral disintegration fundamentally destructive to the national fiber. To dole out relief in this way is to administer a narcotic, a subtle destroyer of the human spirit. It is inimical to the dictates of sound policy. It is in violation of the traditions of America. Work must be found for able-bodied but destitute workers.[24]

New Deal public employment programs like the Works Progress Administration were deliberately temporary. UI was permanent, but states initially set tight limits on benefits. In 1938 only six allowed support lasting more than sixteen weeks. Caution persisted until well past the end of World War II, when it was feared that demobilization would bring back mass unemployment.

In the tight labor markets of the 1950s states at last felt they could expand benefits, which was popular, without competing unduly with available jobs. Most extended support to twenty-six weeks, still the norm for the basic UI program. The idea grew that Washington should finance further benefits during recessions, when it was more difficult to find jobs. By the time worrisome levels of joblessness returned in the 1970s, unemployment was seen as a reason to expand benefits, not restrict them. Congress voted temporary benefit extensions in 1958 and 1961, then established a permanent Extended Benefit (EB) program in 1970. EB benefits are "triggered" (become available) in states where unemployment exceeds specified levels. They provide up to thirteen weeks coverage beyond regular UI benefits and are financed half by the payroll tax, half by federal revenues. In 1974 Congress added a third tier of support, Federal Supplemental Benefits (FSB), which were all federally financed and provided a further thirteen weeks (until 1977, twenty-six weeks) of coverage. Before recent cuts a worker receiving the maximum benefits might stay on UI for as long as sixty-five weeks, several times longer than in the early days of the program.[25]

The benefit extensions were politically understandable, given the chronic recession of the 1970s. Their purpose was not so much to give the jobless extra time for jobhunting as to help them ride out long layoffs until the economy improved. However, the result was rising dependency and spending. Between 1965 and 1982 the number of initial claims for benefits grew from 12.4 to 30.6 million, the average number of workers on UI per week from 1.2 to 3.6 million, and the costs of the program from $2.3 to $25.0 billion a year.[26] That put the solvency of many state programs in jeopardy.

Nonwork became an issue as it became apparent that much of the new unemployment was voluntary. Virtually all Americans knew unemployed workers who used their benefits for a vacation and became serious about seeking work only when they ran out. Studies showing how UI increases the level and duration of unemployment were cited earlier. The benign interpretation is that the unemployed are simply looking hard for the best job.[27] In reality many UI claimants are not looking for work at all. Perhaps 14 percent of UI benefits are paid in error, and the overwhelming reason, extending to 50 to 80 percent of cases, is that claimants do not look actively for work. One study of Seattle and Denver found that during a third of the time claimants were on UI they were not seeking work, and a fifth of the time they were not even available to work if asked. Men were not looking or available about 10 percent of the time, women almost 40 percent. Differences among the races were small.[28]

As in welfare, Congress responded with a combination of benefit cuts and tougher work requirements. Every year from 1980 to 1983 something was done to limit eligibility and benefits in UI and to stabilize finances. One step was to raise the unemployment rates that "trigger" Extended and Federal Supplemental Benefits.[29] Supplemental Benefits were ended entirely in 1985. These measures, plus declining unemployment, have returned the maximum benefit in most states to the twenty-six weeks provided by the basic program.

In the past work enforcement, such as it was, had been left to state programs operating under state laws. Typically claimants had to attest to UI when they picked up their checks every two weeks that they were available for work. In most states they also had to register with the Employment Service and interview for available jobs if asked. What kind of job they had to accept if offered depended on suitable work rules akin to those debated during welfare reform. UI staff were supposed to let them hold out at first for jobs quite close to those they formerly held, then gradually make them step down in pay or status the longer they were jobless. However, the rules were leniently enforced, especially during recessions. Most UI recipients faced little effective pressure even to look for work until their benefits ran out.

In 1977 Congress instituted the first federal work requirement in UI. PL 95-19, sec. 104, required that recipients of FSB, the third tier of benefits, be "engaged in a systematic and sustained effort to obtain work" and provide "tangible evidence to the State agency" of their effort. They also had to accept suitable work defined to mean "any work" they could do, unless they had good prospects of returning to their customary occupation shortly. In 1980 (PL 96-499, sec. 1024) the same stipulations were extended to EB, the second tier of benefits. The Senate Finance Committee contemplated extending them even to the regular UI program, then desisted. But many states did that on their own. By 1980, 37 states had active job search requirements.[30] These steps, plus tightening of other state laws surrounding UI, have significantly restricted abuse of the program.

There was a direct collision between the new attempt to balance support with obligations and the traditional, benefit-oriented politics of unemployment. In 1976 a National Commission on Unemployment Compensation was appointed. The chairman was Wilbur Cohen, one of the founders and high priests of American social insurance. The commission members were mostly establishment labor, business, and government officials, many with professional ties to UI. The commission funded research showing that nonwork in UI was serious, yet its recommendations concentrated on financing the generous benefits of the 1970s, not on cuts or work requirements. The commission endorsed no federal work test, recommended that state-level active search requirements be rescinded, and deprecated the increasing severity of the states toward voluntary unemployment. But its report appeared in 1980 just as Congress, the states, and the Reagan Administration moved decisively in the other direction.

As in the welfare programs the new requirements had palpable effects. The 1977 job search stipulation in FSB raised the number of claimants disqualified for benefits, mainly for not looking for work, by percentages ranging from 78 to 287 across the states. The impact was least in states that already had work search rules akin to the new requirements.[31] The potential of tough administration to cut expense and nonwork in UI is clear from research. If states disqualify more claimants for declining to look for jobs or accept suitable work, fewer claimants exhaust their benefits before taking new jobs. If every state in 1971 had doubled the rate at which it denied UI claims, unemployment would have dropped 1.4 percentage points, or nearly a quarter.[32]

But as in welfare the political will to enforce work, and the impact of enforcement, are still quite limited. Congress has not contemplated anything close to required work in UI, and at the local level rates of benefit denial are still very low. Of 194 million benefit checks claimed in 1979, only 4.3 million, or 2.2 percent, were denied, and only 1.4 million of those, or less than 1 percent, because the claimant was unable to work, not seeking work, or refused suitable work.[33] Enforcement has barely scratched the surface of the third or more of UI recipients who apparently do not look for work seriously.

Disability

There is a work issue even in Disability, a program that supports the most "deserving" of all dependent groups. The program, closely tied to Social Security, pays pensions to workers who have become disabled and thus supposedly unemployable. Disability, like UI, presumes that its beneficiaries have already worked and paid payroll taxes. It seems to offer little room for voluntary nonwork, since eligibility hinges on a medical determination that the applicant is indeed disabled.

Yet conservatives in Congress long resisted disability programs for fear they would promote nonwork. Even welfare benefits for the disabled were approved only in 1950. The Disability insurance program was enacted in 1956 only with the stipulation that the disabilities covered be of "long continued and indefinite duration" and so serious as to prevent any gainful employment.

But as in UI, once the program was established, pressures built to liberalize it. Starting in 1960 the work history required of recipients was reduced, and disabilities projected to last as few as twelve months were covered. At the same time benefits were increased and then indexed to inflation. Between 1970 and 1978, a period when average wages rose by 70 percent, the average Disability payment rose by 120 percent. Administration also became more lenient. Impaired workers found it easier to qualify for benefits, and easier to win appeals if benefits were denied. Between 1965 and 1975 the number of people potentially eligible for Disability rose by 56 percent, but the number of new awards to claimants rose by 134 percent—from 253,000 to 592,000 a year.[34]

The consequence was explosive increases in costs and dependency. Spending for Disability rose from $1.6 billion in 1965 to $8.4 billion in 1975, then to $15.4 billion in 1980. If Disability is added to other, smaller programs for the disabled such as veterans benefits, the equivalent figures are $4.9, $19.3, and $33.1 billion. By 1981 those programs together were supporting 8 to 9 million workers and their families at a cost of $37 billion.[35]

Disability is politically attractive as a rubric for social policy, because it seems to involve no judgement about the motivation of recipients. They are disabled or they are not. But as the disability boom proceeded, policymakers found that they could not ignore motivation. The surge in claims could not be blamed on health conditions in the population, which by all accounts were improving. A lot of disability turned out to be "softer" than originally intended. The law allowed local agencies to consider vocational as well as medical factors in determining eligibility, and Social Security, with its client-centered ethos, urged them to do so. As early as 1962, according to Martha Derthick, "Non-medical factors . . . such as the individual's intelligence, psychological adaptability, age, education, work experience and skills, and motivation" were crucial to 40 percent of admissions to Disability. According to a government survey, 31 percent of the impairments claimed by the disabled are mental.[36]

Furthermore, the Disability caseload is far from a cross-section of the working population. Poorer, older, and less skilled workers predominate. In 1978, 61 percent of Disability recipients had family incomes under $10,000, 54 percent were over fifty-five, 63 percent were male, and 16 percent were black. The comparable figures for workers not on Disability are only 37, 28, 42, and 12 percent, respectively. Severly disabled workers are poor twice as often as the nondisabled.[37] It is understandable that more manual workers than others would be physically disabled. The mental disabilities, however, are often another name for the nonphysical problems of work discipline that are now so central to the predicament of the disadvantaged. The main role of Disability has been to let older unskilled workers escape those pressures by retiring early. Thus, despite its insurance label, Disability is in large measure a welfare program.

Workers were tempted to leave work for Disability, then not to return even when they could, because the benefits included not only a guaranteed income but Medicare health coverage. Disability benefits were indexed and large relative to what many workers could earn. In 1977, 28 percent of recipients received over three-fifths of their prior earnings from the program, and 14 percent received more than 100 percent; the latter were low-paid workers receiving extra benefits for large families. If income from other disability programs is added in, those figures rise to 46 and 19 percent. In the 1970s multiple benefits were quite common; 44 percent of Disability recipients received income from at least one other program, most often veterans benefits. Recipients also left the program less often than earlier. Between 1969 and 1976, although the Disability rolls doubled and the nature of covered impairments softened, the proportion of recipients returning to work each year actually fell, from 2.8 percent of cases to 1.5 percent.[38]

To reduce work disincentives, Congress in 1977 and 1980–81 reduced the benefits paid to large families and limited the income a recipient could receive from all disability programs together to 80 percent of prior earnings. The cuts, however, applied only to new awards, not to past ones. In 1980 Congress also mandated that recipients with nonpermanent disabilities be reviewed every three years to see if they could return to work.[39]

The periodic reviews, however, exposed the political limitations of trying to solve nonwork simply by cutting back the welfare state. The Reagan Administration, denied important legislative cuts in Disabililty by Congress, tried to curb the program administratively by vigorously prosecuting the case reviews mandated in 1980. In 42 percent of the reviews, or 485,000 cases, it would have cut off benefits entirely. But in more than 60 percent of these cases the recipients successfully appealed and had their benefits restored, while 30,000 court cases were brought against the government. The reviews provoked such an uproar that Congress forced the Administration to halt them in early 1984.[40] A change in the law has since placed the burden of proof in revocation cases squarely on the government. Politically it was simply too painful to withdraw benefits once granted, even if many of the recipients were in fact employable.

The less clearcut disability has become, the more the program has been forced to embrace explicit work policies. Since 1960 it has allowed clients to start working without immediately losing their Disability eligibility, should they have to return to the rolls. In 1980 (PL 96-265) the period of "trial work" was extended from nine months to two years, and former recipients were allowed to keep Medicare benefits for a further three years. Recipients could also keep Disability eligibility while entering Vocational Rehabilitation (VR), a federally aided, state-run program that retrains the handicapped. The number of clients Disability paid VR to serve grew by 170 percent in the 1970s.[41]

Social Security, which runs both Disability and welfare for the disabled (under Supplemental Security Income, or SSI), even has some authority to force recipients to participate in work-oriented programs on pain of losing their benefits, in the WIN manner. It can require Disability clients to accept VR services, if VR offers them, and it can make drug addicts and alcoholics in SSI enter either rehabilitation or work programs.[42] These powers could be the germ of a more general work requirement if the problem of nonwork in Disability continues.

Structural Problems

Work policies seem unavoidable if support is to be extended to the employable and still limit nonwork. Why then have they been so ineffective? One reason is simply that policies at the legislative level are still ambivalent. They do not yet unambiguously require the dependent to work (in the case of welfare) or to look for work (in the case of social insurance). Even if they did, however, enforcement would face difficult problems, most of them inherent in any effort to make people work when they are already receiving support.

The most fundamental problem is that none of those immediately involved in the work test may truly support it. That is clearest for recipients, whom the tests require to seek work or accept training *after* they have established eligibility in a program. Since they are already receiving benefits, the requirement necessarily assumes a negative character. It is an attempt to make clients do something for income they are already receiving for nothing. That gives them an incentive to evade the requirement or comply with it only *pro forma*, without a serious effort to work.

Furthermore, leverage over the client is limited to the value of the benefits. With even the toughest test, work is only a condition placed on grant funds. Noncompliance means, at worst, a loss of benefits, nothing more. Clients can escape obligations simply by abandoning what the program gave to them. Recipients of AFDC who are employable but refuse to work sometimes extricate themselves from WIN just by giving up their share of the family's welfare grant. Limited leverage is one reason why, as mentioned above, the YIEPP youth project that tied school attendance to government jobs failed to reduce dropout rates. The dropouts had too many other sources of income—families, underground jobs, other programs—to have to accept the proffered jobs and the school obligation linked to them. They did not *need* the benefits enough truly to be *bound* by them. Potentially requirements tied to welfare probably are the most binding simply because single parents with children are loath to do without assistance and thus must accept stipulations tied to it.

Even the interests of work program staffs may oppose enforcement. In any bureaucracy there is little incentive for individuals to perform, because their personal contribution is seldom recognized. Even if they do seek job placements, their individual interest is to do so with as little effort as possible. That biases work personnel toward working with the most, not the least, employable clients. In WIN the labor staff prefer to place recipients who are motivated to work and have some skills. The social service staff prefer to work with mothers who are willing to arrange their own child care rather than demand it from the agency. Those preferences diminish WIN's impact, by causing it to help mainly clients who might well have gone to work without WIN. The program is less likely to enforce work on the unwilling, so work does not become a norm for the welfare population as a whole.

WIN and the Employment Service must also maintain good relations with the employers to whom they refer clients. Businesses can always find their own employees or use private employment agencies. When they come to WIN or ES, they demand "good" referrals, meaning workers with skills and positive work attitudes. The staff are often afraid to send them welfare recipients, for fear the clients will not interview well and cost the office its customers. The employers also have little interest in reporting back to WIN when a referral fails to show or behaves poorly, information WIN needs in order to discipline clients.[43]

Other traditions and incentives peculiar to the Employment Service and welfare, which together run WIN, undercut serious work enforcement. The ES plays the central role in enforcement in Unemployment Insurance and food stamps as well as AFDC. Yet the agency has a voluntarist ethos. Its self-image, dating from its origins in the Depression, is that of a labor exchange helping willing workers locate willing employers. ES personnel tend to take work motivation for granted, not to question it as work enforcement often requires. They prefer to work actively with "volunteer" clients, those who come to them freely, rather than with welfare or UI recipients who come only to satisfy a registration requirement. To the extent they do serve recipients, they tend, again, to "cream," or favor the clients who need the least help getting jobs.

The funding incentives in the ES cut the same way. Federal authorities fund ES state programs on a competitive basis. Each receives funds, in part, according to how well it performed relative to the others in the previous fiscal cycle. Performance is defined to mean mainly the number of job entries achieved per staff member. That forces ES offices to seek maximum numbers of placements, which they usually try to do by serving volunteers and the most employable recipients. The funding system gives no credit for the savings in welfare or UI monies that result from placing the more reluctant recipients.

Since WIN is staffed largely by the ES, some of that ethos carries over, even though WIN works entirely with welfare recipients. The WIN funding system gives the program more incentive than the ES to work with a wide range of clients, and the most effective offices do so. The quality (e.g. wage level) as well as quantity of jobs counts, and credit is given for savings in welfare grants. But because of their ES background, most WIN staff assume anyway that they are only supposed to "make placements."[44] So they tend to cream, just like regular ES offices.

For different reasons, welfare agencies tend also to neglect work enforcement. In the early days of WIN many were positively opposed to work, especially for welfare mothers. Today, in a more conservative climate, they seldom are. However, work is still peripheral to the main welfare mission, which is to pay out grant funds efficiently. Departments tend to think of WIN registration in procedural terms, as a formality employable recipients must satisfy before they can go on welfare, not as something that might lead to work and keep them off welfare. In New York State welfare executives often favor work, but local personnel typically tell applicants that they must "put in an appearance" at WIN before their "case can be opened." WIN staff say derisively that "It's like paying your bill at Con Ed. Or getting your driver's license renewed."[45] Welfare management wants to reduce assistance costs, but mainly through getting ineligible recipients off welfare entirely, not through employment.

As in the ES, federal funding incentives are reinforcing. WIN can lead to cuts in a state's federal AFDC funding only if it works actively with fewer than 15 percent of its registrants, a low figure that most states easily satisfy. However, the agencies also face fiscal sanctions if they fail to reduce error and fraud rates in grant payment below specified levels or fail to enforce child support in AFDC, standards they find much more threatening. So welfare administrators strive mainly to streamline grant administration, not to avoid welfare through work.[46]

Another difficulty is that in many respects compliance with work requirements cannot be monitored. The test mandates that employable recipients work, or look for work, in good faith, but staff find it difficult to tell if they do. If clients fail to get or keep jobs, or say they are unavailable, the program usually lacks the information to second-guess them. When recipients are sanctioned, that is, cut off from welfare for noncooperation, it is usually for offenses inside the program such as failing to register or keep appointments with WIN staff, precisely because these can be monitored.[47]

Without direct knowledge of behavior, work enforcement hinges on judgements of motive that are inherently dubious. Work test personnel have to decide, in WIN's words, "whether the individual intentionally is performing at or near his/her potential."[48] Unless noncooperation is obvious, the staff are continually tempted to believe clients' excuses, not to press work demands, and thus let benefits be paid essentially without conditions. It is the perennial problem of any system that supports the poor without requiring a degree of surveillance or institutionalization. Alexis de Tocqueville commented on the problem as early as 1835:

> Nothing is so difficult to distinguish as the nuances which separate unmerited misfortune from an adversity produced by vice. . . .What profound knowledge must be presumed about the character of each man and of the circumstances in which he has lived. . . Where will you find the magistrate who will have the conscience, the time, the talent, the means of devoting himself to such an examination? . . . .

> And if any of these intrepid beings can be found, how many will there be? . . . Poverty is verified, the causes of poverty remain uncertain: the first is a patent fact, the second is proved by an always debatable process of reasoning. Since public aid is only indirectly harmful to society, while the refusal of aid instantly hurts the poor and the overseer himself, the overseer's choice cannot be in doubt. The laws may declare that only innocent poverty will be relieved; practice will alleviate all poverty.[49]

In England in Tocqueville's time the monitoring problem was solved by replacing an overextended system of "outdoor relief" with one requiring recipients to live in a public "workhouse." That deterred some paupers from asking for aid and forced many others to labor, slowly dissolving a substantial welfare class.[50] The modern-day equivalent would be workfare. Once jobs are assured, even the work behavior of clients can be monitored and held accountable. Workfare also turns around the uninterest of recipients in work. Since the obligation is now assessed before, not after, support is given, they are likely to view it more positively. But workfare is costly, and it does not overcome the other impediments to enforcement.

Short of workfare, compliance could be improved simply by more staff to work closely with clients and check up on them. All the work enforcement operations are underfunded relative to their caseloads. WIN, the most important, spent an average of $342 million annually in the years 1978–83. That money, to put AFDC families to work, was less than 5 percent of the amount spent supporting them over the same period. Yet rather than build up WIN, the Reagan Administration first cut its funds by more than a third, then tried to abolish it in favor of compulsory workfare, as against the optional workfare Congress allowed in 1981.[51] If more were spent on work enforcement, some of the cost would be recouped from savings in grant expenses due to more work by recipients.

A further problem is that welfare work is inherently complicated. To put recipients to work while supporting them requires that they be funded by an income maintenance system, given necessary support services such as child care by a social services staff, then trained and placed by an employment staff. In WIN those functions are discharged, respectively, by local welfare departments, services staff from the Separate Administrative Unit (SAU) attached to welfare, and job developers from the Employment Service. If clients are referred outside WIN for training, yet further structures are involved. There have been proposals to reduce the complexity by vesting all operations in welfare, the ES, or federal training programs like CETA. But these programs would then have to perform the same three functions, duplicating the agencies that now perform them. The complexity is inherent in the task.[52]

The result is often that responsibility for enforcement falls through the cracks. There is a tendency in welfare work for clients to be referred around among welfare, WIN, and training programs with no one authority really helping the client or insisting on work. The division of authority between WIN and welfare is especially troublesome. While WIN has the formal power to remove clients from welfare for work offenses, welfare often has more real authority in the eyes of recipients because it controls the welfare grant. Welfare departments sometimes neglect to reduce the grant to implement a WIN sanction, and they are still sometimes reluctant to enforce work. When the messages welfare gives about expectations differ from WIN's, clients become confused and are less likely to work.

More than anything, local discretion has allowed the work agencies to uphold the work requirement in principle while, in practice, forcing few recipients to labor. Work tests are embodied mainly in requirements that recipients register for work, but the rules themselves exempt most adults, especially mothers, and give the agencies some choice about the rest. WIN staff sometimes try to get difficult or unskilled recipients reclassified as disabled so they will be exempt from registration and not burden the office. Most important, staff have almost complete control over which of the registrants they call to participate actively in training or job placement. WIN regulations require only that the staff put each client in the most "appropriate" status for him or her. WIN programs do face the Talmadge requirement that at least 15 percent of registrants be active, and state policy may set caseloads per worker. But over these levels staff may decide for themselves how many clients they want to work with, in light of their own work loads or the jobs or training slots they think are available. Since only the active participants face any real obligation, staff effectively control who is and is not subject to a work test.

The process of sanctioning clients is also highly discretionary. Registrants can have their grants reduced if they refuse to participate in WIN without "good cause," a term that has some recognized meanings, such as illness, but is subject to wide interpretation by WIN staff. That allows staff members in practice to avoid adjudication if they want to, which they often do because of the onerous procedures and paperwork involved.[53]

Discretion helps explain why even workfare seems to obligate few clients. All able-bodied adults are supposedly subject, but somehow only some are found employable, only some of those participate actively, and only a handful are ever disciplined. Through these judgments the grip of the work demand is loosened, and most recipients—even the employable—escape it. It would be easy to conclude, with George Gilder, that the attempt to make recipients work when they do not want to is "as hopeless a venture as has ever been undertaken by government." Adds Henry Aaron, in tones much like Tocqueville's:

> [I]f work does not pay, a work requirement . . . would be ineffectual and inoperative, a costly and largely futile effort to compel the poor to behave in ways contrary to their own self-interest. It is unimaginable that a large bureaucracy would be capable of sifting millions of individual cases, each fraught with special problems, needs, and ambiguity, all requiring judgment if not wisdom. To inspire hard work is a laudable goal, but one not likely to be achieved through a work requirement without more authoritarian administation than most Americans are likely to accept.[54]

If a work test exists, then, it must be seen at present largely as an exercise in symbolic politics, as homage to a widely held value that government cannot actually achieve.[55]

Political Problems

Aaron's crucial assumption is that serious work enforcement would be impolitic *in America*. In some sense that is true. The reluctance of Congress to strengthen enforcement further certainly suggests hesitations. The political resistance to functioning requirements of any kind is strong, especially among political leaders.

At the same time politics is also an answer to enforcement problems. The structural difficulties in requiring work all arise because recipients and staff behave in self-interested ways. They have no personal reason to interest themselves in work effort. Like other civilities, it benefits society more than the individual and is difficult to verify and enforce. "In the end," Thomas Schelling has written, "personal morality is a public asset; there is not much else to keep us from throwing bottles out our car windows . . . . Virtue may be its own reward, but the reward is too often a collective good, shared only minutely by the virtuous individual."[56]

But on a strict assumption of self-interest, the work obligation would not be honored even to the extent it is. Most people fulfill social obligations, even at personal cost, because they feel them to be *legitimate.* In any compliance question, David Hume wrote, "Force is always on the side of the governed," and "the governors have nothing to support them but opinion."[57] In forming such an opinion politics is crucial. Government must persuade individuals, in certain key respects, to give up their own preferences and instead serve society's. An interaction between public mandates and public opinion seems to be involved. To elicit compliance, public obligations, including work, must be specified in *both* law and opinion, and in congruent terms. The laws that spell out duties must be acceptable to opinion, but through enforcement they also shape opinion to support the laws.[58] Compliance can grow or decline as the supporting enforcement and opinion strengthen or weaken.

The tax obligation is a good illustration. The American income tax is based largely on self-assessment, since citizens figure and file their own tax returns. If taxpayers were only self-regarding, compliance would be no better than it is with work obligations. In fact around 90 percent of taxpayers have traditionally filed their returns honestly; the percentages run considerably lower in some other Western countries. The reason is partly tough enforcement. The Internal Revenue Service disposes of powers to levy taxes, investigate noncompliance, and punish offenders that are the envy of welfare work agencies. Taxes are withdrawn from paychecks *before* individuals have a chance to claim overpayments, much as workfare—if enforced—exacts the work obligation in advance of benefits.

However, the tax authority really rests on opinion no less than law. The IRS exceeds the work agencies, not only in legal powers, but in the respect in which it is held. That esteem goes back to the high view taken of the tax obligation in the English political tradition, inherited by the United States. Most Americans do not resent tax payment but see it almost as a badge of citizenship. Tax evasion is commonly seen as a serious offense, to be prosecuted against rich and poor alike. Most Americans believe the IRS has lived up to that mission. It is seen as implacable but also impartial and incorruptible. Without such feelings government could never enforce compliance. The IRS, like the work agencies, is quite small, with nothing like the resources it would need to monitor every taxpayer.

The recent decline in tax compliance shows how fragile compliance is. In 1982, 13 percent of taxes owed were not paid, up over half in a decade. The IRS could do little about it, since only 1.55 percent of returns were audited, down from 2.59 percent in 1976. The agency prosecuted only 1,624 taxpayers, and only 917 went to jail. It simply lacks the staff and computers to do more. Noncompliance has grown because tax levels have risen and more Americans feel that paying up is unfair. The shame of evasion has declined. If these feelings grow, efforts to enforce taxes will be overwhelmed with evasion.[59] To restore authority is both a legal and a political task. It will require tougher enforcement backed up by appeals to opinion by officeholders. A few well-publicized prosecutions of prominent tax evaders would probably help.

The authority problems in work enforcement are more serious but not different in kind.[60] Most grant recipients already seem to accept the work obligation in principle. The difficulty is to make it operative through enforcement. That involves increasing WIN's powers, but also building support for them, especially among the elites who have resisted serious requirements. The structural problems of work enforcement will not disappear, but they will ease as the behavior of clients and staff alike becomes less self-interested and more compliant. Only when the work obligation seems as certain as "death and taxes" will nonwork be overcome.

The political limitations on WIN, and the chance to strengthen enforcement, both center in the first instance on the program's legal powers, which are now quite limited. Their weakness is an important reason why so few of the employable actually face a work test. WIN staff must clear many hurdles before they can obligate clients to participate actively in the program. The recipients must be found nondisabled and employable under WIN eligibility rules. They must be provided with child care and other services so they can leave home and join WIN activities. Many recipients know that WIN faces these requirements, and they sometimes invoke them in order to avoid or delay participation. If they claim illness or disability, WIN must arrange a medical before they can participate. If they say they cannot find their own child care, the agency must arrange it, which is usually tougher to do than for the mother to make informal arrangements.[61]

To sanction clients for noncooperation also poses problems for WIN. It is costly in time and staff effort. The client must fail to cooperate on several occasions, go through a thirty-day period of conciliation, and be sent an official notice that a sanction is planned. The recipient may then request a fair hearing before an administrative law judge, and an adverse finding may be appealed to state-level and federal-level review boards. At every stage WIN must document all charges and provide the client with legal assistance if asked. Until 1980 WIN also had to offer up to sixty days of further counseling after adjudication before it could actually reduce the grant.[62]

Even when a sanction is invoked, it may be quite mild. Since in WIN only welfare for the noncompliant recipient is usually cut off, many clients tolerate the sanction rather than accept jobs they do not want; often the reason is that they are already making more money working off the books. The penalty may also be short. Federal court decisions of the late 1970s held that WIN could penalize recipients only for as long a time as they had been uncooperative, usually a brief interval.[63] Powers to levy sanctions for fixed intervals, now three or six months, were restored by statute only in 1980. WIN staff universally complain that their sanctions lack the "teeth" to command respect from recipients. It is little wonder that they often decline to invoke them, though that further undercuts the authority of the program.

Welfare departments have greater powers, which helps explain their greater authority in the eyes of recipients. Welfare mothers have to keep appointments with the agency every six months to continue their eligibility for support. If they fail to or infringe other rules, welfare can close their cases, cutting off the whole grant. Welfare's adjudication procedure is also more summary than WIN's. In consequence, mothers will routinely break a WIN appointment if they must in order to keep one with welfare. Since the rules are largely federal, welfare's greater authority ultimately reflects the fact that federal politicians are more comfortable cutting mothers off welfare entirely than they are forcing them to work in return for welfare.

Toward Welfare Work

Because of the legal features just outlined, WIN can seldom clearly obligate its registrants to do anything serious about work. The responsibility for making welfare work happen rests too much on the staff, not enough on the clients. That puts the staff in the position of bargaining with clients, persuading them to work, instead of directing them from a position of authority. With effort the staff can still cause many to work, but they have to do so on their own, with little support from the institutions.[64]

Like other features of federal social policy the work rules express the sociological view of disadvantage. They tend to confirm, rather than change, the belief recipients have that their fate turns on forces outside themselves. Clients are supposed to work, the rules say, but only if the program first solves their health problems, arranges child care, finds them a job, and so on. The structure ratifies dependency.

To shift more responsibility for work to the client would require rule changes such as:

- A definition of mothers as employable when their youngest child was three, not six, as now. Currently, the age three limit applies only in AFDC workfare (CWEP), not WIN
- A requirement that the mothers normally arrange their own child care, unless they furnished evidence to WIN that they could not. Welfare would still pay for the care, as it does now
- A shortening of the adjudication process, for instance by eliminating the conciliation stage and restricting appeals
- A strengthening of sanctions so that the grant was normally canceled for the entire family, not just the noncompliant member

Such changes would communicate a much stronger political will to enforce work. They would link benefits more closely to the work obligation, so staff would have more authority and recipients would take work more seriously. However, the point here is less to advocate these specific steps than to suggest how crucial the legal balance in social programs is. Washington is used to thinking of programs economically, in terms of the benefits and incentives they transfer to the needy. How recipients *respond* to support, however, seems to depend just as much on the legal aspects of programs, since these determine how much leverage the programs obtain over clients in return for benefits.

Another essential step is to make sure work staffs implement the expectations once they are on the books. What undercuts work tests now, as much as anything, is the power the staffs have to set the requirements aside for most recipients. They too must be obligated to function. The following changes, especially the first, would do something to make participation in WIN, not nonparticipation, the norm for the employable:

- An increase in the proportion of registrants that WIN programs must work with actively to avoid fiscal penalties, from the current 15 percent to perhaps 30 percent, then with additional increases over time
- A requirement that staff adjudicate clients after two failures to keep appointments without good cause, not two to five as the policy is now[65]
- More staff to serve and check up on participants, with some of the cost to be recouped from savings in grants due to more clients working

To mandate workfare probably is less critical than to achieve higher participation in the existing work programs. The workfare programs too have suffered from low participation rates, and for similar reasons. If that problem were solved, more clients would go to work even in job-search programs like WIN, and the heavy costs of workfare, both political and economic, could be minimized. If participation is not raised, workfare will probably achieve little. Workfare's best role probably is to backstop WIN-style work search. The employable would be required to look for work, then placed in government jobs if they failed to take priviate jobs in, say, thirty to ninety days. The Reagan Administration's proposal to mandate workfare in AFDC is much along those lines.

The idea of giving WIN staff such powers to enforce work may conjure up specters of "arbitrary" welfare administration, a bugaboo of the liberal welfare reformers. Actually the tradition of discretionary administration as it existed until the 1960s arose mainly because demands on clients were *not* levied federally. Because of the liberalizing policy changes of the 1960s and 1970s local staffs now exercise discretion mainly in *not* enforcing norms rather than in doing so. Firmer work rules would mean, not a return to arbitrary administration, but a renewal of obligations based for the first time on federal authority.

Furthermore, work demands are a good deal less sensitive than those that characterized the earlier discretionary regime. Then, welfare staffs were mainly concerned to limit eligibility for benefits. That meant discovering, above all, whether welfare mothers were really separated from their husbands, as eligibility required, or were still seeing them or other men. Surveillance was concentrated on recipients sexual and family lives, the most sensitive areas. Work, in contrast, is a public obligation involving public behavior, outside the home. Recipients recognize that whether they work or not is a proper agency concern, and they accept inquiries about it.[66] Work requirements would levy functioning demands at the point where they are most, not least, legitimate to the poor themselves.

While all those steps would improve work enforcement, however, they would face stiff resistance at a policymaking level in Washington. Despite recent political shifts to the right, the conviction that government is supposed to solve the problems of the poor remains deep-seated. The kind of work mandate needed to improve enforcement may be one thing, the kind that is acceptable quite another. While unambiguous, workfare-oriented policies might make a large dent in the work problem in welfare, they may be too tough to be politic, at least in the short term. Politics is the instrument of enforcement but also the leading barrier to it.

7

Welfare Work: A Closer Look

THE most important federal work program is the Work Incentive (WIN) program attached to AFDC. WIN is supposed to place employable AFDC recipients in work or training. The program has been only marginally effective, but it can demonstrate something very important, that public authority is the key to the work problem. We already know that WIN's impact has risen as its authority has. My own studies of WIN show that the main thing that sets effective WIN offices apart from ineffective ones is that they use their authority well. Whether the office clearly expects WIN clients to work is the main determinant of whether they do. Economic conditions such as the availability of jobs matter also, but less than is commonly believed.

The staff in the effective WIN offices believe that standards are a *good* thing for recipients, not a bad thing as is so often assumed in Washington. They have developed a way of interacting with their clients that is demanding, yet positive. They expect them to work exactly *because* they believe they can. Standards express the social interest in work, but they also testify to the potential competence of recipients, an affirmation they vitally need.

WIN AND ITS RECORD

WIN was once the universal AFDC work program. It no longer is because of the alternatives allowed under the 1981 Reagan reforms.[1] The changes arose from widespread dissatisfaction in Washington and many states with WIN's record. The program has raised work levels in AFDC hardly at all. WIN training improves the earnings of clients very little. Earnings gains have been greatest for the least skilled clients but are seldom sufficient for them to leave welfare. WIN's services seem to do little long-term good for clients, and no one form of service is better than another. Since the Talmadge amendments of 1971 WIN has deemphasized services and stressed placement in available jobs, but many clients leave their jobs quickly and return to welfare within a short period. Quite possibly WIN has little impact of any kind. Clients, that is, may obtain jobs or improve their earnings no more than they would have without WIN. In its disappointments WIN's record resembles that of other federal employment programs.[2]

Why has WIN achieved so little? The commonest explanations make no reference to the problem of obligating recipients to function. The emphasis is on the many barriers that allegedly keep the poor from working. The recipients are too unskilled to get their families off welfare. WIN lacks sufficient funding to serve them well. Especially since Talmadge, it has spent too little on training to overcome the skills problems. WIN also lacks enough child care to serve all the welfare mothers who would like to work. Above all, there are not enough jobs—especially "decent" jobs—for all the recipients who want to work. Says Leonard Goodwin, "The key issue . . . is whether the federal government will take the next step beyond WIN and guarantee the kinds of jobs to all those willing and able to work which will provide enough income to live above the poverty level.[3]

Limited skills, inadequate education, and other personal characteristics, however, seldom actually bar recipients from employment. According to Judith Mayo, "the amount of time a welfare mother spends working is not chiefly the product of her personal characteristics and employability." A recent government study found that such factors as the race, education, and age of mothers have very little effect on whether they leave welfare by working. The low-skilled are apparently almost as able to work as the higher-skilled.[4] Nor is child care usually a barrier, since most mothers, even with preschool children, manage to arrange care informally if they seriously want to work. Only 8 percent of WIN children under twelve are in day care centers; most of the rest are lodged with relatives or friends during the day, arrangements that most WIN mothers find satisfactory.[5] As for jobs, low-paid work usually is available to welfare clients in most localities, even if more attractive positions are not.

Furthermore, the evaluators have tended to ask the wrong question. The purpose of WIN is not mainly to help recipients improve their lot, desireable though that is. It is to have them discharge the work obligation linked to welfare. For that any job will do. Recipients need not earn enough to get off welfare entirely, but they must work at something. The scandal in WIN is, not that few recipients gain from the program, but that so few participate in it, let alone actually go to work.

The performance of WIN naturally varies across the state programs, and across the local offices in each program. Only about a fifth to a half of the variation seems due to differences among the programs or offices in how employable the clients are and how favorable the labor market is.[6] What goes on *inside* an office seems to matter even more than the conditions around it. The worst administrative dilemmas in WIN have already been mentioned: its parent agencies' uninterest in work enforcement and the complexity of that task. In addition WIN often suffers from bureacratic mediocrity. Employees from the ES or welfare rarely seek assignment to WIN, because the clients are difficult and it means leaving the main career ladders in their agencies. Those assigned to WIN, therefore, are often unproductive workers who are "dumped" there from regular ES or welfare offices because they cannot be fired under civil service.[7]

Much of the lethargy of WIN can be attributed to the old-line character of the parent agencies. The ES and welfare have existed in much their present form since the 1930s. Set in their ways, neither has adjusted fully to the demands for work enforcement made by Congress since 1967.[8] ES agencies have often escaped accountability to state governments because virtually all their funding is federal. AFDC costs the states and localities much more (the federal subsidy averages about half), so welfare agencies have felt more pressure to get tough about work. Some have become more work-oriented than the ES, and they are frustrated that the latter gives WIN low priority. Some would like to return work activities entirely to welfare control, the situation before 1967. Such pressures explain why an all-welfare work program was one of the alternatives to WIN allowed by the 1981 Reagan reforms.

Recent research has systematically compared ES and WIN programs and offices to discover what distinguishes the more effective ones. In these studies, as in the ones I report below, performance was assessed relative to what could be expected of an office given its particular clients and labor market.[9] That way, the variations in performance have to be due to differences in what goes on inside WIN. The high-performing programs and offices were those that most avoided the evils of bureaucratic sclerosis. Most of them manifested:

- Innovative, entrepreneurial leadership not afraid to try new things
- A flat bureaucratic hierarchy, with few levels between leadership at the state level and operating staff in the offices
- Organization in many small offices, each with close ties to the neighborhood and local employers
- An informal mangement style, allowing flexibility about rules, much delegation to service-level staff, and a lot of communication among staff at all levels
- Yet at the same time, clear accountability for performance due to effective performance monitoring of offices and staff
- Personnel with energy, commitment, and a sense of responsibility for results
- Little political interference from local or state politicians

Conversely, the low-performing programs and offices tended to manifest the problems of old-line agencies:

- Cautious, custodial leadership with fixed ways of doing things
- A many-layered hierarchy, too many managers, and too few staff serving clients
- Large, bureacratic offices, especially in urban areas
- A formal management style with strict routines, little delegation to staff, and mainly downward communications

- Little accountability for performance, partly due to poor monitoring
- Staff with limited ability and commitment to the program
- Frequent political interference, especially in decisions about personnel and the location of offices

The contrast between one kind of office and the other could be seen in New York State, the focus of my studies. New York was not generally a high performer in WIN, but it had several top-flight offices where, staff said, there was more concern with getting the job done than with bureaucratic "formality." Workers developed "procedures within procedures" in order to move clients into jobs. They "hustled" to "take care of business."[10] Managers pitched in to help them with little sense of hierarchy, yet demanded results. Staff put out the sheer eneregy necessary to energize the clients—and get through the paperwork. Because they worked hard, clients did too. Recipients were constantly coming and going, meeting with the staff, joining training activities, or going out on job interviews. The atmosphere was upbeat. You could feel the electricity just walking into these offices.

The poor offices, on the other hand, were deathly quiet. Staff were more concerned with following procedures, less with placing clients. Managers were often remote, defensive, attuned mainly to placating their superiors. Staff were passive, largely going through the motions. Many were demoralized by the demands of the job, as well as low pay. Yet they felt trapped in WIN because they seldom could earn as much outside government. Overbureaucratization was common, in part because some of the New York offices were among the largest in the country.

However, organization in the usual sense of bureaucratic structure and management is not WIN's central problem. Even WIN programs and offices that are well run in these senses perform only marginally better than those that are not, if differences in client characteristics and the labor market are allowed for.[11]

Authority Problems

WIN's main difficulties, rather, stem from limitations of authority that are only loosely related to administrative arrangements. The program needs authority simply because its clients are so ambivalent toward the unattractive jobs most available to them.

One study of WIN mothers found that, though they wanted to work, 70 percent of the women rejected many of the unskilled jobs they most easily qualified to do, for example work as waitresses, domestics, or nurses aides:

> The jobs that most respondents appeared to want clearly required extensive . . . training--jobs as dieticians, medical technicians, stenographers, counselors, and the like. In general, they expressed distinct dislike for the menial jobs often held by unskilled black women. For example, more than 90 percent . . . said that they would not want to do private household work. Only a handful of the women felt equipped to undertake the jobs that interested them. Almost all were looking to WIN to provide them with the education and training necessary to obtain and perform the jobs they wanted.[12]

Thirteen percent of the jobs recipients wanted presupposed training on a professional or academic level, 46 percent extensive training, 30 percent moderate training, and only 11 percent minimal or no training. One welfare caseworker explained the psychology as follows:

> Let's face it, if you're poor you'd like to have a job so you can say, "I'm an office worker, I'm a white collar worker," instead of being a maid, which for many of them is their background. So, they want something that is going to give them prestige in the eyes of their neighbors and friends and children. And many times they are unrealistic because of that.[13]

Most of the women in fact were able to get only rudimentary jobs, mainly because of limited education. Only 2 percent of those who were working after WIN obtained jobs that required professional or academic training; 18 percent required extensive training, 35 percent moderate training, and 45 percent minimal training or none. The distribution was only slightly better than the positions the participants had held before entering WIN. And 43 percent of the trainees left WIN with no jobs at all. Only a third managed to get off welfare through WIN, something 90 percent had hoped to do. Clearly, WIN "did not provide what most participants seemed to want: a road out of the world of welfare and marginal employment."[14]

The national interest in work, however, still requires that recipients accept the low-skilled jobs. WIN is like other employment programs in that it raises the income of its clients mainly by getting them to put in more hours in available jobs, not qualifying them for better ones. For that task WIN must *require* people to work. Yet such are the limits to its powers, researchers find, that recipients usually have only the vaguest grasp that WIN is in any sense mandatory. They seldom understand why they have to register and cooperate with the program, and what will happen to them if they do not.[15]

WIN, like other federal employment programs, also tends to objectify attitudes and actions that impede work as if they were barriers outside the recipients. WIN's official handbook allows the staff to exempt registrants from participation for "work motivation factors" such as "acceptance of the work ethic," among other reasons. Staff should not demand participation from clients with "severe emotional problems" or for whom jobs are "unavailable or are unlikely to develop." To be sure, clients may be guilty of "inappropriate behavior," but the policy is to trace the problem to the "environment" or "lack of information" if possible.[16]

Official communications with recipients, too, tend to emphasize the rights and service aspect of the program, not its obligatory work aspect. A pamphlet for clients from the early WIN period said brightly that "With WIN, anyone on AFDC who has attained age 16 can get off welfare and get a good job." "People are placed in good full-time jobs—where there is a chance for advancement and a chance to get ahead in life," a promise much beyond what WIN has delivered. The mandatory side of WIN was hardly hinted: "If a person can't work, he will not be forced to. . . . But anyone referred to WIN must give his reason for not participating before he can be excused. " Only on the last page was it indicated that "For such persons, unless there is a good reason, AFDC payments may be cut off." Yet the pamphlet immediately added, "But payments won't be stopped without a fair hearing if requested, and the family may still receive payments." And anyone sanctioned "will be informed of his rights and told where to appear along each step of the way."[17] WIN offices are commonly festooned with signs informing clients of their rights to complain or appeal if they suffer discrimination or are denied benefits.

Recent literature on WIN is more sober. Pamphlets used in the New York program now discuss clients' obligations as well as rights. Signs stressing appeal rights are less in evidence; some managers have deliberately taken them down. Yet obligations are still rarely emphasized. Welfare centers still have a tendency to tell employable recipients that they are being referred to WIN for "training," not for work, though training has not been WIN's main purpose since 1971. Federal rules and policy still do not say clearly that the work test mainly involves an obligation to accept available jobs, even if they are unrewarding. Without a climate of public, formal expectations, the burden of conveying the work obligation falls too heavily on WIN staff.

Just as individual WIN programs and offices differ in their economic environment and organization, so do they differ in how rights-oriented they are toward clients. Within the limits set by federal policy some states manage to levy much firmer work obligations than others. States that do well in WIN relative to national norms (for example, West Virginia, North Carolina, Wisconsin, and California) do tend to have favorable labor markets and effective WIN organizations. But more important, there is strong political support for the enforcement mission, so WIN offices are able to convey more obligation to clients.

The political background is different in each case. West Virginia is tough about work because it has a blue-collar economy and a severe local work ethic. Since manual, often unskilled work is common for poor and nonpoor alike, politicians resist the idea that anyone employable, especially men, should be on welfare. The state also has a tradition of tough welfare administration, to the point where the welfare department virtually ran WIN and is now participating in AFDC workfare. In Wisconsin the style is much more solicitous. Progressivism left a tradition of service to the individual in social service administration. But because staff identify clients' interests with independence, and work with them intensively to achieve it, the result is still a highly insistent WIN program. In California an effective WIN is the legacy of Reagan conservatism, with its suspicions of permissive, big-city welfare.

Lower-performing states (for example, New York, Massachusetts, Maryland, and Michigan) are less demanding about work. They do tend to have worse WIN organizations and labor markets (though recently Massachusetts has improved sharply on both counts). But more important, their political cultures are less supportive of enforcement. The welfare caseload in these states is concentrated in large cities, where a welfare culture ambivalent about work has become dominant. In New York and Massachusetts liberal politics distinctive to the states has encouraged an entitlement view of welfare. The result is that WIN programs face entrenched urban caseloads without the higher-level support they need to make the work test credible.

The impact of political culture is apparent in how the liberal and conservative states have greeted the advent of workfare in AFDC. In New York and Massachusetts recipients and activists demonstrate, their signs saying "Workfare is Slavery." But in West Virginia recipients express quiet satisfaction that they are now working and "earning" their support.[18]

Studies of WIN

My own studies of WIN focused on the twenty-two offices in New York State.[19] The offices varied widely in size, organization, and administrative style, as WIN offices do nationwide. Staff in the offices ranged in number from eight to sixty-nine, the number of registrants, or clients, from 786 to 22,411. The largest offices were in Buffalo and New York City, the smallest in upstate towns and cities.

My objectives were to show the affect of work obligations on functioning and also *how* the expectations are conveyed, or not conveyed, to the clients. The approach was to see how well all the influences that have been mentioned could explain the performance of the twenty-two offices. The test was done statistically, using data from fiscal years 1978–1980. In addition, interviews, either by phone or by visit, were done in 1981–82 in all the offices to help interpret the results and find out how expectations of clients were communicated.[20]

The analysis required that WIN's performance and all the forces upon it be expressed in measured form. Performance was rated using the following indicators:

- *Total job entries*: the proportion of registrants in an office who entered jobs during the fiscal year, whether they obtained the jobs themselves or were placed by WIN staff
- *Placed entries*: the proportion of registrants who entered jobs arranged by the staff
- *Obtained entries*: the proportion of registrants who found jobs themselves

- *Working registrants:* the proportion of registrants who were working while still on welfare
- *Retention rate*: the proportion of all registrants entering jobs who were still on the job after thirty days

All of these measures are used officially in WIN to monitor performance except the fourth, "working registrants," which I added because the goal of putting recipients to work while still assisting them was important to welfare reform.[21]

The following were the factors that might influence WIN performance, with the specific indicators used to approximate each:

- *Obligations*: the proportions of registrants in an office put through the administrative processes leading to active participation or nonparticipation in the program
- *Services:* the proportions of the participants assigned to each kind of training or service available in WIN
- *Bureaucratic*: the numbers of employment, social service, and total staff available to an office in relation to its caseload[22]
- *Demographic*: the proportions of registrants with characteristics linked to employability, including sex, race, age, and education
- *Labor Market*: the availability of entry-level jobs in the county where an office was located, as measured by the unemployment rate, growth in employment over the previous year, and other measures

The indicators were drawn from past research on WIN. Much WIN evaluation has concentrated on which of the WIN services are most effective; the service factor asks whether the mix of services preferred by an office affects performance. The bureaucratic factor captures the most important organizational influence on performance, simply staff resources relative to caseload. The demographic and labor market factors capture the environmental influences that explain a good share of WIN's performance.[23]

To these four factors I added work obligation. The degree of work expectation in an office may seem to be an intangible, and economists, who have done most of the work on WIN, have doubted that it could be measured.[24] However, the main reason WIN and other work programs have slight authority is that so few employable recipients have to participate actively in the programs. Thus the proportion of registrants who do participate is a good measure of how tough a WIN office is in expecting work.

Participation hinges on the specific things WIN does with clients after they register in the program. Essentially it is clients put in specific training or work-readiness activities (called components) or in job placement (for referral to available jobs) who have to participate actively;[25] most others are designated unassigned recipients (UR) and effectively exempted from the work test. A number of specific procedures, discussed further below, govern who is chosen for active status. The proportion of registrants put through all those processes can be used to estimate the proportion on active status, which in turn estimates obligation for the office.[26]

All the factors were measured for the twenty-two New York offices, and the data were put into a computer. The factors were then pitted against each other in explaining the performance indictators using correlation and regression methods. What these methods do is look at variation in each explanatory factor across the twenty-two offices and measure how closely it matches corresponding variation in each of the performance indicators. The factors that vary most nearly in step with performance are deemed to have had the greatest influence on it. That strategy makes a virtue out of the discretionary nature of WIN. Staff largely control how many clients they obligate to participate and how they serve them, and the differences should affect performance.

Overall, the results dramatize the crucial role of public authority in achieving welfare work. Table 5 shows how the factors stacked up in explaining the five performance terms.[27] On average, obligation is the strongest, though its importance varies from term to term. It matters most for placing clients in jobs and getting them to stay there for thirty days; those were the kinds of performance, the interviews also suggested, where pressure on clients by staff had the most effect. Obligation is less important for obtained placements and working registrants, probably because here clients are getting jobs on their own or keeping them beyond thirty days; therefore, labor market conditions matter more than the suasions of the WIN office.

But notice that in the two latter cases the bureaucratic factor ranks first or second, taking over much of obligation's leading role.

TABLE 5
Rank of Factors in Explaining WIN Performance, New York State WIN Offices, Fiscal 1979

	Obligation Factor	*Services Factor*	*Bureaucratic Factor*	*Demographic Factor*	*Labor Market Factor*	*Percent of variation explained*
Total job entries/ registrants	2	4	3	1	5	91
Placed entries/ registrants	1	3	5	2	4	67
Obtained entries/ registrants	3	5	1	4	2	93
Working registrants/ registrants	5	3	2	4	1	80
Retention rate	1	2	4	3	5	62
Average	2.4	3.4	3.0	2.8	3.4	79

NOTE: The entries in each row show how the indicated factors ranked in explaining variation across the offices in the performance measure to the left. The bottom row shows the average rank for each factor for all five performance terms. The last column to the right shows the share of the total variation in each of the performance measures accounted for by all five factors together.

SOURCE: Lawrence M. Mead, "Expectations and Welfare Work: WIN in New York State," *Polity*, vol. 18, no. 2 (Winter 1985), table 4.

The reason staff resources matter for obtained entries is probably that a lot of staff activity in an office convinces clients that the work test is serious, so many of them get jobs on their own. The results confirm that welfare work is a political question much more than an economic one. Whether recipients work is determined mainly by factors policymakers can control. Many welfare people will work if government seriously expects them to. Social and economic conditions are important too, but on balance less so.

The obligation factor was powerful because the administrative processes that led to participation were themselves strongly tied to performance. In New York City each client placed in training or job-readiness activities was worth *more* than one additional job entry to the office. Conversely, the more clients put in inactive status (UR), the worse an office performed.

Surprisingly, the procedures for adjudicating and sanctioning clients for noncooperation proved to be weakly or negatively linked to performance, even though they might seem to embody WIN's authority. Overall, the more registrants an office proceeded against in this formal way, the *worse* it performed. However, two explanations sustaining the role of authority emerged from the interviews. One was that the analysis was done for years when, as mentioned earlier, WIN's sanctions had been undercut by court decisions. That caused even some effective offices to deemphasize sanctions, weakening their tie to performance. The other reason was that formal authority was not the best way to levy work expectations. The interviews made clear that the best way to convey obligations was *informally*, earlier in the administrative process. If clients realized when they first entered WIN that the work obligation was serious, they rarely needed discipline later.

The services an office preferred were weakly tied to performance, confirming other research that no one service in WIN is much better than another. But at the same time the total number or proportion of clients assigned to services had a tremendous payoff. The interviews suggested the key to the puzzle: The main thing the services convey is not skills but work obligation. To be assigned to any of those activities involves an obligation to participate regularly, and that is what motivates people to work. WIN's services have much less impact than the expectations conveyed *through* them.

These findings apply, strictly speaking, only to New York State. They might not hold entirely for other states or the nation.[28] While the New York offices were fairly representative of WIN offices nationally, New York WIN was below average in both work obligations and performance (the state ranked fifth lowest among the states in job entry performance in 1979, though above average in retention rate).[29] That is one reason obligations explained performance variations within the state so powerfully. Offices with higher participation rates than others realized large gains.

Work obligations seem most important in WIN *at the margin*. At the low levels of expectations usual in WIN today, nothing can improve performance like higher participation. But if participation rose, at some point declining returns would set in. At that point WIN would face tougher limitations from its economic environment than it does now. Efforts to train the unskilled or create jobs for them would then be more necessary than they seem to be at present.

A problem with work expectations is that this factor was strongly associated with several of the others. Offices with strong oligations more often than not also had a lot of staff resources, many job-ready clients, and favorable labor markets. Conversely, offices weak in expectations tended to be undermanned and to have less placeable clients and worse job markets. The first kind of office tended to be found outside the center city, the second inside. Maybe, then, the degree of obligation was not independently chosen. Maybe the successful offices were demanding only because they had the staff to be, and they knew their clients could get jobs. Maybe the less successful failed to expect much because they saw the futility of doing so.

The interviews suggested, nevertheless, that obligations were substantially independent. The demanding and undemanding offices were actually quite diverse. The first group included some urban offices, the second some suburban and rural ones. Whether an office was demanding was no simple reflex of its environment but rather a *response to* that environment, especially by the office manager. The demanding offices were those that decided to confront the welfare culture's ambivalence about work, the passive ones those that took it as a given.

Perhaps the most important thing the results do not show is effects over time. While the degree of work obligation clearly affects welfare work at a given moment, what would the impact be—on the recipient, on work and dependency levels—over several years? Would a recipient subject to work requirements work more consistently after leaving welfare, or relapse into the pattern of irregular work that is usual now? Definite answers would require a longitudinal social experiment akin to the national supported work demonstration or the income maintenance experiments. While the results of those studies suggested the role that public standards might have in work, neither was designed to address that question. A study of AFDC workfare now under way is likely to yield the best information yet on the impact of firmer work requirements. But further experimentation may well be necessary.[30]

The interviews clarified how offices that performed well, relative to their environment, used their administrative procedures to impress work expectations on their clients. To the staff of these offices the processes were not just busy work; they were used purposively to convey to recipients that work was expected. It was the less effective offices that went through the motions passively, and hence to little effect.

When an effective office first registered recipients in the program, it gave greatest stress to the obligations they faced, in part to counteract the contrary messages they might have received from welfare. The lower-performing offices more often let those messages stand. The registrants next underwent appraisal, meaning a review of their work history and skills by WIN staff. An employability plan was drawn up stating the employment goal for the client and the steps both he and the program would take to reach it (the program would typically promise child care and perhaps training). In the higher-performing offices the plan was often taken seriously, almost as a contract stating the mutual obligations of client and staff. In the lower-performing ones it was usually downplayed as paperwork.

Next, the office faced its major decision: Which of the registrants would participate actively in WIN? Typically staff would make active the clients they believed were placeable, hence likely to yield job entries for the office. Registrants could participate only if the social service staff attested that they had been provided with child care and other necessary services, a process known as certification. The numbers show that the more clients an office certifies, the better it performs. Staff themselves tend to regard certification as the real work test, since only the active registrants face any real pressure to work.

Certification required effort from WIN staff to arrange support services for the clients, then effort to place them or get them ready to work. The mark of the high-performing offices was that they nevertheless certified widely. They regarded a wide range of clients as employable, excepting only those with "impassable" barriers to work as unemployable. These offices rejected the conventional wisdom in employment programs, that the way to perform well was to "cream," that is, work only with the most job-ready registrants. If they had only creamed, they could not have raised participation very high. Nor could they have created the ethos—essential to their success—that work was the norm for the office, to be demanded in principle of every registrant.

The lower-performing offices, in contrast, certified many fewer registrants. They defined the employable more narrowly, the unemployable more broadly. Whereas the better offices made a point of certifying troublesome or unmotivated clients, just to insist on the work obligation, the weaker offices would often let them off. Said one employment worker, "If they don't want to work . . . there's no sense fighting with them." The note of fatalism was characteristic of these offices.

Most of the certified registrants were put in job placement. The employment staff sent them out to interview for available jobs. The effective offices worked hard to find a client a job with good pay, working conditions, and prospects. But if the client did not find a preferred job, the offices would press him or her to take "any" legal job, even a menial one. That, they believed, was the "bottom line" in WIN. Continued unemployment would not discharge the work obligation connected to welfare. Said one social service administrator, "The most menial job is no job" at all.

The weaker offices made less attempt to tailor the job to the client, but they were also more loath to "push clients up against the wall" about accepting lesser jobs. They were deterred by the "resentment" many clients felt at having to take jobs "beneath" them. They doubted it was "fair" to make them accept "just any job," for instance "washing dishes" or "cleaning toilets." If these jobs were all they could get, they were "better off on welfare." Such comments reflect a mild view of the work obligation. Admitted one office manager, "We certainly don't want to force them to work." But the result was less success in moving clients into jobs.

Active clients not ready for job placement were usually put in some form of training or job preparation, officially called components. The ineffective offices often preferred components that made light demands on either the clients or themselves, for example classroom instruction in office skills. That kind of training, much emphasized in the early days of WIN, took clients away to separate training agencies and spared WIN staff having to interact with them.

The demanding offices, in contrast, favored components that allowed them to work with clients intensively.[31] They often emphasized intensive employment services (IES), a form of counseling where clients would meet with employment staff on a daily basis, then go out on job interviews and report back. This allowed the staff to convey work expectations personally, impress constructive attitudes on the clients, and monitor them closely. The staff sought, by their own energy and commitment, to energize the recipients to take work seriously.

Another strategy was group job hunting, sometimes known as job clubs, where groups of clients would meet to discuss their problems and prospects, then support each other while seeking work. Job clubs were often surprisingly effective at moving recipients into jobs. The main reason was that the groups themselves levied work expectations in a strong but positive way. The clients, as fellow unemployed, were sympathetic to each other's problems, but they also brought "peer pressure" to bear in favor of "positive attitudes" toward work. They enforced on *each other* the work expectations that they had difficulty living up to themselves. Clients would often accept work demands from other clients that they resisted if made by WIN staff.[32] It is "hard for us to tell them," one employment worker said, what they tell each other. Thus, the groups helped solve, but also dramatized, the authority problem in WIN.

The best way to exercise authority in WIN was informally, by making expectations clear to clients early in the administrative routine. To "throw the book" at recipients through sanctions indicated the *breakdown* of authority rather than its exercise. At the same time most of the effective offices said they were quite willing to sanction if they had to. They were watchful for "professional welfare people" who would "beat the system" unless taken to task. That attitude usually deterred noncooperation and foreclosed the need to adjudicate. The less effective staffs felt sanctions were not "productive," to be invoked only as a "last resort." But the result was, they admitted, that they often had to "bargain" with clients over compliance. They ended up sanctioning more than the less permissive offices.

The key to effective adjudication was to get across that the office would "follow through" *automatically* if clients failed to co-operate. Ideally, from the moment recipients entered the program, they confronted standards that were not in question. To minimize discretion actually threw responsibility on the clients and gave them control. It established a direct connection between how they behaved and the treatment they were given. That contrasted sharply with the lives many of them had lived, in which authority figures often had not set standards consistently.

While administrative processes were the key to communicating work obligation in WIN, or failing to, staff in the effective and ineffective offices also had distinctive styles of interacting verbally with the clients. The first group sought to exercise authority over clients, the second to avoid it.[33] The stronger staff were blunt about expressing obligations to recipients. WIN was "mandatory," they said, and it meant "work." They rejected "bleeding heart, living room liberals" or "suzie social workers" who tried to shield their clients from the labor market. The less effective staff were much more passive. They saw themselves in a "helping" role, offering "services" and not "hassle" to recipients. They declined the role of "policemen" enforcing work. They wanted to provide help to "human beings" without making demands. Said one social service worker, "pleasant professionalism should be the tone." "We don't want them to feel they're on welfare." Far from obligating the clients, these staff people felt they bore the onus to "find them a job."

Yet surprisingly the demanding staff were usually more positive toward the recipients. They imposed expectations because they thought the clients actually could meet them. "All of us have something to offer the job market" was the credo of one forceful social service worker. These staff members intended their demands to motivate the clients, not defeat them. When Wilbur Mills first introduced the work test in 1967, he said he was trying to be "rough in a constructive manner."[34] That was very much the style of the more effective staff. The lesser staff were usually more negative toward their clients as well as more passive. To them, the recipients were "walking wounded" of whom little could be expected. Some responded with "compassion," but others felt hostility, contemning in the clients a life-style to which they, because of their own disadvantages, felt all too close. When WIN fails to expect work of recipients, the reasons are seldom affirming.

The two groups of staff disagreed about what it meant to help the welfare poor. The effective staff tended to identify with the strength of recipients, the ineffective with their weakness. The demanding staff saw in their clients people who, if they only overcame certain problems, could be full-fledged members of society. They refused to "condescend" to them with a "double standard" about work. Recipients should meet the "same social obligations" as the staff did by coming to work every day. Some of these workers claimed to "level" and "talk turkey" with clients about their obligations as equals. The more passive staff saw only that the recipients were "terribly, terribly limited." You had to "put yourself in the person's position" and say, "There but for the grace of God go you."

All the staff "sold" work to recipients mainly by stressing the practical advantages—more income and an end to hassles with WIN and welfare. The more demanding staff, however, also made moral appeals in which they personally believed. Work, they felt, was good for people, not just a source of income. It expressed a person's "integrity" and "dignity," and it brought "self-respect." It put an end to the welfare stigma even if a mother, while working, still needed some assistance to support her family. The more passive staff seldom made such arguments, often because they did not believe in them. To them the work obligation was "negative," not positive. They might enforce it, but they often attributed it to distant "federal requirements."

In the comments of the effective staff could be discerned the civic approach to social policy that emerged during the welfare reform debates. Welfare was a "two-way street," these workers told their clients. Employment was "part of the package" along with support. To discharge the work obligation was also the mark of the "citizen." To work made you the equal of other Americans, even if they were making more money. One social service worker put it most graphically: Recipients who worked could "pay taxes and bitch about the government like everybody else." Those staff workers, like the public, supported welfare work not so much to save money as to remove the shame of dependency. "At least they are functioning," said one social service manager. "They're not just sitting at home having babies."

Behind those different styles stood different perceptions of two central issues in welfare work: client motivation and the availability of jobs. The effective WIN staff mostly believed that motivation was a problem, so they tried to provide "direction." Said one office manager, expressing a common sentiment, "We try to lead 'em to work, then we push 'em." The lesser staff more often took the motivation of clients as a given. To "elicit their cooperation" was the goal, not to tell them what to do. But given the reluctance of many recipients to accept available jobs, that stance less often led to work.

The better WIN staff also believed work was available. They could always find some kind of job for most of their clients, they insisted, even if they had to go down to the "corner gas station" and drum up the openings themselves. The less effective workers more often said jobs were lacking, though they usually meant "good" jobs that recipients wanted to take. Only a very few staff said *no* jobs were available. On the firing line, as in Washington, the real issue in welfare work is not whether there are jobs but whether recipients should have to take them.

Obligation and Affirmation

The conclusion of these studies is clear. To overcome nonwork, WIN offices must be demanding of clients. They must also be affirming. And there is no contradiction. Demands themselves are an affirmation to the clients that they actually can realize mainstream norms like work. There is no point of expecting things of people that they cannot do.

One office in New York especially dramatized the point. The office, traditionally a low performer, had been accustomed to working with few registrants, and thus placing few. Under pressure to improve it was forced to adopt as more authoritative style. The staff instituted job clubs and certified many unassigned registrants who had never participated in WIN before. "We stopped listening to all the problems," one worker reported. The new approach was to "tell [clients] they are capable, responsible people with a whole lot to offer." Many clients previously deemed unemployable began going to work. They also reacted "very positively" to the demands made upon them. At last they were getting some attention from the program. WIN was helping them achieve employment, as they always wanted. That gave them a kind of standing, and a kind of hope, which benefits without obligations never could.

One moral is that generalizing about helping the poor is treacherous. Rigid obligations can harm the vulnerable, but so can the lack of them. Policymakers must above all really wish to help the poor and do what that requires. Today it requires setting standards. But due to political conventions, politicians tend to prefer undemanding programs and to regard the style of the effective WIN offices as punitive. Just for that reason standards, not solicitude, are likely to be the scarce commodity in federal policy. When programs like WIN manage nevertheless to assert obligations, they provide recipients a resource that is as vital to them as income.

8

Why Washington Has Not Set Standards

THERE are federal programs or policies in all the areas where standards seem most necessary to improve functioning—employment, education, crime—but they set few, if any, standards themselves. The work tests on the books are profoundly halfhearted, and in the other areas Washington has deferred almost entirely to local authorities. Federal politicians increasingly recognize that programs should set standards, yet the government seldom acts to institute them.

The reluctance to obligate is deep-seated. Washington's powers to regulate in the social area are more limited than they appear. The incentives of federal politicians are simply to subsidize salient interests; to control them in any way has been quite secondary. The way policy analysts as well as politicians approach social programs tends to emphasize their benefits, not the powers they might have to obligate recipients. Government is seen predominantly as a distributor of benefits to deserving groups, not as an authority that might govern them for larger social ends. The *scale* of government is an issue over which parties contend. The permissive *character* of the regime passes almost unnoticed.

Nevertheless, there are some causes for which federal authority has mobilized decisively. To emancipate the slaves, to tame the excesses of big business, and, most recently, to guarantee more equal rights to black Americans, Washington has not feared to force change on the nation. The interesting question is how the development of functioning standards for the disadvantaged could become such a cause.

The Constitution

The most fundamental limitation on federal authority in social policy is constitutional. Washington simply lacks the power to impose work or comparable requirements on individual citizens directly. The powers given to Congress in Article I, section 8, of the Constitution are those of an eighteenth-century regime. They allow Washington to tax and borrow money, regulate commerce and the money supply, run a post office and a military. Those are the only purposes for which the government can directly coerce its citizens. The more general "police power," to regulate for broader public purposes, rests with the states. The federal powers make no direct provision for what we now call social policy—programs in welfare, health, education, housing, and so on. Nor have the most noted expansions of federal authority changed the situation. Since the 1930s the federal courts have forced the states to abide by most of the protections specified in the Bill of Rights, and the federal tax and interstate commerce powers have been interpreted broadly enough to allow Washington to regulate the economy for virtually any purpose. Neither development empowers the government to run social programs or use them to set standards like work tests.

Instead, social policy rests largely on the "spending power," the authority given Congress in Article 1, section 8, paragraph 1, to tax and spend to "provide for the . . . general welfare." The courts have held that the spending may be for virtually any purpose, not only those specified in the rest of section 8. That has empowered Washington to do many more things by spending money than it can by mandates. Specifically it can institute benefit programs run either under its own authority, like Social Security, or through grants to state authorities, like AFDC.

The courts have also held that the government can attach virtually any conditions to its spending. Stipulations such as the work test are binding as strings tied to federal grants. States must enforce them and recipients must obey them as the price of receiving federal benefits.[1] Both states and recipients are viewed legally as contractors of Washington. They need not accept the grants, but neither may they demand them without conditions. That doctrine has made the government virtually sovereign, at least in legal terms, within the reach of the grant system. Agencies, firms, or individuals that accept its funding may have to adhere to stipulations stretching much beyond what federal authorities could demand without paying money. In recent years the regulations have included civil rights, affirmative action, and environmental rules that have little directly to do with the programs themselves.[2]

This strong constitutional position has meant that requirements like work tests are difficult to challenge in court. Federal judges have disallowed some restrictions on welfare on constitutional grounds, but they have never admitted the claim of some rights advocates that welfare or other social benefits are entitlements under the Constitution. The Supreme Court stated in 1976 that "Welfare benefits are not a fundamental right, and neither the State nor Federal Government is under any sort of constitutional obligation to guarantee minimum levels of support." The government may also regulate the beneficiaries in return for support, provided civil liberties are not infringed.[3] Consequently, according to government lawyers, federal work requirements have never faced a serious constitutional challenge. Usually all opponents can claim is that such regulations are more stringent than allowed under the Social Security Act, the basis of welfare law.[4] The issues in most welfare litigation are thus statutory, not constitutional. That means issues like work tests are political much more than legal. Legislatures decide them, not judges.

Nevertheless, the dependance of work or similar requirements on the spending power also entails serious weaknesses. Such stipulations are binding only on parties that have first received something from the government. Washington must purchase their concurrence and cannot simply demand it. Since benefits must come first, attempts to enforce the rules assume a negative cast, undermining implementation. The government also has no authority over recipients prepared to give up their benefits. YIEPP, the experimental youth program mentioned earlier, found that low-paid government jobs did not suffice to persuade dropouts to accept a school obligation. To be effective, requirements must be linked to income to which the recipients have no alternative, and that may require limiting their recourse to other programs or the underground economy, which is difficult to do.

Furthermore, grant programs usually govern recipients only indirectly, through the states. While Washington probably could run all its own social programs, most federal welfare and service programs operate through grants to state and local agencies. The government, therefore, can obligate recipients only indirectly, by getting these agencies to enforce federal rules. Since they seldom comply completely, federal authority is weakened.

Most important, what the courts uphold is, from a political perspective, too narrow a definition of the constitutional. What is legal may still lack the legitimacy to be enforced. In economic affairs, for example, the government's power to regulate widely has been legally unquestioned since the New Deal. Since 1887 Congress has created a large number of agencies, resting mainly on the commerce clause, with the power to control prices, other policies, and competition in many industries. While the price and competition rules have benefited some industries, recent health and environmental regulations have been very costly for business. The economic agencies have a power to compel without giving direct benefits that the social agencies lack. Yet many businessmen have never accepted their authority. Industry petitions to Congress, lawsuits against regulations, and plain noncompliance have seriously impeded the implementation of many rules. The attempt of the Reagan Administration to roll back many of these programs indicates that antigovernment feeling is very much alive among business men and conservatives. In that larger political sense a constitutional problem in regulation persists.[5] How much less effective must be social rules linked to grants, since federal authority is more indirect?

Politics

Even without constitutional difficulties, however, federal programs would tend to be benefit-oriented for political reasons. The federal government encounters special political problems because it is not very visible to the average voter. Its most critical functions lie in national security and economic management, while basic public services are vested in state and local government. Unless they go to a Social Security office or are audited by the IRS, most Americans never meet a *federal* official; even the Postal Service, which used to be federal, is now a separate corporation. Therefore federal politicians, Martha Derthick has said, have a special need "to provide benefits to voters for which credit may be claimed."[6] They do so largely by distributing economic advantages to a wide range of interests. The government may provide few essential services, but it has ample power to tax, spend, and regulate in favor of this or that group, industry, region, or class.

Programs are benefit-oriented, as well, because of the pluralist structure of the government. The Founders decided to disperse power among the branches of the federal government, and between it and states and localities, rather than concentrating authority in the hands of a governing elite, the pattern in other modern regimes. The idea, James Madison wrote, was to frustrate "factions" by preventing any one of them from capturing a controlling position. In practice, instead of checking each other, interest groups have come to colonize different parts of the government. Each has its own programs and subsidies, and leading estates—Labor, Commerce, and Agriculture—have whole departments dedicated to their interests. In much of federal domestic policy the public interest is identified with serving group claims.[7]

The expansion of benefit programs in the last fifty years has extended distributive politics to a new level. The welfare state has given rise to a whole new set of interests dependent on government: the social welfare staffs, education and training institutions, and other organizations that Washngton pays to deliver benefits. The programs that tie those interests to government, David Stockman has written, constitute a "social pork barrel" alongside older subsidies like water projects and farm programs. The benefits have also given federal politicians for the first time a way to subsidize much of the general population. According to a recent survey, a startling 31 percent of all Americans and 47 percent of all households are now recipients of one or another federal benefit program.[8]

Congressmen find that they can use these programs to court their districts and stay in office even if they differ politically from most of their constituents. Their staffs engage in "casework," or helping voters work out problems getting benefits from the bureaucracy. There is constant pressure to expand eligibility for popular programs like Social Security or Disability, so they can serve more voters. Some analysts say these new resources may be one reason why incumbent Congressmen have become more secure than they used to be. There are fewer marginal House seats than before 1960, and in each election over 90 percent of House members who stand are returned.[9]

The power of benefit politics was dramatized during the welfare reform period, when proposals for guaranteed income or work tests were often debated alongside more routine measures to increase Social Security and other benefits. The same Congressmen who opposed welfare reform, from either the left or the right, usually scrambled to endorse the Social Security increases, and even to demand greater ones. Middle-class Americans, not only the poor, now demand many perquisites from government, and their representatives know their survival depends on complying.

The way the parties approach federal policy is another force for permissive government. The parties are more inclined to differ over the extent of government than over its nature. In part that reflects the marginal role of Washington in domestic governance. If the central government were responsible for essential public services, the scope of its responsibilities would be fairly clear. Parties would differ over the philosophy, management, and details of government, as they most often do in Europe. Without a clearly defined federal role, the scope of federal programming became a natural focus of partisan differences.

The division, furthermore, has been over *economic* policy much more than social. Much of Great Society policymaking was bipartisan, and Republicans have played an important role in expanding the various benefit programs. The main partisan dispute has been over public intervention in the private economy, especially through taxes and regulation. Most Democrats believe business will not serve the public interest without government control over harmful pricing, selling, employment, and pollution practices, while most Republicans are readier to trust the free market. The division dates mainly from the New Deal and is in many ways outmoded. Some newer issues, such as the environment, do not seriously allow government the option of doing nothing. The real issue in policymaking today is usually *what* govenment will do, not whether. Today, furthermore, policymakers more often have to manage existing programs than debate proposals for new ones. As long as the partisan division persists, however, questions about the legitimacy of policy will bedevil efforts to improve it. Recent Reagan Administration efforts to eliminate many programs have given new life to this long-standing struggle.

One consequence of partisanship is that federal politicians advance proposals in social policy, not really to solve social problems, but to carry on the primal struggle over the *economic* organization of society. Liberals and most Democrats use problems like poverty or unemployment to prove that the private economy cannot guarantee income or jobs without greater government involvement. Conservatives and most Republicans use the same problems to demonstrate that earlier interventions have failed and that taxes and regulations must be reduced. Because both sides are really talking about economic policy, neither finds it easy to address behavioral problems like family breakup, nonwork, or crime, none of which has any direct connection to the scope of economic controls.[10] Given their focus on the scale of government, both sides are understandably skeptical about proposals for requirements like work tests. Many liberals fear that they will be made a substitute for the real necessity, an expansion of the public sector. Some conservatives fear they would tend to legitimize welfare, thus deflecting efforts to reduce or eliminate it.

The patterns of federal politics all conspire to make Washington, in the most literal sense, the servant and not the master of its people. All that most Americans directly know of the government is the stream of benefits and other advantages flowing from federal programs. What Washington expects from most people in return is only the income tax, and that is extracted as unobtrusively as possible through the withholding system. So Americans rarely think of the federal government as an authority at all, but rather as a willing benefactor that funds good things. To them, government must above all be "responsive."[11] A regime that must always buy support from its constituents finds it difficult to be anything else.

Such a government can be faulted for serving no higher vision of the public good than group benefit. That is the gist of Theodore Lowi's criticism:

> Interest-group liberalism possesses the mentality of . . . universalized ticket-fixing. Destroy privilege by universalizing it. Reduce conflict by yielding to it. Redistribute power by the maxim of each according to his claim. Purchase support for the regime by reserving an official place for every major structure of power.

But Lowi's main objection is simply that government so often serves business and other narrow interests rather than broader popular ones. He hardly questions the conventional view of Washington as a fount of benefits. He simply wants them to flow more widely.[12]

In social policy the greater problem is that so little in the federal tradition equips the government to demand things from ordinary people in exchange for benefits. With some difficulty Washington can regulate business, but it has hardly attempted to uphold the standards for work, law-abidingness, and other civilities that undergird everyday society. Even to see the problem requires a perspective like George Will's, drawn from European political theory, with its much greater concern for public authority:

> [M]odern liberalism . . . has given us government that . . . is big but not strong; fat but flabby; capable of giving but not leading. It is invertebrate government, a servile state . . . . But a government obsessed with responsiveness is incapable of leadership. Leadership is, among other things, the ability to inflict pain and get away with it—short-term pain for long-term gain. . . . The one thing we do not have is strong government.[13]

For such a system the attempt to use programs to enforce social order must always cut against the grain.

Policy Analysis

Another reason for permissive programs is the way policy analysts tend to approach social problems in Washington.[14] The methods of analysis, most of them drawn from economics, seem to have shaped themselves to the demands of pluralist politics. Like politicians, analysts tend to see government as a distributor of benefits to specific groups or classes, not as an authority that might govern society for larger ends.

"Policy analysts" in Washington mean staff who study policy issues and how to resolve them for political executives in the bureaucracy or for Congressmen on Capitol Hill. Since 1960 thousands of analysts have joined the government, working either directly for it or for the think tanks or universities doing government studies under contract.[15] While decisions ultimately rest with the politicians, the analytic class has increasingly shaped the choices, especially in areas like social policy where there has been rapid innovation.

Contrary to conservative fears of a "new class," that influence has not always favored larger government. While social policy experts helped develop the Great Society programs, evaluations done by analysts also revealed the shortcomings of those efforts. Analysts in the Defense Department criticized some weapons systems as unnecessary, and regulatory economists called for less government control over the energy, transportation, communications, and securities industries, recommendations that were largely carried out in the 1970s.[16]

The main influence of the analysts, rather, has been to entrench the view that government distributes resources without governing. Most federal analysts have been economists by training or in the methods they use.[17] In several respects the economic outlook emphasizes the benefits that programs give; it downplays the political and adminisrative aspects of policy that are uppermost in any attempt to enforce requirements like work.

Such standards presuppose that society can state a preference for certain behavior by the dependent and enforce it. Economics as a science, however, interprets society as a market place of individuals interacting only for personal advantage. The preferences they seek to realize are usually viewed as arbitrary, falling outside analysis. Much of economics consists of methods for choosing optimally among means *after* the goals have been set. Economists tend to treat the preferences of government as no less arbitrary. In economic theory government must undertake certain tasks, such as the prevention of monopoly and pollution, that arise from imperfections in the market place. But its role is circumscribed. Anything further that it does, such as pay social benefits, either is unjustified in economic terms or expresses preferences that are beyond discussion.[18]

This agnostic view of preferences does not equip government economists to question the range of claims that outside interests press upon Washington. Unless the demands clearly offend the few missions economists specify for government, they usually see their role as staffing out ways to realize the goals rather than judging them. That attitude reinforces the tendency of a pluralist government to try to serve all claims. Without a comprehensive public ethics, most policy analysts are unable—at least as analysts—either to affirm or deny the kind of noneconomic values expressed in social standards like work tests.

Economists tend to view government, not as an authority *over* society, but as one actor among many *within* it. Government is richer and more powerful than private individuals, but it too interacts with others in a search for mutual benefit. That vision causes analysts to imagine government as obtaining its ends through manipulation rather than the exertion of authority. Through penalties and rewards, government will lead individuals to serve public purposes. Since self-seeking motivation is assumed, there is no way within economics to propose or explain behavior, such as voluntary tax payment, that serves society's interests instead of the individual's. But virtuous action of just that kind is indispensable if work and other civilities are to be sustained.

Economists tend to think that the main problems in federal policy and administration can be solved by the adroit use of incentives. Rather than try to regulate industries that could be competitive, such as airlines, deregulate them and let the market direct them to serving the public good. Rather than levy regulations against pollution that are hard to enforce, tax discharges or pay firms not to pollute, so they have an incentive to clean up. Rather than serve the poor through training and employment programs that are hard to implement, give them cash or vouchers so they can buy the services they want on their own. Community Action was also an incentives strategy in a way, since it organized the poor to bring pressure on local agencies for services themselves, without depending on inefficient bureaucratic hierarchies stretching from Washington. The popularity of those ideas among analysts explains why experiments in incentives-oriented reform have been implemented or studied in every area of social policy since the late 1960s.[19]

But some behaviors that government needs from individuals, such as tax payment and low-wage work, can never be made to serve their personal interests, at least in a narrow economic sense. Therefore they must be enforced bureaucratically. There is no alternative to the difficult process of building up, in tandem, the legitimacy of requirements and their administrative enforcement. It is a kind of policy development for which most economists have little sympathy. The disciplines of law and public administration in this respect have much more to offer, but analysts from these backgrounds have been crowded out of the senior government social planning positions by economists.

The neglect of administrative structure was dramatized by the perfunctory attention given to bureaucratic arrangements in the drafting of welfare reform. The framers of both the Nixon and the Carter reform plans gave exhaustive attention to the eligibility and benefit structures and the work incentives that would supposedly flow from them. How eligibility, payments, and work requirements would actually be administered was thought through much less fully. The initial thinking for FAP was entrusted to Richard P. Nathan, a political scientist, and a committee of experts and officials with long experience in welfare administration. But the detailed planning fell into the hands of HEW economists. Nathan feared that their relative inattention to administrative problems like fraud and abuse would undermine the credibility of the plan in Congress, and so it did. "For too long," he later testified, "a purist kind of economic thinking has dominated in HEW," to the detriment of reform itself.[20]

Another, subtler effect of economic analysis is to downplay the less tangible, attitudinal and political dimensions of social problems. Most analysts prefer to deal with the material dimensions, because these are the only ones that can easily be measured for inclusion in the kind of quantitative analyses economists prefer. Much of economic analysis in social policy consists of relating measurable problems like poverty or dependency to putative causes that are also measurable. The causal variables usually must be confined to characteristics of people on which the government regularly collects statistics, for example age, sex, race, income, years of education, and so on. "Softer" determinants, such as the attitudes of the poor and political or administrative influences, tend to be omitted because they seldom are measured.[21]

In consequence economic analysis tends to reinforce the sociological ideology that has dominated federal social policy-making. The measurable forces that surround the poor, such as inadequate income, education, or employment, are presumed to shape their behavior in some irresistable way. Both the clients and the influences upon them tend to become abstractions, connected only statistically. The much more concrete ways the dependent are governed, or not governed, by benefit programs almost always fall outside the analysis.

Such analyses easily seem academic and unreal to those who actually administer social benefits. Seen from outside Washington, Arnold Meltsner says, federal analysts often appear to operate in a "protective cocoon of computers, models, and statistical regressions" out of touch with reality. When Representative Martha Griffiths made her own inquiry into the welfare problem, she was careful to hold hearings among welfare administrators in the field.

"[T]he farther you get from Washington and HEW," she remarked, "the more commonsense everybody has who is connected with this thing."[22]

Economists realize the behavioral dilemmas in social policy, but they usually play down regulative solutions. They prefer to see welfare nonwork, for instance, not as a moral issue but as a "technical problem" to be solved by finding just the right mix of income and work incentives for the dependent. The economic style eschews moral upset at such abuses, and it deprecates the desire simply to forbid them. When economists testified in the welfare hearings, their detachment sometimes infuriated conservative Congressmen. One HEW spokesman, for example, dismissed the low number of welfare clients sanctioned for noncooperation in WIN as a "statistical" anomaly. Russell Long exploded: "Labor says, there is the job, there is the training slot. The [recipient] said, I am not going to work. Now you continue him on welfare anyway. What in the devil is statistical about that?"[23]

Economic analysis makes it difficult to imagine *transferring* some of the responsibility for coping from government to its recipients, the vital step in enforcing work or other civilities. In economic modeling the problem under study is termed the "dependent" term, and the causes of it, "independent" terms—statistical conventions that candidly express the political assumptions of the analysis. People suffering poverty or dependency are understood as the passive products of the forces acting upon them, one of which is government benefits. One early "systems analysis" of welfare imagined that even intangible satisfactions such as "individual fulfillment and social adjustment" could be produced by the detached manipulation of various economic and cultural forces by government.[24] Tacitly the initiative is left with government to provide some new benefit, and to keep trying new benefits, until something is found to which the subjects respond. Such models ratify the sociological presumption that government is an econcomizer that must adjust to the needs of the recipients, not vice versa.

But Great Society education and training programs based on that kind of analysis showed only slight impact on the skills or behavior of their recipients. This led to soul-searching in the analytic community. Admitted one welfare economist:

> I . . . do not know quite what to make of this, but it seems to be true in area after area . . . that when we study, econometrically and statis-

> tically, the effects of some policy instrument on some dependent variable, the result is that it does not make any difference. . . . It may be true that nothing makes a difference, or it may not be true, for our measures may be bad, our theories may be bad, our specification of relationships may be bad.[25]

The problem was most likely the passive role assigned to the recipient. The dependent were expected to react to government benefits in self-seeking ways but not to conform to mainstream norms, such as work, simply because they were right. That expectation faithfully reflected economic psychology, but it blocked the idea, essential to effective government, that clients should actively help government realize its objectives.[26] The idea of responsibility *shared* between government and the individual is too complex to model easily. The recipient becomes an economizer alongside programs, an ally in solving the social problem, an independent and not just a dependent term.

At the dawn of the Great Society economic methods seemed to offer the promise of a true policy science, one that could link policy inputs to the achievement of key government objectives. Problems such as poverty or the work problems of the low-skilled could be overcome, it was believed, by discovering optimal combinations of benefits and services and transferring them to the needy.[27] In the early and mid-1960s, when the expert influence on programming was greatest, economists were not just impartial students of policy problems; they advocated an economic approach to policymaking.[28] With the failures of Great Society programs, however, policymakers have begun to turn, through benefit cuts and work and child support requirements, toward just the kind of authoritative, administrative solutions that lie outside economic analysis.

The eclipse of analysis is dramatized by the career of Daniel Moynihan, planner and politician. Moynihan, trained as a political scientist, had used economic methods for his report on the black family, and he praised the economic analysis that went into FAP, of which he was a drafter.[29] But he parted company with other experts over their political naïveté and refusal to confront the behavioral problems in welfare. Community Action, he believed, had aroused claim-making by the poor but had not truly helped them, much to the discredit of the antipoverty program.[30] As a Senator he found that the economists who drafted the Carter welfare plan were unwilling to recognize, let along address, the family and work problems that underlay dependency. Later he blamed the failure of the plan, not only on political ineptitude, but on the "dominance of economic models" in all the research and analysis behind reform:

> What happened during the development of PBJI is that the economists took over. The entire process got caught up with economic models of how people behave and an absolute absorption in the equations and marginal tax rates of how one fools around with earnings. . . . One must remember that they set up an incredible policymaking apparatus that produced nothing. . . . These bureaucrats were *idiot savants*—a term the French use to describe a witless person who exhibits skill in some limited field.[31]

The influence of economists reached its apogee in the Carter Administration. More Carter Cabinet appointees and their principal lieutenants were economists—21 percent—than in any previous Administration.[32] That was one reason why the Administration was very expert about its policymaking but, at the same time, passive, prone to serving all interests, and blind to the behavioral side of social problems. The Reagan Administration has launched an assault, not only on Democratic programs, but on the analytic style. The Reagan cuts have been justified mainly on ideological grounds, and Reagan welfare policy has stressed the enforcement of work and child support norms that planners previously neglected. Economic analysis has played a peripheral role except in technical areas like regulation. It is as if the Administration deliberately rejected the focus of economics on means in order to expose the questions of goals, of the proper limits of programming, which had been buried under layers of technical analysis in Washington.

Implementation

Further impediments to a more authoritative social policy arise from the trouble the government has in implementing social programs, especially when they try to couple benefits with requirements like work tests. The idea of mandating work or other standards from Washington supposes that the government can create a bureaucratic chain of command stretching from Washington down to the local offices where recipients are put to work. In fact the difficulties are immense. They stretch beyond the problems, considered earlier, that are peculiar to work programs.

Most federal domestic programs are carried out, not directly by Washington, but by means of grants that pay state and local authorities to provide the desired benefits or services. Large grant programs, including AFDC, began in the 1930s, but had fairly loose rules that allowed states to use the money for a wide range of purposes, much like revenue sharing programs today. During the Great Society the grant system was vastly expanded on the supposition that it could serve much more focused federal goals. Between 1960 and 1980 the number of federal grant programs grew from 132 to more than 500, and many of them were social benefits or services designed specifically to help the poor, disadvantaged, or nonwhite. In the same period spending for grants grew from $7 billion to $91 billion a year, a jump of more than four times even allowing for inflation, before falling 17 percent by 1982 because of the Reagan cuts.[33]

The states, however, have shown a tendency to bend those programs, like earlier ones, to their own ends. They use the money more to carry on existing state programs than to achieve federal objectives. Their inclination, especially in education and training programs, is to channel many of the benefits to white and better-off recipients whom Washington does not view as deprived.[34] That blunts the ability of federal officials to "target" their programs, leading to protracted quarrels between the states and the federal bureaucracy. States for their part resent the burdensome application and reporting paperwork that goes along with federal grants. Some observers say the frictions have virtually paralyzed the grant system. A simplified system may be needed, based on fewer, broader grants carrying fewer federal requirements.[35]

In those compliance battles the states have the resources to resist federal direction. They possess the administrative apparatus Washington needs to conduct domestic policy, and they do not view themselves as its subordinates. Unlike local governments in other countries, they antedate the federal government constitutionally and are not the creatures of it. Politically they can appeal to Congress against the compliance demands of federal officials. In consequence, the bureaucracy can rarely deploy its tough armory of fiscal sanctions against the states. In theory, states are supposed to enforce child support, provide family planning to recipients, reduce fraud and payment errors to specified levels, and certify at least 15 percent of WIN registrants, among other things, or face reductions in their federal AFDC funding. But in practice when officials invoke these penalities, Congress intervenes, causing negotiation and compromise. The story is similar with threats to cut off education funding to force school or university integration.[36]

The history of work enforcement is an object lesson in the trials of implementation through the grant system. Federal leaders have favored increased work by welfare recipients since at least 1962, when states were first given authority to set up welfare work programs. But few states acted on the offer. In 1967, when the WIN program was mandated, most states referred few recipients to it. Since 1971 when referrals were mandated, most states have required only small proportions of registrants to participate actively. Since 1981 the Reagan Administration has tried to enforce participation through workfare, but Congress has allowed it only as an option.

Federal politicians, whether in the Executive or Congress, have little incentive to worry about administrative problems because the public is little conscious of them. Publicity and political rewards come to them mainly from proposing or enacting new programs, not from managing or reforming old ones.[37] Policy analysts, besides the inattention to structure that stems from economic methods, have tended to look down on state and local government as less enlightened than federal. There is a story that whenever the drafters of the antipoverty program discussed the role of the states, "the name of the Alabama governor, George C. Wallace, would be mentioned and the discussion would promptly terminate."[38] That prejudice persists even though state governments have become considerably more modern, efficient, and progressive since 1960.[39]

When faced with administrative problems in programs, politicians tend to denounce the abuses to the press and public, while analysts propose incentives-oriented alternatives such as vouchers. The national distaste for bureaucracy as a means of social organization runs deep. The attraction of electoral or market mechanisms is that they offer choice. The voter can select a candidate, or the buyer a seller, then later make a different choice if the first fails to satisfy. There is no need for the sustained labor to improve a given hierarchy that bureaucratic statecraft requires.[40]

Federal authority is most often used, not to impose requirements like work on the dependent, but to keep state or local governments from doing so. Washington demands rights for its recipients much more than it imposes obligations. In federal income programs requirements for recipients such as work or child support are heavily outnumbered by protections. Under the AFDC law states may not deny aid to welfare mothers merely for illegitimacy, force recipients to accept family planning, give them assistance other than in cash in most instances, or tell them how to spend their money unless the welfare of other recipients is in danger. Under the Unemployment Insurance law there was until 1977 no federal work provision, but there are detailed stipulations mandating that "compensation shall not be denied" to claimants by states for such causes as pregnancy, preference for an approved training program over work, or refusal to accept work for a variety of reasons (e.g. the job is open only due to a strike, pays below the prevailing wage, or would forbid union membership).[41]

Like these legal rules, federal administration has usually been client-oriented and opposed to "moralism" by the state agencies running programs. Federal officials have also used administrative stipulations, such as requirements that states have merit-based personnel systems, to force states to raise civil service standards and rein in localities that restrict benefits, steps that in turn promote client-serving administration. In a rights-oriented political culture an entitlement approach to administration easily seems more value-free, less judgmental, than attempts to restrict benefits according to client behavior.[42] It is also easier to implement than authoritative policies, since recipients can be counted upon to bring local restrictions to the attention of federal administrators or courts, as they do not overly generous benefits.

Local authorities, then, can usually expect opposition, not support, from Washington in any effort to enforce standards on the recipients of federal benefits. That places them in a quandary: They need federal funds to afford the programs, but the money comes bearing libertarian conditions that make it harder to solve the social problems to which the programs are addressed. In education policy the dilemma has been that federal programs are supposed to elevate the skills of disadvantaged students, but the regulations accompanying them often get in the way. The rules emphasize the rights of minorities, women, the handicapped, and so on, and it is on these provisions—not performance standards—that compliance disputes have focused. James Coleman comments:

> [C]ontrol of a community's schools has been taken largely out of the community's hands by federal (and to a lesser extent state) intervention. Public schools have become an overregulated industry, with reg-

> ulations and mandates ranging from draconian desegregation to mainstreaming of emotionally disturbed children, to athletic activities that are blind to sex differences. It is in part these regulations . . . which are responsible for the slackening of academic demands and the breakdown of disciplinary climate that many public schools have experienced in recent years.[43]

Given the predilection of federal authority to undermine social standards in programs rather than uphold them, why not return welfare and other programs for the poor entirely to state and local control, the traditional conservative prescription? Those authorities could then levy work or other requirements on recipients free from the permissive rules and politics that seem inseparable from federal funding. The current drift of American social administration is certainly in that direction. Federal grants to states for law enforcement were ended in 1979, and the Reagan Administration originally proposed to phase out federal education and welfare programs as well. In employment, urban development, and social services, as well as education programs, the trend has been toward looser, revenue-sharing arrangements that relax federal controls on grant money. The grant programs, furthermore, have borne the brunt of the Reagan budget cuts.

However, there is little likelihood that the states could do without federal social spending, and as long as they receive this funding they will be subject to federal conditions. More important, what demands to make of recipients in return for support are such important questions that they must be decided federally. Thus, while greater state control of programs may be desirable, there is no alternative to building up the *federal* capacity to set social standards.

The Politics of Obligation

How might federal social authority increase? The Supreme Court might give the government more power to obligate recipients, independent of benefits, or to impose policy on the states. Some liberals say that the underclass and minorities will never be integrated until Washington asserts something more like sovereign power over subordinate authorities.[44] Stronger political parties might appear having the authority to implement truly national policies rather than just distribute benefits to constituency groups.[45] A less agnostic form of policy analysis might appear, in which analysts would be more able to take stands on questions of value and seriously contemplate authority and administration as tools of governance.[46]

None of these developments is likely. Recent Supreme Court decisions have left federal powers essentially unchanged.[47] The parties are weak and getting weaker, while interest groups grow in power in Washington. Recent failures of policy analysis, especially in economic policy, seem only to have increased the commitment of practitioners to economic methods.[48] Most of all, the changes are impolitic because they contradict the pluralist nature of federal politics. In different ways each would vest the authority to decide policy in a smaller range of interests than has access now. Those excluded would have the political resources to resist.

But fortunately such changes are probably not necessary. History shows that great expansions of federal authority can occur and have occurred through decisive shifts in public opinion, without changes in the balance of power within the political system. As a result of the Civil War, the Progressive and New Deal reform periods, and civil rights, Washington has fundamentally more power to regulate the states and private interests than it had at the Founding. That change came about even though it would be hard to say that power in federal politics is any more concentrated today than it was earlier. The national government must still bargain with groups, states, and other interests to decide what to do, but it has been given undoubted authority to act in areas related to equal rights and control of the economy. The mechanism seems to be, not political centralization, but the appeal of some national objectives to political culture. Certain goals come to seem so vital that a consensus forms that centralized power must be available to pursue them.

The added powers are largely the residue of what Mark Roelofs has called the "mythic" moments in American history. In normal times political influence is as dispersed as the Founders intended, and political energies seem consumed in wasteful bickering among interests. But in times of great crisis—Lincoln's presidency, Roosevelt's hundred days—the Madisonian fragments have fused together to create a transcendent national will.[49] In those moments the public has authorized new extensions of federal authority to solve critical national problems even though the constitutionality of the actions was in question. While factionalism returned afterward, the heritage was lasting agreement that the issues behind the crises are federal questions. That conviction has been codified in seminal legislation, for example the Social Security Act and the Civil Rights Act of 1964. Those documents committed the government to guarantee new protections to important groups and gave it the new powers needed to do so.

As yet Washington has ample authority to finance its programs, some authority to regulate those who run them, but very little, in practice, to obligate the recipients themselves. To expect recipients to function in minimal ways, even for their own good, is not yet among the purposes for which the nation is willing to mobilize federal power. It is somehow a national priority to provide social benefits like welfare, but not to enforce the functioning standards that recipients today also need if they are to be integrated. What was it about earlier causes that allowed them to tap federal authority? How might a more complex antipoverty strategy, combining benefits with requirements, do the same? That is the serious political question facing federal social policy.

9

Attitudes Against Obligation

POLITICAL culture will ultimately decide whether functioning standards are acceptable in American government. However necessary requirements like work tests may be on policy grounds, they must be justified in the face of the highly suspicious attitudes that many Americans have toward government, particularly in Washington. In a society as individualistic as the United States, so prone to assert rights against government, the idea of obligating people to function is inherently problematic. How could a servant government ever justify making such demands?

Worse than that, the subject of social policy seems to mobilize attitudes among elites even more libertarian than those of the public in general. Even in a democracy, V. O. Key wrote, leaders are the only full-time participants in politics. Their attitudes are critical for the potential of a regime.[1] American political leaders have been especially preoccupied with the control of authority rather than its use. Nowhere is that more true than in dealing with welfare and poverty, to judge from the debates on work tests and welfare reform. Even conservatives were prone to counter dependency by cutting back government rather than by seeking to use it to enforce functioning. The hard-line kind of conservatism portrayed here ultimately earned less support in Congress than the more authoritative, civic variety studied in the next chapter. But combined with liberal opposition, it helped to make the work tests we have more symbolic than real.

The tragedy is that suspicions of government have made it difficult to deploy federal authority even for democratic ends. The problem is an old one in American politics but is especially acute in social policy. The public would like greater order, but action is blocked by the government-blaming reflexes native to federal politics.

The American Political Style

The American political identity is founded around opposition to authority rather than support for it. The result is that most Americans, although they are orderly, seldom think of government as the basis for order.

Americans have never thought they needed government as much as some other societies. In John Locke's philosophy, on which the Founders relied, people leave the state of nature, where there is no authority, by contracting to form a government. But they do so only reluctantly, because nature is relatively benign. It offers its inhabitants freedom and much sustenance. Only certain "inconveniences," chiefly the lack of a common judge for disputes, make government desirable. Even under government citizens retain rights, in Jefferson's formulation, to "life, liberty, and the pursuit of happiness." They have, as it were, one foot in government and one foot out. They do not feel the alternative to public order is utter barbarism. The danger to rights is more likely to come from government itself than from other citizens.

The Lockean model fits well the formative American experience. The nation emerged from a conflict with foreign authority. Its citizens primarily sought economic opportunity across a rich continent. Inevitably politics focused on the need for authority, on where the boundary between government and a healthy society should fall. The *degree* of government would always matter more in America than in the more settled, less fortunate countries of Europe. Its nature would matter less.

The chief divisions in American politics seem not to be social. The main reason, as Tocqueville noted, is that Americans were "born equal instead of becoming so."[2] As a new society the nation avoided the class divisions of feudalism, and the tensions of overcoming them, that afflicted Europe. The American meaning of class is shallow and economic, not cultural. Other than a small upper and lower class, all Americans participate in much the same way of life. All groups and classes swear allegiance to the same Lockean political beliefs, including the Constitution, liberty, and preservation of property.[3]

There is more division over social issues, with workers and racial minorities more in favor than other people of public measures to redistribute opportunity, income, and status. But the differences are small.[4] Efforts to advance equality—the New Deal, civil rights—have seldom strayed from the liberal consensus. Their goal has been to expand opportunity for individuals, not, like socialism, to create a fundamentally different kind of society.[5]

The important political division has been between society as a whole and government. American political culture is not ideological so much as moralistic. It seeks, not to reorder society, but to make claims on government in the name of higher ideals—freedom, equality, and participation among them. The main political danger is, not revolution by one class against the others, but an overload of demands on government from all classes.[6] Left and right disagree most deeply, not about any social question, but about the proper relationship of the federal government to society.[7] Each side makes demands on government in its own way, the one to expand the federal role and the other to cut it back. The divisions in American society are not unimportant, but they seem to take fire politically mainly from contention about the proper and improper use of public power. Workers, blacks, and business groups most offend each other, not over what they want socially, but over how they would use *governmental* power to achieve it.

The regime is nevertheless stable, because Americans view their institutions, in Robert Lane's phrase, as "eternally settled." The political culture has what Almond and Verba call a "subject" dimension alongside the "participatory" one. Americans may press their claims on government, but most of them are also "good citizens" who obey the law and discharge other obligations stemming from government.[8] That obedience seems to stem from British political culture, the main source of American belief, with its strong commitment to the rule of law.

Dutiful attitudes seem to be grounded in the favorable images young children form of political authority. At a very early age they idealize the local policeman and, even more, the President. Easton and Dennis remark ironically:

> We will, perhaps, disappoint those readers who are accustomed to think of the American as one who is brought up on the raw meat of rugged individualism. We find that the small child sees a vision of holiness when he chances to glance toward government—a sanctity and rightness of the demigoddess who dispenses the milk of human kindness. The government protects us, helps us, is good, and cares for us when we are in need, answer most children.

While people become more cynical about government as they grow up, their early belief in the legitimacy of government remains, providing a reservoir of support for the regime.[9] Such feelings differ even less across social groups than do the more issue-oriented beliefs of participatory politics; blacks and low-income people share them right along with the better-off.[10]

The trouble is that the subject culture can conflict with participatory attitudes. Ideally, as in British experience, the two kinds of attitude should complement one another. Over a long history the British public first learned to obey government, then, through the vote, to direct it. The outcome was a political culture that is democratic but highly respectful of government and thus able to *use* it for a wide range of social ends.[11] In America the participatory reflex often undercuts government authority. Leaders tend to deal with problems in the society by directing popular disquiet against the regime itself. They often seek benefits for individuals or narrow groups at the expense of any overall policy. According to Almond and Verba,

> . . . participant orientation in the United States appears better developed than subject orientation and to some extent dominates it. . . . This cultural imbalance . . . is the result of American historical experience with governmental and bureaucratic authority—an experience that began with distrust and revolution against the British Crown, and that has been consolidated by the American tendency to subject all governmental institutions, including the judiciary and bureaucracy, to direct popular control.[12]

In Mark Roelof's formulation the "mythic" values of the political culture, the drive for popular freedom and equality, demand responsiveness from government, but there is also strong loyalty to the established institutions, which tend to disperse power and stymie action. The result can be political paralysis, frustration, and crisis.[13]

The patterns mean that society is more likely to force change on the regime than vice versa. The impulse to demand things of government is actually strongest among the politicians and officeholders closest to power. Among the public, most people profess self-reliance, and the impulse to demand help from government is latent. But the politicians have electoral incentives to promise new programs, and the voters respond. The regime *invites* pressures on itself. Over time the latent needs surface, and demands on the system increase.[14]

Recently there has been rising alienation from politics, mainly due to government's failure to solve chronic economic problems.[15] Many people have simply withdrawn from political interests, always a danger in a society that still feels it can take or leave government, especially at the federal level. Tocqueville warned:

> If men continue to shut themselves more closely within the narrow circle of domestic interests and to live on that kind of excitement, it is to be apprehended that they may ultimately become inaccessible to those great and powerful public emotions which perturb nations, but which develop them and recruit them.[16]

But withdrawal has not meant deference to government. Americans were always more conscious of their rights against government than their duties, and the imbalance has increased.[17] Pressures on the regime have, if anything, strengthened. A good many of the alienated have simply shifted their energies from party politics to single-interest groups whose demands—to safeguard the environment, stop nuclear power, abolish abortion, and so on—are even harder for government to satisfy than those of the parties.

The outcome of this culture, seen in few other societies, is that groups and individuals find security in *separation* from government rather than conformity to it. Localities, interests, professions—all characteristically profess distrust of authority, especially in Washington, and set themselves against it, even though American government is very undemanding by the standards of Europe. Even civil servants tend to see themselves as separate from government rather than a part of it.[18] Whereas in much of the world, especially the non-West, the pattern is just the opposite—to adjust to authority and seek its protection.[19]

Some have seen in that reflex a sign of self-reliance that should simply lead to less government. Americans do say they would rather be free of government than receive economic security at its hands. Individualist attitudes may have restrained the growth of the welfare state in the United States, in contrast with Europe.[20] But at the same time one aspect of individualism is an active conscience, an insistence that government serve people in need.[21] The humanitarian impulse has driven development of the American welfare state.

Nor has individualism prevented Americans from claiming assistance for themselves. Those who are doing as well as they can without assistance easily think they deserve some. Americans want a government that is limited and not paternalist, but also helpful. Such a government may become quite large. Tocqueville caught the logic, so regretted by conservative critics big government:

> There is always a multitude of men engaged in difficult or novel undertakings, which they follow by themselves without shackling themselves to their fellows. Such persons will admit, as a general principle, that the public authority ought not to interfere in private concerns; but, by an exception to that rule, each of them craves its assistance in the particular concern on which he is engaged . . . . If a large number of men applies this particular exception to a great variety of different purposes, the sphere of the central power extends itself imperceptibly in all directions, although everyone wishes it to be circumscribed.[22]

Many Americans also seem to feel, illogically, that making demands on government is a way of controlling it. Programs may swell the budget, but they also keep government subject to the popular will, which is the important thing.

The result of American attitudes is not necessarily a small government but a servant government that helps people rather than telling them what to do. The political culture easily admits claims by people against government, but not claims by programs against them, even in return for benefits.

Conservative Freedom

The attitudes that prevail in social policy, at least among leaders, seem to be even more libertarian. Perhaps that is because social policy, more than any other kind, raises questions about how self-sufficient people really are. The response of both left and right, in different ways, is to reaffirm the orthodoxy. The cost is that programs lose the authority to set standards for their recipients. These attitudes were dramatized during the congressional debates on welfare work and reform. I have traced through the rhetoric the lines of argument characteristic of each political extreme, though of course actual speeches were often less coherent. The conservatism portrayed here is approximately that of the Congressmen who opposed passage of FAP in the climactic House votes in 1970, while the liberalism is that of the members who opposed stiffer work rules. Many of the most militant spokesmen at either extreme joined the rump that opposed both steps.

The conservatives who opposed welfare expressed great gloom about government, but their pessimism actually rested on optimism about society. They saw little need for welfare, and less for welfare reform, in a country where, they believed, income and opportunity were available to anyone willing to work. They might use hard-line formulations like the need to preserve "the free enterprise system," but behind their defensive words hovered a bountiful vision. Conservatives believed, said one witness, that "our present system . . . is essentially productive." It rewarded effort. "You work longer and you get more." The Senate Finance Committee, in opposing the Nixon reform plan, evoked an idealized past: "Several generations ago, before there was any AFDC program, poor families improved their economic conditions by taking advantage of this country's opportunities through a commitment to work, and through the strengthening and maintenance of family ties."[23]

The free society, however, was far from a Garden of Eden. To seize its opportunities still required individual effort, a willingness to labor and defer gratifications. Conservatives saw this *individual* discipline, instead of collective organization, as the keystone of the American system. Americans tend to regard attacks on work discipline, Daniel Moynihan wrote, as in themselves a form of political radicalism.[24] Conservative Congressmen charged that a guaranteed income would overthrow "the work ethic that has made our country great." Russell Long said it would "tear down" "American institutions." Conservatives opposed liberal efforts to abolish the shame associated with welfare. For, as Congressman Philip Crane argued, the "social stigma" of dependency was essential "to encourage individuals, capable of doing so, to stand on their own two feet."[25]

Belief that opportunity was real explains why conservatives

gave such stress to personal responsibility for social problems. Seeing an open society, they could not believe that people in difficulties had anyone but themselves to blame. One business representative asked why there was "so much sympathy and concern for . . . those individuals in our society who are apparently lazy, indifferent, shiftless, or unwilling to assume their responsibility as Americans to earn their bread by the sweat of their brow?" Senator Carl Curtis was driven to conclude that many recipients must simply lack the "moral fiber" to make good use of their opportunities.[26] Such judgments sound harsh, but they were spoken more in sorrow than in anger. The conservatives, like other Americans, did not lack compassion for the "deserving poor." Their vision of a fair society open to talents simply left them no other conclusion.

However, these conservatives had no thought of using government to instill greater responsibility in dependent people. They wanted simply to reduce welfare. To make it more authoritative by adding work tests or other requirements was decidedly second best. To some extent that was because the right saw even dependency on benefits without requirements as a form of unfreedom. A representative for the Liberty Lobby in the FAP hearings reasoned: "For a man to be totally free, he must have some measure of independence, and handouts from the Government only exacerbate his dependency, and correspondingly reduce his freedom." John Rarick, a Louisiana Democrat, in the second House debate on FAP, insisted on viewing reform as "another major step down the path to a totally controlled environment for the American people."[27]

Most conservatives, however, saw welfare as a force for *dis*order, not for discipline. Their images of it were aquatic. Federal welfare was a dissolving force that broke down the individual discipline conservatives counted on to order society. To Representative Herbert Burke, a Florida Republican, welfare reform would just lead to a further "outpouring" of tax money to pay for "socialism." To Russell Long it threatened "the dissolution of our form of government," unless some way were found to stuff the welfare "genie back in the bottle."[28] We often assume that collectivism must mean Orwellian regimentation. Many conservatives feared exactly the opposite—a welfare state even *less* disciplined than private society.

Furthermore, they doubted many Americans would resist the temptation to live off a guaranteed income without work, if it came at the hands of government. In a moment of candor Senator

Abraham Ribicoff, a liberal who favored reform, admitted that it would mean "basically changing the social philosophy of the United States." That was just what rightists feared. Once guaranteed income was on the books, they expected remorseless pressures to liberalize eligibility and benefits, just as in earlier income programs. Said Senator Harry Byrd: "Once you write that principle into law, then it is Katie-bar-the-door. There is no stopping then." Soon enough, claimed Willie Gradison, a Republican Congressman, "half the American people are going to be supporitng the other half."[29]

The right-wing conservatives never accepted the idea that the nature of welfare might be changed by attaching work or other requirements to benefits. They agreed with the Finance Committee that "paying an employable person a benefit based on need, the essence of the welfare approach, has not worked." But whereas Finance, under Russell Long's leadership, looked toward workfare as an alternative, the more consistent right-wingers simply wanted to cut back welfare. It was a "monster," Representative Ronald Sarasin said, and the duty of Congress was to "destroy" it.[30]

The conservatives noticed only that the Nixon and Carter welfare plan would vastly expand welfare, not at all their idea of welfare reform. Said Al Ullman, a senior Democratic Congress man, "You cannot clean up the welfare mess by doubling the number of people on welfare payments." Said Charles Chamberlain, his Republican colleague on Ways and Means, "what we need is welfare reform that will get people off the rolls and make them independent." In the opinion of the right "true welfare" should not cover the employable at all, but only the "truly needy," meaning mainly the aged, blind, and disabled,[31] who alone could not support themselves from the economy's bounty.

Many conservatives also feared economic scarcity. The wealth of society was not unbounded. Government was a parasite on the "hard-earned money" of individual taxpayers. Society's productive forces were in the private not the public sector, and they could not bear too great a burden. William Colmer, the conservative chairman of the House Rules Committee, reminded reformers in 1970 that "the people have to support the Government; the Government can't support the people." Said Congressman Samuel Devine, an Ohio Republican; "You know, if everybody climbs in the wagon, who is going to pull it?"[32]

The incentives of welfare were to produce a larger parasitic class, whom working people would groan to support. Some conservative Congressmen dared to say that guaranteed income would promote, not only "indolence," but "illegitimate children" and a "population explosion."[33] In a free economy people had to limit their children to the number they could support, or starve; once on welfare, they did not. There is a hint here of that Malthusianism, or fear of overpopulation, that has gone along with belief in the free market since Adam Smith. Again, the public sector imposed less, not more, discipline than the private.

Many conservatives also opposed a more directive form of welfare out of opposition to federal authority. In their view Washington was simultaneously lenient toward government's dependents but all too demanding of taxpayers, the states, and other local authorities. Roger Freeman, a conservative economist, contended in the FAP hearings that the "impetus for expansion" in welfare had always come from the "federal level," from the courts and bureaucracy as well as Congress; there would be "no limit" to further expansion unless liberal reform were defeated and all responsibility for assistance returned to the states. Senator Carl Curtis asked how a "far-removed Federal Government" ever could enforce serious work tests in welfare. The conservative credo was well summed up by the Council of State Chambers of Commerce: "National programs of income maintenance . . . are incompatible with a welfare program based on need and rehabilitation."[34]

The answer to both permissiveness and "federal controls" of states and localities was to get welfare out of Washington. It should be "managed and funded closer to home," the Liberty Lobby recommended, "at the lowest possible level of government." Some Congressmen even questioned whether the federal government had had any business in welfare at all. To Omar Burleson, a conservative Democrat, public assistance was "a mission for which this Government was never designed."[35]

In a statement that struck many conservative themes, Representative John Rarick questioned even Washington's power to have a social policy:

> The Constitution contains no authority that provides that the Federal Government shall force the taxpayers to pay for health services, food, clothing, transportation, housing, legal services, jobs, birth control devices, or even education to citizens. And failure of States to provide these services is no justification for the Federal Government to intervene and preempt the functions of State and local governments.

> The only guarantee owed by the Federal Government to the States is a republican form of government.
>
> If local and State governments do not provide the services such as health, housing, and education as desired by the citizenry, the answer lies with the people, not the Federal Government.

The problem of poverty was real, Rarick admitted, but the responsibility for it lay with "private charities . . . aided by local and State governments." "The solution to the welfare mess is to return to the Holy Bible and to the Constitution." "My dipping into my pocket to give my money earned by my toil to another is an act of love—the Government's taking it from me to give to another is legalized theft."[36]

Rightists also felt strong suspicions of the federal bureaucracy. They viewed the Department of Health, Education, and Welfare as a bastion of permissive attitudes that had not always dealt openly with Congress. Finance Committee conservatives accused HEW of deliberately underestimating the cost of new programs, notably Medicaid and Medicare, to get them past Congress. The department, Carl Curtis declared, was "lost in its own regulations and its own statistics"; its "abuses" could never be "weeded out." Nor did conservatives believe, despite the department's professions, that it would seriously enforce a work test. No "bureaucrat" with "compassion running out of his eyes and drooling out of his mouth," Rules Chairman Colmer said, would ever force a recipient to work.[37]

The conservative response to the idea of the work test was ambivalent at best. Few opposed it outright, but most preferred simply to do away with federal welfare. They suspected, correctly, that the work requirements in the leading reform plans were largely "illusory."[38] The hard-liners would have used the work test, if at all, simply to keep the employable out of welfare, thus limiting assistance to the "truly needy." For if the test were serious, Roger Freeman argued, employable people would not apply for welfare, and no other eligibility test would be needed.

To many conservatives it was nonsensical to require work of people receiving welfare. For "if they work," Senator Curtis retorted, "why do they need it?"[39] Work was the alternative to welfare, not something to be combined with it. Income would be balanced with a work obligation in the private sector, by keeping the employable out of welfare—not within the public sector, as the work test proposed. The answer, said the Liberty Lobby, was "more individual responsibility and less government"[40]—not individual responsibility *through* government.

On some other social questions, such as abortion and school prayer, the right has been readier to invoke federal authority than over welfare work. The goal, however, has mainly been to remove federal bars to restrictive measures by lower-level governments, not to set standards from Washington. So far, even these efforts have failed. The reason may be, not only liberal opposition, but conservative ambivalence toward invoking federal authority even in these limited ways.

The conservatives wanted greater social order, but the combination of Lockean beliefs and suspicions of Washington led them *away* from government rather than toward it. Federal authority could not be *used* for conservative ends, they believed, but only weakened and avoided.

Liberal Freedom

Liberals were led away from the idea of program requirements by different but equally libertarian beliefs. They might differ from conservatives on whether to expand welfare, but they concurred in deprecating any need to combine benefits with a work test.

In addressing the problems of welfare and nonwork, liberal politicians and client groups offered up heavy doses of the same sociological reasoning planners used to justify the welfare reform proposals. Recipients, said William Ryan, a liberal New York Congressman, were "trapped in conditions beyond their control which our Nation has failed to overcome." A spokesman for welfare employees termed the conditions—"hunger, economic deprivation, illness, oppression, and racism,"—the real "perpetrators of family instability," not the recipients. Like welfare planners, witnesses at the welfare hearings often merged indiscriminately the socioeconomic and behavioral problems of recipients. Their dependency, according to the American Public Welfare Association, was due to "lack of education and marketable skills, discrimination in employment and housing, poor health, social disorganization, technological change, and lack of a full employment economy." The "illness," said a welfare mother, lay not in the recipients but "in the society around them."[41]

The responsibility for change thus passed to government. "The poor have placed their faith in the American dream," Whitney Young declared, and it was for government, not the poor themselves, to fulfill that "promise." Said Vernon Jordan of the National Urban League, government must "fulfill their faith, to prove to them that their hopes have not been in vain." That meant filling the material deficits suffered by the poor. Welfare families were "weighed down by a multiplicity of overwhelming problems," said one social service group, but "Given adequate . . . education, decent housing, employment, and skilled counseling most of them would respond to the opportunity to become self-supporting." The only question was the best combination of benefits. Even the Nixon Administration accepted a responsibility, in planning FAP, to discover some "structural reform which will break people out of this cycle of dependency."[42]

Knowing the sensitivity of the work issue, liberal witnesses were at pains to explain away nonwork among many poor people. On the one hand, according to Allard Lowenstein, "the vast majority of AFDC recipients, as much as 99 percent," were unable to work "for one good reason or another." But at the same time many were willing and able to work if government would only provide them training, child care, and, above all, jobs. Senator Fred Harris, a proponent of liberal reform, contended that there are "simply not enough jobs to go around," a doubtful view. Children's advocacy groups asserted that "The urban ghettos are full of healthy, untrained and unemployed males who want to work." Their failure to do so could only be due to "the failure of our economic system to assure full employment." To hold the poor responsible in any way would just be "blaming the victim."[43]

Sociologism justified a permissive welfare policy with an idea of prior burden. Recipients, liberals believed, had already been sufficiently obligated by poverty, racism, and other disadvantages. Government should accept those private burdens in lieu of any public ones. No work obligation was justifiable, even for the employable, unless "conditions" permitted. A work test might be justified "in general terms," Senator Robert Kennedy said, but recipients should be bound to it only if jobs were "satisfactory" and "adequate child care" was available. They must be able to support their families, said several women's groups, or jobs were not worth taking. In the words of the U.S. Catholic Conference, recipients should have to work only "if they are able"[44]—an "if" that, to conservative ears, drained the work obligation of most of its meaning.

A few liberal spokesman, like conservatives, dared to differ with Supreme Court doctrines about welfare. Where the right wanted to deny any federal role in welfare, liberals presented adequate income as an inherent right. To Congressman Ryan, "a guaranteed annual income is not a privilege. It should be a right to which every American is entitled." Welfare groups viewed social guarantees like welfare as equivalent to political freedoms. "The right to an adequate income is a basic right flowing directly from . . . principles expressed in our Declaration of Independence: the right to life, liberty and the pursuit of happiness." Thus, "certain goods and services are a matter of human rights" just like "civil and political rights."[45]

The idea of prior burden put the onus on government to extend new protections before work could be demanded. Effectively that meant work could occur only through recipients' free choice, for only if they had opportunity to work, yet did not have to, could it be said that their disadvantages were overcome. To deny welfare mothers the "choice" whether to work or not was "invidious" because it forebade them "the privilege which other women have of deciding whether to remain in the home." Hearing such arguments, Senator Herman Talmadge lamented that the idea of an unqualified work obligation for the employable was dead; "the new theory seems to be that you have got to . . . have a certain status before you take that work."[46]

Just as conservatives based their opposition to extensive welfare partly on economic scarcity, so liberals based support for it on a belief in plenitude. As John Kenneth Galbraith wrote on the eve of the Great Society, it is hard to enforce a work expectation once society seems to enjoy a high and rising surplus.[47] In the welfare hearings any number of liberal witnesses deduced support for reform from the fact, as Walter Reuther put it, that "we are the richest nation in the world." To Edward Kennedy, just the possession of "the resources to eliminate hunger and want" turned the elimination of poverty into a question of mere "will." In Robert Kennedy's words—quoted to the Finance Committee by welfare radical George Wiley—"as long as there is plenty, poverty is evil." The Advisory Council on Public Welfare borrowed the same syllogism in 1966 for the title of its report: "Having the Power, We have the Duty."[48]

Though liberals saw more barriers to the poor than conservatives did, the role they imagined for government actually differed little, except in degree, from conservative dictates. They wanted a more generous government, but not a more directive one. In their own way they shared the conservative optimism about existing society. Rightists viewed society as healthy and blamed welfare problems on individuals. Liberals blamed the problems on society, but they viewed the poor as sound. Dependent people, Senator Fred Harris stated, were "like the rest of us." Claimed Charles Rangel, another liberal New York Congressman, the "vast majority" of them "desperately want to work." Or rather, that is what policymakers must assume to avoid making "moral judgments" that would just entrench the "stigma" of welfare. If programs were to deal with "causes" and not just the symptoms of poverty, Senator Mike Mansfield reasoned, then they "must assume . . . that everybody who is dependent wants to become self-supporting."[49]

Liberals admitted that most Americans lived prosperous and desirable lives. They simply wanted to include the welfare poor in the same kind of life. The problem was seen as social exclusion, the solution as integration, the obstruction as merely political. In a revealing image, one witness characterized the poor as "disconnected" from society by lack of "opportunity." There was no need to rebuild society, only to remove specific barriers such as racism or lack of jobs or skills. If poverty remained, therefore, the reason could only be lack of political determination. As one welfare mother told the Ways and Means Committee, "The Nation"—that is, government—"is the cause of the problem."[50]

In their own way liberals made government the whipping boy just as much as conservatives did. The latter blamed Washington for insulating the dependent from their duties, while liberals demanded that it accept "responsibility" for the poor. George Wiley, the founder of the National Welfare Rights Organization, declared to the Senate Finance Committee, pointing to welfare children he brought to the hearing, "Now, every one of you here has to take personal responsibility for the starvation, for the malnutrition, for the hunger, for the ill housing that happens to these children." Democrats and liberals were inclined meekly to agree. Senator Ernest Hollings said, speaking of welfare illegitimacy, "Regardless of what we think about the mother's morality or deservedness, the child . . . is coming, and it is society's child."[51]

Government's role might be extensive and expensive, but it was not *in*tensive. It was not to reshape either society or welfare recipients, but only to assure recipients the income, jobs, and other resources they needed to live a normal life on their own. HEW Secretary Joseph Califano used the narrow language of economics: Government must compensate for "labor-market failures" over which the poor had "no control." Said his colleague, Labor Secretary Ray Marshall, government's role was to "insure" that the "expectation" society had of the employable, to support their families, could "become a reality."[52] Government was a fount of assistance and resources, but not of discipline.

The public role, if successful, would also be transitional. Liberals did not see public resources permanently replacing private ones any more than conservatives did. In the short run, militants like George Wiley might insist, generous welfare was the "solution" for poverty and not the "problem." But most liberal spokesmen claimed that generosity in the short run would actually reduce dependency later on.[53] Welfare programs, if well designed, could transmute dependence into independence. They would somehow "give self-determination to these people." Government income and services would provide them with "adequacy," "self-direction," and "dignity." With guaranteed income, said John Conyers, a Democratic Congressman, the poor would be "free to feel that they are directing their own lives."[54] Conservatives might view such claims as an abuse of language, but they do show that liberals wanted to confine government to the margin of recipients' lives.

Liberals, furthermore, shared conservatives' suspicions of federal authority. Liberalized benefits for the poor were fine. But attempts to regulate the poor were to be resisted, said Congressman William Ryan, as "alien to individual choice and freedom." In that cause liberals could inveigh against public control with the most strident conservatives. Welfare mothers had a right to choose whether to work, insisted Common Cause—"No bureaucracy should want to second-guess" them. Senator Walter Mondale, a supporter of liberal reform, opposed Russell Long's workfare plan on grounds that it would create "a totally federally controlled and dominated organization," a virtual "Federal czar" over the lives of children.[55]

Liberals evoked images of a remote, pitiless government bearing down on miserable, defenseless poor people. The 1967 WIN amendments established the mildest kind of work test, but to Robert Kennedy they bespoke "a punitive attitude reminiscent of medieval poor law philosophy." The resort to "coercion," liberals feared, would "alienate the poor" and inflame divisions in the cities. John Lindsay, the liberal Republican Mayor of New York, raised the specter that the attempt to "force" solutions in welfare would lead to an "explosion."[56] His reasoning was Lockean: A victimized people would inevitably rebel against an oppressive government.

Liberals took a very vulnerable, interior view of the individual, particularly if he or she were poor. Conservatives paid employable recipients the compliment of thinking they were exploiting government and were thus able to live without support. Liberals were much more solicitous but less complimentary. They believed the dependent could approach independence only if given "patient and dignified help, not punishment and coercion." To motivate them, one had first to get inside their heads and see the world as they did. That meant, in the words of one Catholic spokesman, to sympathize with "the meaning of their person, their unlimited potential, their restless desire, their need and want of family love and neighborhood respect, protection and development."[57] Such statements mirror at the policy level the threatened view of recipients taken by the less effective staff members in WIN.

Government, therefore, could promote work among the poor only by therapeutic means, never coercion. It had to rely on what Senator Mike Gravel called "volunteerism." Anything tougher would just defeat and demoralize recipients. A "constructive solution" to the work problem was possible, the American Public Welfare Association (APWA) claimed, only "through patient and perhaps time-consuming effort, to encourage and support and enable, and to instill some motivation."[58]

As that statement indicates, during the Great Society social workers moved away from the role of controlling recipients for which liberal reformers had criticized them. The National Association of Social Workers publicly regretted that its members had been "forced to take on the role of a parent or an authority." That was "not the role that the social workers are to play today vis-à-vis people who need income support from society and are entitled to it." Instead, social work adopted the more impersonal, systems-oriented view of the social problem taken by planners in Washington. Said the APWA, "Solving human problems and promoting social competence are complex undertakings which require the knowledge and skills of many disciplines and the deep involvement of a wide variety of governmental and voluntary agencies and of individual citizens."[59] To overcome dependency apparently required a great deal of money and expertise, but no authority.

Unfortunately, the potential power of programs over recipients grew as more people became dependent on government. The danger distressed liberals, even though federal policy was in fact permissive. Their fear prompted a desire to clarify yet further the claims of recipients against government. Clients must have vested legal rights to their benefits, even if they had not earned them, so that a program could not condition the benfits on behavior. The Advisory Council on Public Welfare reasoned:

> There are many today who express a sincere anxiety or alarm lest the growing interdependence of people in the modern world, reflected in . . . their growing dependence on . . . government, throw into imbalance the carefully designed weighting of rights reserved to the individual and powers assigned to the State. These people fear that a beneficent State may become, in effect, an oppressive State. . . . The only practical remedy . . . is to accompany each new assignment of responsibility to governmental programs with equivalent protections for the rights of those affected by those programs.[60]

Evidently, liberals refused to recognize obligations for recipients under any circumstances. Such burdens were unwarranted even if they rested on claims the dependent had first made on government. The answer to potential obligations arising from claims could only be yet further claims against government. In reality, the recipients were vulnerable precisely because they had *only* rights. Without functioning in expected ways, such as work, they could never truly be *entitled* to their benefits.

Liberal Theories

In addition to the general beliefs just described, liberals from different backgrounds asserted a number of specific beliefs about the role of government in social policy. Those theories, though different, all converged on the conclusion that government must solve the social problem with benefits and without authority. All schools favored government but opposed govern*ing*.

The economic approach to poverty and welfare, considered earlier, rested on a market view of society that excluded the tutelary role of govenment implied by work or other functioning requirements. The presumption that society was composed of competent people interacting in the market place for mutual advantage concealed from economists the coping problems of many government dependents. It left no basis for viewing welfare behavior as dysfunctional. The poor were simply responding to the "incentives" around them, and government had no right to second-guess. Poverty was a purely economic problem, to be solved by cash transfers. That belief persisted over the decade of welfare reform debate even as behavioral problems mounted. In 1978, Russell Long noted, HEW planners still believed that "people are poor because they do not have money, and the way to solve that problem is to mail them a check."[61]

Similarly, the doctrine that work must be an expression of self-interest by the worker kept economists from confronting the trends that had brought the individual and social interest in work into conflict, at least for low-skilled workers. George Shultz, President Nixon's Secretary of Labor, testified that to expect recipients to work without adequate monetary incentives was "to expect individuals to behave in a manner adverse to their own economic interests." One might just as well ask why individuals should pay taxes or obey the law, duties that equally do not serve personal interest. President Carter's Labor Secretary, Ray Marshall, made little effort to defend even the vestigal work requirements in PBJI. "A job program," he candidly told the Finance Committee, "is, by its very nature, voluntary. Even a rigorously enforced work requirement cannot make people work." Government should motivate work only by funding work incentives. "No army of bureaucrats," Labor said, "can nor should be relied upon to fulfill this function."[62]

There was no point in government's defining who was and was not employable, many economists argued, when only economic forces, outside government, could really decide that. Wrote the Heineman commission:

> Employment tests imposed by current programs often are based on largely irrelevant criteria such as age, sex, and the like. . . . The only meaningful determination of employability for an individual is the outcome of a freely operating labor market; no timeless definitions of employability can be drawn.

And since government could not easily monitor the market, "the claims of the individual in regard to his own employability must be relied upon in cases of doubt."[63]

Closely related to the economic theory was the position advanced by labor union spokesmen during the welfare hearings. But for the force of labor ideology, organized workers might well have opposed welfare. Labor was socially conservative. No one resented welfare dependency more than working-class people struggling in jobs that paid them little more than recipients received, at least in the major cities, for doing nothing at all. Senator Howard Baker noted that "the most explosive social issue in the United States is the simmering resentment that the working population has against the abuses of the welfare system."[64]

But labor leaders generally refused to see an oppositon between their interests and those of the welfare class. The only proposed new benefit they questioned was guaranteed jobs for the poor in government. Public employees feared that recipients, working only for welfare, would take their jobs away from them or reverse the hard-won gains they had made in pay, benefits, and conditions. The American Federation of State, County, and Municipal Employees (AFSCME), the main public employee union, expressed "considerable difficulty with the notion that welfare recipients can somehow move into the same kinds of jobs as regular public employees at less pay, or no pay at all."[65]

Otherwise, labor favored reform, and of a generous and permissive kind. Labor leaders refused to blame the welfare poor for their condition, but instead allied with them in pressing claims on government. Unionists easily saw the welfare predicament through progressive eyes. They remembered labor's formative experiences in the 1930s, when an economic collapse overwhelmed many workers' effort to support themselves without government help. "The welfare problem is not a problem of people," the AFL-CIO stated. "It is a problem of institutional failures," especially "the chronic failure of the economy to provide enough jobs." Government therefore had a "dual obligation," to guarantee jobs to those seeking work and adequate income to those unable to work.

Labor refused to countenance any serious work requirements until government had done all the things for workers and the poor that were really necessary to permit work. Declared the AFL-CIO:

> How can people be compelled to take jobs that aren't available, or take training programs that aren't yet functioning, or put their children in day care centers that haven't been built? We should provide people with adequate education, provide upgraded training where needed for the unemployed, make jobs available which pay at

> least the statutory minimum wage, make day care centers available for children of mothers who want to work and make decent health care available to everyone. After all this is done, if we find welfare rolls still expanding with qualified, educated, able-bodied adults while at that time truly productive good paying jobs go begging, we may then wish to consider whether compulsory work requirements would be desireable.[66]

If government was so obligated, the idea of burdening recipients, even in return for benefits, was difficult even to contemplate.

Labor might at least have demanded that welfare people work for less than ordinary workers, in deference to their lower productivity, dependency, and debt to society. To make welfare work less expensive, the Nixon welfare plan required recipients to accept some jobs paying below the minimum wage, while the Carter plan set wages in PSE below those paid to regular workers in comparable jobs. The AFL-CIO, however, insisted that "substandard" wages, even for recipients, threatened "wage slavery" and a derogation of "hard-won labor standards" for all workers.[67]

Labor preferred measures, such as a higher minimum wage, that would benefit workers generally, not just the poor. George Meany, president of the AFL-CIO, declared that "the way out of poverty is good jobs at decent wages for all who can work." Government must ensure such jobs as a "right" to all workers instead of placing special burdens on the dependent. If recipients got "the wages they are entitled to, the prevailing wage," they could better support themselves and not need "to depend on a welfare payment to supplement inadequate wages."[68] Battles over these wage and standards issues, not opposition to reform as such, came the nearest to threatening labor support for FAP.[69]

As much as any economist or capitalist, labor leaders cherished the ideal of the free market. They fiercely defended their right to settle wages and conditions with employers free of government interference. To conservatives, unionism itself might be an interference with the market, but to unionists government was much more of one. Forced work inevitably meant, in the words of one Democratic Congressman, "the deterioration of the kind of free labor and free-enterprise system in which labor and management have bargained together." Mandatory, rather than voluntary, work was "completely contrary," Russell Long admitted, "to the general theory of organized labor." Even most wage subsidy schemes for the poor violated that theory, for they meant that a worker's wages reflected the size of his family more than his productivity, a departure from the labor ideal of "equal pay for equal work."[70]

Most unionists also preferred employment in the private sector rather than the public. They believed with Jerry Wurf, the president of AFSCME, that "every American is entitled to a basic decent income." But except for public employees government was supposed to provide that income through the *private* economy. Labor leaders supported PSE if needed to guarantee jobs to the unemployed, yet they also doubted whether government itself ever could provide "real jobs at decent wages."[71]

For unionists, as much as other Americans, life *outside* government has been the norm. Like other interests, labor prefers to find security by separating from authority instead of identifying with it. The cost is that labor's political goals are overwhelmingly defensive, *against* government. In Europe unions often obstruct the policies even of their own socialist governments by insisting on wage increases that conflict with economic policy. Union freedom *from* government impedes the constructive use of authority for social ends.[72]

Racial politics played a large role in the welfare debates simply because so many recipients were black. By 1979 blacks were a plurality of AFDC recipients nationally—43 percent, versus 40 percent for whites and 14 percent for Hispanics[73]—and a majority of the urban and long-term dependent. Blacks had suffered more than any group from the permissive cast of federal programs, yet black leaders fiercely resisted any suggestion that recipients bear heavier obligations. Their resource was that blacks could assert better than anyone the liberal theory of prior burden. By appealing to a history of victimization, they could avoid responsibility for welfare work and family problems and shift the onus to others. Their credo, as President Johnson stated in his Howard University speech, was that apparent differences in competence between low-income blacks and other Americans were "not racial differences. They are solely and simply the consequence of ancient brutality, past injustice, and present prejudice. . . . For the Negro they are a constant reminder of oppression. For the white they are a constant reminder of guilt."[74]

From the time of the controversy over the "Moynihan report," the civil rights movement rejected "self-improvement" as a route toward racial progress in the United States. Social workers, who dealt most directly with the personal problems of welfare clients, faced increasing hostility from them. They found themselves confronted both locally and in Washington, Moynihan wrote, by "angry black women reviling the genteel world of the professional." They were "utterly incapable of responding in any terms save agreement and concession." Except on the far right, "deference to the ways in which blacks defined black problems" went unquestioned.[75]

The welfare committees in Congress did press proposals for work tests, but they met fierce resistance from black leaders who shifted the blame for welfare onto white society. Asserted Representative Shirley Chisholm, "the reason we have so many black women heading up welfare families in this Nation is . . . that their men never had a chance." They were "victims" of a discriminatory job market. They had never been allowed "to become proud, self-sustaining citizens in this country." Accordingly, said welfare radical George Wiley, to aim policy at the "personal failures and/or anti-social behavior" of recipients would only deny blacks "basic fundamental liberties."[76]

Given their history, the idea of work tests or workfare was even more alarming for blacks than for other recipient groups. Even the very mild 1967 work registration requirement spurred protests by welfare rights advocates against "slavery" and "dictatorship." In asking for lenient work rules in the FAP hearings, former New York City welfare chief James Dumpson, himself a black, reminded Ways and Means that "Slave labor, indentured servitude, are specters from our own unhappy past—let us not revive them in 1969–70." Said another public official, welfare work meant turning recipients into "the lackies and coolies of our society."[77] Such feelings explain why it is in some ways easier for conservatives to cut back welfare than to combine benefits with serious work tests. Then, at least, blacks will be "enslaved" by private poverty rather than public action.

The racial welfare theory justified the demands made by the National Welfare Rights Organization (NWRO) under George Wiley's leadership in the late 1960s. The organization at first had considerable success staging demonstrations in city welfare offices. It demanded added benefits for welfare mothers, and local authorities frequently acquiesced.[78] NWRO also played a flamboyant role in the welfare hearings in Congress. Three times Wiley staged demonstrations in the hearing rooms of the welfare committees. He demanded guaranteed income and jobs with no work requirements at all. He carried on a running feud with Finance Chairman Russell Long. His members threatened to "disrupt" the government unless their demands were met.[79]

Though few said so publically, many Congressmen were alienated from reform by the extreme stance NWRO took in the official hearings, and in unofficial hearings that Senator Eugene McCarthy staged for the group in November 1970.[80] Even in Washington, where blacks are accorded special deference, there was a limit to what they could demand without recognizing more reciprocity. But any idea that blacks could have responsibilities toward society was repudiated by civil rights ideology.

In light of black history the rights-claiming style of welfare politics is thoroughly understandable. The permissive character of social programs may demonstrate better than any other problem the terrible price America has paid for unjust obligation in the past. Because authority was once misused against blacks, it is now struck from the hands even of well-meaning policymakers seeking to help disadvantaged blacks. The civil rights ideology, like the others, was too much opposed to government even to realize its own goals. Race politics, though it seemed to demand everything of Washington, actually set sharp limits to what blacks could achieve *through* government. Once NWRO had obtained all the welfare local and state governments would allow, it withered away. It could not offer welfare mothers what they really wanted, an escape from dependency. For that would have required facing up to the work and family problems of the mothers themselves, not simply their need.

The strongest claims for guaranteed income, however, came from the representatives of organized religion. Churchmen in the welfare hearings espoused the sensitive, liberal conception of the individual in an extreme form. According to the Presbyterian Church, all persons, but especially "the weakest and most deprived members of socity," must be given "the freedom to choose how they may express the meaning of their lives." For the National Council of Churches, the "God-given worth of persons" was enough to establish a right to welfare without obligations. Said Whitney Young, "Simply because one exists in the image of God, he is entitled to certain basic human rights, to the realization of his full potential."[81] Strictures like work tests were an illegitimate "encroachment upon the independence" of recipients, for they meant that people's lives were "no longer controlled by themselves but rather by the Government." Such uncompromising individualism implied, one Episcopal group admitted, that government must abandon any attempt to "legislate morality."[82]

While churchmen saw recipients as individuals with rights, they saw taxpayers in communitarian terms that denied them any comparable claims. Theologically the better-off were not allowed to separate their interests from those of the dependent. Said the Methodist Church, "Social welfare . . . implies the concern of all persons, organized for the welfare of all persons." According to the U.S. Catholic Conference, "each member of a national or local community has some responsibility for and should feel some sense of solidarity with all the other members. A particular obligation rests on the more fortunate to help those not so fortunate."[83] Such formulas obliterate the individual and the claims of property.

Indeed, from a theological perspective there was no such thing as private property. All possessions were of God, and humans only the stewards of them. According to the Episcopal Church, "God has created life and the resources that sustain life. Man does not have the right to withhold the abundance of God's resources from those in need, nor can he rightly determine who does and who does not 'deserve' what God has given freely and lovingly." The National Council asserted that "economic institutions exist only to meet the needs of persons in community," and this established "a claim upon the individual to contribute to the well-being of his neighbor."[84] In principle, all wealth was collective.

The poor had not only a claim but a paramount claim on the resources of the community. All Christian ethics reflects the solicitude that Jesus shows toward the poor in the Gospels. According to the Episcopalians:

> The poor are a special charge of God. . . . Provision and opportunity for the poor is the primary standard by which individuals and nations are to be judged. Giving to the poor and destitute from the leftovers is to be condemned; rather the poor have prior claim for adequacy on our resources.

An adequate social policy, said the Lutheran Church, demanded that the nation "rise to a new level of moral commitment" to the needy. Otherwise, said the National Council, it would "earn an 'eternal curse'."[85]

Some welfare recipients were all too aware that churchmen

made government their servant. One NWRO member told the Finance Committee that welfare recipients were "people . . . you are supposed to take care of," and if Senators refused, "God isn't going to stand for it."[86] But by the 1970s simply giving things to the poor was no longer a sufficient way to help them. Perhaps it is the otherworldly character of their faith that prevents churchmen from seeing this. The primitive political ideal in Christianity has always been a small, harmonious community in which all decisions are taken by consensus and there is no authority or coercion of an impersonal kind. Only there could open-ended charity be practicable, since informal social suasions would enforce reciprocity. It is not an ideal feasible for large modern states.[87]

There is, however, another tradition in theology that accepts government as a necessary, if fallen, part of God's design. St. Paul wrote that public authorities "have been instituted by God," and all subjects must obey them (Romans 13:1–7). He even wrote, as if to justify the work test, that "if any one will not work, let him not eat. For we hear that some of you are living in idleness, . . . not doing any work. Now such persons we command . . . to earn their own living." (2 Thess. 3:10–12).[88] While there is little explicitly about politics and government in the New Testament, St. Augustine, medieval thinkers, Luther, and Calvin elaborated a Christian political theory which, though it held government to principled standards, also allowed it the authority needed to maintain order in the world.[89]

Dietrich Bonhoeffer spoke out of that tradition when he decried the permissive tendencies of much liberal theology:

> The justification of the good has been replaced by the justification of the wicked, the idealization of good citizenship has given way to the idealization of its opposite . . . ; the forgiving love of Jesus . . . has been misrepresented, for psychological or political reasons, in order to make of it a Christian sanctioning of anti-social "marginal existences" . . . . In seeking to recover the power of the gospel this protest unintentionally transformed the gospel of the sinner into a commendation of sin. And good, in its citizen-like sense, was held up to ridicule.[90]

Bonhoeffer is usually reckoned a liberal theologian himself, but as a German he was also freer than most Americans from the impulse to subordinate authority to individual claims. The Bible can justify many polilitical theories. American churchmen are permissive, perhaps, because they *are* Americans. Like other liberals, they call for programs that are generous but undemanding.

Culture and Obligation

"England is a free country," wrote Elie Halévy of Britain in 1815. He was, like Tocqueville, a French admirer of Anglo-Saxon civic virtue. But, he added, England was also "the country of economic freedom, unbridled competition, and class war." The British ruling class was so averse to strong central government, and so complacent about stability, that the regime was for a time helpless to assuage the growing class conflicts of the Industrial Revolution. Halévy believed that only evangelicalism, a conservative religious sentiment shared by all classes, staved off revolution. Only later did government develop the bureaucratic apparatus needed to ameliorate economic and social conditions.[91]

Something comparable could be said of the United States today. To all but radical eyes, America is a free country. The political culture, no less than the institutional arrangements, stoutly resists the control of individuals that would be needed to make it unfree. But a libertarian regime carries the risk, if not of class conflict at present, then of ethnic separation due to dysfunction and dependency.

Despite their disagreements, conservatives and liberals both see individual freedom as something opposed to government. The thread that connects them is trust in the individual at the expense of authority, a desire to make the realization of his or her desires the basis of social order. They differ on how much government should do to help people but agree that it should not tell them what to do. In that respect, the punitive side of welfare policy, the impulse to exclude and punish the poor, is really just the inverse of the humanitarian impulse to give them everything they ask. Liberals bemoan the one, conservatives the other, but they are really blaming themselves. Neither will use authority in social policy in a benevolent *and* directive way.

The opposition Americans see between freedom and authority, especially in Washington, is an old problem for American government. It has forced all expansions of the federal role to be justified in the name of freedom, a value opposed to the very essence of government, which is control. That was true of the initial federal regulatory programs, established around the turn of the century. Only if government prevented such evils as monopoly, unstable money, and railroad exploitation, reformers said, could there be opportunity for the little man in American life, the small businessman or farmer. The difficulty, Herbert Croly wrote in *The Promise of American Life*, a manifesto of Progressivism, was to get Americans to admit that a degree of "national organization" served freedom and was not opposed to it.

The deeper problem, Croly saw, was that Americans defined their "national idea" against government rather than through it. The American mind had a "Jeffersonian" tendency to identify democracy simply with an open society, a free economy, and a suspicion of public interference. There was also a "Hamiltonian" tradition willing to use government for certain national ends, but it was less democratic. Croly hoped the Progressives would bring the two traditions together. They realized that "a certain measure of discipline" from the center was now necessary to serve popular ends. That would bring an end to the traditional "democracy of suspicious discontent" and inaugurate one of "individual and social improvement."[92]

That juncture is not yet complete. That is the central political problem in social policy. The connection was made in economic policy; Washington now regulates the economy for a range of purposes, though not without continuing resistance. In social policy, however, federal programs dispense benefits without truly regulating. In some ways the problem is traceable to the New Deal, the formative period of federal benefit programs. Roosevelt's cornucopia of new economic and social agencies seemed the fulfillment of Croly's vision.[93] But where the economic programs exerted clear-cut authority, the new benefits never did. The new welfare state was based chiefly on social insurance, that is, on prior work, and a hope that welfare would fade away. In their zeal to prevent stigma, federal officials never established that recipients could bear explicit obligations in return for support. When, by the 1960s, welfare burgeoned, there was no tradition of governing the dependent to fall back on. The work test is a tardy effort to create one.

The separation between the Jeffersonian and Hamiltonian strands lives on in the stance the major parties take toward domestic policy. Democrats are the more "democratic" party in the sense of responding to group claims on government. Republicans are the more "republican" in the sense of resisting claims and defending the institutions.[94] Democrats are thus the party of big government, yet Republicans may be the more truly statist in the sense of willingness to govern. But Republicans have never fully accepted the vast expansion of social programs since the New Deal, just as Democrats have never accepted the need to limit claims. Republicans seem to want to exert authority without programs, while Democrats want programs without authority. Neither has truly governed *through* programs. In that sense we still suffer, in Croly's words, from "a democratic theory and tradition which blocks the process of national development."[95]

The problem goes back, ultimately, to the Lockean nature of American political culture. That culture is essential to national unity, but it also makes very limited demands on the citizenry. It allows them to engage mostly in a private "pursuit of happiness." It does not require of them much attention to public questions, or to other people. The idea of authoritative social programs supposes a more intimate involvement of government with the dependent, and vice versa, than most Americans can ever entirely accept.

10

The Civic Conception

In the welfare debates also appeared what I have called the civic conception, or the idea of linking welfare benefits to obligations like work. The Congressmen who asserted that viewpoint may be called civic conservatives or moderates, because they fell in some senses between the extremes of conventional conservatism and liberalism. They also, however, fell off the usual political spectrum entirely because of their willingness to use federal authority as an instrument in social policy. Like more conventional viewpoints, the civic idea must be abstracted from the flow of argument for or against reform. It seldom appears in the developed and coherent form suggested here. Nor were all those I assign to this position always consistent; some of them spoke in conventional liberal or conservative terms on other occasions.

Not by accident, most of the civic spokesmen were members of Ways and Means or Finance, the committees with immediate responsibility for welfare in the House and Senate. They seem to have been driven toward the civic position because it was the only way they could reconcile Congress's desire to help the poor with its equally strong upset at nonwork and other abuses in welfare. Of these members the most trenchant was Martha W. Griffiths, Democratic Representative from Michigan and a senior member of Ways and Means. In hearings and on the House floor, hers was the strongest voice for the civic position, though even she was not entirely consistent. Her special authority stemmed from her willingness to confront the abuses *and* support generous aid for the poor. Her toughness was not a mask for unconcern.

The moderate leaders spoke for a much larger number of Congressmen who wanted to reform welfare without yielding to the extreme counsels of the far right or left. The civic stance, as noted earlier, tended to define the consensus in Congress on the critical work and eligibility questions posed by welfare reform. Under moderate leadership Congress did not deny assistance to the employable, but neither did it guarantee them an income without requirements. Instead it took the first steps toward combining existing welfare benefits with work obligations. While work measures did not go as far as some moderates wanted, the *nature* of welfare was changed much more than its scope.

The civic position was successful, in part, because it accorded better than orthodox liberalism or conservatism with what we know of public opinion about welfare and related issues. The public, too, is humanitarian toward the poor yet concerned that helping them not undermine social standards. In Washington politics is largely about rights and claims on government, but to the average American citizenship appears to entail a mix of rights *and* obligations, including work.

The Participatory Ideal

The civic conservatives downplayed the usual concern in Washington for the scale and control of government in order to use government to enforce work. Something was more important to them than freedom *from* government. Their motive could be found in a vision, shared by politicians of all persuasions, of a common society in which all Americans participated. That ideal runs through the welfare debates like a minor theme. The moderates obtained their influence, perhaps, because theirs was the only position that plausibly might realize that vision.

When Congressmen phrased their social ideal in the debates, they invariably emphasized, not equality of a status or income kind, but the *participation* of all Americans in a common web of political and econcomic activity. To them energetic *interaction* with others *in public*, whether in political or economic affairs, was the quintessential American experience. As early as 1835 Tocqueville commented on the "bustle" of America, the "activity that pervades all parts of the body politic in the United States."[1] To Congressmen, an activist, participatory society was still the ideal.

Welfare announced, however, that some 10 million Americans did not engage fully in that interchange. The fact that they were *out of circulation*, with so few working, was much more disturbing to politicians than their poverty or their dependence on government. Congressmen of all parties, when they dared to face that reality, expressed pain about it, not just opposition. To Thomas Curtis, a Republican member of Ways and Means, it was "negative" and "hopeless" that "a portion of our society" should be consigned to "a permanent welfare situation." Martha Griffiths voiced the common conviction that "the end of the welfare system is to go out of business. Unless welfare is a self-liquidating enterprise, it is a failure. . . . [It] should seek to move people into a dignified and rewarding participation in the economic life of the Nation."[2]

Welfare was seen as a problem in integration more than economics. To Senator Abraham Ribicoff, a liberal Democrat, the question was "how to take that world and make it like the rest of America." To many, the *passivity* of the poor, not their poverty as such, was what barred integration. Congressmen and witnesses groped for ways to *energize* recipients so they would participate more actively in the life of society, particularly by working. Said John Volpe, the Governor of Massachusetts, recipients needed "the maximum amount of self-reliance, self-respect, self-esteem, ours being an individualized society." Said John Byrnes, the senior Republican on Ways and Means, they must somehow "work for their self-respect," since "that is the American system." Even welfare radicals pleaded for the chance "to participate in this country, to be a part of this country."[3]

Clearly, benefits and dependency alone could never bring the poor into this activist life. Rather, government must somehow instill greater activity in the dependent. Declared Ways and Means, "a mechanism has to be developed which would make it possible for welfare recipients to develop into citizens who play a significant role as workers in the economy of the Nation." The purpose of welfare reform was to discover that "mechanism." The goal was that "all those who are capable of participating in the economy of this country should have the opportunity and the responsibility of doing so."[4]

No problem arose politically as long as government merely helped the dependent toward independence. Congressmen on all sides warmly endorsed "rehabilitiation." It was easy to support what Herman Talmadge, a Finance Committee conservative, called "education and training our citizens to become useful and productive citizens."[5] As time went on, however, the need to enforce work became clear, and that was much tougher to support. Some Congressmen, therefore, did so disingenuously, by characterizing the work test as one more benefit or opportunity to be *given to* recipients, rather than as something demanded *from* them.

When he first proposed the work test, Wilbur Mills, the chairman of Ways and Means, described it vaguely as a way to "lead" people toward "independence and self-support." In the Senate George Smathers, a Florida Democrat, said it meant "opening the door to a new and better world for hundreds of thousands of unfortunate citizens." Senator Charles Percy, a liberal Republican, denied that the test was "hardhearted," for "In the end it is compassionate to give people a chance to stand on their feet and to give them dignity." To Senator John Tunney, a liberal Democrat, the meaning was "not that we somehow punish welfare recipients but that we provide a means so that men and women work to support their families."[6]

A popular rubric was to portray the work test as helping recipients who were already seeking to better themselves. The "only way you can help anybody," said Wilbur Mills, "is to try to help him to help himself," as the work test tried to do. Said Bill Frenzel, a Republican Congressman: "The hand up instead of the handout has always been the way we in this country have helped our fellow citizens."[7] Aiding the self-reliant, of course, cast the work problem in New Deal terms as a lack of opportunity. It ignored the awkward reality of nonwork among many of the dependent.

Even Martha Griffiths, normally so forthright in defending the work test, sometimes tried to present it as a form of liberation for welfare mothers. She claimed that "social workers" often took the choice to work away from mothers, deciding that they should stay home with their children. "I think the social workers make that choice," Griffiths declared. "I think most of these women want to work and they can work . . . . But they have to be given an opportunity to work." Illogically, she wanted to take the "choice" not to work away from mothers, yet asserted that they were "going to have an opportunity to work." Griffiths even presented compulsory work as a form of feminism, in the belief that welfare mothers, like other women, had to get out of the home and work if they were "ever to participate in the decisions of the world."[8]

These formulations reveal the intense uneasiness American politicians feel at giving up their usual benefit-oriented stance in social policy, even when they have accepted the need for functioning requirements in principle. They are simply much more comfortable *giving* things to people than demanding things of them. They are loath, at least rhetorically, to *transfer* obligation from government to recipients, the step that is vital to an authoritative policy.

Nevertheless, the participatory ideal was of great importance for federal policy. The vision it articulated was noticeably different from those painted by the ideologues of either left of right. Participation did not mean a regime for the poor consisting only of rights or entitlements. Neither did it offer them only equal opportunity, or the chance to compete for success, without any guarantees at all. The ideal implied that individuals deserved certain assured chances and supports from society, but also that they had obligations to function independent of how successful they were. The participatory vision did not share the preoccupation of the usual federal ideologies with the control of power. Rather, it reflected a *social* ideal, drawn from everyday American life, that power might be used to achieve.

The Civic Approach

The civic spokesmen were much blunter in asserting the need for social obligation than other politicians. They rejected the views conventional conservatives and liberals took of the key issues in social policy in order to avoid obligation. They emerged in a distinctive position where *both* government and the individual bore responsibility for solving the social problem, tutelary functions for government like work tests were legitimate, and functioning requirements were closely coupled with benefits.

The moderates sided with liberals and against the right on the government's duty to do something about poverty and dependency. Martha Griffiths, despite her willingness to enforce work, never wavered in her conviction that welfare was a "national responsibility." The moderates criticized the "abuses" of welfare but not the principle that Washington should assist the needy.[9] It will be recalled that the key committee chairmen, Wilbur Mills and Russell

Long, did not attack welfare, or welfare reform, primarily on grounds of cost or principle. They were willing to spend generously for reform if only it would solve the work problem. Asserted Long, "it is not the cost that bothers me, but whether this thing will work."[10]

Wilbur Mills first touted the work test as a "new direction" for welfare, but his hopes for it were actually fairly minimal. Its purpose was "restoring more families to employment and self-reliance." It might prevent welfare from becoming "a way of life" for successive generations.[11] There was no suggestion that forced work would eliminate welfare entirely, even for the employable. Nor has the development of work tests since 1967 put the federal commitment to welfare in question.

At the same time, however, the civic Congressmen sided with orthodox conservatives and against liberals in emphasizing the personal responsibility of welfare recipients. Government's duty toward the needy did not cancel their own obligation to function in ways other Americans expected. The sociological doctrine that traced the blame for poverty only to society was rebuffed. In the words of Senator Carl Curtis, one of Long's allies on the Finance Committee, "I do not accept the premise that everybody is guilty but nobody in particular is responsible for their own acts" or, in other words, "that nobody is to blame but everybody is."[12]

Once recipients were held responsible for themselves, they could be expected to work, on grounds that they were able to and others did. Wallace Bennett, the senior Republican on Finance, asked, "Can this Nation treat mothers of school-age children on welfare as though they were unemployable and pay them to remain at home when more than half of mothers with school-age children in the general population are already working?" Faced with that argument, even liberals and welfare reform planners reluctantly admitted that it was "reasonable" to expect some kind of work effort from recipients.[13]

The moderates also insisted that at least low-paid work was generally available to recipients, despite high official unemployment, and they forced Administration witnesses to admit as much. Russell Long insisted that "in practically every city in America there are jobs available as waitresses and dishwashers." The fact that they were menial jobs was no excuse for not taking them, said Martha Griffiths, for the same was "true of every job for every woman in America, and for a very large number of men."[14]

These themes of personal responsibility, antisociologism, and fairness to others clashed with the far more solicitous approach to the poor taken by conventional liberals. Griffiths recalled discussing welfare with a church group concerned about the poor:

> I will never forget some of those hostile questions in that church: "But the woman must pay some money for the food stamps." Answer: "We have considered that. She is still getting a substantial amount of free food." Question: "But she waits all day for a doctor." Answer: "Who doesn't. But the woman who works may give up a day's pay, wait all day, pay $15 to the doctor and $50 for prescriptions." Question: "But she has to take three buses to get to the place to get the food stamps, welfare, etc." Answer: "The woman who works may take three buses twice a day, 5 days a week to get back and forth to work."
>
> The theory of comparing what is given in welfare with what is needed is foolish. "What is needed" is a phony standard set up by a paternalistic middle class. The real standard is what similar people earn, and how they are treated. Few have ever asked what those who work need. Those who have bled for people who have nothing have not demanded that people who work be treated at least as well as people on welfare.[15]

The moderates wanted, not to abandon the poor, but to see that responsibility for their situation was *shared* between them and government. The difficulty was to prevent government from absorbing all the responsibility simply by virtue of giving benefits. The work test would *transfer* some of that duty to the client. Argued Wilbur Mills, "we're putting the onus on the individual. You don't get one penny out of this program until you cooperate by going to that employment office." Martha Griffiths told the employable that it was government's duty to provide them with a job and training, but what use they made of the opportunity was "your problem."[16] In economic language, the burden of economizing, of reconciling individual and social need, was no longer to rest solely with government.

If individuals were morally responsible, then government could deal openly and directly with functioning problems like nonwork. It need not approach them only indirectly, as liberals wanted, by manipulating the material conditions around the disadvantaged. It could simply expect people to behave otherwise than they did. Nixon Administration officials explained their welfare plan to Congress with the usual sociological reasoning that the right mix of income and incentives could overcome poverty. The irreverant voice of Martha Griffiths broke the spell. All they were adding to welfare was "money." she contended, and "to break this terrible pattern of life" would take a lot more than that. At intervals through the House hearings on FAP she demanded to know how the new program would forestall illegitimacy, family breakup, nonwork, and poor school performance—the behavioral problems central to welfare. Other than a belief, grounded in economic theory, that the incentives in their plan would restrain breakup and promote work, the witnesses had little to offer. It was "mythical" to think, Griffiths asserted, that economics alone could overcome dependency.[17]

Al Ullman, the moderate Democrat who was later to chair Ways and Means, objected that there was no real "rehabilitiation" in the Nixon plan. He declared, invoking the participatory ideal, "I want to bring every [recipient] within the mainstream of constructive activity in this Nation." How could FAP do that if it "put people on the shelf" by paying them simply to "exist"?[18] Again, no sufficient answer was forthcoming. Thus Griffiths, Ullman, and their fellows tore down the taboo that had blocked serious discussion of functioning problems in federal politics.

The critics even dared to question the work motivation of recipients, taken as axiomatic by liberals and planners. How, Wilbur Mills asked, could it be said that the poor wanted to work when many welfare families had been on the rolls for three generations? The widespread presence of low-wage jobs made clear that the barriers to work were not mainly economic. "These jobs await the willing hand," said Earl Landgrebe, a Republican Congressman, "but a person on a guaranteed annual income may not be so willing."[19]

The moderates raised these issues, not to stigmatize the recipients, but to insist that social programs set some standards for acceptable behavior in American society. Existing welfare tended to reinforce the very behavior society deprecated. Fathers could leave their families, and mothers could have illegitimate children and refuse to work, yet society guaranteed support. In her welfare hearings Martha Griffiths commented often on the "immoral" promises that AFDC seemed to make to the poor:

> Chairman Griffiths. Aren't we . . . saying to a wife and a mother of several children, "If you want to live with this man, your husband and the father of these children, why, do so; but if you would rather leave him, why, leave him; the rest of us will take care of you"?
>
> We are saying that, aren't we? The law says that in so many

> words, really: "You don't have to put up with anything; the rest of us are going to take care of you."
>
> Now we have gone a step further. When you have no investigation and no authority to investigate and you cannot compel the mother to admit where the father is, or that he is the father, we are then saying, "Why, you can continue to have the father live right in the house, just don't marry him, and we will support you. And he can have a job that pays $25,000 a year." Aren't we saying that?

Russell Long refused to endorse a benefit-oriented approach to reform that "encouraged people to do all the wrong things." Somehow government, while helping the poor, must lead them to "do the right thing" rather than what was "basically wrong."[20]

The moderates spoke for the deep hunger of the general public, after the social disruptions of the 1960s, to reaffirm the legitimacy of their basic institutions. Barber Conable, a Ways and Means Republican, said people "want something done with their social structure so it will make more sense."[21] The incentives approach to work, which counted on self-interest and the market to induce work, could not communicate such moral messages well. A work requirement like WIN, whatever its faults, was morally more satisfying. It defined who was employable much more plainly and *told* them to work.

To the moderates the main point of the test was not, as it was for hard-line conservatives, to keep people off the rolls and save money. It was to force recipients, even if still on welfare, to behave in integrating ways. Work measures, admitted Wilbur Mills, were "not just for economy, because they do not being economy in the short run." What they would do, wrote the Finance Committee, was bring "intangible benefits to society, such as the fact that the children in these homes will have the example of a working parent to emulate, and the fact that the working parent may have a more positive attitude toward society in general." Moderates were unmoved by economists' argument that work tests would cost more in training and child care than they saved in grant money. That was to miss the moral point. Russell Long would reply, according to one HEW official, "That's okay, you can't put a value on those children seeing a mother get up at 5:30 to go to work."[22]

Like orthodox conservatives, the civic Congressmen wanted recipients to bear a responsibility for work. But unlike them they wanted to impose that burden through public authority, not simply by excluding the employable from the rolls. Claims and obligation would be balanced *within* welfare, rather than just in the private sector. The moderates emphasized, more than other Congressmen, that without public enforcement work for the poor would become a "sucker's game," given the alternatives available. Here is Martha Griffiths dueling with Ronald Hayes, an advocate of guaranteed income from the National Conference of Catholic Charities:

> Representative Griffiths. The point that bothers me very greatly is the assumption that everybody is owed a living. Supposing everybody chooses to collect. What do you do then? Who pays?
>
> Mr. Hayes. Well, . . . we have the resources with which to solve this problem. . . .
>
> Representative Griffiths. In my judgment, everybody is owed a job. Society should be so set up that everybody has a chance to work. Once you fail that, then I will agree that the rest of us may owe you a living. . . .
>
> Mr. Hayes. I would agree . . . but I would include that . . . they are owed a living. In other words, they are owed a way to make a living. . . .
>
> Representative Griffiths. Then I find great difficulty with the suitability of work. . . . I cannot understand somebody who comes in before this committee and says to me, I am not going to work at that job. Well, . . . as far as I am concerned, you can go hungry. Why not work?[23]

Griffiths, a New Deal Democrat from blue-collar Michigan, here articulates the values of an earlier age, when workers less often expected status from their labor than they do today. The jobs of most workers did not flatter their egos, but they were obligatory nonetheless.

If obligation served a social good, it was also good for the recipients. The moderates rejected unreflective, humanitarian interpretations of what it meant to help people. After all, said John Byrnes, the ranking Republican on Ways and Means, AFDC was "humanitarian on its face" yet had "harmful effects" on individuals as well as "the fabric of our society." Senator Ernest Hollings, a Southern Democrat, said "throwing money" at poverty might "salve a nagging conscience" but was not, by itself, a solution. Both Russell Long and Edward Brooke, a liberal Republican, worried about the toll on the "human spirit" of prolonged dependency on welfare. Those who just wanted higher benefits for the needy were not helping them, Martha Griffiths declared, but were "really espousing the philosophy of a slave."[24]

While liberals sought to protect the poor by entitlements, the moderates realized that the dependent must be in some ways *less* protected if they were to be integrated. Said Senator Wallace Bennett, "Welfare, for all its faults, is security," but for the recipients truly to participate in the economy and society there had to be a "movement from security to risk." For this, public authority was indispensable. Admonished Russell Long, "[W]e have to recognize that the least successful people in our society need to be prodded, they need to be pushed," language very much like that of many WIN staff. Unless there were requirements, Griffiths said, there was "great danger" of creating "a permanent welfare class." Without "some compulsion at some point," reasoned Representative George Bush, a Texas Republican, there was no way to "break the back" of dependency.[25]

A memorable confrontation on this issue occurred in the House hearing on FAP between Griffiths and Allard Lowenstein, a nationally known liberal Democrat. Lowenstein made the standard liberal case for guaranteed income for all the poor with only weak work aspects. "We can afford to eliminate poverty," he said. "Knowing that, can we afford not to?" But Griffiths accused him sharply of being, not a "revolutionary," but "a supporter of the status quo." For to give mothers money without work requirements, though it would raise their income, would only confirm their social subordination. Far more real change would follow, Griffiths proposed, from making them work, if necessary under the threat of taking their children away. Lowenstein recoiled at the thought of such "compulsory" measures, so foreign to the liberal mind. "I begin to see what you mean," he confessed, "about who is and who is not a revolutionary."[26]

Out of the crucible of obligation, the moderates believed, functioning citizens should emerge. A recipient might not work freely, but he would still enjoy what Russell Long called the "dignity of employment." He would have to function, and from that, said the Finance Committee, would follow the "dignity, self-worth, and confidence which will flow from being recognized as a wage-earning member of society." "Gainful employment," said Congressman John Byrnes, was simply "the best individual and family therapy we can provide."[27]

The civic conservatives occasionally made the further claim, seldom heard openly in American politics, that obligations, including work, were as much a badge of citizenship as rights. In the Finance hearings on WIN in 1967, a parade of welfare groups indicted the proposed work test as inhuman and coercive. Senator Carl Curtis made the disarming reply that it was wrong that "any particular segment of our population should be protected from all forms of compulsion." "I believe the average citizen is compelled to do a lot of things," he went on, such as attend school and pay taxes. [P]rofessional welfare workers are wrong in rejecting any compulsion because there are people in the world that do things that they have to." In the 1970 Finance hearings on the Nixon welfare plan, Clifford Hansen, another Finance Republican, made a similar rejoinder:

> What 10 million Americans [i.e., the recipients] . . . would regard as involuntary servitude . . . is something that the other 190 million Americans quite readily accept as a responsiblity that they believe is theirs to accept the duties of citizenship, the duties of parenthood, the time-old responsibility of taking care of one's family. . . .
>
> I do not believe at all that to expect able-bodied people to have to work in order to help take care of their families is . . . the application of the power of a despotic government upon citizens that violate[s] their constitutional rights or anything else.[28]

Curtis and Hansen were conservatives who would have resisted new federal controls on the economy. But even a "free" society, they seemed to say, presupposed some minimal discipline on the part of individuals. For the dependent that obligation necessarily had to come from government.

There is even a touch here of the classical idea that the citizen must in some senses be *un*free. He is not simply a natural man possessing rights carried over from the state of nature, as in Locke. He is also a civic man, the product of his own polity, and stamped by the rights *and* obligations that derive from it. As Rousseau once wrote, "It is national institutions which shape the genius, the character, the tastes and the manners of a people." Only if citizens are thoroughly schooled in their obligations can duty have

> . . . a vigour which will supplant the abusive operation of vain precepts, and which will make them do through preference and passion that which is never done sufficiently well when done only for duty or interest. These are the souls on which appropriate legislation will take hold. They will obey the laws without evasion because those laws suit them and rest on the inward assent of their will.[29]

The work test was a humble attempt to teach such virtue, in the belief that willing work in available jobs was a defining obligation of the American polity.

In their arguments the moderates and their opponents appealed implicitly to notions of a Lockean natural condition, of the way society would be without government. Whatever rights or obligations recipients enjoyed in that condition they should also encounter in welfare. Liberals assumed that society was naturally rich enough to guarantee an income to everyone. Hence, for government to refuse welfare, or condition it on work, was to deny a basic right. Conservatives, who believed society was open but less bountiful, offered the poor the opportunity to work for their living but no assurance of an income. While government might support the unemployable, assistance even for them was best left to private, charitable auspices. The employable and their families must labor for their sustenance, and the market place would determine whether they succeeded.

The moderates borrowed elements from both positions. They shared the conservative view that society could not afford a guranateed income for the employable. "If every person chose not to work," said Martha Griffiths, "we could all starve together." Senator John Stennis, a conservative Democrat, warned that "when all we have to do to qualify is just be a human being, then we undermine the basic foundation of self-government."[30] Individuals would not govern themselves, nor could claims on government be limited.

But, as liberals wished, the moderates would have guaranteed an income to the unemployable, and they would have guaranteed jobs, if not income, to those who could work. As Martha Griffiths framed the standard in her report on welfare:

> Most Americans believe that the government should assume the duty of assuring that jobs exist for all who are willing and able to work, that able-bodied individuals are responsible for working at available jobs to earn enough to support themselves and their families, and that the government should aid persons unable to work steadily.

Again, Griffiths resurrected the social policy of the New Deal: income from work or work-based social insurance for the able-bodied, and welfare for the unemployable. Many Congressmen seem to have yearned for a kind of welfare reform never proposed in Congress, one that would eliminate benefits but not jobs for the employable. Instead of guaranteed income they wanted schemes of "guaranteed opportunity" that would "guarantee jobs rather than income."[31]

Viewing work as an obligation, the civic conservatives rejected attempts by liberals to base welfare work on self-interest and choice by the recipients. Asked Griffiths, "Why should some people be offered a choice at the expense of the rest of us?" The moral objection to work incentives, as Senator Carl Curtis put it, was that "no one should have to give any ablebodied person a cash incentive to go to work. That is his responsiblity." The same objection cut against paying recipients the minimum or prevailing wage in guaranteed jobs; they should be entitled only to the value of the welfare they were already receiving. Said Russell Long, "You don't have to pay someone a minimum wage to be a good citizen."[32]

Welfare for the employable, then, was contractual, just as the courts have viewed it. There was no public work obligation for the nondependent, who could decline to work and take the consequences. But there was for the dependent if employable, because they received an assured government income. Russell Long always denied that he was "forcing" anyone to work. "I do not want to *make* anybody go to work," he exclaimed. "I just do not want to pay them a lot of money for *not* working." Neither the dependent nor the independent had to work other than in return for income; "the right to go hungry, if you don't want to work," Long declared, "should be preserved in this country."[33]

Concretely, the civic approach to welfare implied an effort to tie work requirements as closely as possible to benefits for the employable. The ideal, perhaps realized only in workfare, was to make clear to all potential recipients that the employable could have support and work only *together*. As a practical matter, reasoned Russell Long, "Welfare is so much more attractive than work" for many unskilled recipients that they would not look seriously for jobs unless the work requirement were stiff. Only then could placement programs like WIN be effective.[34] Accordingly, the moderates paid more attention to the legal aspects of welfare work than they did to the benefits and other economic dimensions of welfare. They realized, as many Congressmen did, that the rules defining employability and suitable work have as much or more to do with motivating work than the work incentives stressed by planners.

The governing ideal was one of moral, not economic, reciprocity.

Wrote Martha Griffiths, "no society has promised subsistence without expecting or exacting a quid pro quo. Like other societies, ours is based on the principle that individuals should pull a share of the load." But this required only, said Wilbur Mills, that the employable do "some work" in return for support. It did not require any precise correspondence between earnings and needs. The obligation was that a recipient work, not necessarily that he make enough to support his family and leave welfare, desireable though that was. Said Russell Long, again invoking the participatory ideal, "Now, to me it is not as important what he is doing as the fact that he is doing something. We are moving him toward being a working, deserving citizen of the community and of this Nation."[35]

Whereas antigovernment conservatives saw dependency itself as an affront, for moderates nonwork was the chief abuse in welfare. It infringed the common obligation to work. The ideal in welfare, Martha Griffiths said, was to "treat everybody equally." That meant all the needy getting an income—and all employables working. AFDC, however, placed most adult recipients in "a completely different category" exempted from work. It created, said Wilbur Mills, a "difference in status between neighbor and neighbor," anathema to the participatory vision. Somebody had to stand up for the taxpayer and even more, said George Bush, for "the man who is working for a living."[36]

Liberals left to the labor market whether recipients worked at all, conservatives whether the employable made enough to survive. For moderates, who both demanded and guaranteed work, the market determined only how good a job a recipient received. For discharging the work obligation, any legal job would do. Reformers had no right to complain that the jobs available to the low-skilled were beneath them. "It is not for us," Russell Long said, "to pass on the job that is available to them."[37] On the other hand, even the most low-paid work, if necessary in government jobs, sufficed to qualify a family for assistance. Provided the employable discharged the work obligation, society would help them meet their needs.

Finally, the moderates were prepared to take decisions about welfare standards nationally. The question of the benefits and requirements to be attached to welfare were too important to be devolved to varying decisions by lower levels of government, as conservatives wanted. Nor could Washington any longer fund welfare while letting local authorities enforce norms on a discretionary basis. The question, said Paul Fannin, another Finance Committee

Republican, was whether the federal government would now "set a standard" for recipients. Requirements had to be stiffened if only to prevent local administrators from exempting most of the employable. Work standards were no longer to be hostage to "the philosophical inclinations of social workers and administrators," declared Wilbur Mills, but would be set in "national policy laid down by Congress."[38]

Social Attitudes

As far as existing studies show, public feeling toward welfare issues corresponds most closely with civic conservatism, which may be why that viewpoint tended to prevail in the welfare debates. The logic of the civic position even helps to unravel some apparent puzzles in opinion.

The public seems to assign responsibility for the social problem to both government and the individual, just as the moderates did in Congress. On the one hand public support for government social spending is unambiguous. Critics of the welfare state, from either right or left, sometimes suggest that Americans' commitment to the welfare state is halfhearted. That is not the message of public opinion polls.[39] At least two-thirds of the public supports the principal social insurance programs, such as Medicare and Unemployment Insurance; the figure for Social Security is well over 90 percent. These programs are as near to untouchable as anything in American politics. That is why Congress has been most reluctant to cut their benefits in spite of chronic financial problems.

More recent, Great Society programs have also been popular, especially education and training programs that promise expanded opportunity rather than income to the poor, in spite of doubts about their effectiveness in Washington. Only "welfare" is unpopular, and even here the opposition bears close examination. Support for social programs also varies surprisingly little by social group. The well-off support them right along with the low-income, even though it is less in their interest, narrowly speaking, to do so. Support has also been solid for a long time, in the case of the insurance programs since the New Deal.

Even the recent national turn toward the right has not put social commitments in question. On examination the "tax revolt" signaled by Propostion 13 in California in 1978 was a call for more efficient government, not less government. Like the civic conservatives average Americans apparently want to change the nature of government much more than its size. They want it to be less wasteful and lenient with the dependent, but they also want it to go on responding to social needs.[40] Politicians of either right or left who focus only on the scale of government are responding to the conventions of federal politics. They apparently do not speak for unpolitical, social opinion.

Of course, the public does not understand well the cost or operations of programs. For most people, whether or not to support benefits for the elderly, ill, or needy is a "motherhood" question, unless costs are stressed. Support for programs does drop if respondents are asked, at the same time, to support the taxes necessary to pay for them. Nevetheless, the popularity of benefit programs —other than "welfare"—is still not seriously in doubt. The breadth and rapid growth of the American welfare state would be inexplicable on any other presumption.

That support exists, despite the national "individualism," because the humanitarian impulse in American politics is very strong. When a group is clearly unable to provide for itself, the public desire to help overrides any notion that the responsibilities of government are limited. Even the foes of guaranteed income in Congress shared that feeling. "We should take care of people in need," said Wilbur Mills, for "That is the American way of life." Deserving groups, such as the aged, blind, and disabled, should receive, said Russell Long, "the most adequate support we can afford."[41]

At the same time Americans hold individuals responsible for social problems, especially when behavior is a cause, contrary to sociological reasoning. Surveys show that even city dwellers, including blacks, who are surrounded by crime and other disorders trace them mostly to the incivilty of people, not to impersonal social or economic conditions. Planners may look to environmental changes as the key to poverty, but ordinary Americans believe that the problems would abate if only the individuals involved would behave better.[42]

Most people see a difference between the hardships of the Depression, caused by an economic collapse, and the kind of poverty or unemployment prevalent today. When Americans are asked to explain poverty, they show a preference for individualist explanations such as lack of thrift or foresight by the poor themselves, as against reasons that appeal to luck, fate, or social factors such as discrimination. Those attitudes, too, differ little among social groups. The low-income and the undereducated assert them as well as the better-off. Blacks are the only group where a majority cite social explanations for poverty, and large numbers of blacks also cite individualist or random causes.[43] None of this means that the respondents live by the values they profess, but the norms themselves are not in doubt.

The great mystery in attitudes toward social policy is that most Americans oppose "welfare" even though they favor helping the poor and needy, things which to a policy planner are equivalent. Respondents to surveys will often reject "welfare" in general while supporting specific programs meant for the poor. A poll at the time of the Carter welfare plan found 58 percent of Americans against government welfare programs, but at the same time 81 percent favored AFDC and food stamps and 82 percent favored health care for the poor. Many government employment and training programs are means-tested, yet they too are popular. As before, the reactions are much the same for all groups, except that blacks are more tolerant of welfare than others.[44]

One interpretation is that the public is simply confused. It wants to help the needy but fears that many of them are abusing programs and not really "deserving." Alternatively, the public may understand the "poor" and "welfare" recipients to be distinct groups. The first means the "deserving poor," mainly the aged, blind, and disabled, while the second means the "undeserving"—shiftless men and female-headed families. The "deserving" groups, as unemployable, are not held responsible for need or dependency, while the "undeserving" are.[45] This interpretation would explain why Congress was willing to federalize and liberalize welfare for the aged and disabled in 1972 at the same time as it refused to do so for family welfare.

More probably, however, public opinion has a logic of its own. The same two-sidedness appears in attitudes about welfare specifically for the "undeserving." Sixty percent or more of Americans oppose guaranteed income for the employable, yet majorities just as large favor helping them through some kind of work or guaranteed job system. According to a 1972 Gallup poll 81 percent of the public would choose to replace cash welfare with a work-based relief system even if it cost more because of child care and other expenses. That vociferous preference for "work relief" over cash relief stretches across all strata. Blacks are the only group where a majority supports guaranteed income, and much higher majorities of blacks prefer guaranteed jobs instead.[46] This suggests that the public, like many Congressmen, opposes, not so much welfare *per se*, as the failure of existing programs to demand functioning from the employable *in return* for support. If the "undeserving" poor commonly worked while on welfare, they too would be "deserving" and the resistance to aiding them would dissipate.

Welfare reformers sometimes intimated that popular opposition to "welfare" was based on envy. Struggling working people supposedly resented that they were not normally eligible for assistance, while female-headed families were. The Nixon reform planners made a great play in Congress of showing how AFDC was "inequitable" and "unfair to the working poor," while FAP would cover them for the first time.[47] But as Congressmen pointed out, this misread popular psychology entirely. The public wanted, not welfare for itself, but conformist behavior from existing recipients. "Most people will gladly pay taxes at personal sacrifice to help needy children break the welfare cycle," said one Congressman. "But they insist that any such program . . . weed out adult chiselers who use the welfare payments for their own indulgence." Said Russell Long, people were "not demanding welfare payments for themselves; they do not expect it." Their demand was that employable recipients work alongside the taxpayers, or leave welfare.[48]

The public apparently holds a contractual view of welfare much like the civic viewpoint. Alice Rivlin testified, "We would like to have everyone have a minimum decent standard of living, but we would also like to see work be the main source of income for people of working age who are not sick or disabled." The central problem in income policy, Lee Rainwater has written, is "so to govern the society" that both those goals are met.[49] The main impediment is, not public attitudes against the poor or welfare, but problems specific to federal governance that have made it difficult to combine welfare and work. Federal politicians find it easier to enact benefits than requirements, and work tests pose demanding implementation problems. As a result welfare benefits usually only help the poor without enforcing the obligations the public also want. Welfare is unpopular because it satisfies only half the public mind. To eliminate welfare would satisfy only the other half. The public will remain uncomfortable until a civic version of welfare is realized.

The Meaning of Equality

American attitudes toward equality seem, as well, to express an idea of equivalent rights and obligations.

Equality is one of the leading values in American politics. Why then, many authors ask, has American democracy never pursued equality in the socialist sense of expropriation of business or the rich? The American people apparently control their government, but they have never voted for public control of the economy or explicit income redistribution even to the extent seen in Western Europe. A lot of economic regulation and some redistribution have occurred, but the rationale has always been to advance individual freedoms, not to construct a more egalitarian society in economic terms. Researchers find that even working-class and low-income people have the individualist view that economic inequalities must be respected because they reflect the verdict of the market place. Americans want equal political rights and equal social opportunity regardless of background, but not equal outcomes in the sense of equal income or status.

One explanation is that political equality and equal opportunity have been so close to realities for most Americans that they simply cannot muster the grievance to turn to socialism. No group holds a social vision opposed to Lockean liberalism. A more critical view is that the American mind is internally conflicted. It harbors irresolvable tensions between the desire for equality for all and respect for freedom, capitalism, and the existing political system, whose capacities for change are limited. A further, more radical view is that social individualism is a form of false consciousness. It is the tribute that capitalist influence forces Americans to pay to the forces of property, when their democratic beliefs should properly lead them to socialism.[50]

It may be naïve to think that political democracy should logically entail socialism. To raise people's income is not, even in other societies, a panacea that produces equality, and the public appears to sense this. Studies done in a wide range of countries find that the absolute level of income people have has little to do with their happiness. How they compare in income or status with others in the same society is much more important, yet people tend to make such comparisons in a highly constrained way. In rating their own success, they compare themselves to people close to them in status and income, not more distant classes that may be doing much better or worse.[51] Ordinary people tend to ask limited and concrete things of government: jobs, pensions, health care. Where governments have instituted more explicit socialism, the impetus has usually come from elites with an intellectual commitment to equality, not from popular demands.

Nor does equality have to mean a leveling of social and economic distinctions, the meaning that has come out of socialism. In the United States, rather, it seems to mean common citizenship. Americans seem to feel equal when they possess a bundle of rights *and* obligations that they view as normal for their society. Citizenship does encompass certain minimal rights to income and employment. In a study of social standards Lee Rainwater found that most respondents agreed closely, regardless of class, that a little over half the average family income was a minimum that every family should have. But if that minimum were assured, they had little further interest in income redistribution. They opposed eliminating high incomes simply because they were high.[52]

To a great extent, equality is simply detached from economics or status. Instead, Rainwater found, "American equalitarianism means that everyone is treated the same regardless of what he has." There was "a strong desire to ignore resources, to treat them as irrelevant from a social interactional point of view." It was sufficient that differences or status or privilege receive no *public* deference. In fact, "great disparities in resources" were acceptable provided they did not "intrude themselves in . . . public encounters," that is, in the everyday social and economic interactions central to the participatory vision. In that sense, said one respondent, "equality is fairness." It meant to be treated as "a person of equal merit," not through an end to status differences, but *in spite of* them. Equality meant, not to end social distinctions, but to *devalue* them in the light of equal citizenship. None of this means that advantages of status or income were unimportant to people; they competed fiercely for them. But such differences were not *politically* divisive provided that Americans were equal in public things.

This popular idea of equality is quite different from the economic conceptions prevalent in Washington:

> Conspicuously absent . . . is any clearly formulated conceptualization of inequality issues as involving relative shares. This . . . is important, because policy discussions in this area inevitably revolve around an understanding of relative shares and therefore on some dis-

> tributions being more unequal than others. The idea of relative shares seems to be a very abstract one that individuals do not use and only barely grasp . . . .

The American ideal is not socialist equality but the realization of "a nation of average men." There is no felt opposition between freedom and equality. Rather, equality *is* equal freedom in the sense of equal citizenship.[53]

American equality seems to entail common obligations, not only rights as politicians and intellectuals tend to assume. Equality is not so much an entitlement, a status, as an *activity*. To be equal an American must *do* things, not just claim them. From that perspective duties such as obeying the law or paying taxes become, not just burdens, but badges of belonging. The planners of welfare reform wanted to exempt the poor from paying taxes, the better to tax them "negatively." To economists, taxation could only seem a cost to the poor. Some Congressmen, however, wanted welfare recipients to pay taxes, as well as work. Since both activities were among the common obligations, they could give recipients a status they were unlikely to obtain from more competitive forms of striving. The poor could at least be "taxpayers instead of taxtakers." To remove them from the tax rolls might be demeaning. "I don't think that any American ought to be in a situation where he is not paying taxes," said Martha Griffiths. Better to keep taxing the dependent and increase their grants to allow for it.[54]

The opposition that some see between "political" and "economic" values, or between equality and free enterprise, in American thinking[55] may really be an effort to balance rights and claims. Since American government is permissive while the economy is demanding, "political" values have come to connote the claims Americans and their leaders make on the system, while "economic" values represent the competences they also want individuals to display.[56] But neither correspondence is perfect. There are some obligations, such as tax payment, that Americans clearly expect to come from government, and there are some claims, such as for jobs, that tend to be met by the private economy. A just balance of claims with obligations seems to be more important to most people than whether either comes from the public or private sector. Whether the regime is fair in that sense has little to do with where the dividing line between government and society falls, the question that has preoccupied federal politics.

Once we credit that American equality requires equal obligations, as well as equal rights, demands that welfare recipients work no longer seem so punitive. Studies of attitudes to equality, no less than polls about specific policies, uncover the public's deep yearning to guarantee the poor jobs rather than income.[57] The motivation is moral, not just self-interested. A substantial class of nonworking adults simply violates the American idea of equality. Those who function in the ways citizenship requires cannot feel equal to others who do not, when it seems they could. The stigma of welfare stems mainly from the frequent incompetence of the dependent, and the shame is felt by society as well as the recipients.[58] The moral purpose of functioning requirements is to ensure, for their own benefit and others', that recipients do in fact discharge the common obligations of citizenship.

11

The Common Obligations

WHAT exactly are the common obligations that Americans expect of one another? We cannot be sure from the available information, but there are a number of specific competences in which government at some level has taken an interest. Work is only one. These expectations, so much less visible than claims or rights in federal politics, provide a hidden basis for community in the United States, and also for social policy. Programs that enforce those standards, as well as offer support, have the best chance to satisfy social expectations and thus integrate their recipients.

To meet the common obligations, as well as to claim benefits from government, is a form of equality accessible even to the most disadvantaged, though it may involve a greater degree of paternalism than Americans have been used to. The connection of this minimum competence to common citizenship and to equality in the American sense is the idea that might finally legitimize functioning requirements in federal policymaking.

Social Obligations

The common obligations seem to specify certain *social* duties alongside political ones. Social expectations relate to interacting with others and getting along in everyday life rather than satisfying the demands of government. We are inclined to think of such obligations as private, but Americans seem nevertheless to regard them as mandatory.

Political rights and duties are the easiest to specify. They are all directly related to government and defined in law. The most obvious duties include obedience to civil and criminal laws and payment of taxes. In addition, adults may be obligated to serve on juries and, if there is a draft, in the military. For the average citizen the laws behind these requirements stem mostly from the general "police power" of state and local governments. Federal requirements, other than taxes, impinge mainly in the form of regulations on business and state or local agencies. In addition, voting is sometimes viewed as a political duty, though it is not mandated and is also seen as a right, along with other political and civil liberties.

The social dimension of citizenship is less clearly defined, because it is less governmental. Social rights, like political ones, tend to be legally stated, in the shape of the benefits programs provide to protect people against need, unemployment, health expenses, and so on. Social obligations are less clear. They are public in the sense that they are necessary to the community, are decided in some collective way by it, and are not subject to individual choice. But they are not all governmental in the sense of being specified in law. All have the force of public opinion behind them, only some that of government.

Nevertheless, we can infer some of those expectations from the social capacities in which government has taken an interest, often short of enforcement, as well as from the welfare debates and opinion studies seen earlier. The following seem to be the main social obligations expected of adults in the United States today:

- Work in available jobs for heads of families, unless aged or disabled, and for other adult members of families that are needy
- Contributing all that one can to the support of one's family (But public assistance seems acceptable if parents work and cannot earn enough for support.)
- Fluency and literacy in English, whatever one's native tongue
- Learning enough in school to be employable

- Law-abidingness, meaning both obedience to law and a more generalized respect for the rights of others

Work for the employable is the clearest social obligation, and not only because there are work tests. Belief in the work ethic resounds through American culture. Perhaps Americans are less truly committed to that ethic than formerly, but they still profess it and they prize work involvement as a basis for belonging. John Rawls has truly written, "What men want is meaningful work in free association with others."[1] The need appears especially great in the United States because of the comparative weakness of some other forms of community. There is no common ethnicity, small towns have declined in favor of faceless urban areas, and the family is less stable than it was. For many Americans today the workplace *is* their family, and the price of admission is the capacity to labor in some way others are willing to pay for.

The meaning of work—and social obligation in general—is dramatized in recent beer advertisements on television. Miller and Budweiser ads show workers, usually blue collar, struggling with some challenging task, then knocking off and socializing in the nearest tavern. The emphasis is on work effort and reward, and especially on the *connection between* them. The effort and the relaxation are *both* necessary, and neither would be meaningful without the other. Only men who have worked hard have earned the right to play, while work would be pointless unless rewards lay at the end of it. "For all you do," the jingle runs, "this Bud's for you." Men who have proven themselves on the job can also trust one another in private life. Competence in public things leads to community.

Such is the value of work that even the aged and disabled, whom society exempts from labor, now often insist on a right to employment. The "earnings test"—the rule that retirees can earn only small amounts without having their pensions cut—is one of the most unpopular restrictions in Social Security, and Congress has progressively eased it. When Supplemental Security Income for the aged, blind, and disabled was enacted in 1972, Congress included economic incentives to reward the recipients for working, even though they did not have to. During hearings on PBJI, groups representing the aged and blind complained that the plan offered weaker work incentives to them than to the able-bodied. Declared one spokesman, "[t]he blind do not want to see this country move further away from the principles of independence and self-sufficiency."[2]

The obligation to contribute to the support of families is reflected in welfare work requirements and also in federal and state child support laws. The idea is that parents are responsible in some sense for themselves and the families they have brought into being. Yet, to judge from the welfare debates and public opinion, the common obligations do not at present include self-sufficiency, or an ability to cope without any assistance from society. Congress rejected that standard when it refused to deny all welfare to the employable. Most politicians and the public seem more upset by moral offenses than economic incompetence in welfare. They oppose nonwork, nonpayment of child support, and fraud or abuse of programs by recipients, but not welfare or dependency *per se*. If adult dependents are making an honest effort to support their families, that is enough to justify at least some assistance. Indeed, since work is the strongest social obligation, the mere fact of working establishes a strong presumptive claim to assistance.

The importance of English literacy and competence in school is most apparent at the level of state and local government, which have the main responsibility for education. Schooling is not just a benefit those authorities provide to people but a means they use to set standards for some public kinds of competence. The Supreme Court has repeatedly upheld their power to do so. In 1972, for example, it affirmed the power of states to require whatever "degree of education" was "necessary to prepare citizens to participate effectively and intelligently in our open political system" and also to be "self-reliant participants in society."[3] The demands of an individualist interactive society, that is, may justify public obligations.

The standard-setting role of education has come to the fore in recent years because of public concern over falling standards in the schools. The decline in SAT scores, seen in Table 1, and other test results suggest that the losses have been greatest in the higher-level reasoning and writing skills most necessary for higher education.[4] There is some reason to think that standards fell during the Great Society period because the nation's priorities in education shifted toward goals—racial integration, student rights, "mainstreaming" of the handicapped—that could undercut learning, at least as they were implemented. But recently several national reports have raised the alarm over quality,[5] and most states have raised standards for teacher certification, graduation from high school, or both. "Minimum competency" tests that students must pass to progress between grades or to graduate are now commonplace.

During the Great Society, programming theory in education, as in other policy areas, was resource-oriented. Sociological reasoning traced the learning problems of disadvantaged children to material deprivations, and it was thought that some of these could be made up by special remedial programs, funded largely from Washington. The Coleman report and other studies, however, implied that there was no simple connection between spending or services and the production of educated students.[6] Gradually policy thinking and research recognized the important role of authority. Good schools seem, in the main, to be those that set clearcut standards for children and monitor their progress closely.[7] As in welfare and employment, the challenge is to *express* social expectations more clearly *through* government.

Law-abidingness is in part a political obligation, because it includes obedience to law, but it also connotes a more generalized respect for the rights of others in ways not legally enforced. As in education, local authorities take the lead in this area, and the Great Society was a period of laxness. The crime boom had a number of causes, but one of them was overly discretionary enforcement by local prosecutors and judges. Plea-bargaining reduced serious offenses to lesser ones, and indeterminate sentences plus heavy use of parole spared even violent criminals from having to spend much time behind bars. Recently most states have legislated mandatory sentences for major crimes, to reduce discretion, and have built more prisons. A sharp increase in incarceration has resulted. Between 1972 and 1982 the number of prisoners doing time per 100,000 population rose from 93 to 177.[8] The rate of major offenses peaked in 1980, then fell 9 percent by 1983, as shown in Table 1. Tougher enforcement is evidently one of the reasons, along with the passing of the "baby boom" generation.

As in education, there has been a shift from resources to authority as the main policy instrument. In criminology the main expression of sociological reasoning was rehabilitatory approaches to punishment, but special programs to train and educate convicts have not measurably reduced their propensity to commit future crimes. That has forced governments increasingly to use punishment in ways that are less liberal but apparently more effective—not to reform criminals but simply to immobilize and deter them.[9] Effectively, this shifts much of the responsibility for crime that government had assumed back onto the criminals. Society has begun to worry less about their problems and more about its own.

The role of the social obligations is to balance the array of social rights guaranteed by government. While individuals make claims for sustenance through politics and their own labors, they also must contribute to a reservoir of resources, both economic and moral, shared by all the citizens. Fulfilling the obligations is a matter of both prudence and morals. Compliance usually serves self-interest, but it is mandatory in any event. The social ideal behind the obligations is the participatory vision evoked by Congressmen—a single, strenuous society in which everyone is working simultaneously for himself and for others.

Authority and Compliance

What may be most disquieting about the idea of enforcing social obligations is the paternalism involved. Enforcement means more than just levying standards. It means local authorities instructing people how to behave. Government to some extent takes over the socializing role of parents. For teachers, whose clients are children, that role is explicit and noncontroversial. However, social workers, employment counselors, and other local staff often play the same role for the adult recipients of welfare, employment, and training programs. They are more than clerks dispensing benefits. Through personal suasions, backed up by their official authority, they may try to motivate their clients to obey program rules, function better, and overcome their problems. Necessarily, a more directive social policy would build up this authoritative role of local service provision.

However, there has been disquiet in Washington over paternalism even in existing social administration. That is one of the reasons reform thinking in federal social policy has been anti-institutional. Liberals wanted to guarantee income or give benefits in the form of vouchers, in part, so that recipients would be independent of, and even have power over, local program staffs.[10] The trend in welfare policy was to cut staff power and pay benefits essentially as entitlements. The conservative tactic of abolishing programs for the employable came to much the same thing. While it reduced support for the needy, it also freed them from the toils of the welfare state.

Reformers, left and right, assumed that the dependent could learn to live successfully without personal guidance, simply by the experience of interacting with other people in public, especially in the marketplace. By being responsible for their own choices, recipients would learn what behavior did and did not serve them. If they spent unwisely or refused to work or otherwise function, they would "pay" for it in the coin of hostility from others. Conservatives rightly emphasize that demands to perform that come from one's own boss or customer have a special force, and not only because compliance is closely linked to self-interest. The demands spring from the other person's *own* needs, not the impersonal dictates of society. They have an authenticity that strictures imposed by bureaucratic authority figures like social workers can never have.

Those arguments assumed away the problem, however, for if the poor really could learn and cope in this self-reliant way, social programs would be unnecessary. Ghetto culture does not make it easy for the young and uneducated to see that "behaving well" will serve their interests. Local authorities have the crucial advantage that they can interpret social norms to clients directly. The suasions they can exert *personally* may well be essential to make obligations meaningful. Otherwise clients are unlikely to assume obligations like work or school that often seem unrewarding to them in the short run. Unless authorities whom they can see confront them, they are unlikely to comply with more impersonal powers that they cannot see, and which have much more power to harm them. Today socialization of the poor essentially is left to the market, the courts, and the street, and most of them are seriously injured or stigmatized before society's requirements become clear to them.

There is much fear among liberals that clearer standards in school, work, or other areas of functioning will simply lead to more failure and ostracism for the unfortunate. Undoubtedly there is a danger of that. To shift more responsibility for functioning to the dependent does mean that failure in some senses would be allowed. Society must give up at least some of its fear of "blaming the victims" if it is to help them more effectively. In part the choice it faces is whether to stigmatize the least cooperative of the disadvantaged in order to integrate the rest.

However, widespread failure is likely only if, as now, routine obligations are not forcefully communicated to the poor. The evidence indicates that if standards were clear and enforced, many more disadvantaged people would meet them than do now. The main problem lies not with the poor themselves but with political authorities who refuse to govern them firmly. In making standards clear, local officials like teachers and welfare staff play an essential role. Admittedly, to judge from the record of programs, it is not a role they have played well in recent decades. But much of the reason is the limitations of authority that have flowed from federal policies. Local workers cannot guide the poor on their own authority, as many of them try to do now. They need stronger mandates from Washington.

The assumption, orthodox in Washington, that helping the poor is synonymous with the removal of restraint was much truer for the well-functioning beneficiaries of New Deal reforms than today's needy. The current poor and disadvantaged seem to need, not just support or opportunity, but *contact* with those better integrated than themselves. "Healthy human beings," Edward Wynne has written, "are . . . the product of . . . engagement, caring, persistent attention, and—most importantly—of demanding relationships."[11] One-sided support for the poor is no substitute for institutions, such as effective schools or work programs, that tie recipients to society in this reciprocal way. These structures must allow government and its dependents to make demands on *each other*.

Because of the authority problems in public programs, the archetype of this effective kind of local authority comes from the private sector—nuns teaching in parochial schools. Traditionally nuns are tough on their students precisely *because* they believe in them and are concerned about their futures. On average, parochial high schools today seem to outperform public ones, and one reason is that they are freer to set and enforce standards than most public schools.[12] Norms, however, were once clearer in the public system, even in low-income areas. This is Kenneth Clark's memory of the schools he went to in prewar Harlem:

> [T]he teachers were concerned with holding *all* of us to high standards, because they were convinced *all* of us were educable. We had not yet come to that particular breakdown in the public education of minorities which is due to . . . the sloppy, sentimental good intentions of certain educators, who *reduce* learning standards for low-status youngsters, because they believe . . . it impossible for them to learn as much as suburban children. . . . But when I was going to public school we had teachers who did not consider themselves . . . ra-

> tionalizers of educational inequities. They were asked to teach reading, arithmetic, grammar, and they *did*.[13]

That note of insistence is what distinguishes effective schools and other programs for the disadvantaged in our own time, as in Clark's. By it they say that their clients *can* fulfill social standards, and also that they *must*. Those suasions, positive and negative, spur them to find in themselves the capabilities society will later demand of them.

The Competence Dimension

The trend is toward government specification of social, like political, rights and obligations. In the United States, as in other countries, the state has gradually taken over the provision of social insurance, welfare, and support services from churches, labor unions, and other voluntary organizations. The purpose was to expand and guarantee the benefits in a way that private agencies never could.

In the United States and elsewhere, there has recently been stock-taking about the costs of these benefits and their negative effects on functioning, especially on work effort. Recent federal efforts to enforce work and child support, alongside local efforts to toughen law enforcement and educational standards, suggest that government is taking over the obligations side of social citizenship as it already has the benefits side. The moral may be simply that the welfare state must finally *be* a state. If benefits are guaranteed in the ironclad way possible only with government, they will inevitably provoke dysfunction. Government then must mandate functioning as well as benefits. The costs, social as well as economic, of letting obligations lapse are simply too great.

A welfare state that sets standards as well as provides benefits has an enlarged political importance. It constitutes an *operational definition of citizenship* in its social dimension, and it becomes a means for deciding what that dimension should mean. The structure of benefits and requirements states quite concretely what American society gives to, and expects from, its members. It does so not only for recipients but implicitly for all citizens, since the balance within programs is meant to match the balance that nondependent people face. Changes in benefits and rules effectively change the terms of belonging in American society. Especially, shifts in explicit requirements like the work test alter the kinds of functioning that are viewed as mandatory. Such rules become the mechanism by which America can decide collectively how demanding a society it wants to be.

To some extent social obligations can be understood in conventional, progressive terms simply as cuts in some of the rights and privileges government had previously extended to the public. Government is taking away the entitlements that seem to undercut social competence. However, only canceling benefits really undoes the welfare state. The effort to combine benefits with obligations is something new. What the standards should be is a different question from the scale-of-government issues that earlier dominated American social politics.

Figure 1 portrays those two issues as separate dimensions of politics. The horizontal axis is the conventional, left-right spectrum concerning the size of the welfare state and the degree of intervention in the private economy. The vertical axis is the degrees of competence that might publicly be expected of citizens. The position chosen on one axis determines the extent of government, on the other its nature, that is, how authoritative or permissive it should be. On each axis a number of positions are plausible. Conventional conservatives favor small government, but also a free-market society that would be quite demanding of people. Conventional liberals favor a large but undemanding government. Civic conservatives accept a large government but want it to expect work or other civilities from the needy as well as supporting them. The fourth position, that of private charity, opposes statism but is relatively undemanding of citizens. It occurs, not so much in the United States, as among churches and other private organizations in Communist societies, where the state, not the market, is the basis of social discipline. In those countries people who want to protect the needy from social demands tend to turn away from government programs, rather than toward them as in the West.

As the functioning issue has surfaced in American social policy, the main axis of political dispute has shifted from the horizontal spectrum toward the dotted line connecting quadrants 2 and 3. Conservatives still defend the private sector against government, but they are more explicit than they used to be in demanding that dependent groups function better without assistance. Liberals still

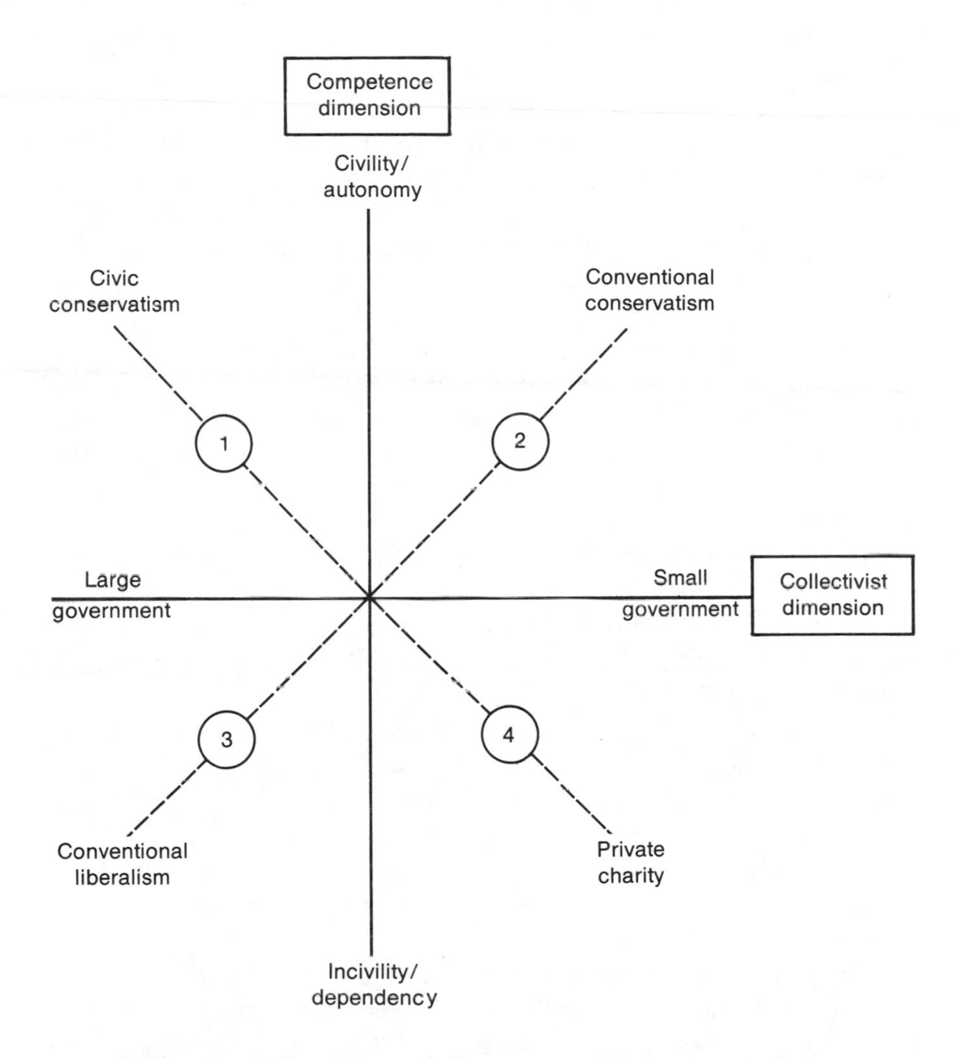

Figure 1 Collectivist and Competence Dimensions in Politics

defend the welfare state, but increasingly they also have to defend the dysfunction of benefit recipients, as they did in the welfare debates. Politicians between those extremes are torn between a desire to preserve popular benefits and the conviction that something must be done about nonwork and other social problems that benefits seem to promote. The civic conservatives held a strategic position in the welfare struggle because they alone proposed a way to do both these things, though one requiring the difficult development of a more authoritative kind of program.

The idea of setting standards through deliberate choice conflicts with other conservative approaches to order in social policy. It means that decisions would be taken nationally, not devolved to local or private "mediating structures," whose decisions would be more variable and less legitimate. It also suggests that competence standards pose a political question with no single best answer. The issue cannot be settled by appeals to tradition or moral absolutes. All depends on the degree of discipline which the public, through its leaders, decides is necessary to a civilized society at a given time.[14] Answers rest, in part, on judgments about economic weath. At present, society feels rich enough to assure the employable income only in return for certain minimum civilities. If it were wealthier, it might guarantee income without conditions. If poorer, it might demand that families live on just what they can earn.[15]

To respond to conditions, however, society needs the full range of options. The difficulty in American social policy is that Figure 1 is effectively truncated. Quadrants 2 and 3 are readily available, but not quadrant 1. American politicians find it easiest to raise functioning standards by *reducing* public authority, that is, through the small-government tactics of conventional conservatism. But that approach cannot work in the instances where public standards are indispensable to order. In welfare, education, or law enforcement, either government sets requirements or no one does.

Federal politicians have begun to accept a duty to set work and child support standards, partly because federal funding dominates the income programs where those obligations most need enforcement. In education and crime, however, state funding dominates, and federal authorities have been much more diffident. Accordingly, efforts to toughen standards in these areas have come mainly from the state level, not from Washington. There is actually as good a case to require young welfare mothers to stay in school as there is to make them work, since finishing high school is critical to their earning enough to support their families. At several points in the welfare hearings Martha Griffiths proposed such a requirement for AFDC. But the Administration replied that it was unready "to write into the Social Security Act educational requirements that have traditionally been the states responsibility."[16] For similar reasons, it would be politically very difficult to use federal education grants to force states to raise standards in the schools.

Washington has probably done more to undermine the primacy of English than to uphold it. The Supreme Court decided in 1974 that foreign-speaking children were denied equal opportunity unless schools adjusted to their language problems, typically by teaching them initially in their native tongue. However, the federal bilingual education program, first enacted in 1968, has been used by Hispanic educators more to preserve Spanish-speaking education in the schools, and jobs for themselves, than to teach English. Efforts to change the bilingual rules to mandate English have so far failed. That has reduced the chances that the large numbers of Hispanics and other non-English-speakers now entering the country can be integrated. Some localities have tried to enforce English usage on their own, and a movement has arisen to amend the Constitution to specify English as the national language.[17] The pattern, as in other policy areas, is for the grassroots to impose discipline on Washington rather than the other way around.

The difficulty is still greater for new obligations where local authorities have not first broken ground. During the Carter Administration HEW Secretary Joseph Califano launched a campaign to discourage cigarette smoking. The health benefits of reducing smoking were undoubted, but the plan was stymied by virulent opposition from tobacco interests. In spite of its social costs smoking was still seen as private behavior over which government, at least in Washington, had very little say.[18] Local restrictions on smoking are accumulating, however, and eventually federal policies may be able to follow suit.

If the work question is any guide, principled resistance to enforcing standards will probably decline over time. Which civilities to enforce, and at what level, will increasingly become practical questions to be settled according to the needs of the time. The most important functioning standards must be set nationally, because of their implications for citizenship. At the same time there is little prospect of the country's becoming highly regimented. The political culture remains Lockean, specifying only limited duties to the collectivity. While obligations of a social kind seem bound to increase, they should never become ends in themselves, but only means to realize the civic society that individuals need for the private "pursuit of happiness."

Competence and Equality

The common obligations all set *minimum* requirements for functioning. That is why they can be a basis for equality in American society. All the standards are limited, and none is competitive in the sense that only some people can meet it. In that respect the public competences society demands from people are quite different from the talents they need to "succeed" in competitive senses. To "make it" in economic or career terms is competitive and takes a much higher order of excellence than specified by any of the common obligations. Americans vie fiercely for competitive eminence, but just because they cannot all have it, they also seem to want the national community defined on a more inclusive basis.

Federal social policymaking has been dominated by two extreme views of behavioral issues like work. There has been the liberal impulse to avoid all "value judgments" about behavior, leading to the permissive regime generally embodied in federal programs, and there has been the orthodox conservative impulse to make very severe judgments, to be executed by denying all support to the "undeserving." The liberal position is untenable because it sets no standards, even those the dependent need, while the conservative view sets a "success" standard that is arbitrary and too competitive to be broadly realized.

The civic conservatives, avoiding these extremes, proposed a *limited* moral judgment, confined to standards that were essential to the poor and in some sense common to the public, hence not arbitrary. Such stipulations could save social benefits from permissiveness, but they still set a standard that was achievable by all but a very few competent adults. Most adult recipients would meet that standard if they were seriously expected to. Most of the rest would be disabled enough to be institutionalized and exempted. The category of potentially competent, uninstitutionalized, yet nonfunctional adult that today dominates welfare would, over time, disappear.

This scheme would extend to social policy one of the traditional virtues of American society, which was to separate the essential worth of people from competitive distinction. The American working class does not feel the inferiority toward the more affluent and better-educated that working classes have traditionally felt in Europe. Provided they function in minimal ways, ordinary people feel accepted even if they lack the refinement of the elite.[19] The New Deal achieved the integration of workers *as* workers. The average man could feel *equal* to the better-off without having to become the *same*.

Institutions like the schools and the economy are morally complex because society wants them to reward competence in both the minimal and competitive senses. The classroom and the workplace nurture the capabilities that society universally expects, but they are also arenas for competitive striving. Public schools tend to emphasize general skills, the more so due to the "minimum competency" movement, while private schools are more meritocratic. Blue-collar workers tend to set a more egalitarian, minimalist standard for work effort than do managers or professionals.

Minimum obligation inhibits social hierarchy, because public burdens are not differentiated by class. It is hard for Americans to have a political elite in the aristocratic, Old World sense because the competence people expect in public is too limited. Eminence won in private life does not carry over intact into public. The privately successful certainly have an edge getting into politics and government, but there is little of the sense, common in Europe, that they are specially, *ascriptively* qualified to govern. Americans continue to believe that public affairs can be handled by the "common man"—the minimally competent man of the American public imagination. Accordingly, the electoral and civil service systems allow many people of modest background to achieve office.[20] The public world is much less meritocratic than the private.

The error in recent federal social policy has been precisely to focus on status considerations that have never been central to the American public identity. New Deal programs tried to help workers in limited ways, in return for their labor, without seeking directly to change their social position. But Great Society programs aimed to improve the status and income of disadvantaged groups, especially blacks, *relative* to others. That goal was only partly realized, and it distracted attention from the minimum capacities that the least competent need much more if they are to be accepted, as well as to succeed competitively in the long run. The underclass cannot be made middle-class in a single generation, except at the cost of government guarantees that deprive the achievement of meaning. But it can become working-class if its members learn to do somewhat better in school, at work, and in coping with their families. And that is all the integration requires.[21]

Beyond Entitlement

Common obligation might provide the ideological means to legitimize requirements like work tests for the first time. The requirements face political and implementation problems, in the end, because they are not yet among the special purposes for which the nation is willing to deploy federal authority. Large-scale expansions of federal power in the past were justified rhetorically in the name of freedom. But looked at more closely, those exertions were really to defend, not freedom in the simple sense of no restraint, but a common citizenship comprising both rights and obligations. The evils of slavery, racism, and unregulated capitalism threatened the rights aspect of citizenship and prompted federal protections. The functioning problems characteristic of the ghetto—crime, nonwork, family breakup—threaten fulfillment of the common obligations. The response should be federal obligations attached to the programs that support the poor.

In the past the nation transcended its fears of federal authority because common citizenship was ultimately more important than freedom. As a new and polyglot society the nation could not find its unity in a shared history or ethnicity, like the nations of Europe, but only in common rights and obligations politically defined. American citizenship came to be a *public* characteristic that all citizens shared regardless of their private differences. That citizenship made limited but definite demands. It respected differences of cultural background but insisted on the competences, such as working and speaking English, that were essential to constitute a single society, at least in political and economic affairs. In these limited senses to be an American still stamped a person with a new identity.[22] The greatest threat to the community was anything that endangered equal citizenship, and it was to vindicate that ideal that federal authority could be mobilized. Writes Theodore Lowi: "In a democratic system citizenship is the only thing people absolutely, involuntarily, and perpetually have in common. And it is in regard to this public dimension of people and things that government has its really effective claim."[23]

Nation-building has in fact been an important goal of social policy. The central purpose of the New Deal was to attach the national identity for the first time to the programs of the *federal* government, the goal laid out by Herbert Croly. The drafters of the antipoverty program, Daniel Moynihan wrote, were among other things state builders, "fiercely loyal to the Republic and still trying to fashion a nation out of a continent." Great Society policy was an attempt to redefine the terms of belonging in American society to encompass, more surely than before, the poor, disadvantaged, and nonwhite. The goal, the Kerner commission wrote, was the "creation of a true union—a single society and a single American identity."[24]

The difficulty, of course, was that it no longer sufficed to liberate people to achieve this. To provide benefits to the excluded runs with the grain of federal politics, while to demand things of them cuts very much against it. The first coerces only the strong, who are taxed and regulated; the second obligates the weak themselves, whom government wants to help. The libertarian reflexes of federal politics served the cause of equal citizenship when rights were threatened; they endanger it when the need is for firmer requirements.

Somehow the rhetoric of equal rights that dominates federal politics must be turned around to justify equal obligations as well. The civic conservatives in Congress began to show how to do that. Martha Griffiths expressed outrage at the lack of work or education requirements for welfare mothers *as if* it were denying them their rights, and in a sense it was. Today, the poor, dependent, and nonwhite must demand equal obligations from government the way they once demanded equal rights. Equality demands that they take back the duties to work, get through school, contribute to families, and so forth, that programs have assumed on their behalf. For, given the evenhanded nature of citizenship, only those who bear obligations can truly appropriate their rights.

Abraham Lincoln realized the dilemma at the heart of equality. "As I would not be a *slave*," he wrote, "so I would not be a *master*. This expresses my idea of democrary."[25] He meant that, to achieve equality, it is not enough to do away with obvious oppressions. The masters the poor relay on must also be eliminated, and for this they must be able to live their own lives well. In the short run that calls for more public authority rather than less. To require the dependent to function in minimal ways, onerous as it seems, is essential to banish the worse bondage of unequal citizenship.

As Croly wrote, a tutelary role for government is now supportive of the national purpose and not adverse to it:

> The modern nation, particularly in so far as it is constructively democratic, constitutes the best machinery as yet developed for raising the level of human association. It really teaches men how they must feel, what they must think, and what they must do, in order that they may live amicably and profitably.[26]

To require functioning in the name of equality is the first, but vital, step in solving the authority problems that have so far enervated federal social policy.

Congressional Materials and Abbreviations

The following were the main congressional hearings, reports, and debates on welfare reform and work tests between 1967 and 1979. They are cited in the notes using the conventions shown. The abbreviation used for each is listed and, under it, the full citation of the item and a précis of the subject involved. The materials are listed in order of date. In the notes, each abbreviation is followed directly by the page numbers referred to, without any abbreviation for pages.

67 H. hearings

U.S. Congress, House, Committee on Ways and Means, *President's Proposals for Revision in the Social Security System, Hearings* before the Committee on Ways and Means, on H.R. 5710, 90th Cong., 1st sess., March 1–April 11, 1967. Hearings on Johnson Administration proposals to liberalize welfare and other Social Security Act programs.

67 H. report

U.S. Congress, House, Committee on Ways and Means, *Social Security Amendments of 1967*, H. Rept. 544 to accompany H.R. 12080, 90th Cong., 1st sess., August 7, 1967. Work tests and requirements are proposed for AFDC.

67 H. debate

U.S. Congress, House, 90th Cong., 1st sess., August 16–17, 1967, *Congressional Record*, vol. 113, part 17, pp. 22779–86, 23048–133. Debate on the 1967 amendments, including the welfare work provisions.

67 S. hearings

U.S. Congress, Senate, Committee on Finance, *Social Security Amendments of 1967, Hearings* before the Committee on Finance, on H.R. 12080, 90th Cong., 1st sess., August 22–September 26, 1967. Hearings on the welfare work proposals, among other amendments.

67 S. report

U.S. Congress, Senate, Committee on Finance, *Social Security Amendments of 1967,* S. Rept. 744 to accompany H.R. 12080, 90th Cong., 1st sess., November 14, 1967. The House welfare work provisions are endorsed with some changes.

67 S. debate

U.S. Congress, Senate, 90th Cong., 1st sess., November 15–17, 20–22, 1967, *Congressional Record,* vol. 113, part 24, pp. 32584–626, 32821-53, 33057–85, 33109–20, 33166–99, 33489–590, and part 25, pp. 33620–37. Debate on the 1967 amendments, especially the work provisions.

67 H. final debate

U.S. Congress, House, 90th Cong., 1st sess., December 13, 1967, *Congressional Record,* vol. 113, part 27, pp. 36342–93. Passage of the conference report on the 1967 amendments.

67 S. final debate

U.S. Congress, Senate, 90th Cong., 1st sess., December 15, 1967, *Congressional Record,* vol. 113, part 27, pp. 36887–88, 36911–27. Passage of the conference report on the 1967 amendments.

68 JEC hearings

U.S. Congress, Joint Economic Committee, *Income Maintenance Programs, Hearings* before the Subcommittee on Fiscal Policy, 90th Cong., 2d sess., June 11–27, 1968. Initial Martha Griffiths hearings on welfare.

69 H. hearings

U.S. Congress, House, Committee on Ways and Means, *Hearings on the Subject of Social Security and Welfare Proposals,* 91st Cong., 1st sess., October 15–November 13, 1969. Initial hearings on the Nixon welfare reform plan.

70 H. report

U.S. Congress, House, Committee on Ways and Means, *Family Assistance Act of 1970,* H. Rept. 904 to accompany H.R. 16311, 91st Cong., 2d sess., March 11, 1970. The Nixon plan endorsed with minor changes.

70 H. Rules hearings

U.S. Congress, House, Committee on Rules, *Hearings on H.R. 16311 (Family Assistance Act of 1970)*, 91st Cong., 2d sess., April 7, 13–14, 1970. Ways and Means obtains a rule for House debate limiting amendments.

70 H. debate

U.S. Congress, House, 91st Cong., 2d sess., April 15–16, 1970, *Congressional Record*, vol. 116, part 9, pp. 11863–904, 12028–106. Initial House debate and passage of the Nixon plan.

70 S. hearings

U.S. Congress, Senate, Committee on Finance, *Family Assistance Act of 1970, Hearings* before the Committee on Finance, on H.R. 16311, 91st Cong., 2d sess., April 29–September 10, 1970. Hearings on the Nixon plan.

70 S. report

U.S. Congress, Senate, Committee on Finance, *Social Security Amendments of 1970*. S. Rept. 91-1431 to accompany H.R. 17550, 91st Cong., 2d sess., December 11, 1970. First Finance report on FAP, demanding major changes.

70 S. debate

U.S. Congress, Senate, 91st Cong., 2d sess., December 16–29, 1970, *Congressional Record*, vol. 116, parts 31–33; pp. 41798–3868. First, abortive Senate debate on FAP and rival plans.

71 H. report

U.S. Congress, House, Committee on Ways and Means, *Social Security Amendments of 1971*, H. Rept. 231 to accompany HR. 1, 92d Cong., 1st sess., May 26, 1971. Report on revised version of Nixon plan included in H.R. 1.

71 H. debate

U.S. Congress, House, 92d Cong., 1st sess., June 21–22, 1971, *Congressional Record*, vol. 117, part 16, pp. 21082–106, 21329–463. Second House debate and passage of the Nixon plan.

71 Talmadge debate

U.S. Congress, House, 92d Cong., 1st sess., December 14, 1971, *Congressional Record*, vol. 117, part 36, pp. 46769–79. House debate on Talmadge WIN amendments.

71–2 S. hearings

U.S. Congress, Senate, Committee on Finance, *Social Security Amendments of 1971, Hearings* before the Committee on Finance, on H.R. 1, 92d Cong., July 27, 1971–February 9, 1972. Further hearings on the Nixon plan.

72 JEC hearings

U.S. Congress, Joint Economic Committee, *Problems in Administration of Public Welfare Programs, Hearings* before the Subcommittee on Fiscal Policy, 92d Cong., 2d sess., March 20–June 8, 1972. Griffiths welfare hearings, held mostly in New York, Detroit, and Atlanta.

72 S. report

U.S. Congress, Senate, Committee on Finance, *Social Security Amendments of 1972*, S. Rept. 1230 to accompany H.R. 1, 92d Cong., 2d sess., September 26, 1972. Long's workfare alternative to the Nixon plan.

72 S. debate

U.S. Congress, Senate, 92d Cong., 2d sess., September 27–October 6, 1972, *Congressional Record*, vol. 118, parts 25–26, pp. 32470 ff. The final Senate showdown on welfare reform. Only SSI is passed.

72 H. final debate

U.S. Congress, House, 92d Cong., 2d sess., October 17, 1972, *Congressional Record*, vol. 118, part 28, pp. 36914–38. Passage of the conference report on H.R. 1, deleting all reform plans for AFDC.

72 S. final debate

U.S. Congress, Senate, 92d Cong., 2d sess., October 17, 1972, *Congressional Record*, vol. 118, part 28, pp. 36804–25. Passage of the conference report on H.R. 1, deleting all reform plans for AFDC.

74 JEC report

U.S. Congress, Joint Economic Committee, Subcommittee on Fiscal Policy, *Income Security for Americans: Recommendations of the Public Welfare Study*, 93d Cong., 2d sess., December 5, 1974. Report and proposal concluding the Griffiths welfare inquiry.

77 H. prelim. hearings

U.S. Congress, House, Committee on Ways and Means, *Special HEW Report on Welfare Reform, Hearings* before the Subcommittee on Public Assistance and Unemployment Compensation, 95th Cong., 1st sess., May 4, 1977. Hearings on the basic principles of the Carter reform plan.

77 S. prelim. hearings

U.S. Congress, Senate, Committee on Finance, *President's Statement on Principles of Welfare Reform, Hearings* before the Subcommittee on Public Assistance, 95th Cong., 1st sess., May 5, 12, 1977. Hearings on the basic principles of the Carter reform plan.

77 H. hearings

U.S. Congress, House, Committee on Agriculture, Committee on Education and Labor, and Committee on Ways and Means, *Administration's Welfare Reform Proposal, Joint Hearings* before the Welfare Reform Subcommittee, 95th Cong., 1st sess., September 19–November 4, 1977. Hearings on the Carter plan.

78 S. hearings

U.S. Congress, Senate, Committee on Finance, *Welfare Reform Proposals, Hearings* before the Subcommittee on Public Assistance, on S. 2084, 95th Cong., 2d sess., February 7–May 4, 1978. Hearings on the Carter plan.

79 H. debate

U.S. Congress, House, 96th Cong., 1st sess., November 7, 1979, *Congressional Record*, vol. 125, part 24, pp. 31333–84. Debate on the Carter incremental reform plan.

Notes

Chapter 1. The Problem of Obligation in Social Policy

1. "Libertarian" and "permissive" will be used to connote the view that individuals should not be obligated to function well, whether by government or by private pressures like the market place. "Authoritative" connotes the view that they should. This distinction is different from that between "liberal" and "conservative," which connotes different views of the scale of government. See chapter 11.
2. George Gilder, *Wealth and Poverty* (New York: Basic Books, 1981); Charles Murray, *Losing Ground: American Social Policy, 1950–1980* (New York: Basic Books, 1984).
3. Sar A. Levitan and Clifford M. Johnson, *Beyond the Safety Net: Reviving the Promise of Opportunity in America* (Cambridge, Mass.: Ballinger, 1984); John E. Schwarz, *America's Hidden Success: A Reassessment of Twenty Years of Public Policy* (New York: Norton, 1983).
4. Michael Harrington, *The New American Poverty* (New York: Holt, Rinehart & Winston, 1984).
5. Harold D. Lasswell, *Politics: Who Gets What, When, How* (New York: Meridian, 1958).
6. Angus Campbell et al., *The American Voter* (New York: Wiley, 1960), chs. 3–11, 20. There is some evidence that the public has become more ideological and issue-oriented due to the divisive controversies of the 1960s and 1970s—see, e.g., Norman H. Nie et al., *The Changing American Voter*, En-

larged Ed. (Cambridge, Mass.: Harvard University Press, 1979)—but it has remained substantially ignorant of the details of government policy.

7. Samuel P. Huntington, *Political Order in Changing Societies* (New Haven: Yale University Press, 1968), p. 4. The phrase is from Tocqueville's *Democracy in America*. Huntington's thesis is that developing countries suffer mainly from insufficient government, not government that is insufficiently democratic, the usual subject of American rhetoric. My thesis here is similar: The main problem with the welfare state is that it lacks authority, not that it is too large or too small. Welfare institutions require further political development, even within otherwise highly developed Western polities.
8. Joseph E. Garvey, *Testing for College Admissions: Trends and Issues* (Arlington, Va.: Educational Research Service, 1981), pp. 25–28.
9. Alongside the decline in social functioning went changes in public attitudes that in some ways undercut political functioning. The public since the middle 1960s has grown more distrustful of government and parties, more supportive of groups making demands on government, and less likely to vote. See chapter 9, note 15.
10. James Q. Wilson, *Thinking About Crime* (New York: Vintage Books, 1977), ch. 3.
11. A list of these materials, and the abbreviations used to cite them, is placed before the Notes.
12. For discussions of how to combine political and economic reasoning in public policy studies, see Lawrence M. Mead, "A Meaning for Public Policy," *Policy Studies Journal*, 12, no. 2 (December 1983): 247–50, and "Policy Studies and Political Science," *Policy Studies Review*, vol. 5, no. 2 (November 1985).
13. Gertrude Himmelfarb, *The Idea of Poverty: England in the Early Industrial Age* (New York: Knopf, 1983).

Chapter 2. Functioning: The New Shape of the Social Problem

1. Richard Hofstadter, *The Age of Reform: From Bryan to F.D.R.*(New York: Knopf, 1955); Samuel H. Beer, "In Search of a New Public Philosophy," in Anthony King, ed., *The New American Political System* (Washington, D.C.: American Enterprise Institute, 1978), pp. 9–13.
2. Gabriel Kolko, *Railroads and Regulation, 1877–1916* (Princeton, N.J.: Princeton University Press, 1965); Marver H. Bernstein, *Regulating Business by Independent Commission* (Princeton, N.J.: Princeton University Press, 1955).
3. James T. Patterson, *America's Struggle Against Poverty, 1900–1980* (Cambridge, Mass.: Harvard University Press, 1981), chs. 3–4.
4. Frances Fox Piven and Richard A. Cloward, *Poor Peoples Movements: Why They Succeed, How They Fail* (New York: Pantheon Books, 1977), chs. 2–3, contend that the New Deal movements had influence only by threatening disorder. But their treatment makes clear that the violence of workers and the

unemployed was limited, directed, and political in purpose, not unpolitical, anomic disorder of the kind reflected in Table 1.

5. On the underclass, see Daniel P. Moynihan, ed., *On Understanding Poverty: Perspectives from the Social Sciences* (New York: Basic Books, 1969), chs. 2, 7–9; Ken Auletta, *The Underclass* (New York: Random House, 1982), pp. 27–43, 220–1; and Frank Levy, "How Big Is the American Underclass?" working paper 0090–1 (Washington, D.C.: Urban Institute, September 1977). Experts disagree not about the character of the underclass but about its causes and cures. Those like Lee Rainwater who think it arises from social exclusion think its character will change rapidly to permit integration once exclusion ends. Those like Oscar Lewis who think it is rooted in a "culture of poverty" believe that socialization in new mores is necessary, not just more income and opportunity.
6. John R. Petrocik, "Voter Turnout and Electoral Oscillation," *American Politics Quarterly*, 9, no. 2 (April 1981): 161–80; James DeNardo, "Turnout and the Vote: The Joke's on the Democrats," *American Political Science Review*, 74, no. 2 (June 1980): 406–20; Raymond E. Wolfinger and Steven J. Rosenstone, *Who Votes?* (New Haven: Yale University Press, 1980), pp. 80–88, 104–14.
7. See the Moynihan and Auletta citations in note 5 above and Hyman Rodman, "The Lower-Class Value Stretch," *Social Forces*, 42, no. 2 (December 1963): 205–15. On work attitudes, see Leonard Goodwin, *Do the Poor Want to Work? A Social-Psychological Study of Work Orientations* (Washington D.C.: Brookings, 1972).
8. U.S. Department of Commerce, Bureau of the Census, *Statistical Abstract of the United States, 1984* (Washington, D.C.: U.S. Government Printing Office, December 1983), pp. 6, 471. For discussion of the poverty measure and the 8 percent estimate, see note 40 below.
9. Sar A. Levitan, *The Great Society's Poor Law: A New Approach to Poverty* (Baltimore: Johns Hopkins Press, 1969), pp. 86–88.
10. *Statistical Abstract, 1984,* pp. 36, 471.
11. U.S. Department of Health and Human Services, Social Security Administration, *Aid to Families with Dependent Children, 1979 Recipient Characteristics Study, Part 1: Demographic and Program Statistics* (Washington, D.C.: Social Security Administration, June 1982), p. 1; U.S. Department of Labor, *Employment and Training Report of the President, 1982* (Washington, D.C.: U.S. Government Printing Office, 1982), p. 190; Greg J. Duncan et al., *Years of Poverty, Years of Plenty: The Changing Fortunes of American Workers and Families* (Ann Arbor: Institute for Social Research, University of Michigan, 1984), pp. 49, 76, 80.
12. Charles E. Silberman, *Criminal Violence, Criminal Justice* (New York: Random House, 1978), pp. 118–20; *Statistical Abstract, 1984,* p. 194.
13. *Statistical Abstract, 1984,* pp. 144, 146.
14. Ibid., p. 405.
15. Lloyd Ulman, "The Uses and Limits of Manpower Policy," *The Public Interest*, no. 34, Winter 1974, pp. 97–98; Robert A. Levine, *The Poor Ye Need*

Not Have With You: Lessons from the War on Poverty (Cambridge, Mass.: MIT Press, 1970), p. 46; Thomas Bailey and Roger Waldinger, "A Skills Mismatch in New York's Labor Market?" *New York Affairs*, 8, no. 3 (Fall 1984): 9–10, 15–18.

16. *Statistical Abstract, 1984*, p. 431.
17. Jerome T. Murphy, *State Education Agencies and Discretionary Funds: Grease the Squeaky Wheel* (Lexington, Mass.: D.C. Heath, 1974); Paul Berman et al., *Federal Programs Supporting Educational Change*, Vol. IV (Abridged): *A Summary of the Findings in Review* (Santa Monica, Calif.: Rand, April 1975).
18. "Antipoverty" or "War on Poverty" programs refers to programs authorized under the Economic Opportunity Act of 1964; including later renewals. "Great Society" refers to the overall period of compensatory and other social programming from the early 1960s through the late 1970s, including but not limited to the antipoverty programs.
19. Council of Economic Advisors, *Annual Report*, in *Economic Report of the President*, transmitted to the Congress, January 1964 (Washington, D.C.: U.S. Government Printing Office, 1964), p. 74; Robert J. Lampman, "What Does It Do for the Poor?—A New Test for National Policy," *The Public Interest*, no. 34, Winter 1974, pp. 66–82.
20. Sar A. Levitan and Robert Taggart, *The Promise of Greatness* (Cambridge, Mass.: Harvard University Press, 1976), pp. 121–23, 136; Office of Management and Budget, *Budget of the United States Government, Fiscal Year 1980* (Washington, D.C.: U.S. Government Printing Office, 1979), pp. 211, 221; Charles Murray, *Losing Ground: American Social Policy, 1950–1980* (New York: Basic Books, 1984), p. 70.
21. This assessment is based on Levitan and Taggart, *Promise of Greatness*, ch. 6; Harry M. Levin, "A Decade of Policy Developments in Improving Education and Training for Low-Income Populations," in Robert H. Havemen, ed., *A Decade of Federal Antipoverty Programs: Achievements, Failures, and Lessons* (New York: Academic Press, 1977), pp. 153–71; and Henry J. Aaron, *Politics and the Professors: The Great Society in Perspective* (Washington, D.C.: Brookings, 1978), ch. 3. On the Coleman report and its critics, see James S. Coleman et al., *Equality of Educational Opportunity*, Office of Education, U.S. Department of Health, Education, and Welfare (Washington, D.C.: U.S. Government Printing Office, 1966), and Frederick Mosteller and Daniel P. Moyihan, eds., *On Equality of Educational Opportunity: Papers Deriving from the Harvard University Faculty Seminar on the Coleman Report* (New York: Random House, 1972). Later studies suggest that preschool programs may have some delayed benefits that were missed in the early Head Start evaluations. See Gene I. Maeroff, "Early Remedial Teaching Cited as Success," *New York Times*, May 19, 1981, pp. C1, C6, and "Support of Early Schooling Grows as U.S. Threatens Retrenchment," *New York Times Winter Survey of Education*, January 10, 1982, pp. 1, 35.
22. This assessment is based on Aaron, *Politics and Professors*, pp. 125–28; Levin, "Decade of Policy Developments," pp. 171–79; Levitan and Taggart, *Promise of Greatness*, ch. 7; Ernst W. Stromsdorfer, "The Effectiveness of

Youth Programs: An Analysis of the Historical Antecedents of Current Youth Initiatives," in Bernard E. Anderson and Isabel V. Sawhill, eds., *Youth Employment and Public Policy* (Englewood Cliffs, N.J.: Prentice-Hall, 1980), ch. 4; Michael E. Borus, "Assessing the Impact of Training Programs," and Bernard E. Anderson, "How Much Did the Programs Help Minorities and Youth?" in Eli Ginzberg, ed., *Employing the Unemployed* (New York: Basic Books, 1980), chs. 2 and 3; and Congressional Budget Office, *CETA Training Programs—Do They Work for Adults?* (Washington, D.C.: U.S. Government Printing Office, July 1982.

23. Daniel P. Moynihan, *The Politics of a Guaranteed Income: The Nixon Administration and the Family Assistance Plan* (New York: Random House, 1973), pp. 50–56, 107–9, 148–52, 356–57.
24. Patterson, *America's Struggle* (note 3), p. 179; Barbara Boland, "Participation in the Aid to Families with Dependent Children Program (AFDC)," in U.S. Congress, Joint Economic Committee, Subcommittee on Fiscal Policy, *Studies in Public Welfare, Paper No. 12 (part 1): The Family, Poverty, and Welfare Programs: Factors Influencing Family Stability*, 93d Cong., 1st sess., November 4, 1973, pp. 139, 141, 153, 156.
25. Levitan and Taggart, *Promise of Greatness*, pp. 193–96.
26. Ibid., pp. 59–61, 80–81.
27. For statements of the dual labor market theory and its policy implications see Aaron, *Politics and Professors*, pp. 44–48, 92–97, 128–39; Peter B. Doeringer and Michael J. Piore, *Internal Labor Markets and Manpower Analysis* (Lexington, Mass.: D.C. Heath, 1971); and Bennett Harrison, *Education, Training, and the Urban Ghetto* (Baltimore: Johns Hopkins Press, 1972).
28. Congressional Budget Office, *CETA Reauthorization Issues* (Washington, D.C.: U.S. Government Printing Office, August 1978), pp. 17–19; Manpower Demonstration Research Corporation, *Summary and Findings of the National Supported Work Demonstration* (Cambridge, Mass.: Ballinger, 1980); Ginzberg, ed., *Employing the Unemployed*, chs. 7–9; Robert H. Haveman, "Direct Job Creation: Potentials and Realities," in Paul M. Somers, ed., *Welfare Reform in America: Perspectives and Prospects* (Boston: Kluwer-Nijhoff, 1982), ch. 10; Thomas Sowell, "Are Quotas Good for Blacks?" *Commentary*, June 1978, pp. 39–43.
29. Business sponsored Job Opportunities in the Business Sector (JOBS), 1968, and has helped shape CETA and JTPA training programs. See Levine, *The Poor Ye Need Not* (note 15), pp. 86–87, 109–16.
30. Howard E. Shuman, *Politics and the Budget: The Struggle Between the President and the Congress* (Englewood Cliffs, N.J.: Prentice-Hall, 1984), pp. 262, 272, points out that the budget that House Democrats proposed in 1981 proposed three-quarters of the same cuts contained in the Reagan plan. Liberal and conservative analysts agree that the cuts enacted left the social "safety net" largely intact; see D. Lee Bawden, ed., *The Social Contract Revisited: Aims and Outcomes of President Reagan's Social Welfare Policy* (Washington, D.C.: Urban Institute, 1984), and John C. Weicher, ed., *Maintaining the Safety Net: Income Redistribution Programs in the Reagan Administration* (Washington, D.C.: American Enterprise Institute, 1984). The estimates of

the cuts come from Congressional Budget Office, "Major Legislative Changes in Human Resources Programs Since January 1981," unpublished memorandum, August 1983, sections 1–3, and D. Lee Bawden and John L. Palmer, "Social Policy: Challenging the Welfare State," in John L. Palmer and Isabel V. Sawhill, eds., *The Reagan Record: An Assessment of America's Changing Domestic Priorities* (Washington, D.C.: Urban Institute, 1984), pp. 184–187.

31. Daniel P. Moynihan, "The Professionalization of Reform," *The Public Interest,* no. 1, Fall 1965, pp. 6–16.

32. Haveman, ed., *Decade of Federal Antipoverty* (note 21), p. 6.

33. Wolfinger and Rosenstone, *Who Votes?* (note 6), pp. 90–91. Blacks do vote at lower levels than whites, but this is attributable to their generally lower education and class rather than race.

34. *Statistical Abstract, 1984,* p. 144; Sar A. Levitan et al., *Still a Dream: The Changing Status of Blacks Since 1960* (Cambridge, Mass.: Harvard University Press, 1975), p. 103.

35. Duncan et al., *Years of Poverty* (note 11), ch. 5; Levitan and Taggart, *Promise of Greatness,* p. 207; Martin Kilson, "Black Social Classes and Intergenerational Poverty," *The Public Interest,* no. 64, Summer 1981, pp. 63–66; Richard Freeman, "Black Economic Progress Since 1964," *The Public Interest,* no. 52., Summer 1978, pp. 54–59, 66.

36. John G. Condran, "Changes in White Attitudes Toward Blacks: 1963–1977," *Public Opinion Quarterly,* 43, no. 4, Winter 1979: 463–76; Victoria Sackett, "Ignoring the Public," *Policy Review,*no. 12, Spring 1980, pp. 9–22; Angus Campbell and Howard Schuman, "Racial Attitudes in Fifteen American Cities," in National Advisory Commission on Civil Disorders, *Supplemental Studies for the National Advisory Commission on Civil Disorders* (Washington, D.C.: U.S. Government Printing Office, July 1968), pp. 1–67.

37. *Statistical Abstract, 1984,* p. 405.

38. William Serrin, "'High Tech' Is No Jobs Panacea, Experts Say," *New York Times,* September 18, 1983, pp. 1, 28; Bailey and Waldinger "A Skills Mismatch" (note 15).

39. For estimates of the number of illegals, see Edwin P. Reubens, "Alliens, Jobs, and Immigration Policy," *The Public Interest,* no. 51, Spring 1978, pp. 113–14, 116, n. 1; Edwin Harwood, "Can Immigration Laws Be Enforced?" *The Public Interest,* no. 72, Summer 1983, p. 110; and *New York Times,* January 16, 1980, p. Al, and March 24, 1980, p. B1.

40. For the official poverty figures, see *Statistical Abstract, 1984,* p. 471. The most sophisticated adjusted estimate is probably Timothy M. Smeeding, *Alternative Methods For Valuing Selected In-Kind Transfer Benefits and Measuring Their Effect on Poverty,* Technical Paper 50, U.S. Department of Commerce, Bureau of the Census (Washington, D.C.: U.S. Government Printing Office, March 1982). Smeeding estimates the poor as 6 to 9 percent of population in 1979, depending on which in-kind benefits are counted as income and how their value is appraised. A number of estimates in the 4 percent range for 1975–1980 appear in Sommers, ed., *Welfare Reform in America* (note 28),

chs. 3–5. An often-cited estimate is 8.3 percent of families in 1976, from Congressional Budget Office, *Poverty Status of Families Under Alternative Definitions of Income* (Washington, D.C.: U.S. Government Printing Office, June 1977), pp. 7–9. An estimate of 8.8 percent for 1982, a recession year, appears in Peter Gottschalk and Sheldon Danziger, "Macroeconomic Conditions, Income transfers, and the Trend in Poverty," in Bawden, ed., *Social Contract Revisited* (note 30), p. 195. I have assumed that the subsequent economic recovery has dropped the rate to about 8 percent.

41. Daniel P. Moynihan, "The Schism in Black America," *The Public Interest*, no. 27, Spring 1972, pp. 3–24; Andres F. Brimmer, "Economic Developments in the Black Community," *The Public Interest*, no. 34, Winter 1974, pp. 146–63; Kilson, "Black Social Classes."
42. *Statistical Abstract, 1984*, pp. 54, 70; Robert Pear, "Many Households Get U.S. Benefits," *New York Times*, April 17, 1985, p. A23.
43. Cited in Blanche Bernstein, *The Politics of Welfare: The New York City Experience* (Cambridge, Mass.: Abt Books, 1982), p. 5. Income ratios calculated from *Statistical Abstract, 1984*, p. 463.
44. Bawden and Palmer, "Social Policy" (note 30), p. 198; Gottschalk and Danziger, "Macroeconomic Conditions," pp. 195–97; Marilyn Moon and Isabel V. Sawhill, "Family Incomes: Gainers and Losers," in Palmer and Sawhill, eds., *The Reagan Record* (note 30), ch. 10; U.S. Department of Commerce, Bureau of the Census, *Changing Family Composition and Income Differentials*, Report CDS–80–7 (Washington, D.C.: U.S. Government Printing Office, August 1982).
45. *Statistical Abstract, 1984*, p. 407.
46. Donald O. Parsons, "The Decline in Male Labor Force Participation," *Journal of Political Economy*, 88, no. 1 (February 1980): 117–34 and "Racial Trends in Male Labor Force Participation," *American Economic Review*, 70, no. 5 (December 1980): 911–20.
47. Miriam Ostow and Anna B. Dutka, *Work and Welfare in New York City* (Baltimore: Johns Hopkins Press, 1975), p. 8.
48. Three out of five illegals earn above the minimum wage, and the average illegal earns 60 percent of the prevailing wage. See Reubens, "Aliens," pp. 114–20, and John M. Crewsdon, "Illegal Aliens Are Bypassing Farms for Higher Pay of Jobs in the Cities," *New York Times*, November 10, 1980, pp. A1, D9.
49. Duncan et al., *Years of Poverty* (note 11), pp. 18–26, 28, 55–58; Levitan et al., *Still a Dream* (note 34), pp. 37–40; Bureau of the Census, *Changing Family Composition*, p. 14.
50. Fiscal 1981, of course, represents the programs at their height, just before the Reagan cuts, but it is the last year on which comparable figures are available on all the programs. And the cuts were marginal (see note 30).
51. *Statistical Abstract, 1984*, p. 11.
52. Ibid., pp. 6, 380. The sum of the Disability and Medicaid caseloads, which have little overlap, is 26.5 million alone. The dependent proportion including Social Security is close to the estimate of a quarter by Roger A. Freeman, *The Wayward Welfare State* (Stanford, Calif.: Hoover Institution Press, 1981), p. 212, for all social programs.

53. Pear, "Many Households Get U.S. Benefits" (note 42).
54. Peter H. Rossi and Zahava D. Blum, "Class, Status, and Poverty," in Moynihan, *On Understanding Poverty* (note 5), p. 59; Patterson, *America's Struggle* (note 3), p. 110.
55. Robert D. Plotnick and Felicity Skidmore, *Progress Against Poverty: A Review of the 1964–1974 Decade* (New York: Academic Press, 1975), pp. 136–39; Sheldon Danziger and Robert Plotnick, "The War on Income Poverty: Achievements and Failures," in Sommers, ed., *Welfare Reform in America* (note 28), pp. 39–40; Timothy M. Smeeding, "The Anti-poverty Effect of In-kind Transfers: A Good Idea Gone Too Far?" *Policy Studies Journal*, 10, no. 3 (March 1982): 499–522; Charles A. Murray, "The Two Wars against Poverty: Economic Growth and the Great Society, " *The Public Interest*, no. 69, Fall 1982, pp. 8–10.
56. Michael K. Brown and Steven P. Erie, "Ethnic Politics and Benefits: Blacks and the Great Society," paper presented at the annual meeting of the American Political Science Association, Washington, D.C., August 28–31, 1980, table 4; Levitan and Taggart, *Promise of Greatness* (note 20), pp. 211–13.
57. Brown and Erie, "Ethnic Politics," table 1.
58. Theodore J. Lowi, *The End of Liberalism: The Second Republic of the United States*, 2d Ed. (New York: Norton, 1979), pp. 216, 222–26, 233–35.
59. Everett Carll Ladd, Jr., with Charles D. Hadley, *Tranformations of the American Party System: Political Coalitions from the New Deal to the 1970s*, 2d Ed. (New York: Norton, 1978,), chs. 4–5; Daniel Bell, *The Cultural Contradictions of Capitalism* (New York: Basic Books, 1976).
60. Alexis de Tocqueville, *Democracy in America*, trans. Henry Reeve, ed. Phillips Bradley (New York: Knopf, 1980), vol. 2, book 2, ch. 11, p. 133.
61. Duncan et al., *Years of Poverty* (note 11), pp. 12–14; Freeman, "Black Economic Progress," (note 35), pp. 52–68.
62. Michael Harrington, *The Other America: Poverty in the United States*, Revised Ed. (Baltimore, Md.: Penguin Books, 1971), and *The New American Poverty* (New York: Holt, Rinehart & Winston, 1984); William Ryan, *Blaming the Victim* (New York: Pantheon Books, 1971); Frances Fox Piven and Richard A. Cloward, *Regulating the Poor: The Functions of Public Welfare* (New York: Pantheon Books, 1971): *Poor People's Movements* (note 4); and *The New Class War: Reagan's Attack on the Welfare State and Its Consequences* (New York: Pantheon Books, 1982).
63. Charles E. Lindblom, "Another State of Mind," *American Political Science Review*, 76, no. 1(March 1982): 9–21.
64. "A Letter from Mr. Burke to a Member of the National Assembly," in Edmund Burke, *Reflections on the Revolution in France* (London: Everyman, 1967), p. 282.
65. Orlando Patterson, "The Moral Crisis of the Black American," *The Public Interest*, no. 32, Summer 1973, p. 52.
66. *On Liberty*, in John Stuart Mill, *The Philosophy of John Stuart Mill: Ethical, Political and Religious*, ed. Marshall Cohen (New York: Modern Library, 1961), pp. 197, 276.

67. Piven and Cloward, *Regulating the Poor*, pp. 148–49.
68. Ibid., pp. 343–44.

Chapter 3. Functioning Ignored: Permissive Programs

1. William A. Gamson, *Power and Discontent* (Homewood, Ill.: Dorsey Press, 1968), p. 134.
2. The following three sections expand Lawrence M. Mead, "Social Programs and Social Obligations," *The Public Interest*, no. 69, Fall 1982, pp. 17–32.
3. *New York Times*, September 16, 1982, pp. A1, A22–23. See also George Gilder, *Wealth and Poverty* (New York: Basic Books, 1981), chs. 14–16, 18; and Martin Feldstein, "The Retreat from Keynesian Economics," *The Public Interest*, no. 64, Summer 1981, pp. 92–105.
4. See Chapter 1, note 2, and Martin Anderson, *Welfare: The Political Economy of Welfare Reform in the United States* (Stanford, Calif.: Hoover Institution Press, 1978), ch. 2.
5. See Chapter 1, notes 3 and 4. Some analysts contend that poverty should be defined not as some low absolute level of resources but as some share of the median family income, commonly a half. That would mean poverty could not be overcome simply by economic growth or transfers. The income distribution would have to be flattened, at least at its bottom end. See Robert D. Plotnick and Felicity Skidmore, *Progress Against Poverty: A Review of the 1964–1974 Decade* (New York: Academic Press, 1975), pp. 42–43, 187–88; Robert H. Haveman, ed., *A Decade of Federal Antipoverty Programs: Achievements, Failures, and Lessons* (New York: Academic Press, 1977), pp. 10–12, 18–19; Lee Rainwater, *What Money Buys: Inequality and the Social Meanings of Income* (New York: Basic Books, 1974), ch. 11; and Victor R. Fuchs, "Redefining Poverty and Redistributing Income," *The Public Interest*, no. 8, Summer 1967, pp. 88–95.
6. Ken Auletta, *The Underclass* (New York: Random House, 1982), pp. xiii–xviii, 268–97, 319; Lawrence M. Mead, "Welfare: More Harm Than Good?" *New York Times Book Review*, December 16, 1984, p. 7.
7. The term "new class" seems to have been coined by Milovan Djilas, *The New Class* (New York: Praeger, 1957), and John Kenneth Galbraith, *The Affluent Society* (New York: Mentor Books, 1958), ch. 24, and then appropriated by conservatives. See B. Bruce-Briggs, ed., *The New Class?* (New Brunswick, N.J.: Transaction Books, 1979); Everett Carll Ladd, Jr., with Charles D. Hadley, *Transformations of the American Party System: Political Coalitions from the New Deal to the 1970s*, 2d Ed. (New York: Norton, 1978), ch. 4; Irving Kristol, *Two Cheers for Capitalism* (New York: Basic Books, 1978).
8. John C. Donovan, *The Politics of Poverty*, 2d Ed. (Indianapolis: Bobbs-Merrill, 1973), pp. 112–20, 123–32; Daniel P. Moynihan, *Maximum Feasible Misunderstanding: Community Action in the War on Poverty* (New York: Free Press, 1970); James L. Sundquist, *Politics and Policy: The Eisenhower, Kennedy, and Johnson Years* (Washington, D.C.: Brookings, 1969), chs. 1, 11.

9. U.S. Department of Labor, Office of Policy Planning and Research, *The Negro Family: The Case for National Action* (Washington, D.C.: U.S. Government Printing Office, March 1965), pp. 1–4.
10. Sar A. Levitan and Robert Taggart, *The Promise of Greatness* (Cambridge, Mass.: Harvard University Press, 1976), p. 271.
11. Lawrence M. Friedman, "Social Welfare Legislation: An Introduction," *Stanford Law Review*, 21, no. 2 (January 1969): 217–47.
12. Martha Derthick, *Policymaking for Social Security* (Washington, D.C.: Brookings, 1979), chs. 10–13, 17, 19.
13. James L. Sundquist, ed., *On Fighting Poverty: Perspectives from Experience* (New York: Basic Books, 1969), p. 245; 69 H. hearings 2456.
14. Rainwater, *What Money Buys*, p. 9.
15. William Julius Wilson, *The Declining Significance of Race: Blacks and Changing American Institutions*, 2nd Ed. (Chicago: Chicago University Press, 1980); Louis Ferleger, "A Critique of Conventional Explanations of Labor Market Conditions for Employed Blacks," *Policy Studies Journal*, 10, no. 3 (March 1982): 539–55.
16. Robert E. Hall, "Prospects for Shifting the Phillips Curve through Manpower Policy," *Brookings Papers on Economic Activity*, 1971, no. 3, pp. 681–89; Stephen T. Marston, "Employment Instability and High Unemployment Rates," *Brookings Papers on Economic Activity*, 1976, no. 1, pp. 188–99, 201–2; Greg J. Duncan et al., *Years of Poverty, Years of Plenty: The Changing Fortunes of American Workers and Families* (Ann Arbor: Institute for Social Research, University of Michigan, 1984), ch. 4. For a learned critique of the labor market theory, see Glen G. Cain, "The Challenge of Segmented Labor Market Theories to Orthodox Theory: A Survey," *Journal of Economic Literature*, 14, no. 4 (December 1976): 1215–57.
17. The following discussion of administrative requirements bearing on recipients and administrators is based on interviews of federal officials in the Departments of Defense, Labor, and Education. I am unaware of any systematic treatment of performance standards bearing on clients and administrators in the social policy literature.
18. Auletta, *The Underclass* (note 6), chs. 1–17; Manpower Demonstration Research Corporation, *Summary and Findings of the National Supported Work Demonstration* (Cambridge, Mass.: Ballinger, 1980).
19. Joel F. Handler and Ellen Jane Hollingsworth, *The "Deserving Poor": A Study of Welfare Administration* (New York: Academic Press, 1971), pp. 16, 34–37.
20. Auletta, *The Underclass*, pp. 236–45; Ernst W. Stromsdorfer, "The Effectiveness of Youth Programs: An Analysis of the Historical Antecedents of Current Youth Initiatives," in Bernard E. Anderson and Isabel V. Sawhill, eds., *Youth Employment and Public Policy* (Englewood Cliffs, N.J.: Prentice-Hall, 1980), pp. 100–103; Judith M. Gueron, *Lessons from a Job Guarantee: The Youth Incentive Entitlement Pilot Projects* (New York: Manpower Demonstration Research Corporation, June 1984).

    According to Nat Semple, a congressional staff member who helped draft the legislation, YIEPP was meant to test whether requirements linked to benefits could improve functioning, as proposed in this book. The recipients in this case had too many alternatives to work for the educational requirements to be binding. See further discussion in Chapters 6 and 8.

21. Daniel A. Mazmanian and Paul A. Sabatier, *Implementation and Public Policy* (Glenview, Ill.: Scott, Foresman, 1983), ch. 6; Michael Kirst and Richard Jung, "The Utility of a Longitudinal Approach in Assessing Implementation: A Thirteen-Year View of Title I, ESEA," in Walter Williams et al., *Studying Implementation: Methodological and Administrative Issues* (Chatham, N.J.: Chatham House, 1982), ch. 6.
22. See Chapter 2, note 31. Moynihan, *Maximum Feasible Misunderstanding* (note 8), pp. xxix–xxxiii, 189–201, and Henry J. Aaron, *Politics and the Professors: The Great Society in Perspective* (Washington, D.C.: Brookings, 1978), emphasize that the experts greatly exaggerated what the new social science could deliver. The claims were disproved by experience and negative program evaluations. Later researchers have been much more circumspect.
23. Aaron, *Politics and Professors*, p. 77.
24. Sar A. Levitan, *The Great Society's Poor Law: A New Approach to Poverty* (Baltimore: Johns Hopkins Press, 1969), pp. 11–15.
25. Ibid., pp. 33–34; Sanford Kravitz, "The Community Action Program: Past, Present, and Its Future?" in Sundquist, ed., *On Fighting Poverty* (note 13), pp. 56, 56, *n*. 3; Moynihan, *Maximum Feasible Misunderstanding*, pp. 81–82.
26. Dwight Macdonald, "Our Invisible Poor," *The New Yorker*, January 19, 1963, pp. 82–132.
27. Max Weber, "The Social Psychology of the World Religions," in Max Weber, *From Max Weber: Essays in Sociology*, eds. H. H. Gerth and C. Wright Mills (New York: Oxford University Press, 1958), pp. 284–85.
28. Daniel P. Moynihan, "The Professors and the Poor," in Daniel Moynihan, ed., *On Fighting Poverty: Perspectives from the Social Sciences* (New York: Basic Books, 1969), p. 31.
29. William Ryan, *Blaming the Victim* (New York: Pantheon Books, 1971), p. 248 and passim.
30. Council of Economic Advisers, *Annual Report*, in *Economic Report of the President*, transmitted to the Congress, January 1964 (Washington, D.C.: U.S. Government Printing Office, 1964), pp. 55, 70.
31. U.S. Congress, Senate, Committee on Human Resources, *Adolescent Health, Services, and Pregnancy Prevention and Care Act of 1978*, *Hearings* before the Committee on Human Resources, on S. 2910, 95th Cong., 2d sess., June 14, 1978, pp. 25–40.
32. Nadine Brozan, "The Abortion Repeaters," *New York Times*, September 16, 1979, pp. C1, C10. In the same vein the *Times* recently editorialized that women suffering unwanted pregnancies are "victims of contraceptive failure, ignorance or innocence" (January 28, 1984, p. 22).
33. Michael Harrington, *The Other America: Poverty in the United States*, Revised Ed. (Baltimore: Penguin Books, 1971), pp. 16–17.
34. "To Fulfill These Rights," reprinted in Lee Rainwater and William L. Yancey, *The Moynihan Report and the Politics of Controversy* (Cambridge, Mass.: MIT Press, 1967), pp. 126, 131.

35. Council of Economic Advisers, *Annual Report, 1964,* p. 75.
36. *Public Papers of the Presidents of the United States: John F. Kennedy, 1963* (Washington, D.C.: U.S. Government Printing Office, 1964), p. 816.
37. Lawrence M. Mead, "The Interaction Problem in Policy Analysis," *Policy Sciences,* 16, no. 1 (September 1983): 45–66; Samuel H. Beer, "In Search of a New Public Philosophy," in Anthony King, ed., *The New American Political System* (Washington, D.C.: American Enterprise Institute, 1978), pp. 15–32.
38. Rainwater and Yancey, *Moynihan Report.*
39. Kenneth B. Clark, *Dark Ghetto: Dilemmas of Social Power* (New York: Harper Torchbooks, 1967), pp. 107, 109.
40. National Advisory Commission on Civil Disorders, *Report of the National Advisory Commission on Civil Disorders* (Washington, D.C.: U.S. Government Printing Office, March 1, 1968), pp. 129, 229.
41. See the articles in the *New York Times* by Judith Cummings, November 20–21, 27, 1983, and by Kenneth Noble, January 29, 1984. The articles discuss the revival of interest in the black family among black leaders but avoid the functioning issue.
42. Heather L. Ross and Isabel V. Sawhill, *Time of Transition: The Growth of Families Headed by Women* (Washington, D.C.: Urban Institute, 1975), pp. 101–6; Barbara Boland, "Participation in the Aid to Families with Dependent Children Program (AFDC)," in U.S. Congress, Joint Economic Committee, Subcommittee on Fiscal Policy, *Studies in Public Welfare, Paper No. 12 (part 1): The Family, Poverty, and Welfare Programs: Factors Influencing Family Stability,* 93d Cong., 1st sess., November 4, 1973, pp. 139, 153.
43. Frances Fox Piven and Richard A. Cloward, *Regulating the Poor: The Functions of Public Welfare* (New York: Pantheon Books, 1971), ch. 10; James T. Patterson, *America's Struggle Against Poverty, 1900–1980* (Cambridge, Mass.: Harvard University Press, 1981), ch. 11; Robert B. Albritton, "Social Amelioration Through Mass Insurgency? A Reexamination of the Piven and Cloward Thesis," *American Political Science Review,* 73, no. 4 (December 1979): 1003–11.
44. Congressional Budget Office, *CETA Reauthorization Issues* (Washington, D.C.: U.S. Government Printing Office, August 1978), pp. 3–13.
45. Articles by John M. Berry and Art Pine on federal employment and youth programs, *Washington Post,* April 24–26, 1979.
46. Robert A. Moffitt, "The Effect of a Negative Income Tax on Work Effort: A Summary of the Experimental Results," in Paul M. Sommers, ed., *Welfare Reform in America: Perspectives and Prospects* (Boston: Kluwer-Nijhoff, 1982), ch. 11.
47. For summaries of research on the effects of AFDC and interpretations of the income maintenance experiments, see Ross and Sawhill, *Time of Transition,* ch. 5; John H. Bishop, "Jobs, Cash Transfers and Marital Instability: A Review and Synthesis of the Evidence," *Journal of Human Resources,* 15, no. 3 (Summer 1980): 301–34; Sheldon Danziger et al., "How Income Transfer Programs Affect Work, Savings, and the Income Distribution: A Critical Review," *Journal of Economic Literature,* 19, no. 3 (September 1981): 975–1028; and testimony during hearings on the Carter welfare reform plan:

77 H. hearings 895–926, 1193–1288, and 78 S. hearings 205–24, 351–80, 814–51. See key to abbreviations before the Notes.

For summary and analysis of the Seattle/Denver experiment, see U.S. Department of Health and Human Services, Office of Income Security Policy, *Overview of the Seattle-Denver Income Maintenance Experiment Final Report* (Washington, D.C.: U.S. Government Printing Office, May 1983), and the Fall 1980 issue of the *Journal of Human Resources*.

48. U.S. Department of Health and Human Services, *Overview of Seattle-Denver*, pp. 18–21, 26.
49. Morton Paglin, "How Effective Is Our Multiple-Benefit Antipoverty Program?" in Sommers, ed., *Welfare Reform in America*, pp. 86–88, 96–97.
50. According to Charles Murray, *Losing Ground: American Social Policy, 1950–1980* (New York: Basic Books, 1984), p. 152, the rise in marital instability was negligible in the income maintenance experiment conducted in Gary, Indiana, because the Gary participants, unlike those in Seattle and Denver, were told that they would be *denied* assistance if their families divided.
51. Auletta, *The Underclass* (note 6), chs. 3–15.
52. This was a sentiment I heard frequently from WIN and CETA staff while interviewing them for the studies of employment programs in New York and other states reported in Chapter 7.
53. Gilder, *Wealth and Poverty* (note 3), p. 122; Edward A. Wynne, *Social Security: A Reciprocity System Under Pressure* (Boulder, Colo.: Westview Press, 1980); Alvin W. Gouldner, "The Norm of Reciprocity: A Preliminary Statement," *American Sociological Review*, 25, no. 2 (April 1960): 161–78.
54. James P. Comer and Alvin F. Poussaint, "PUSH-EXCEL: Setting High Achievement Goals for Black Youth," *Washington Post*, April 26, 1979, p. D.C.14.
55. Samuel P. Huntington, *American Politics: The Promise of Disharmony* (Cambridge, Mass.: Harvard University Press, 1981), pp. 75–81.

Chapter 4. Why Work Must Be Enforced

1. This section expands Lawrence M. Mead, "Expectations and Welfare Work: WIN in New York State," *Policy*, 18, no. 2 (Winter 1985), sections 1–2.
2. Daniel P. Moynihan, *The Politics of a Guaranteed Income: The Nixon Administration and the Family Assistance Plan* (New York: Random House, 1973), p. 94.
3. U.S. Department of Commerce, Bureau of the Census, *Statistical Abstract of the United States, 1984* (Washington, D.C.: U.S. Government Printing Office, December 1983), p. 407.
4. William E. Schmidt, "Growing Problem: Finding People to Work," *New York Times*, October 28, 1984, p. 26.
5. George L. Perry, "Changing Labor Markets and Inflation," *Brookings Papers on Economic Activity*, 1970, no. 3, pp. 411–41. Figures cited are from U.S. Department of Commerce, Bureau of the Census, *Statistical Abstract of the*

United States, 1977 (Washington, D.C.: U.S. Government Printing Office, September 1977), p. 395; U.S. Department of Commerce, Bureau of the Census, *Statistical Abstract of the United States, 1978* (Washington, D.C.: U.S. Government Printing Office, September 1978), p. 408; and *Statistical Abstract, 1984,* p. 422. The survey is from Kay Lehman Schlozman and Sidney Verba, *Injury to Insult: Unemployment, Class, and Political Response* (Cambridge, Mass.: Harvard University Press, 1979), pp. 38–40.

6. *Statistical Abstract, 1978,* p. 410; *Statistical Abstract, 1984,* p. 423; Congressional Budget Office, *Promoting Employment and Maintaining Incomes with Unemployment Insurance* (Washington, D.C.: U.S. Government Printing Office, March 1985), pp. 8–12, 25.
7. Martin Feldstein and James Poterba, "Unemployment Insurance and Reservation Wages," Working Paper No. 1011 (Cambridge, Mass.: National Bureau of Economic Research, July 1982); Carl Rosenfeld, "Job Search of the Unemployed, May 1976," *Monthly Labor Review,* 100, no. 11 (November 1977): 39–43. For a separate but similar analysis of the survey, see Alfred Tella, "How to Be an Expert on Joblessness Figures," *New York Times,* July 18, 1983, p. A15.
8. *Statistical Abstract, 1984,* p. 422. See the series on the nature of unemployment in the *Brookings Papers on Economic Activity*: Robert E. Hall, "Why Is the Unemployment Rate So High at Full Employment?" 1970, no. 3, pp. 369–402; George L. Perry, "Unemployment Flows in the U.S. Labor Market," 1972, no. 2, pp. 245–78; Stephen T. Marston, "Employment Instability and High Unemployment Rates," 1976, no. 1, pp. 169–203; and Kim B. Clark and Lawrence H. Summers, "Labor Market Dynamics and Unemployment: A Reconsideration," 1979, no. 1, pp. 13–72. Also Nancy S. Barrett and Richard D. Morgenstern, "Why Do Blacks and Women Have High Unemployment Rates?" *Journal of Human Resources,* 9, no. 4 (Fall 1974): 452–64. Clark and Summers show that the long-term unemployed account for most of measured unemployment, but they admit that joblessness for most unemployed is short and consistent with the "turnover" theory, even for the groups with the highest rates.
9. Hall, "Why Is Unemployment," p. 389; Robert E. Hall, "Prospects for Shifting the Phillips Curve through Manpower Policy," *Brookings Papers on Economic Activity,* 1971, no. 3, pp. 682–89. For a review of the evidence on voluntary unemployment, see Roger A. Freeman, *The Wayward Welfare State* (Stanford, Calif.: Hoover Institution Press, 1981), pp. 245–60.
10. Mary Jo Bane and David T. Ellwood, "The Dynamics of Dependence: The Routes to Self-Sufficiency," study prepared for the Office of Planning and Evaluation, Department of Health and Human Services (Cambridge, Mass.: Urban Systems Research and Engineering, June 1983), ch. 3. For a summary of evidence that most working mothers can arrange their own child care, see Suzanne H. Woolsey, "Pied-Piper Politics and the Child-Care Debate," *Daedalus,* 106, no. 2 (Spring 1977): 127–45; and B. Bruce-Briggs, "'Child Care': The Fiscal Time Bomb," *The Public Interest,* no. 49, Fall 1977, pp. 87–102. Middle-class and professional women are most in favor of day care programs; they have more difficulty than welfare mothers in arranging day care informally, because they tend to have fewer ties to their neighborhoods.

11. David M. DeFerranti et al., *The Welfare and Nonwelfare Poor in New York City* (New York: Rand Corporation, June 1974), pp. 109–10; Miriam Ostow and Anna B. Dutka, *Work and Welfare in New York City* (Baltimore: Johns Hopkins Press, 1975), p. 80, *n*. 3.
12. *Statistical Abstract, 1984*, p. 414.
13. 72 S. debate 32716; 71–2 S. hearings 1354; Ostow and Dutka, *Work and Welfare*, p. 75.
14. 67 S. hearings 255.
15. Ostow and Dutka, *Work and Welfare*, pp. 25–26, 36; 78 S. hearings 358; Bane and Ellwood, "Dynamics of Dependence," ch. 2.
16. Greg J. Duncan et al., *Years of Poverty, Years of Plenty: The Changing Fortunes of American Workers and Families* (Ann Arbor: Institute for Social Research, University of Michigan, 1984), pp. 37–38, 40–43; Frank Levy, "How Big Is the American Underclass?" Working Paper 0090–1 (Washington, D.C.: Urban Institute, September 1977), p. 13.
17. Hall, "Prospects," p. 661. For a review of economic theories of unemployment, none of them adequate, see Lester C. Thurow, *Dangerous Currents: The State of Economics* (New York: Random House, 1983), ch. 7.
18. Leonard J. Hausman, "The Impact of Welfare on the Work Effort of AFDC Mothers," in President's Commission on Income Maintenance Programs (Heineman Commission), *Technical Studies* (Washington, D.C.: U.S. Government Printing Office, November 1969), pp. 83–100; Anne McDougal Young, "Job Search of Recipients of Unemployment Insurance," *Monthly Labor Review*, 102, no. 2 (February 1979): 50; John M. Barron and Wesley Mellow, "Search Effort in the Labor Market," *Journal of Human Resources*, 14, no. 3 (Summer 1979): 389–404; Congressional Budget Office, *Unemployment Insurance: Financial Condition and Options for Change* (Washington, D.C.: U.S. Government Printing Office, June 1983), p. 2.
19. Feldstein and Poterba, "Unemployment Insurance" (note 7), pp. 22–39; Congressional Budget Office, *Promoting Employment* (note 6), pp. 19–20.
20. Martin S. Feldstein, "The Economics of the New Unemployment," *The Public Interest*, no. 33, Fall 1973, p. 25.
21. Clark and Summers, "Labor Market Dynamics" (note 8), pp. 51–55, 58–59.
22. National Advisory Commission on Civil Disorders, *Report of the National Advisory Commission on Civil Disorders* (Washington, D.C.: U.S. Government Printing Office, March 1, 1968), pp. 93, 232.
23. Kenneth B. Clark, *Dark Ghetto: Dilemmas of Social Power* (New York: Harper Torchbooks, 1967), chs. 2–5; William A. Gamson, *Power and Discontent* (Homewood, Ill.: Dorsey Press, 1968), chs. 3–8.
24. For a review of research on the "disemployment" effects of minimum wages, see Steven P. Zell, "The Minimum Wage and Youth Unemployment," *Federal Reserve Bank of Kansas City Economic Review*, January 1978, pp. 3–16.
25. This is the problem with the argument that the minimum wage deters black employment made in Walter E. Williams, *The State Against Blacks* (New York: McGraw-Hill, 1982), ch. 3. William's case that government rules pre-

vent better-socialized blacks from getting into higher-paying jobs and professions (chs. 5–9) is more persuasive.

26. Richard B. Freeman and Harry J. Holzer, "Young Blacks and Jobs—What We Now Know," *The Public Interest*, no. 78, Winter 1985, pp. 27–30.
27. Elijah Anderson, "Some Observations of Black Youth Employment," in Bernard E. Anderson and Isabel V. Sawhill, eds., *Youth Employment and Public Policy* (Englewood Cliffs, N.J.: Prentice-Hall, 1980), ch. 3.
28. Ken Auletta, *The Underclass* (New York: Random House, 1982), pp. 228–29, 236–45.
29. Leonard Goodwin, *Do the Poor Want to Work? A Social-Psychological Study of Work Orientations* (Washington, D.C.: Brookings, 1972), pp. 82–84, 101, 112. See also his *Causes and Cures of Welfare: New Evidence on the Social Psychology of the Poor* (Lexington, Mass.: D. C. Heath, 1983).
30. Goodwin, *Do the Poor Want to Work?* p. 46; 78 S. hearings 1257.
31. Committee for Economic Development, Research and Policy Committee, *Improving the Public Welfare System* (New York: Committee for Economic Development, April 1970), p. 39.
32. Lee Rainwater, "The Problem of Lower-Class Culture and Poverty-War Strategy," in Daniel P. Moynihan, ed., *Understanding Poverty: Perspectives from the Social Sciences* (New York: Basic Books, 1969), p. 238; Hyman Rodman, "The Lower-class Value Stretch," *Social Forces*, 42, no. 2 (December 1963): 205–15.
33. Lon Fuller, *The Morality of Law*, Revised Ed. (New Haven: Yale University Press, 1969), ch. 1.
34. Samuel Z. Klausner, *Six Years in the Lives of the Impoverished: An Examination of the WIN Thesis* (Philadelphia: Center for Research on the Acts of Man, 1978).
35. Martha S. Hill et al., *Motivation and Economic Mobility of the Poor: Final Report, Part 1* (Ann Arbor: Institute for Social Research, University of Michigan, August 3, 1983); Thomas Sowell, *Ethnic America: A History* (New York: Basic Books, 1981); David C. McClelland, *The Achieving Society* (Princeton: Van Nostrand, 1961), ch. 9 and passim. The Hill study finds, however, that motivation is not closely related to the mobility of the poor on an individual basis. See also note 60 below.
36. Daniel T. Rodgers, *The Work Ethic in Industrial America, 1850–1920* (Chicago: University of Chicago Press, 1978), p. 28 and passim.
37. Connie de Boer, "The Polls: Attitudes Toward Work," *Public Opinion Quarterly*, 42, no. 3 (Fall 1978): 414–23; U.S. Department of Health, Education, and Welfare, Special Task Force to the Secretary of Health, Education, and Welfare, *Work in America*, December 1972, reprinted in U.S. Congress, Senate, Committee on Labor and Public Welfare, 93d Cong., 1st sess., committee print, February 1973; William Serrin, "Study Says Work Ethic Is Alive but Neglected," *New York Times*, September 5, 1983, p. 8.
38. Winifred Bell and Dennis M. Bushe, *Neglecting the Many, Helping the Few: The Impact of the 1967 AFDC Work Incentives* (New York: Center for Studies

in Income Maintenance Policy, New York University School of Social Work, 1975).

39. Frederick Doolittle et al., "The Mirage of Welfare Reform," *The Public Interest,* no. 47, Spring 1977, p. 83; 70 S. hearings 1831, 1984; 78 S. hearings 214–19, 355. It is possible that work incentives, though they prompt more mothers to work, reduce overall work levels by allowing mothers already working to earn the same with less work and by attracting more eligibles onto AFDC; see Frank Levy, "The Labor Supply of Female Household Heads, or AFDC Work Incentives Don't Work Too Well," *Journal of Human Resources*, 14, no. 1 (Winter 1979): 76–97.
40. U.S. General Accounting Office, *An Evaluation of the 1981 AFDC Changes: Initial Analyses* (Washington, D.C.: U.S. Government Printing Office, April 2, 1984), pp. 5, 34. For a summary of several studies, see University of Wisconsin, Institute for Research on Poverty, *Focus*, 8, no. 1 (Spring 1985): 1–8. Perhaps weaker work incentives actually increased work effort; see note 39.
41. 77 H. hearings 924; Frank Levy, *The Logic of Welfare Reform* (Washington, D.C.: Urban Institute Press, 1980), pp. 48–49, 56–57. See also Chapter 3, note 47.
42. Bane and Ellwood, "Dynamics of Dependence" (note 10), pp. 17–23.
43. Doolittle et al., "Mirage of Welfare Reform," pp. 67–68, 82, 86.
44. Martin Anderson, *Welfare: The Political Economy of Welfare Reform in the United States* (Stanford, Calif.: Hoover Institution Press, 1978), ch. 6; Henry J. Aaron, *Why Is Welfare So Hard to Reform?* (Washington, D.C.: Brookings, 1973), chs. 4–5.
45. Sar A. Levitan et al., *Work and Welfare Go Together* (Baltimore: John Hopkins Press, 1972), pp. 128–31, 136–37.
46. Charles E. Lindblom, *Politics and Markets: The World's Political-Economic Systems* (New York: Basic Books, 1977), pp. 19–20.
47. Duncan MacRae, Jr., "Normative Assumptions in the Study of Public Choice," *Public Choice,* 16 (Fall 1973): 38–39; Lester H. Hunt, "Some Advantages of Social Control: An Individualist Defense," *Public Choice*, 36, no. 1 (1981): 3–16.
48. Michael Walzer, *Obligations: Essays on Disobedience, War, and Citizenship* (Cambridge, Mass.: Harvard University Press, 1970).
49. Frances Fox Piven and Richard A. Cloward, *Poor People's Movements: Why They Succeed, How They Fail* (New York: Pantheon Books, 1977), pp. 275–88.
50. Moynihan, *Politics of Guaranteed Income* (note 2) pp. 295–96.
51. Proponents of the liberal position would include Henry J. Aaron, *Politics and the Professors: The Great Society in Perspective* (Washington, D.C.: Brookings, 1978), ch. 4; and Goodwin, *Do the Poor Want to Work?* (note 29), ch. 8, and *Causes and Cures* (note 29), ch. 7. Conservatives include Martin Anderson, *Welfare*, and George Gilder, *Wealth and Poverty* (New York: Basic Books, 1981), chs. 6, 8–9, 11–12. Moderates would include Richard Zeckhauser and Peter Schuck, "An Alternative to the Nixon Income Maintenance Plan," *The Public Interest*, no. 19, Spring 1970, pp. 120–30; and Charles C.

Holt et al., *The Unemployment-Inflation Dilemma: A Manpower Solution* (Washington, D.C.: Urban Institute, 1971). Of the liberals, Aaron has since come to favor some form of work requirement.

52. For a candid but unconvincing argument that nonwork is acceptable, see David Macarov, *Incentives to Work* (San Francisco: Jossey-Bass, 1970).
53. Harvey Leibenstein, "Allocative Efficiency vs. X-Efficiency," *American Economic Review*, 56, no. 3 (June 1966): 392–415; P.T. Bauer, *Equality, the Third World and Economic Delusion* (Cambridge, Mass.: Harvard University Press, 1981), chs. 4–6.
54. Edward C. Banfield, *The Moral Basis of a Backward Society* (Glencoe, Ill.: Free Press, 1958) and *The Unheavenly City Revisited: A Revision of the Unheavenly City* (Boston: Little, Brown, 1970).
55. Gilder, *Wealth and Poverty*, ch. 5.
56. Urie Bronfenbrenner, "The Origins of Alienation," *Scientific American*, August 1974, pp. 53–57, 60–61; Klausner, *Six Years* (note 34), p. 60. The suggestion is from Oscar Lewis in James L. Sundquist, ed., *On Fighting Poverty: Perspectives from Experience* (New York: Basic Books, 1969), pp. 246–47.
57. Morris Janowitz, *The Reconstruction of Patriotism: Education for Civic Consciousness* (Chicago: University of Chicago Press, 1983).
58. The survey was commissioned by the National Bureau of Economic Research (NBER) and carried out in 1979–80. My summary of the findings is based on Freeman and Holzer, "Young Blacks and Jobs" (note 26), and papers prepared for the Conference on Inner City Youth Unemployment held at NBER in Cambridge, Mass., August 11–12, 1983. For a vivid characterization of the life-style of lower-class black youth, see George Gilder, *Visible Man: A True Story of Post-Racist America* (New York: Basic Books, 1978).
59. Thomas Hobbes, *Leviathan*, ed. Michael Oakeshott (Oxford: Blackwell, 1946), pp. 120 (ch. 18), 221–22 (ch. 30).
60. James S. Coleman, "Equal Schools or Equal Students?" *The Public Interest*, no. 4, Summer 1966, p. 75. Researchers agree that feelings of personal efficacy are linked to success. There is dispute over whether they *cause* success. See these articles, all from the *Journal of Human Resources*: Paul J. Andrisani, "Internal-External Attitudes, Personal Initiative, and the Labor Market Experience of Black and White Men," 12, no. 3 (Summer 1977): 308–28; Greg J. Duncan and James N. Morgan, "Sense of Efficacy and Subsequent Change in Earnings—A Replication," 16, no. 4 (Fall 1981): 649–57; and Paul J. Andrisani, "Internal-External Attitudes, Sense of Efficacy, and Labor Market Experience: A Reply to Duncan and Morgan," 16, no. 4 (Fall 1981): 658–66.
61. Jane E. Brody, "Self-Reliance Held to Be Important In Victims' Recovery," *New York Times*, January 17, 1984, pp. C1, C6.
62. For an introduction to political socialization, see Richard E. Dawson et al., *Political Socialization*, 2d Ed. (Boston: Little, Brown, 1977).
63. Lawrence M. Mead, "Health Policy: The Need for Governance," *Annals of the American Academy of Political and Social Science*, 434 (November 1977): 39–57.
64. Banfield, *Unheavenly City Revisited*, ch. 11.

Chapter 5. The Work Issue Defeats Welfare Reform

1. U.S. Department of Commerce, Bureau of the Census, *Statistical Abstract of the United States, 1972* (Washington, D.C.: U.S. Government Printing Office, July 1972), p. 302.
2. Joel F. Handler and Ellen Jane Hollingsworth, *The "Deserving Poor": A Study of Welfare Administration* (New York: Academic Press, 1971), ch. 7; Scott Briar, "Welfare from Below: Recipients' Views of the Public Welfare System," *California Law Review*, 54, no. 2 (May 1966): 370–85. The abuses that Frances Fox Piven and Richard Cloward discuss in *Regulating the Poor: The Functions of Public Welfare* (New York: Pantheon Books, 1971) occurred mainly in the South before 1960.
3. Robert A. Levine, "Evaluating the War on Poverty," in James L. Sundquist, ed., *On Fighting Poverty: Perspectives from Experience* (New York: Basic Books, 1969), p. 212; 78 S. hearings 3.
4. These cases were, respectively: *King* v. *Smith*, 392 U.S. 309 (1968); *Shapiro* v. *Thompson*, 394 U.S. 618 (1969); and *Goldberg* v. *Kelly*, 397 U.S. 254 (1970).
5. Mirian Ostow and Anna B. Dutka, *Work and Welfare in New York City* (Baltimore: Johns Hopkins Press, 1975), pp. 7–8.
6. 78 S. hearings 444; Blanche Bernstein, *The Politics of Welfare: The New York City Experience* (Cambridge, Mass.: Abt Books, 1982), pp. 51–62, 95–97. The potential for child support is suggested by Massachusetts and Michigan, which, respectively, collect from 43 percent of absent fathers and recoup 8 percent of AFDC costs.
7. Marc Bendick, Jr., "Failure to Enroll in Public Assistance Programs," *Social Work*, 25, no. 4 (July 1980): 268–74.
8. The full citations for the groups and their reports are:

   Advisory Council on Public Welfare, *"Having the Power, We have the Duty,"* Report to the Secretary of Health, Education, and Welfare, U.S. Department of Health, Education, and Welfare, Welfare Administration (Washington, D.C.: U.S. Government Printing Office, June 29, 1966). The council, consisting mostly of welfare experts and administrators, was commissioned to study welfare under the Social Security Amendments of 1962.

   Ad Hoc Steering Committee of the Arden House Conference on Public Welfare, *Report*, in 68 JEC hearings, vol. 2, pp. 445–91. The committee was drawn from a meeting of business executives, public officials, and academics convened by Governor Nelson Rockefeller of New York in 1967.

   National Advisory Commission on Civil Disorders (Kerner Commission), *Report of the National Advisory Commission on Civil Disorders* (Washington, D.C.: U.S. Government Printing Office, March 1, 1968). A body of public, business, labor, and civil rights leaders commissioned by President Johnson to study the urban riots in 1967.

   President's Commission on Income Maintenance Programs (Heineman Commission), *Poverty Amid Plenty: The American Paradox* (Washington, D.C.: U.S. Government Printing Office, November 1969). A committee of government, business, and academic figures commissioned by Johnson in 1968 to assess the entire income maintenance system.

Committee for Economic Development, Research and Policy Committee, *Improving the Public Welfare System* (New York: Committee for Economic Development, April 1970). The CED is an organization of prominent and progressive businessmen with close ties to government.

9. Handler and Hollingsworth, *"Deserving Poor,"* pp. 86–87.
10. Advisory Council, *"Having the Power,"* p. 16; President's Commission, *Poverty Amid Plenty*, pp. 2, 23, 32–33.
11. President's Commission on Income Maintenance Programs, *Background Papers* (Washington, D.C.: U.S. Government Printing Office, November 1969), p. 58; Ad Hoc Steering Committee, *Report*, p. 461; President's Commission, *Poverty Amid Plenty*, p. 23.
12. Advisory Council, *Report*, pp. xi, 103; President's Commission, *Poverty Amid Plenty*, p. 57.
13. President's Commission, *Poverty Amid Plenty*, p. 59.
14. The National Association of Manufacturers (NAM) as well as the Committee for Economic Development endorsed the Nixon welfare plan. The Chamber of Commerce opposed it but proposed a conservative, revenue-sharing alternative to the Carter plan; see 78 S. hearings 663–84. NAM did not testify on PBJI. See Daniel P. Moynihan, *The Politics of a Guaranteed Income: The Nixon Administration and the Family Assistance Plan* (New York: Random House, 1973), pp. 285–94.
15. Gilbert Y. Steiner, *The State of Welfare* (Washington, D.C.: Brookings, 1971), pp. 95–100.
16. For discussion of the economists' approach to reform, see Henry J. Aaron, *Why Is Welfare So Hard to Reform?* (Washington, D.C.: Brookings, 1973); Michael C. Barth et al., *Toward an Effective Income Support System: Problems, Prospects, and Choices* (Madison: Institute for Research on Poverty, University of Wisconsin, 1974); and Lester C. Thurow, "Income Transfers vs. the Public Provision of Goods and Services In-Kind," in Laurence E. Lynn, Jr., with the assistance of Stephanie G. Gould, *Designing Public Policy: A Casebook on the Role of Policy Analysis* (Santa Monica, Calif.: Goodyear, 1980), ch. 22.
17. Sar A. Levitan and Robert Taggart *The Promise of Greatness* (Cambridge, Mass.: Harvard University Press, 1976), pp. 47–49.
18. In 1968, 1,200 economists petitioned Washington for a guaranteed income, and in 1976 seven prominent economists wrote a public letter to President Ford to the same effect. See Steiner, *State of Welfare*, pp. 95–96, and James L. Rowe, Jr., "7 Economists Urge Reform of Welfare," *Washington Post*, April 15, 1976, pp. 1, 8.
19. The Griffiths project is not listed with the welfare studies mentioned earlier because it came later and had less influence, except on academics, for whom the research it commissioned on welfare was a bonanza. A helpful compendium and analysis of all the plans is found in Lester M. Salamon, *Welfare: The Elusive Consensus* (New York: Praeger, 1978), ch. 4.
20. For example, the Income Supplement Program developed by HEW planners in 1974 originally included no work test. An option allowing, but not requiring, states to include work registration was added only at the insistence of HEW Secretary Caspar Weinberger. Martha Griffiths gave extended attention to

work and other administrative aspects of welfare in her welfare inquiry, but the ABLE proposal avoided work tests, saying only that the issue might be "reopened" if guaranteed income proved to deter work. See Lynn and Gould, *Designing Public Policy*, pp. 95, 95*n.;* 74 JEC report 210.

21. Moynihan, *Politics of Guaranteed Income*, pp. 141–42, 219–20, 283–84; Vincent J. Burke and Vee Burke, *Nixon's Good Deed: Welfare Reform* (New York: Columbia University Press, 1974), pp. 75, 85; M. Kenneth Bowler, *The Nixon Guranteed Income Proposal: Substance and Process in Policy Change* (Cambridge, Mass.: Ballinger, 1974), p. 29.
22. Laurence E. Lynn, Jr., and David deF. Whitman, *The President as Policymaker: Jimmy Carter and Welfare Reform* (Philadelphia: Temple University Press, 1981), pp. 126, 221–26; 78 S. hearings 350–51, 382.
23. Richard P. Nathan, "Family Assistance Plan: Workfare/Welfare," *The New Republic*, February 24, 1973, pp. 19–21.
24. 77 H. prelim. hearings 43.
25. For these interpretations, see the works by Moynihan, Burke and Burke, Bowler, and Lynn and Whitman already cited. See also Martin Anderson, *Welfare: The Political Economy of Welfare Reform in the United States* (Stanford, Calif.: Hoover Institution Press, 1978); Christopher Leman, *The Collapse of Welfare Reform: Political Institutions, Policy, and the Poor in Canada and the United States* (Cambridge, Mass.: MIT Press, 1980); Bill Cavala and Aaron Wildavsky, "The Political Feasibility of Income by Right," *Public Policy*, 18, no. 3 (Spring 1970): 321–54; and William P. Albrecht, "Welfare Reform: An Idea Whose Time Has Come and Gone," in Paul M. Sommers, ed., *Welfare Reform in America: Perspectives and Prospects* (Boston: Kluwer-Nijhoff, 1982), ch. 2.
26. 69 H. hearings 2357; 71–2 S. hearings 2, 48, 175, 1064; 77 S. prelim. hearings 14.
27. 72 S. debate 33096; 71 H. debate 21461–62.
28. The hearings, reports, and debates consulted were those listed in the key to abbreviations at the beginning of the notes section.
29. 67 H. debate 23053.
30. 69 H. hearings 51.
31. 70 H. Rules hearings 177–78.
32. 67 H. final debate 36386. Such adjectives were scattered throughout liberal speeches.
33. Leman, *Collapse of Welfare Reform*, p. 82. Under AFDC the entire grant can be forfeited only if the offender is a father, in states covering unemployed fathers.
34. *Congressional Quarterly Almanac, vol. 33, 1977* (Washington, D.C.: Congressional Quarterly, 1978), p. 46E.
35. This was the Congressional Budget Office estimate. The Administration claimed only $9 billion. See Lynn and Whitman, *President as Policymaker* (note 22), pp. 232–38.
36. 68 JEC hearings 219. This view of work as a benefit, not an obligation, also animates Sar A. Levitan and Clifford M. Johnson, *Beyond the Safety Net:*

Reviving the Promise of Opportunity in America (Cambridge, Mass.: Ballinger, 1984), an important recent liberal commentary.

37. 68 JEC hearings 124; 77 S. prelim. hearings 30.
38. 72 S. debate 33107; 71–2 S. hearings 829–31.
39. 70 S. debate 43862; 70 S. hearings 1912.
40. Burke and Burke, *Nixon's Good Deed* (note 21), pp. 163–64; 71–2 S. hearings 2069.
41. 69 H. hearings 306–8, 835, 898–99, 1099, 1748–49, 1753, 1792.
42. 69 H. hearings 307; 70 H. Rules hearings 234.
43. For details of the many changes in the FAP suitable work provisions, see U.S. Congress, Senate, Committee on Finance, H.R. 16311, *The Family Assistance Act of 1970: June Revisions, Revised*, 91st Cong., 2d sess., November 5, 1970.
44. 70 H. debate 12092–93, 12105–6. Notably, Martha Griffiths, the most archetypical of the civic conservatives, voted for the recommittal motion but abstained on passage. She did, however, vote for FAP at its second passage by the House in 1971.
45. Leman, *Collapse of Welfare Reform* (note 25), pp. 178–84; Richard Zeckhauser and Peter Schuck, "An Alternative to the Nixon Income Maintenance Plan," *The Public Interest*, no. 19, Spring 1970, pp. 120–30.
46. 70 S. debate 43636; Moynihan, *Politics of Guaranteed Income* (note 14), pp. 17–18, 89–94.
47. 78 S. hearings 27; 72 S. report 83.
48. 78 S. prelim. hearings 70, 79; 78 S. hearings 54.
49. 77 H. prelim. hearings 7–9, 38; 77 S. prelim. hearings 19–20, 67–69.
50. Bernstein, *Politics of Welfare* (note 6), p. 38; U.S. Department of Labor, Manpower Administration, *The Potential for Work Among Welfare Parents* (Washington, D.C.: U.S. Government Printing Office, 1969).
51. 77. H. prelim. hearings 27–33; Sar A. Levitan et al., *Work and Welfare Go Together* (Baltimore: Johns Hopkins Press, 1972); Judith Mayo, *Work and Welfare: Employment and Employability of Women in the AFDC Program* (Chicago: Community and Family Study Center, University of Chicago, 1975).
52. 67 S. hearings 795–96, 1994; 69 H. hearings 266; 71–2 S. hearings 179.
53. 78 S. hearings 24–26.
54. Irene Cox, "Families on Welfare in New York City," *Welfare in Review*, 6, no. 2 (March–April 1968): 22–26 (a summary of the Podell study); Leonard Goodwin, *Do the Poor Want to Work? A Social-Psychological Study of Work Orientations* (Washington, D.C.: Brookings, 1972).
55. 69 H. hearings 305–6; 70 S. hearings 905–75; Moynihan, *Politics of Guaranteed Income*, pp. 509–12.
56. Lynn and Whitman, *President as Policymaker* (note 22), pp. 79 *n.*, 247–49.
57. Ad Hoc Steering Committee, *Report* (note 8), 68 JEC hearings 473–74; *New York Times*, November 16, 1978, p. A23.
58. Lynn and Whitman, *President as Policymaker*, pp. 240–47.

59. Leonard J. Hausman, "The Politics of a Guaranteed Income: The Nixon Administration and the Family Assistance Plan—A Review Article," *Journal of Human Resources*, 8, no. 4 (Fall 1973): 20, advised liberals to do this.
60. Lynn and Whitman, *President as Policymaker*, p. 63; 78 S. hearings 652–53, 755–56.
61. 77 H. hearings 1063.
62. For these Johnson proposals, see 67 H. hearings 3–194.
63. 69 H. hearings 1616; 72 S. debate 32719.
64. 79 H. debate 31333–84; *Congressional Quarterly Almanac, vol. 35, 1979* (Washington, D.C.: Congressional Quarterly, 1980), pp. 33E–35E, 509–11.
65. Lester A. Sobel, ed., *Welfare and the Poor* (New York: Facts on File, 1977), pp. 122–24.

Chapter 6. Federal Work Tests: Weakness and Potential

1. Judith M. Gueron and Barbara Goldman, "The U.S. Experience in Work Relief," unpublished paper, Manpower Demonstration Research Corporation, New York, N.Y., March 1983, pp. 1–2.
2. Technically, WIN is assigned to a "sponsor" agency at the state level. Usually it is the state labor department. In a few states it has been the welfare department, and some states have recently replaced WIN with welfare-run programs, an option allowed under the 1981 Reagan welfare reforms.
3. Vincent J. Burke and Vee Burke, *Nixon's Good Deed: Welfare Reform* (New York: Columbia University Press, 1974), pp. 35–36.
4. Auerbach Corporation, "The Work Incentive Program," reprinted in 70 S. hearings 384.
5. Jesse E. Gordon, "WIN Research: A Review of the Findings," in Charles D. Garvin et al., eds., *The Work Incentive Experience* (Montclair, N.J.: Allanheld, Osmun, 1978), pp. 28, 33–58; Leonard Goodwin, "What Has Been Learned from the Work Incentive Program and Related Experiences: A Review of Research with Policy Implications," Office of Research and Development, Employment and Training Administration, U.S. Department of Labor, February 1977, p. 99.
6. 70 S. hearings 134, 764, 1261, 1265.
7. Gordon, "WIN Research," pp. 33–38, 55; Goodwin, "What Has Been Learned," ch. 3.
8. Quoted in George Mink, "The Organization of WIN and Its Impact on Participants," in Garvin et al., eds., *Work Incentive Experience*, p. 114.
9. 78 S. hearings 350, 474; U.S. Congress, Senate, Committee on Finance, *Social Security Disability Amendments of 1979*, S. Rept. 96–408, on H.R. 3236, 96th Cong., 1st sess., November 8, 1979, pp. 61–62.
10. Mark Lincoln Chadwin et al., "Reforming Welfare: Lessons from the WIN Experience," *Public Administration Review*, 41, no. 3 (May/June 1981): 373.

A small part of the performance gain could be attributed to WIN agencies' learning how to do their job better.

11. U.S. Department of Labor and U.S. Department of Health and Human Services, *WIN: 10th Annual Report to the Congress* (Washington, D.C.: U.S. Department of Labor, December 1980), p. 1.
12. Further evaluations and studies of WIN are discussed in Chapter 7.
13. U.S. General Accounting Office, *An Overview of the WIN Program: Its Objectives, Accomplishments, and Problems* (Washington, D.C.: U.S. Government Printing Office, June 21,1982), ch. 2, says that half of the registrants, or 19 percent of adult recipients, participate actively. My own calculations from national WIN data indicate about a third in recent years.
14. Mink, "Organization of WIN," p. 116; U.S. Congress, Senate, Committee on Finance, *Implementation of Amendments to Improve the Work Incentive Program*, committee print, 92d Cong., 2d sess., June 26, 1972, pp. 4–10.
15. Gueron and Goldman, "U.S. Experience" (note 1), pp. 8–18, 22–28, 31–33; Christopher Leman, *The Collapse of Welfare Reform: Political Institutions, Policy, and the Poor in Canada and the United States* (Cambridge, Mass.: MIT Press, 1980), pp. 214–19.
16. Gueron and Goldman, "U.S. Experience," pp. 8–33; U.S. General Accounting Office, *CWEP's Implementation Results To Date Raise Questions About The Administration's Proposed Mandatory Workfare Program* (Washington, D.C.: U.S. Government Printing Office, April 2, 1984), pp. 15–22.
17. Blanch Bernstein, *The Politics of Welfare: The New York City Experience* (Cambridge, Mass.: Abt Books, 1982), pp. 47–50, 146–48, makes the valid point that welfare savings due to workfare should be counted in its favor; 20 to 40 percent of general assistance cases assigned to workfare in New York prefer to give up assistance rather than meet the work test.
18. Gueron and Goldman, "U.S. Experience," pp. 33–45; Charles S. Rodgers, "Work Tests for Welfare Recipients: The Gap Between the Goal and the Reality," *Journal of Policy Analysis and Management*, 1, no. 1 (Fall 1981): 5–17.
19. Data from the Bureau of Family Assistance, Social Security Administration; U.S. General Accounting Office, *CWEP's Implementation*, pp. 10–17.
20. Congressional Budget Office, *The Food Stamp Program: Income or Food Supplementation?* (Washington, D.C.: U.S. Government Printing Office, January 1977), pp. 19, 24–30.
21. *Federal Register*, January 16, 1981, pp. 4622–32.
22. U.S. Congress, Senate, Committee on Agriculture, Nutrition, and Forestry, *Food and Agriculture Act of 1977*, S. Rept. 95–180, to accompany S. 275, 95th Cong., 1st sess., May 16, 1977, p. 125.
23. U.S. General Accounting Office, *Food Stamp Workfare: Cost Benefit Results Not Conclusive; Administrative Problems Continue* (Washington, D.C.: U.S. Government Printing Office, February 19, 1982), p. 10, passim.
24. Fred L. Israel, ed., *The State of the Union Messages of the Presidents, 1790–1966* (New York: Chelsea House, 1967), 3: 2814–15.
25. Walter Corson and Walter Nicholson, "Extending Benefits During Recessions: Lessons from the FSB Experience," in National Commission on Unemploy-

ment Compensation, *Unemployment Compensation: Studies and Research* (Washington, D.C.: U.S. Government Printing Office, July 1980), 1: 128–35.

26. U.S. Department of Commerce, Bureau of the Census, *Statistical Abstract of the United States, 1982–83* (Washington, D.C.: U.S. Government Printing Office, December 1982), p. 337, and *Statistical Abstract of the United States, 1984* (Washington, D.C.: U.S. Government Printing Office, December 1983), p. 390.
27. Kim B. Clark and Lawrence H. Summers, "Labor Market Dynamics and Unemployment: A Reconsideration," *Brookings Papers on Economic Activity*, 1979, no. 1, pp. 51–55.
28. Congressional Budget Office, *Promoting Employment and Maintaining Incomes with Unemployment Insurance* (Washingon, D.C.: U.S. Government Printing Office, March 1985), pp. 49–50; Paul L. Burgess and Jerry L. Kingston, "Estimating Overpayments and Improper Payments," and Matthew Black and Timothy J. Carr, "Analysis of Nonsearch," both in National Commission on Unemployment Compensation, *Unemployment Compensation: Studies and Research* (Washington, D.C.: U.S. Government Printing Office, July 1980), 2:487–542.
29. Congressional Budget Office, *Unemployment Insurance: Financial Condition and Options for Change* (Washington, D.C.: U.S. Government Printing Office, June 1983), pp. 51–54.
30. National Commission on Unemployment Compensation, *Unemployment Compensation: Final Report* (Washington, D.C.: U.S. Government Printing Office, July 1980), p. 17.
31. Corson and Nicholson, "Extending Benefits," p. 145.
32. Walter Nicholson, "A Statistical Model of Exhaustion of Unemployment Insurance Benefits," *Journal of Human Resources*, 16, no. 1 (Winter 1981): 117–28; Arlene Holen and Stanley A. Horowitz, "The Effect of Unemployment Insurance and Eligibility Enforcement on Unemployment," *Journal of Law and Economics*, 17, no. 2 (October 1974): 403–31.
33. A further 1.3 million claims were denied because claimants quit work voluntarily. See National Commission on Unemployment Compensation, *Unemployment Compensation: Final Report*, p. 46.
34. Martha Derthick, *Policymaking for Social Security* (Washington, D.C.: Brookings, 1979), p. 309; Congressional Budget Office, *Disability Compensation: Current Issues and Options for Change* (Washington, D.C.: U.S. Government Printing Office, June 1982), pp. 25–26, 37.
35. Congressional Budget Office, *Disability*, pp. 1, 17, 23–25.
36. Ibid., p. 21; Derthick, *Policymaking*, p. 310.
37. Congressional Budget Office, *Disability*, pp. 18–21.
38. Ibid., pp. 40–41, 47–49; L. Scott Muller, "Receipt of Multiple Benefits by Disabled-Worker Beneficiaries", *Social Security Bulletin*, 43, no. 11 (November 1980): 3–19.
39. Congressional Budget Office, *Disability*, pp. 28, 42–44.
40. *New York Times*, April 14, 1984, pp. 1, 12.
41. Congressional Budget Office, *Disability*, p. 51.

42. These powers are found in sections 222(b)(1) and 1611(e)(3) of the Social Security Act.
43. The employers do, however, have an interest in reporting workers to UI who quit jobs voluntarily or are discharged for misconduct. Those workers could otherwise claim UI benefits. That might raise the employers' payroll taxes, since the taxes vary with how often they lay off workers.
44. John J. Mitchell et al., *Implementing Welfare-Employment Programs: An Institutional Analysis of the Work Incentive (WIN) Program*, U.S. Department of Labor, R&D Monograph 78 (Washington, D.C.: U.S. Government Printing Office, 1980), pp. 59–61, 127–29. Performance funding in ES and WIN has been suspended in recent years.
45. Quotations from staff interviewed for WIN studies cited in ch. 7, note 19.
46. The above discussion is based on Rodgers, "Work Tests" (note 18), pp. 12–13; David W. Stevens, "The 'Work Test': Goals and Administrative Practices," in National Commission on Unemployment Compensation, *Unemployment Compensation: Studies and Research* (Washington, D.C.: U.S. Government Printing Office, July 1980), 1: 51–62; and Charles S. Rodgers and David W. Stevens, "Regulating Work: The Application of Work Tests for Income Transfer Recipients," paper presented at the annual conference of the Association for Public Policy Analysis and Management, Washington, D.C., October 22–24, 1981.
47. Rodgers, "Work Tests," pp. 13–14.
48. U.S. Department of Labor and U.S. Department of Health, Education, and Welfare, *WIN Handbook*, 3d ed. (Washington, D.C.: U.S. Government Printing Office, October 1979), p. XI–4.
49. Alexis De Tocqueville, "Memoir on Pauperism," *The Public Interest*, no. 70, Winter 1983, pp. 111–12.
50. For an introduction to the English poor law and its reform, see Steven Marcus, "Their Brothers' Keepers: An Episode from English History," in Willard Gaylin et al., *Doing Good: The Limits of Benevolence* (New York: Pantheon Books, 1978), pp. 39–66, and Gertrude Himmelfarb, *The Idea of Poverty: England in the Early Industrial Age* (New York: Knopf, 1984), ch. 6.
51. The calculation of WIN's share of welfare spending covers fiscal 1978–83; figures from *The Budget of the United States Government* (Washington, D.C.: U.S. Government Printing Office) for fiscal years 1980–85. For the Reagan cuts in WIN, see Congressional Budget Office, "Major Legislative Changes in Human Resources Programs Since January 1981," unpublished memorandum, August 1983, p. 65.
52. An additional complexity is that the various work tests are not all consistent in their requirements and administrative structures. A recipient could be subject to different demands under different programs, though the AFDC and Unemployment Insurance requirements usually take precedence.
53. Sydelle Brooks Levy, *The Workings of WIN: A Field Observation Study of Three Local Offices* (New York: Manpower Demonstration Research Corporation, January 1981). For the relevant policies and regulations, see DOL and HEW, *WIN Handbook*, chs. 8, 11; and *Code of Federal Regulations*

(Washington, D.C.: U.S. Government Printing Office, October 1, 1981), vol. 45, part 224.34–224.77.

54. George Gilder, *Wealth and Poverty* (New York: Basic Books, 1981), pp. 116–18; Henry J. Aaron, *Why Is Welfare So Hard to Reform?* (Washington, D.C.: Brookings, 1973), pp. 49–50. Aaron now favors some work policies.
55. Murray Edelman, *The Symbolic Uses of Politics* (Urbana: University of Illinois Press, 1964).
56. Thomas C. Schelling, "On the Ecology of Micromotives," *The Public Interest*, no. 25, Fall 1971, p. 96.
57. "Of the First Principles of Government," in David Hume, *Essays: Moral, Political, and Literary* (Oxford: Oxford University Press, 1966), p. 29.
58. For interpretations along these lines, see Duncan MacRae, Jr., "Concepts and Methods of Policy Analysis," *Society*, 16, no. 6 (September/October 1979): 22-23; and Harrell R. Rodgers, Jr., "Law as an Instrument of Public Policy," *American Journal of Political Science*, 17, no. 3 (August 1973): 638–47.
59. *Time*, March 28, 1983, pp. 26–33.
60. The following discussion of WIN's legal problems and possible reforms expands Lawrence M. Mead, "Expectations and Welfare Work: WIN in New York State," *Polity*, 18, no. 2 (Winter 1985), part 6.
61. Mitchell et al., *Implementing Welfare-Employment Programs* (note 44), p. 166.
62. See note 53.
63. These cases were *McLean* v. *Mathews*, S.D.N.Y. 1977, 458 F. Supp. 285, and *Crosby* v. *Califano*, U.S. District Court, Central District of Illinois, Docket 78-3067, July 11, 1980.
64. This perception I owe to a WIN social service worker interviewed in New York City. See also Samuel Z. Klausner, *Six Years in the Lives of the Impoverished: An Examination of the WIN Thesis* (Philadelphia: Center for Research on the Acts of Man, 1978), p. 16.
65. DOL and HEW, *WIN Handbook* (note 48), p. XI-3.
66. Joel F. Handler and Ellen Jane Hollingsworth, *The "Deserving Poor": A Study of Welfare Administration* (New York: Academic Press, 1971), pp. 82–85.

Chapter 7. Welfare Work: A Closer Look

1. New York is one of twenty-two states that have implemented workfare versions of WIN since 1981, at least in some localities, but my studies deal with WIN as it functioned before then.
2. This discussion draws on these evaluations: Sar A. Levitan and David Marwick, "Work and Training for Relief Recipients," *Journal of Human Resources*, 8, supplement (1973): 5–18; Audrey D. Smith et al., "WIN, Work, and Welfare," *Social Service Review*, 49, no. 3 (September 1975): 396–404; Ronald G. Ehrenberg and James G. Hewlett, "The Impact of the WIN 2 Program on Welfare Costs and Recipient Rates," *Journal of Human Resources*,

11, no. 2 (Spring 1976): 219–32; Leonard Goodwin, "What Has Been Learned from the Work Incentive Program and Related Experiences: A Review of Research with Policy Implications," Office of Research and Development, Employment and Training Administration, U.S. Department of Labor, February 1977; Bradley R. Schiller, "Lessons from WIN: A Manpower Evaluation," *Journal of Human Resources*, 13, no. 4 (Fall 1978): 502–23; Jesse E. Gordon, "WIN Research: A Review of the Findings," in Charles D. Garvin et al., eds., *The Work Incentive Experience* (Montclair, N.J.: Allanheld, Osmun, 1978), ch. 3; and U.S. General Accounting Office, *An Overview of the WIN Program: Its Objectives, Accomplishments, and Problems* (Washington, D.C.: U.S. Government Printing Office, June 21, 1982).

3. Goodwin, "What Has Been Learned," p. 103; Gordon, "WIN Research," p. 78.
4. Judith Mayo, *Work and Welfare: Employment and Employability of Women in the AFDC Program* (Chicago: Community and Family Study Center, University of Chicago, 1975), p. 65; Mary Jo Bane and David T. Ellwood, "The Dynamics of Dependence: The Routes to Self-Sufficiency," study prepared for the Office of Planning and Evaluation, Department of Health and Human Services (Cambridge, Mass.: Urban Systems Research and Engineering, June 1983), pp. 29–47. According to Bane and Ellwood, demographic characteristics have much more effect on whether mothers escape welfare by remarriage.
5. Dorothy Herbert, "Child Care," in Garvin et al., eds., *Work Incentive Experience*, ch. 10. There seems to be less need for center-based, government day care than advocates suggest. See Woolsey and Bruce-Briggs references in Chapter 4, note 10.
6. Mark Lincoln Chadwin et al., "Reforming Welfare: Lessons from the WIN Experience," *Public Administration Review*, 41, no. 3 (May/June 1981): 373–75.
7. See the Auerbach study of WIN reported in 71–2 S. hearings 402–10.
8. The bureaucratic problems of the Employment Service are not new. See Robert L. Thomas, *The Thomas Report on the United States Employment Service*, Office of Research and Development, U.S. Department of Labor, August 1958.
9. See Chadwin et al., "Reforming Welfare," which is in turn based on John J. Mitchell et al., *Implementing Welfare-Employment Programs: An Institutional Analysis of the Work Incentive (WIN) Program*, U.S. Department of Labor, R&D Monograph 78 (Washington, D.C.: U.S. Government Printing Office, 1980). The same research team, of which I was a member, earlier produced Mark Lincoln Chadwin et al., *The Employment Service: An Institutional Analysis*, U.S. Department of Labor, R&D Monograph 51 (Washington, D.C.: U.S. Government Printing Office, 1977). My own studies are heavily indebted to this research and to guidance on methodological issues from John J. Mitchell.
10. Unless otherwise cited, quotations here and below are from staff interviewed during my own studies of WIN, cited in note 19.
11. John J. Mitchell, *Environmental and Organizational Determinants of Local*

Work Incentive (WIN) Program Performance (Arlington, Va.: Kappa Systems, October 1982), sections 3–6.

12. William J. Reid, "Hope for a Better Life," in Garvin et al., eds., *Work Incentive Experience*, p. 150.
13. 72 JEC hearings 1121.
14. Reid, "Hope for a Better Life," pp. 133–51.
15. Audrey D. Smith and Gregory M. St. L. O'Brien, "The Carrot and the Stick," in Garvin et al., eds., *Work Incentive Experience*, pp. 161–64.
16. U.S. Department of Labor and U.S. Department of Health, Education, and Welfare, *WIN Handbook*, 3d ed. (Washington, D.C.: U.S. Government Printing Office, October 1979), pp. VI-8, VI-15, VIII-51, VIII-57, VIII-58.
17. U.S. Department of Labor, Manpower Administration, *Work Incentive Program: From Welfare to Wages* (Washington, D.C.: U.S. Government Printing Office, July 1969).
18. CBS Evening News, June 19, 1984. The above discussion is based on national WIN performance data and field experience researching various WIN state programs. Among CWEP states, West Virginia has attained participation rates of 50 percent or more, an achievement reflecting the state's long commitment to welfare work. See Joseph Ball et al., *Interim Findings on the West Virginia Community Work Experience Demonstrations* (New York: Manpower Demonstration Research Corporations, November 1984).
19. This section is based on Lawrence M. Mead, "Expectations and Welfare Work: WIN in New York City," *Policy Studies Review*, 2, no. 4 (May 1983): 648–62, and "Expectations and Welfare Work: WIN in New York State," *Polity*, vol. 18, no. 2 (Winter 1985). The current writeup includes material from the interviews not included in the articles.
20. Data averaged over 1978–80 were used for the New York City study, data from just 1979 for the New York State study. Those were the latest possible years before office closings and turmoil connected to the Reagan reforms made valid statistical analysis impossible. Interviews were done only with staff, not recipients. To interview the latter would have posed serious clearance and methodological problems. How the WIN staff characterized the recipients, however, was quite consistent with studies that have interviewed them directly.
21. WIN also uses job entry wage (the wage at which WIN registrants enter jobs) and welfare savings due to WIN jobs as performance measures. The first was omitted here because it differed very little across the New York offices, the second because office-level data on it were unavailable. However, the job entry measures and retention rate suffice to capture the main quantity/quality tradeoff in WIN performance. Offices that require recipients to take any jobs, even poor ones, will tend to make many entries but fall down on retention, because recipients will more often leave the jobs early. Conversely, offices that insist on good jobs will do well on retention but poorly on entries. Effective offices, at least in New York, did well on both.
22. The bureaucratic factor also included a dummy variable for whether an office assigned a specific caseload to each staff member or had staff work with clients randomly on a walk-in basis. The former, it was hypothesized, would lead to

steadier work expectations and higher performance. The findings confirmed this. Since organizational factors other than staff resources are hard to measure and seem to have only marginal influence on performance, they were omitted. But some of the administrative features found to favor performance could be termed organizational.

23. All variables were used in a proportional form (divided by the number of registrants in an office) to avoid scaling problems due to differences in office size.
24. Leonard J. Hausman, "The Impact of Welfare on the Work Effort of AFDC Mothers," in President's Commission on Income Maintenance Programs (Heineman Commission), *Technical Studies* (Washington, D.C.: U.S. Government Printing Office, November 1969), pp. 85–86, 85 *n.* 5.
25. Technically, the recipients on active status are those "certified" to participate in WIN activities, a term defined below.
26. The obligation factor was generated using two-stage least squares (2LS) from the propositions of clients in the various administrative processes leading to active status. The method was appropriate because a causal direction could be assumed running from the processes to active status. The other four factors were generated from their constituent variables using factor analysis, without causal priority. See the New York State article for details.
27. Table 5 is a simplified version of regression results shown in the New York State article, table 1. Regression coefficients have been omitted.
28. A study of WIN nationwide comparable to the New York State study is under way. It uses states, not offices, as the units of analysis. Preliminary results are quite like those for New York State, suggesting that the power of obligations over performance holds for WIN nationally.
29. The state rankings come from the WIN Program Management Information Report, fiscal 1979, obtained from the national WIN office. Data from the WIN reporting system shows that in 1979 New York had only 35 percent of its registrants on active status, as against an average for the states of 39 percent. Moreover, most of the active registrants were in job placement. New York had only 8 percent in training and other job-readiness activities, whose payoff to performance is greater, as against a 24 percent average nationally.
30. The Manpower Demonstration Research Corporation is studying AFDC workfare in eight states. The projects address whether workfare saves enough in welfare and other costs to be worth its expense, the effect on the future income of recipients, and administrative causes of high or low participation rates in workfare, which critically affect impact. Early results tend to confirm the power of obligations to motivate increased work effort by recipients. See especially Barbara Goldman et al., *Findings from the San Diego Job Search and Work Experience Demonstration* (New York: Manpower Demonstration Research Corporation, March 1985). MDRC's effort, however, is spread thin over a wide range of questions about workfare. Further research may be needed to assess the impact of obligation on welfare work and the potential of requirements to increase work.
31. Chadwin et al., "Reforming Welfare," p. 376.
32. DOL and HEW, *WIN Handbook* (note 16), p. VIII-4.

33. These differences in verbal style themselves had a measurable influence on performance. See the New York State study, table 5.
34. 67 H. debate 23058.

Chapter 8. Why Washington Has Not Set Standards

1. *United States* v. *Butler*, 297 U.S. 1 (1936), established the broad interpretation of the spending power. *Steward Machine Co.* v. *Davis*, 301 U.S. 548 (1937), and *Helvering* v. *Davis*, 301 U.S. 619 (1937), upheld the Social Security and Unemployment payroll taxes and the programs based upon them. The cases set no definite limit to the programs Washington might run directly, and there have been no further cases testing the issue. I am thankful for advice on this point to my NYU colleague, Professor Robert F. Cushman.
2. *Massachusetts* v. *Mellon*, 262 U.S. 447 (1923); *Steward Machine Co.* v. *Davis*, 301 U.S. 548 (1937); *Oklahoma* v. *Civil Service Commission*, 330 U.S. 127 (1947). On recent regulation via the grant system, see Advisory Commission on Intergovernmental Relations, *Regulatory Federalism: Policy, Process, Impact and Reform* (Washington, D.C.: U.S. Government Printing Office, February 1984).
3. *Rosado* v. *Wyman*, 397 U.S. 397 (1970); *Dandridge* v. *Williams*, 397 U.S. 471 (1970); *Jefferson* v. *Hackney*, 406 U.S. 535 (1972); *Lavine* v. *Milne*, 424 U.S. 577 (1976). The quote is from the last case, p. 584, *n.* 9. On civil libertarian limits to grant conditions, see *Speiser* v. *Randall*, 357 U.S. 513 (1958), and *Sherbet* v. *Verner*, 374 U.S. 398 (1963). For arguments that welfare and other benefits should be entitlements see Charles A. Reich, "The New Property," *Yale Law Review*, 73, no. 5 (April 1964): 733–87; and Albert M. Bendich, "Privacy, Poverty, and the Constitution," *California Law Review*, 54, no. 2 (May 1966): 407–42.
4. Interviews with attorneys in the Departments of Labor and Health and Human Services. However, several lawyers who testified on WIN's initial enactment disputed its constitutionality. See 67 S. hearings 1229, 1371–87, 1776. The courts have held that federal AFDC work rules preempt tougher state requirements in most but not all circumstances; see *N.Y. State Department of Social Services* v. *Dublino*, 413 U.S. 405 (1973); *Woolfolk* v. *Brown*, D.C. Va. 1975, 393 F.Supp. 263, partially upheld 538 F.2d 598 (1976).
5. James O. Freedman, *Crisis and Legitimacy: The Administrative Process and American Government* (Cambridge, England: Cambridge University Press, 1978).
6. Martha Derthick, *Policymaking for Social Security* (Washington, D.C.: Brookings, 1979), p. 210.
7. Theodore J. Lowi, *The End of Liberalism: The Second Republic of the United States*, 2d. ed. (New York: Norton, 1979), chs. 4–5, 8.
8. David A. Stockman, "The Social Pork Barrel," *The Public Interest*, no. 39, Spring 1975, pp. 3–30; Robert Pear, "Many Households Get U.S. Benefits," *New York Times*, April 17, 1985, p. A23.

9. David R. Mayhew, *Congress: The Electoral Connection* (New Haven: Yale University Press, 1974); Morris P. Fiorina, *Congress: Keystone of the Washington Establishment* (New Haven: Yale University Press, 1977); Samuel C. Patterson, "The Semi-Sovereign Congress," in Anthony King, ed., *The New American Political System* (Washington, D.C.: American Enterprise Institute, 1978), pp. 141–53.
10. See Chapter 3, note 6.
11. Robert E. Lane, *Political Ideology: Why the American Common Man Believes What He Does* (New York: Free Press, 1962), pp. 145–60, 169–76,
12. Lowi, *End of Liberalism*, p. 297. Lowi's ideal of "juridical democracy" does, however, imply the rule of law and might permit a more authoritative kind of policy than at present.
13. George F. Will, *Statecraft as Soulcraft: What Government Does* (New York: Simon and Schuster, 1983), pp. 158–59.
14. This section is based on Lawrence M. Mead, "The Interaction Problem in Policy Analysis," *Policy Sciences*, 16, no. 1 (September 1983): 45–66; "'Policy Science' Today," *The Public Interest*, no. 73, Fall 1983, pp. 165–70; "A Meaning for 'Public Policy'," *Policy Studies Journal*, 12, no. 2 (December 1983): 247–50; and "Policy Studies and Political Science," *Policy Studies Review*, vol. 5, no. 2, November 1985.
15. Arnold J. Meltsner, *Policy Analysts in the Bureaucracy* (Berkeley: University of California Press, 1976), pp. 173–77; Hugh Heclo, "Issue Networks and the Executive Establishment," in King, ed., *New American Political System*, ch. 3.
16. For discussions of these analytic enterprises, see David Novick, ed., *Program Budgeting: Program Analysis and the Federal Budget*, 2d ed. (Cambridge, Mass.: Harvard University Press, 1967), ch. 4; and Stephen Breyer, *Regulation and Its Reform* (Cambridge, Mass.: Harvard University Press, 1982).
17. In his study of federal analysts, Meltsner, *Policy Analysts*, p. 15, 15, *n*. 2, found that 40 percent were economists by training, and most of the rest used broadly economic methods in their work.
18. On the scope and limits of the economic theory of the agenda, see Peter O. Steiner, "The Public Sector and the Public Interest," in Robert H. Haveman and Julius Margolis, eds., *Public Expenditure and Policy Analysis*, 2d ed. (Chicago: Rand McNally, 1977), ch. 1.
19. Charles L. Schultze, *The Public Use of Private Interest* (Washington, D.C.: Brookings, 1977); Thomas C. Schelling, ed., *Incentives for Environmental Protection* (Cambridge, Mass.: MIT Press, 1983); Robert A. Levine, *Public Planning: Failure and Redirection* (New York: Basic Books, 1972). These experiments included the income maintenance tests, vouchers and accountability in education, competing forms of health insurance, and housing allowances.
20. Vincent J. Burke and Vee Burke, *Nixon's Good Deed: Welfare Reform* (New York: Columbia University Press, 1974), pp. 41–67; M. Kenneth Bowler, *The Nixon Guaranteed Income Proposal: Substance and Process in Policy Change* (Cambridge, Mass.: Ballinger, 1974), pp. 161–62; 77 House hearings 1062.
21. Laurence H. Tribe, "Policy Science: Analysis or Ideology?" *Philosophy and Public Affairs*, 2, no. 1 (Fall 1972): 84–97, speaks of "dwarfing the soft

variables." Some information on the attitudes of the poor has come from the Panel Study on Income Dynamics (PSID), the income maintenance experiments, and a number of smaller academic studies, notably by Leonard Goodwin.

22. Meltsner, *Policy Analysts*, pp. 18–30; 72 JEC hearings 844.
23. Sar A. Levitan et al., *Work and Welfare Go Together* (Baltimore: Johns Hopkins Press, 1972), pp. 114–15; 70 S. hearings 556–58.
24. Ad Hoc Steering Committee of the Arden House Conference on Public Welfare, *Report*, 68 JEC hearings 484–85.
25. Robert H. Haveman, ed., *A Decade of Federal Antipoverty Programs: Achievements, Failures, and Lessons* (New York: Academic Press, 1977), pp. 195–96. The speaker is Burton Weisbrod.
26. Gordon P. Whitaker, "Coproduction: Citizen Participation in Service Delivery," *Public Administration Review*, 40, no. 3 (May/June 1980): 240–46.
27. Alice M. Rivlin, *Systematic Thinking for Social Action* (Washington, D.C.: Brookings, 1971).
28. Carl Kaysen, "Model-Makers and Decision-Makers: Economists and the Policy Process," *The Public Interest*, no. 12, Summer 1968, pp. 80–95; Donald N. McCloskey, "The Rhetoric of Economics," *Journal of Economic Literature*, 21, no. 2 (June 1983): 481–517.
29. Daniel P. Moynihan, *The Politics of a Guaranteed Income: The Nixon Administration and the Family Assistance Plan* (New York: Random House, 1973), pp. 189–93.
30. Daniel P. Moynihan, *Maximum Feasible Misunderstanding: Community Action in the War on Poverty* (New York: Free Press, 1970).
31. 78 S. hearings 818; Laurence E. Lynn, Jr., and David deF. Whitman, *The President as Policymaker: Jimmy Carter and Welfare Reform* (Philadelphia: Temple University Press, 1981), pp. 259–60.
32. Steven E. Rhoads, "Economists and Policy Analysis," *Public Administration Review*, 38, no. 2 (March/April 1978): 112–20.
33. Advisory Commission on Intergovernmental Relations, *An Agenda for American Federalism: Restoring Confidence and Competence* (Washington, D.C.: U.S. Government Printing Office, June 1981), pp. 1–6; Congressional Budget Office, *The Federal Government in a Federal System: Current Intergovernmental Programs and Options for Change* (Washington, D.C.: U.S. Government Printing Office, August 1983), p. xiii.
34. See Chapter 2, note 17.
35. Advisory on Intergovernmental Relations, *A Crisis of Confidence and Competence* (Washington, D.C.: U.S. Government Printing Office, July 1980); David B. Walker, *Toward A Functioning Federalism* (Cambridge, Mass.: Winthrop, 1981).
36. Joseph A. Califano, Jr., *Governing America: An Insider's Report from the White House and Cabinet* (New York: Simon & Schuster, 1981), ch. 6.
37. Erwin C. Hargrove, *The Missing Link: The Study of the Implementation of Social Policy* (Washington, D.C.: Urban Institute, July 1975), pp. 110–16.

38. Sar A. Levitan, *The Great Society's Poor Law: A New Approach to Poverty* (Baltimore: Johns Hopkins Press, 1969), pp. 59–60.
39. David B. Walker, "The States and the System: Changes and Choices," *Intergovernmental Perspective*, 6, no. 4 (Fall 1980): 6–12.
40. Albert O. Hirschman, *Exit, Voice, and Loyalty: Responses to Decline in Firms, Organizations, and States* (Cambridge, Mass.: Harvard University Press, 1970).
41. Federal Unemployment Tax Act, sec. 3304(a).
42. Martha Derthick, *The Influence of Federal Grants: Public Assistance in Massachusetts* (Cambridge, Mass.: Harvard University Press, 1970), pp. 197–98, passim.
43. James Coleman, "Private Schools, Public Schools, and the Public Interest," *The Public Interest*, no. 64, Summer 1981, p. 30
44. Lowi, *End of Liberalism* (note 7), pp. 258–67; Charles V. Hamilton, "Blacks and the Crisis in Political Participation," *The Public Interest*, no. 34, Winter 1974, pp. 188–210.
45. Theodore J. Lowi, *The Politics of Disorder* (New York: Basic Books, 1971), chs. 1–2, 8.
46. Duncan MacRae, Jr., *The Social Function of Social Science* (New Haven: Yale University Press, 1976); Mead, "'Policy Science' Today" (note 14), and "The Interaction Problem" (note 14), pp. 61–63.
47. *National League of Cities* v. *Usery*, 426 U.S. 833 (1976), restricted federal powers to set or preempt state policies, but was abandoned in a series of later decisions culminating in *Garcia* v. *San Antonio Metropolitan Transit Authority*, No. 82-1913 (1985). See Linda Greenhouse, "Court Takes the Glow Off the 10th Amendment," *New York Times*, March 13, 1983, p. E9.
48. Lester C. Thurow, *Dangerous Currents: The State of Economics* (New York: Random House, 1983).
49. H. Mark Roelofs, *Ideology and Myth in American Politics: A Critique of a National Political Mind* (Boston: Little, Brown, 1976), ch. 5.

Chapter 9. Attitudes Against Obligation

1. V. O. Key, Jr., *Public Opinion and American Democracy* (New York: Knopf, 1963), chs. 8–11, 16, 21.
2. Alexis de Tocqueville, *Democracy in America*, trans. Henry Reeve, ed. Phillips Bradley (New York: Knopf, 1980), vol. 2, book 2, ch. 3, p. 101.
3. Donald J. Devine, *The Political Culture of the United States: The Influence of Member Values on Regime Maintenance* (Boston: Little, Brown, 1972), chs. 3–5; Robert E. Lane, *Political Ideology: Why the American Common Man Believes What He Does* (New York: Free Press, 1962), parts 1, 3.
4. Michael Mann, "The Social Cohesion of Liberal Democracy," *American Sociological Review*, 35, no. 3 (June 1970): 423–39; Seymour Martin Lipset and William Schneider, "The Bakke Case: How Would It Be Decided at the Bar of

Public Opinion?" *Public Opinion*, 1, no. 1 (March/April 1978): 38–44; Louis Henri Bolce III and Susan H. Gray, "Blacks, Whites, and 'Race Politics'," *The Public Interest*, no. 54, Winter 1979, pp. 61–75; Victoria Sackett, "Ignoring the People," *Policy Review*, no. 12, Spring 1980, pp. 9–22.

5. Louis Hartz, *The Liberal Tradition in America: An Interpretation of American Political Thought Since the Revolution* (New York: Harcourt, Brace & World, 1955); Richard Hofstadter, *The American Political Tradition and the Men Who Made It* (New York: Knopf, 1948).
6. Samuel P. Huntington, *American Politics: The Promise of Disharmony* (Cambridge, Mass.: Harvard University Press, 1981), ch. 3; Paul M. Sniderman, *A Question of Loyalty* (Berkeley: University of California Press, 1981), pp. 114–41, 166–70.
7. Devine, *Political Culture*, pp. 255–60.
8. Lane, *Political Ideology*, p. 155; Devine, *Political Culture*, pp. 58–61; Gabriel A. Almond and Sidney Verba, *The Civic Culture: Political Attitudes and Democracy in Five Nations* (Princeton, N.J.: Princeton University Press, 1963), pp. 17–21, 214–29.
9. David Easton and Jack Dennis, *Children in the Political System: Origins of Political Legitimacy* (New York: McGraw-Hill, 1969), chs. 6–11 (the quote is p. 137); Fred I. Greenstein, *Children and Politics*, rev. ed. (New Haven: Yale University Press, 1969), chs. 1–4, 8; Robert D. Hess and Judith V. Torney, *The Development of Political Attitudes in Children* (Chicago: Aldine, 1967), chs. 2–4, 10.
10. Hess and Torney, *Development of Political Attitudes*, pp. 126–72, 223–24; Almond and Verba, *Civic Culture*, pp. 110–12, 220–21, 384–87. Less privileged groups differ from the better-off more in their level of political participation, which is lower, than they do in subject allegiance.
11. This additive quality can also be seen in Canada, a society that, except for political culture, is very much like the United States. See Michael T. Kaufman, "Canada: An American Discovers Its Difference," *New York Times Magazine*, May 15, 1983.
12. Almond and Verba, *Civic Culture*, pp. 107, 217–24, 440–69.
13. H. Mark Roelofs, *Ideology and Myth in American Politics: A Critique of a National Political Mind* (Boston: Little, Brown, 1976), ch. 6 and passim.
14. Sniderman, *Question of Loyalty*, pp. 157–66; Paul M. Sniderman and Richard A. Brody, "Coping: The Ethic of Self-Reliance," *American Journal of Political Science*, 21, no. 3 (August 1977): 501–21; Robert Nisbet, "Public Opinion Versus Popular Opinion," *The Public Interest*, no. 41, Fall 1975, pp. 166–92.
15. Arthur H. Miller, "Political Issues and Trust in Government: 1964–1970," *American Political Science Review*, 68, no. 3 (September 1974): 951–72; David B. Hill and Norman R. Luttbeg, *Trends in American Electoral Behavior*, 2d ed. (Itasca, Ill.: Peacock, 1983), ch. 4; Norman H. Nie et al., *The Changing American Voter*, enl. ed. (Cambridge, Mass.: Harvard University Press, 1979), ch. 15.
16. Tocqueville, *Democracy in America* (note 2), vol. 2, book 3, ch. 21, pp. 262–63.

17. Lane, *Political Ideology*, p. 362; Morris Janowitz, *The Reconstruction of Patriotism: Education for Civic Consciousness* (Chicago: University of Chicago Press, 1983), pp. 152–63.
18. Grant McConnell, *Private Power and American Democracy* (New York: Vintage Books, 1970), chs., 3–4; Frederick C. Mosher, *Democracy and the Public Service*, 2d ed. (New York: Oxford University Press, 1982).
19. O. Mannoni, *Prospero and Caliban: The Psychology of Colonization* (London: Methuen, 1956).
20. Devine, *Political Culture* (note 3), pp. 192–93; Lane, *Political Ideology*, p. 378; Harold L. Wilensky, *The Welfare State and Equality: Structural and Ideological Roots of Public Expenditures* (Berkeley: University of California Press, 1975), pp. 34, 65, 115–17; W. G. Runciman, *Relative Deprivation and Social Justice: A Study of Attitudes to Social Inequality in Twentieth-Century England* (Harmondsworth, Middlesex, England: Penguin Books, 1972), pp. 341–42.
21. Devine, *Political Culture*, pp. 219–27; Roelofs, *Ideology and Myth*, pp. 51–56, 157.
22. Tocqueville, *Democracy in America*, vol. 2, book 4, ch. 3, p. 294, *n*. 1.
23. 70 H. debate 12033; 78 S. hearings 1123; 72 S. report 4.
24. Daniel P. Moynihan, *The Politics of a Guaranteed Income: The Nixon Administration and the Family Assistance Plan* (New York: Random House, 1973), p. 10.
25. 71 H. debate 21403; 72 S. debate 32911; 70 H. debate 12075.
26. 71–2 S. hearings 1621–22; 67 S. hearings 2026.
27. 70 S. hearings 1604; 71 H. debate 21389.
28. 70 H. debate 11900; 72 S. debate 33411–12.
29. 70 S. hearings 1475; 72 S. debate 33105; 77 H. hearings 232.
30. 72 S. report 85; 77 H. hearings 579.
31. 71 H. debate 21335, 21361; 70 H. debate 12088.
32. 71–2 S. hearings 736; 70 H. Rules hearings 164; 70 H. debate 12033.
33. 70 H. debate 12030, 12069.
34. 71–2 S. hearings 1521–22, 1609–12; 78 S. hearings 592; 70 S. hearings 2104.
35. 67 S. hearings 1268; 78 S. hearings 1121; 71–2 S. hearings 771; 71 H. debate 21352.
36. 71 H. debate 21390–91.
37. 70 S. hearings 226; 72 S. debate 32910, 33108; 70 H. Rules hearings 160.
38. 70 H. debate 11876–77, 12067; 71 H. debate 21370.
39. 71–2 S. hearings 1606; 78 S. hearings 53.
40. 70 S. hearings 1601.
41. 67 H. debate 23098; 69 H. hearings 914; 71–2 S. hearings 1649; 67 S. hearings 1794–95.
42. 69 H. hearings 1544: 71–2 S. hearings 2213–14; 67 S. hearings 1518; 69 H. hearings 162.
43. 69 H. hearings 1097–98; 67 S. debate 33195; 67 S. hearings 2029; 77 H. hearings 2236.

44. 67 S. hearings 793; 69 H. hearings 1332–33, 2267.
45. 70 H. debate 12048; 77 H. hearings 2603; 78 S. hearings 1240.
46. 69 H. hearings 1936; 67 S. hearings 1633–34; 70 S. hearings 2062.
47. John Kenneth Galbraith, *The Affluent Society* (New York: Mentor Books, 1958), p. 255.
48. 69 H. hearings 2211; 67 S. debate 33585; 71–2 S. hearings 2103; Advisory Council on Public Welfare, *"Having the Power, We have the Duty,"* Report to the Secretary of Health, Education, and Welfare, U.S. Department of Health, Education, and Welfare, Welfare Administration (Washington, D.C.: U.S. Government Printing Office, June 29, 1966).
49. 70 S. hearings 692; 78 S. hearings 1232; 67 H. debate 22781, 23077; 67 S. final debate 36925.
50. 67 S. hearings 1095; 69 H. hearings 1035.
51. 67 S. hearings 796; 71 H. debate 21365; 71–2 S. hearings 2062; 72 S. debate 33656.
52. 77 H. hearings 27–28, 245.
53. 69 H. hearings 1015; 67 H. hearings 118; 67 S. hearings 1732.
54. 68 JEC hearings 338, 352; 72 JEC hearings 131; 69 H. hearings 2332.
55. 70 H. debate 12049; 70 S. hearings 1373; 72 S. debate 33669.
56. 67 S. hearings 776; 69 H. hearings 1975; 67 S. hearings 1142.
57. 67 S. hearings 1917; 70 S. hearings 1393.
58. 71–2 S. hearings 2603–4; 67 S. hearings 1013.
59. 68 JEC hearings 338; 71–2 S. hearings 1685.
60. Advisory Council on Public Welfare, *"Having the Power"* (note 48), p. xix.
61. 78 S. hearings 171.
62. 69 H. hearings 259; 78 S. hearings 141, 351–52.
63. President's Commission on Income Maintenance Programs (Heineman Commission), *Poverty Amid Plenty: The American Paradox* (Washington, D.C.: U.S. Government Printing Office, November 1969), p. 59, and *Background Papers* (Washington, D.C.: U.S. Government Printing Office, November 1969), pp. 55–60, 66.
64. 78 S. hearings 589; Moynihan, *Politics of Guaranteed Income* (note 24), pp. 26–34.
65. 78 S. hearings 1199.
66. 78 S. hearings 734; 77 H. hearings 1351; 69 H. hearings 1791–92.
67. 77 H. hearings 2373–76; 71–2 S. hearings 1796–97.
68. 67 S. hearings 1445; 77 H. hearings 1351, 2384.
69. Vincent J. Burke and Vee Burke, *Nixon's Good Deed: Welfare Reform* (New York: Columbia University Press, 1974), pp. 92–93, 138–44.
70. 70 H. debate 12032; 71–2 S. hearings 176, 181.
71. 69 H. hearings 1273; 77 H. hearings 2378.
72. Elie Halévy, *The Era of Tyrannies: Essays on Socialism and War*, trans. R. K. Webb (Garden City, N.Y.: Doubleday Anchor, 1965), pp. 105–207, 249–85.

73. U.S. Department of Health and Human Services, Social Security Administration, *Aid to Families with Dependent Children, 1979 Recipient Characteristics Study, Part 1: Demographic and Program Statistics* (Washington, D.C.: Social Security Administration, June 1982), p. 1.
74. Lee Rainwater and William L. Yancey, *The Moynihan Report and the Politics of Controversy* (Cambridge, Mass.: MIT Press, 1967), pp. 128–29.
75. Ibid., p. 248; Moynihan, *Politics of Guaranteed Income* (note 24), pp. 297, 326–27.
76. 71 H. debate 21363; 71–2 S. hearings 2075.
77. 67 S. hearings 1472; 69 H. hearings 898; 72 JEC hearings 610.
78. Gilbert Y. Steiner, *The State of Welfare* (Washington, D.C.: Brookings, 1971), ch. 8; Frances Fox Piven and Richard A. Cloward, *Poor People's Movements: Why They Succeed, How They Fail* (New York: Pantheon Books, 1977), ch. 5.
79. 67 S. hearings 1463–73; 69 H. hearings 1013–40; 71–2 S. hearings 2059–74.
80. Burke and Burke, *Nixon's Good Deed* (note 69), pp. 159–64, 174.
81. 67 S. hearings 1728, 1739; 71–2 S. hearings 2103.
82. 71–2 S. hearings 1475: 67 S. hearings 1735.
83. 67 S. hearings 1731; 70 S. hearings 1775.
84. 71–2 S. hearings 1495, 1502.
85. 71–2 S. hearings 1502; 69 H. hearings 1628–29, 1938.
86. 71–2 S. hearings 2064.
87. Hannah Arendt, *The Human Condition* (Chicago: University of Chicago Press, 1958), pp. 50–58, 238–43, 316–18; Edward A. Wynne, *Social Security: A Reciprocity System Under Pressure* (Boulder, Colo.: Westview Press, 1980), pp. 99–103, 127, 145.
88. The Thessalonians passage is apparently used in the Soviet constitution to mandate work. See Roger A. Freeman, *The Wayward Welfare State* (Stanford, Calif.: Hoover Institution Press, 1981), p. 231, and 71–2 S. hearings 1480, 1511, 1519–20.
89. Sheldon S. Wolin, *Politics and Vision: Continuity and Innovaton in Western Political Thought* (London: George Allen & Unwin, 1961), chs. 4–6.
90. Dietrich Bonhoeffer, *Ethics*, ed. Eberhard Bethge, trans. Neville Horton Smith (New York: Macmillan, 1965), pp. 62–63.
91. Elie Halévy, *England in 1815*, 2d (revised) ed., trans. E. I. Watkin and D. A. Barker (London: Ernest Benn, 1949), pp. 588–91.
92. Herbert Croly, *The Promise of American Life*, ed. Arthur M. Schlesinger, Jr. (Cambridge, Mass.: Harvard University Press, 1965), pp. 22, 173, and passim. Croly was first published in 1909.
93. Samuel H. Beer, "Liberalism and the National Idea," *The Public Interest*, no. 5, Fall 1966, pp. 70–82.
94. Josiah Lee Auspitz, "A 'Republican' View of Both Parties," *The Public Interest*, no. 67, Spring 1982, pp. 94–117. Tom Wicker has spoken of Democrats as a "party of access," the GOP as a "party of government," *New York Times*, November 25, 1984, p. E17.
95. Croly, *Promise of American Life*, p. 271.

Chapter 10. The Civic Conception

1. Alexis de Tocqueville, *Democracy in America*, trans. Henry Reeve, ed. Phillips Bradley (New York: Knopf, 1980), vol. 1, ch. 14, pp. 248–49.
2. 67 H. debate 23067; 68 JEC hearings 2.
3. 67 S. hearings 1138, 1157; 67 H. final debate 36390; 69 H. hearings 1013.
4. 70 H. report 31; 71 H. report 3.
5. 67 H. final debate 36390; 70 S. hearings. 579.
6. 67 H. debate 23053; 67 S. final debate 36912; 70 S. hearings 1582; 72 S. debate 33417.
7. 71 H. debate 21093, 21360.
8. 69 H. hearings 373, 1104–5, 1197; 70 H. debate 12028–29; 71 H. debate 21400.
9. 70 H. debate 12029; 71 H. debate 21353.
10. 71–2 S. hearings 48, 175. See also Chapter 5, note 26.
11. 67 H. report 96; 67 H. debate 23052–53.
12. 67 S. hearings 808.
13. 72 S. debate 32479; 67 S. debate 32852; 70 S. hearings 610–11.
14. U.S. Congress, Senate, Committee on Finance, *Welfare Reform—Or Is It?*, Address of Hon. Russell B. Long, Chairman, Committee on Finance, and Supporting Material, committee print, 92d Cong., 1st sess., August 6, 1971, p. 9; 67 S. hearings 1813. For the admissions of Administration witnesses, see Chapter 5, note 52.
15. 74 JEC report vi.
16. 70 H. Rules hearings 106, 135–36; 69 H. hearings 1102.
17. 69 H. hearings 168, 272–75, 366–78, 443–45.
18. 69 H. hearings 162. Ullman was one of three dissenters who voted against FAP on Ways and Means in both 1970 and 1971.
19. 71 H. debate 21094, 21361.
20. 74 JEC report 5; 67 H. final debate 36391–92; 72 JEC hearings 203, 503; 72 S. debate 33412; 78 S. hearings 884, 913.
21. Lee Rainwater, *What Money Buys: Inequality and the Social Meanings of Income* (New York: Basic Books, 1974), p. 74; 69 H. hearings 1930.
22. 67 H. final debate 36367; 67 S. report 152–53; M. Kenneth Bowler, *The Nixon Guaranteed Income Proposal: Substance and Process in Policy Change* (Cambridge, Mass.: Ballinger, 1974), p. 89.
23. 71 H. debate 21402; 68 JEC hearings 408.
24. 67 H. debate 23062; 72 S. debate 33655–56; 67 S. debate 32592, 33191; 69 H. hearings 1102.
25. 72 S. debate 32719; 78 S. hearings 913; 68 JEC hearings 409; 69 H. hearings 776.
26. 69 H. hearings 1095–1107.
27. 70 S. hearings 3; 67 S. report 147; 71 H. debate 21339.

28. 67 S. hearings 2041–42; 70 S. hearings 691.
29. "Considerations on the Government of Poland," in Jean-Jacques Rousseau, *Political Writings*, trans. and ed. Frederick Watkins (Edinburgh: Nelson, 1953), pp. 168–69.
30. 67 S. hearings 1812; 72 S. debate 33655.
31. 74 JEC report 110–11; 71 H. debate 21346; 72 S. report 1285.
32. 69 H. hearings 860; 71–2 S. hearings 821; 78 S. hearings 1126–27.
33. 71–2 S. hearings 142; 78 S. hearings 781; 67 S. hearings 1129.
34. 70 S. hearings 401, 780–81; 72 S. debate 33649–50; 71–2 S. hearings 180–82.
35. 74 JEC report 87; 67 H. debate 23058; 70 S. hearings 783.
36. 72 JEC hearings 605, 1074; 70 H. debate 11880; 67 S. hearings 2046; 67 H. final debate 36391.
37. 67 S. hearings 1993–94.
38. 71–2 S. hearings 1483; 70 H. debate 11881; 70 H. report 32.
39. The following summary is based on Michael E. Schiltz, *Public Attitudes Toward Social Security, 1935–1965*, Research Report No. 33, U.S. Department of Health, Education, and Welfare, Social Security Administration, Office of Research and Statistics (Washington, D.C.: U.S. Government Printing Office, 1970); Eva Mueller, "Public Attitudes Toward Fiscal Programs," *Quarterly Journal of Economics*, 77 (1963): 210–35; Seymour Martin Lipset and Earl Raab, "The Message of Proposition 13," *Commentary*, 66, no. 3 (September 1978): 42–46; and the sources listed in note 44 below.
40. Lipset and Raab, "Message of Proposition 13."
41. 67 H. final debate 36366; 71–2 S. hearings 3.
42. James Q. Wilson, "The Urban Unease: Community vs. City," *The Public Interest*, no. 12, Summer 1968, pp. 25–26; Lee Rainwater, "The Lessons of Pruitt-Igoe," *The Public Interest*, no. 8, Summer 1967, pp. 117–19; Kenneth B. Clark, *Dark Ghetto: Dilemmas of Social Power* (New York: Harper Torchbooks, 1967), pp. 55–62. Jennifer L. Hochschild, *What's Fair: American Beliefs About Distributive Justice* (Cambridge, Mass.: Harvard University Press, 1981), p. 280, reports that Great Society rhetoric had had some impact. Her subjects were somewhat readier to attribute the problems of the poor to social conditions than were the respondents interviewed for Robert E. Lane, *Political Ideology: Why the American Common Man Believes What He Does* (New York: Free Press, 1962), two decades earlier.
43. Schlitz, *Public Attitudes*, p. 24; Joe R. Feagin, *Subordinating the Poor: Welfare and American Beliefs* (Englewood Cliffs, N.J.: Prentice-Hall, 1975), pp. 95–102.
44. Robert Reinhold, "Public Found Against Welfare Idea But in Favor of What Programs Do," *New York Times*, August 3, 1977, pp. A1, D15; Schiltz, *Public Attitudes*, ch. 6; Lipset and Raab, "Message of Proposition 13," pp. 44–45; Hazel Erskine, "The Polls: Government Role in Welfare," *Public Opinion Quarterly*, 39, no. 2 (Summer 1975): 257–74; and Natalie Jaffe, "Attitudes Toward Public Welfare Programs and Recipients in the United States," in Lester M. Salamon, *Welfare: The Elusive Consensus* (New York: Praeger, 1978), appendix B.

45. Schiltz, *Public Attitudes*, ch. 6; Jaffe, "Attitudes," pp. 221, 224–25.
46. Feagin, *Subordinating the Poor*, pp. 134–41; Lipset and Raab, "Message of Proposition 13," p. 45; Schiltz, *Public Attitudes*, pp. 97–100, 117. Arthur H. Miller, "Will Public Attitudes Defeat Welfare Reform?" *Public Welfare*, 36, no. 3 (Summer 1978): 48–54, finds somewhat more division among groups over welfare policy, but the questions he cites treat welfare and other issues such as aid to minorities and health insurance as New Deal questions of more versus less government. This formulation brings out the partisan divisions discussed in Chapter 9 rather than the underlying consensus about social standards emphasized here.
47. 70 S. hearings 167, 169, 175–78.
48. 70 H. debate 12086; U.S. Congress, Senate, Committee on Finance, *Welfare Reform* (note 14), p. 4.
49. 68 JEC hearings 171; Lee Rainwater, "The Problem of Lower-Class Culture and Poverty-War Strategy," in Daniel P. Moynihan, ed., *On Understanding Poverty: Perspectives from the Social Sciences* (New York: Basic Books, 1969), pp. 252–53.
50. For the first of these theories see Lane, *Political Ideology*, and Seymour Martin Lipset, "Radicalism or Reformism: The Sources of Working-Class Politics," *American Political Science Review*, 77, no. 1 (March 1983): 1–18. For the second, see Hochschild, *What's Fair;* H. Mark Roelofs, *Ideology and Myth in American Politics: A Critique of a National Political Mind* (Boston: Little, Brown, 1976); and Herbert McClosky and John Zaller, *The American Ethos: Public Attitudes Toward Capitalism and Democracy* (Cambridge, Mass.: Harvard University Press, 1985). For the third, see Feagin, *Subordinating the Poor*, and the writings of Piven and Cloward, Ryan, and Harrington cited in Chapter 2, note 62.
51. Richard A. Easterlin, "Does Money Buy Happiness?" *The Public Interest*, no. 30, Winter 1973, pp. 3–10; Lane, *Political Ideology*, ch. 4; W. G. Runciman, *Relative Deprivation and Social Justice: A Study of Attitudes to Social Inequality in Twentieth-Century England* (Harmondsworth, Middlesex, England: Penguin Books, 1972).
52. Rainwater, *What Money Buys* (note 21), chs. 3–8.
53. Ibid., pp. 163–73; Rainwater, "Problem of Lower-Class Culture," p. 252. For a legal statement of citizenship as a "minimum bundle" of rights, see Frank I. Michelman, "On Protecting the Poor Through the Fourteenth Amendment," *Harvard Law Review*, 83, no. 1 (November 1969): 7–59.
54. 67 H. debate 23108; 72 JEC hearings 1075.
55. Hochschild, *What's Fair*, pp. 44–45, 185–86, 190–91, and passim; McClosky and Zaller, *American Ethos.*
56. Hochschild agreed in a private conversation that this interpretation was a plausible alternative reading of her evidence.
57. Rainwater, *What Money Buys*, pp. 175–87, 202–3; Hochschild, *What's Fair*, pp. 158, 162–63, 170–71, 183–84, 252–53, 279.
58. Bill Cavala and Aaron Wildavsky, "The Political Feasibility of Income by Right," *Public Policy*, 18, no. 3 (Spring 1970): 332–34.

Chapter 11. The Common Obligations

1. John Rawls, *A Theory of Justice* (Cambridge, Mass.: Harvard University Press, 1971), p. 290.
2. 77 H. hearings 2324–50, 2517–60.
3. *Wisconsin* v. *Yoder*, 406 U.S. 205, 211 (1972). See also *Pierce* v. *Society of Sisters*, 268 U.S. 510, 534 (1925), and *Lemon* v. *Kurtzman*, 403 U.S. 602, 613 (1971). The education requirement, however, need not be imposed through public schools. *Wisconsin* v. *Yoder* upheld the right of Amish parents to withdraw their children from school before the usual leaving age if they provided equivalent education privately.
4. Kay Barrow et al., *Achievement and the Three R's: A Synopsis of National Assessment Findings in Reading, Writing, and Mathematics*, National Assessment of Educational Progress, Education Commission of the States, March 1982, pp. 18, 56–62. The National Assessment of Educational Progress, the best data available on school performance, is based on national examinations given to samples of nine-, thirteen-, and seventeen year-olds in various subjects since 1969.
5. The most noted of these reports was National Commission on Excellence in Education, *A Nation at Risk: The Imperitive for Educational Reform* (Washington, D.C.: U.S. Government Printing Office, April 1983), which found that school standards were threatened by "a rising tide of mediocrity."
6. Eric A. Hanushek, "Throwing Money at Schools," *Journal of Policy Analysis and Management*, 1, no. 1 (Fall 1981): 19–41; James E. Prather and Frank K. Gibson, "The Failure of Social Programs," *Public Administration Review*, 37, no. 5 (September/October 1977): 556–64.
7. Edward B. Fiske, "Studies Dispute View that Schools Cannot Overcome Effect of Poverty," *New York Times*, December 26, 1979, pp. A1, B12, and "New Look at Effective Schools," *New York Times Education Spring Survey*, April 15, 1984, pp. 1, 35–36, 55–56.
8. Stuart Taylor, Jr., "Strict Penalties for Criminals: Pendulum of Feeling Swings," *New York Times*, December 13, 1983, pp. A1, B8; "A Growing Crisis Behind Bars," *Time*, December 5, 1983, pp. 64–65.
9. Robert Martinson, "What Works?—Questions and Answers About Prison Reform," *The Public Interest*, no. 35, Spring 1974, pp. 22–54; Prather and Gibson, "Failure of Social Programs"; James Q. Wilson, *Thinking About Crime* (New York: Vintage Books, 1977), chs. 3, 8, passim.
10. See Chapter 5, note 16, and Chapter 8, note 19.
11. Edward A. Wynne, *Social Security: A Reciprocity System Under Pressure* (Boulder, Colo.: Westview Press, 1980), p. 138; S. M. Miller and Pamela Roby, "Poverty: Changing Social Stratification," in Daniel P. Moynihan, ed., *On Understanding Poverty: Perspectives from the Social Sciences* (New York: Basic Books, 1969), pp. 79–80.
12. James S. Coleman et al., *High School Achievement: Public, Catholic and Private Schools Compared* (New York: Basic Books, 1982), summarized in James Coleman, "Private Schools, Public Schools, and the Public Interest," *The Public Interest*, no. 64, Summer 1981, pp. 19–30.

13. Nat Hentoff, "The Integrationist," *The New Yorker*, August 23, 1982, p. 40.
14. For the "mediating structures" conception, see Peter L. Berger and Richard John Neuhaus, *To Empower People: The Role of Mediating Structures in Public Policy* (Washington, D.C.: American Enterprise Institute, 1977). Neighborhoods, churches, and voluntary associations might perhaps take over the benefits side of social policy, but standards-setting would have to occur through accountable public institutions, probably at the national level.

    For a provocative attempt to derive standards for civility from Kant and Aristotle, see Hadley Arkes, *The Philosopher in the City: The Moral Dimensions of Urban Politics* (Princeton, N.J.: Princeton University Press, 1981). Such an approach argues for the impartial treatment of citizens, on important principle, but it does not furnish norms sufficient to deal with all the issues of desert and standards in social policy at the federal level.

    George F. Will, *Statecraft as Soulcraft: What Government Does* (New York: Simon & Schuster, 1983), calls for government to instill duties, but he suggests, following Burke, that the norms are to be found in tradition or in institutions outside government, not defined through public decisions, as seems inescapable in social policy. Will calls for a "sociology of civic virtue" (p. 135) without specifying how to achieve it through actual policy.
15. Jennifer L. Hochschild, *What's Fair: American Beliefs about Distributive Justice* (Cambridge, Mass.: Harvard University Press, 1981), ch. 3.
16. 69 H. hearings 272–75, 367, 373–74, 1104, 1197; 70 H. debate 12029.
17. Joseph A. Califano, Jr., *Governing America: An Insider's Report from the White House and Cabinet* (New York: Simon & Schuster, 1981), pp. 312–14; Morris Janowitz, *The Reconstruction of Patriotism: Education for Civic Consciousness* (Chicago: University of Chicago Press, 1983), ch. 5; Francis X. Clines, "The Mother Tongue Has A Movement," *New York Times*, June 3, 1984, p. E8.
18. Califano, *Governing America*, pp. 182–97.
19. W. G. Runciman, *Relative Deprivation and Social Justice: A Study of Attitudes to Social Inequality in Twentieth-Century England* (Harmondsworth, Middlesex, England: Penguin Books, 1972), pp. 323–35, 340–41; Hochschild, *What's Fair*, ch. 3.
20. Frederick C. Mosher, *Democracy and the Public Service*, 2d ed. (New York: Oxford University Press, 1982), chs. 1–2.
21. S. M. Miller and Frank Riessman, "The Working Class Subculture: A New View," *Social Problems*, 9, no. 1 (Summer 1961): 86–97.
22. Samuel P. Huntington, *American Politics: The Promise of Disharmony* (Cambridge, Mass.: Harvard University Press, 1981), ch. 2; Charles F. Andrain, *Children and Civic Awareness* (Columbus, Ohio: Merrill, 1971), pp. 29–30, 107–12. Janowitz, *Reconstruction of Patriotism*, p. 19, speaks of American integration as involving "acculturation" into citizenship norms without full, ethnic "assimilation."
23. Theodore J. Lowi, *The End of Liberalism: The Second Republic of the United States*, 2d ed. (New York: Norton, 1979), p. 261.
24. Daniel P. Moynihan, *Maximum Feasible Misunderstanding: Community Action in the War on Poverty* (New York: Free Press, 1970), p. 147; National Advisory Commission on Civil Disorders, *Report of the National Advisory Commission on Civil Disorders* (Washington, D.C.: U.S. Government Printing Office, March 1, 1968), p. 11.

25. *The Collected Works of Abraham Lincoln*, ed. Roy P. Basler (New Brunswick, N.J.: Rutgers University Press, 1953), 2: 532.
26. Herbert Croly, *The Promise of American Life*, ed. Arthur M. Schlesinger, Jr. (Cambridge, Mass.: Harvard University Press, 1965), p. 284.

Index